Teaching with the Common Core Standards for English Language Arts, PreK–2

Also available

Teaching with the Common Core Standards
for English Language Arts, Grades 3–5
*Edited by Lesley Mandel Morrow,
Karen K. Wixson, and Timothy Shanahan*

Teaching with the
Common Core
Standards
for English Language Arts,
PreK–2

EDITED BY

Lesley Mandel Morrow
Timothy Shanahan
Karen K. Wixson

Foreword by Susan B. Neuman

THE GUILFORD PRESS
New York   London

© 2013 The Guilford Press
A Division of Guilford Publications, Inc.
72 Spring Street, New York, NY 10012
www.guilford.com

Printed in the United States of America

This book is printed on acid-free paper.

Last digit is print number: 9 8 7 6 5 4 3 2 1

Library of Congress Cataloging-in-Publication Data

Teaching with the common core standards for English language arts, preK–2 / edited by
Lesley Mandel Morrow, Timothy Shanahan, Karen K. Wixson.
    p. cm.
  Includes bibliographical references and index.
  ISBN 978-1-4625-0760-3 (pbk.)—ISBN 978-1-4625-0766-5 (hardcover)
  1. Language arts (Elementary)—Curricula—United States—States.   2. Language arts
(Elementary)—Standards—United States—States.   I. Morrow, Lesley Mandel.
II. Shanahan, Timothy.   III. Wixson, Karen K.
  LB1576.T428 2013
  372.6—dc23
                                                                    2012018929

About the Editors

Lesley Mandel Morrow, PhD, holds the rank of Professor II at the Graduate School of Education at Rutgers, The State University of New Jersey. Her research deals with early literacy development and the organization and management of language arts programs. Dr. Morrow has published more than 300 journal articles, chapters, and books. Her work has been recognized with awards including the Outstanding Teacher Educator of Reading Award and the William S. Gray Citation of Merit from the International Reading Association (IRA), and the Oscar S. Causey Award from the Literacy Research Association. Dr. Morrow is past president of the IRA and is a member of the Reading Hall of Fame.

Timothy Shanahan, PhD, is Professor of Urban Education at the University of Illinois at Chicago, where he is Director of the Center for Literacy and Chair of the Department of Curriculum and Instruction. He served on one of the expert panels that helped develop the Common Core State Standards. Dr. Shanahan's research emphasizes reading–writing relationships, reading assessment, and improving reading achievement. In 2006, he was appointed to serve on the Advisory Board of the National Institute for Literacy. Dr. Shanahan is past president of the IRA and is a member of the Reading Hall of Fame.

Karen K. Wixson, PhD, is Dean of the School of Education at the University of North Carolina at Greensboro. She has published widely in the areas of literacy curriculum, instruction, and assessment. Dr. Wixson co-directed the federally funded Michigan English Language Arts Framework standards project, and served as Co-Director and Principal Investigator of the U.S. Department of Education's Center for the Improvement of Early Reading Achievement. She also served as a member of the extended work team for the Common Core English Language Arts standards. Dr. Wixson is a former board member of the National Reading Conference and the IRA.

Contributors

Peter Afflerbach, PhD, Department of Curriculum and Instruction, University of Maryland, College Park, College Park, Maryland

Allison Breit-Smith, PhD, School of Education, University of Cincinnati, Cincinnati, Ohio

Kristin Conradi, PhD, Department of Curriculum, Instruction, and Counselor Education, North Carolina State University, Raleigh, North Carolina

Jennifer Renner Del Nero, MA, Graduate School of Education, Rutgers, The State University of New Jersey, New Brunswick, New Jersey

Nell K. Duke, EdD, Department of Educational Studies, University of Michigan, Ann Arbor, Michigan

Kristin M. Gehsmann, EdD, Department of Education, St. Michael's College, Colchester, Vermont

Sandra L. Gillam, PhD, Department of Communicative Disorders and Deaf Education, Emma Eccles College of Education and Human Services, Utah State University, Logan, Utah

Juliet L. Halladay, PhD, Department of Education, University of Vermont, Burlington, Vermont

Jane Hansen, PhD, Curry School of Education, University of Virginia, Charlottesville, Virginia

Kellyanne M. Healey, MEd, Graduate School of Education, Rutgers, The State University of New Jersey, New Brunswick, New Jersey

Elfrieda H. Hiebert, PhD, TextProject and University of California, Santa Cruz, Santa Cruz, California

Bong Gee Jang, MA, Curry School of Education, University of Virginia, Charlottesville, Virginia

Michael C. McKenna, PhD, Curry School of Education, University of Virginia, Charlottesville, Virginia

Lesley Mandel Morrow, PhD, Graduate School of Education, Rutgers, The State University of New Jersey, New Brunswick, New Jersey

Susan B. Neuman, EdD, Department of Educational Studies, University of Michigan, Ann Arbor, Michigan

P. David Pearson, PhD, Graduate School of Education, University of California, Berkeley, Berkeley, California

D. Ray Reutzel, PhD, School of Teacher Education and Leadership, Utah State University, Logan, Utah

Kathryn L. Roberts, PhD, Department of Reading, Language, and Literature, Wayne State University, Detroit, Michigan

Timothy Shanahan, PhD, Department of Curriculum and Instruction, University of Illinois at Chicago, Chicago, Illinois

Shane Templeton, PhD, College of Education, University of Nevada, Reno, Reno, Nevada

Diane H. Tracey, EdD, College of Education, Kean University, Union, New Jersey

Susan Watts-Taffe, PhD, School of Education, University of Cincinnati, Cincinnati, Ohio

Karen K. Wixson, PhD, School of Education, University of North Carolina at Greensboro, Greensboro, North Carolina

Craig A. Young, PhD, Department of Early Childhood and Adolescent Education, Bloomsburg University of Pennsylvania, Bloomsburg, Pennsylvania

Foreword

Susan B. Neuman

This is an exciting time for those of us in the field of reading and language arts education. Although state standards have been with us for many years, the Common Core State Standards (CCSS) in English language arts represent a landmark in the history of educational reform, a shared vision of what children should know and be able to do. The goal of the CCSS is to provide a clear and consistent framework to ensure that all students, regardless of where they may live, receive a top-notch, high-quality education, helping to prepare them for college and the workforce.

Yet as previous reforms have taught us, even the best of frameworks are dependent on the quality of their implementation. Great teaching can turn a meager curriculum into a gold mine of opportunities for students to learn; similarly, poor teaching of even the best scientifically based materials won't yield their desired results. It is the implementation of the vision that is at the heart of this reform movement. What goes on behind classroom doors will mark whether or not these standards are, at best, a great success or, at worst, one more failed initiative.

Unfortunately, we have yet to identify a science of implementation. Recent evidence, however, suggests a number of important elements. First, teachers will need a great deal of knowledge. School districts will be seriously remiss if they approach these standards as if they were a scripted curriculum. In contrast to other reforms, the CCSS require deep knowledge about text and its complexities and the scaffolds that are necessary for children to be successful readers. The CCSS are based on a theoretical approach that will be new to many teachers, both novice and midcareer. Second, we now have an accumulated evidence base that indicates that knowledge alone is insufficient. Teachers and administrators may know a great deal about instruction, but putting these reforms into practice will require a deep understanding of how to teach—the pedagogical content knowledge that enables teachers to convey these understandings to students. Third, teachers will need a strong foundation in understanding children's development and the cumulative progress of mastery, refined and applied at increasingly high levels for various purposes and in various contexts.

No doubt, it will be a challenge—for teachers and administrators who are directly responsible to our children and for evaluators and researchers who may be responsible for examining student progress. These standards are akin to "tough love" in many ways, demanding that those of us in the reading and language arts community up the ante in terms of requiring higher-level learning and higher-order thinking. They represent a pretty strong dose of knowledge and content for children, starting from the very beginning of their schooling all the way through the high school years.

From my point of view, it's about time. Reforms in education have reflected just about everything you could think of except what matters most: what we teach. When children are fed a heavy diet of nonsense—low-level curricula that reflect a little of this and a little of that—they fail to thrive. When we teach children in a way that engages their minds, involving in-depth learning that allows them to master content, we support not only greater learning but greater motivation to learn more. Furthermore, we give them the gift of information capital, the ability to traverse the knowledge economy, enabling them to direct their own future rather than have their future "directed" for them by limited job prospects.

Consequently, as a scholarly community, we should recognize that these standards represent an unparalleled opportunity for learning—for both teachers and students. Although not all will be comfortable with some of the nuts and bolts of the framework, these standards embrace the notion of equity more than any other single reform in recent decades. Essentially, they state that all students in all grades in all areas of our country must receive a rigorous, content-rich literacy program in order to be successful in the 21st century. It is a laudable goal and one worthy of our resources and strong commitment.

This book is designed to help make the CCSS a reality in classrooms. It brings together all the elements that teachers need to know: implementation strategies for use in the classroom, an understanding of child development, and how these standards may progress throughout the grades. Recognizing that early literacy begins before kindergarten, it sets out to map out the qualities of a good curriculum and its implementation in preschool. It then carefully details throughout the chapters how these standards are expressed with increasing complexity from grade to grade, providing an ongoing and cumulative progression of skills. Specialists in their fields, the contributors provide practical guidelines for implementing these standards in classrooms, along with vignettes that bring them vividly to life. Chapters provide classroom activities and questions to consider as a professional community.

As scholars, practitioners, and policymakers, we cannot afford to fail in our implementation of more rigorous standards for our students. In my experience, students are far more capable than we have traditionally given them credit for. They want to learn. They want to become expert in a domain of their interests. They want to dig deeper in content areas and read closely in order to develop knowledge and expertise. To the extent that this reform movement promotes this kind of in-depth learning, thinking, and collaborating with others in communities of practice, I applaud it and look forward to tapping children's potential in a way we have never fully done before.

Introduction

Jennifer Renner Del Nero

The Common Core State Standards (CCSS) are the first academic standards to be independently adopted by almost every state in the country. National assessments will eventually follow these standards. The purpose and intent of the Common Core standards for English language arts (ELA), as well as those for literacy in history/social studies and science education, are the focus of this book. How should these standards be put into practice for daily instruction? *Teaching with the Common Core Standards for English Language Arts, PreK–2*, attempts to provide answers to this question. The purpose of these standards—universalizing the skills that all K–12 students in the United States will learn—is a worthwhile and necessary endeavor, yet the standards are mere words on a page unless successfully executed in the classroom. Like the children under their guidance, educators and administrators need detailed explanations and models to support them in understanding and implementing these new standards.

This volume is aimed at educators, administrators, graduate students, university professors, and others working with students in PreK through grade 2. Although the Common Core standards technically begin with kindergarten, this book deliberately expands its focus to include preschool. Where the CCSS kindergarten standards are appropriate to PreK instruction, this is noted; where related but distinct standards make sense for PreK, these are also examined. Each of the eight core chapters addresses one of the major ELA domains: literature, informational texts, foundational skills, writing, speaking and listening, language, technology, and assessment. They contain invaluable information, insight, and research from literacy leaders in their respective fields. These authors are fully aware of the challenges that enactment of the Common Core standards presents to educators; the chapters are written candidly and with full appreciation of the efforts it will take for educators to accomplish this goal. Their objective is twofold: to provide a theoretical background and detailed explanation of each of the CCSS/ELA standards as well as practical suggestions, classroom vignettes, models, instructional resources, and unit ideas to implement the standards. Appendix A lists all of the ELA standards for K–2, organized by grade level. Appendix B, unique to this volume, contains a full thematic unit with the CCSS/ELA standards embedded throughout the daily lessons.

There are many interpretations of how the CCSS should be put into place in the classroom. There isn't one right answer. Be cautious when implementing them; think first about the instruction that works well for you right now. For example, we need to teach children in small groups and differentiate instruction using materials with which they can learn and be successful. However, in whole-class instruction, we need to use grade-level text to be sure that children are exposed to and guided through complex materials. Likewise, we need to read lots of informational text to our children, but that doesn't mean we should give up narrative text. They are equally important. We need to focus on the language arts when we teach reading and writing, but also integrate the Common Core standards in content-area subjects. Thematic units help not only to integrate the CCSS into science and social studies, for example, but they are also motivating and relevant and bring meaning to reading. When we pay attention to these things, reading is no longer just a skill to be learned but rather a skill to be used to learn other things. We need to hold on to the explicit instruction that we've learned is so important when teaching reading. But when we embed the CCSS into other content areas, children are getting reading instruction *all day* in school, not just during the language arts period. In short, we should not swing all the way toward either embracing or rejecting the new Common Core standards. Keep what you know is good in your classroom and refine it with these standards to bring more sophistication to your reading instruction.

In Chapter 1, Pearson and Hiebert orient the reader with an introduction to the Common Core standards. The authors begin with a brief history of standards in American education. They then discuss how the CCSS are necessary for successful infusion of literacy instruction throughout all the content areas, followed by an explanation of how these particular standards are distinct from those of the past, including an emphasis on close critical reading and interdisciplinary connectivity. The authors provide two readings of the 10 anchor standards for ELA—one that adheres closely to the original text and another that is their personal interpretation of the content and their speculation as to its implications, including general measures that teachers can enact to meet them. Pearson and Hiebert conclude by turning a critical lens toward the standards, examining their potential complications and the further questions they pose, so that educators can successfully navigate any potential pitfalls.

Turning to the first ELA strand, reading literature, Morrow, Tracey, and Healey, in Chapter 2, discuss how teachers can embed literature in meaningful and motivational ways. The authors begin with a rationale for the importance of regularly incorporating literature into all aspects of daily instruction. They then consider the four subareas (or "organizing elements") of reading literature—key ideas and details, craft and structure, integration of knowledge and ideas, and range of reading and level of text complexity— and unpack each with a brief theoretical background and relevant literature in support of each domain. Following this are illustrative classroom vignettes, resources, and numerous lesson plan ideas for teachers to directly utilize in meeting these goals. The authors conclude the chapter with a comprehensive model thematic unit, with literature and the aforementioned skills infused throughout.

Duke, Halladay, and Roberts take up the discussion of the second strand, reading informational texts, in Chapter 3. The authors reflect on the importance of including informational text in the elementary classroom as well as how the overarching category of "informational texts" includes a wide range of subgenres. This is followed by a consideration of the four subareas of reading informational texts, including detailed explanations, classroom examples, print and digital resources, and lesson plan ideas for each.

The authors stress how instructors must make thoughtful choices in text selection, with an emphasis on matching texts to children's interests in order to nurture motivation.

Within the strand of foundational skills for reading, Gehsmann and Templeton, in Chapter 4, discuss how foundational literacy skills—the basic understandings of language—serve as the backbone for later literacy development. The authors present the four elements of foundational skills—print concepts, phonological awareness, word recognition, and fluency—and support each with lesson plan ideas and illustrative classroom models. They emphasize how the key to successful foundational skills instruction lies in contextualizing the skills through meaningful instructional integration throughout the school day. The chapter concludes with a list of children's books that can be used for teaching foundational skills as well as additional instructional activities.

In Chapter 5, Hansen focuses on the importance of celebrating students as writers and authors in their own right. After a brief history of the evolving idea of students as writers and the significance of the social context in writing instruction, Hansen provides an overview of the three elements of the writing standards that pertain to grades K–2: text types and purposes, production and distribution of writing, and research to build and present knowledge. She then details each component through the use of classroom lessons and various student writing samples. Embedded in the classroom examples is Hansen's analysis of what is occurring and how each of the standards is being successfully addressed by the classroom teacher without "teaching to the test." She insists on the importance of infusing the writing standards throughout the school day and across content domains. Included at the end of the chapter are mentor text suggestions as well as additional writing lesson ideas.

In Chapter 6, Gillam and Reutzel consider the speaking and listening strand, beginning with the critical link between oral language proficiency and academic achievement. They explore comprehension and collaboration and the presentation of knowledge and ideas—two subareas of speaking and listening—and offer suggestions for putting each of these into practice through expanded descriptions, classroom examples for each grade level, and author commentary on the examples. The chapter concludes with additional activity suggestions that support Gillam and Reutzel's philosophy that speaking and listening instruction is most efficient and effective when meaningfully integrated throughout the school day rather than being taught as an isolated lesson.

To introduce their exploration of language in Chapter 7, Watts-Taffe and Breit-Smith emphasize the critical link between language and identity; educators must be vigilant in striking a balance between helping students acquire standard English conventions and celebrating language diversity. The authors guide the reader in exploring each of the two subareas—conventions of language and vocabulary acquisition and use—through classroom vignettes and analysis and illustrate how one teacher infused language best practices throughout the course of a school day. The chapter ends with supplementary text resources and activities.

The importance of having students navigate and negotiate multiple text modes is the focus of Chapter 8. McKenna, Conradi, Young, and Jang highlight the CCSS shift away from technology as an isolated component; this deliberate and welcomed integration in literacy instruction reflects the principle that current literacy practices in classrooms naturally must include digital as well as print media. In support of this, the authors examine points where the new standards explicitly call for technology use and offer sample approaches. Also included is an extensive list of resources and considerations for student assessment.

Afflerbach takes up the topic of assessment in relation to the Common Core standards in Chapter 9. He acknowledges that the new standards represent a series of challenges and opportunities for educators and details how new approaches to literacy assessment can help teachers meet evolving demands. Afflerbach also emphasizes the connection between formative and summative assessment and the need for a balance between the two. Assessments can form the foundation for literacy success. Moreover, well-devised assessments can serve as tools for teachers to help students in raising the bar of academic achievement that the standards mandate.

In Chapter 10, Shanahan brings together the various voices within this volume. Noting the ambitious nature of the CCSS and the challenge they pose to teachers, he offers some valuable points of advice for successful infusion of the standards throughout grades K–2, with the understanding that the birth of new guidelines for administrators and teachers is the easy part. The successful adoption of the standards in classrooms across the country is where the real challenge lies. Shanahan provides a variety of other useful information, including curricular maps integrating the Common Core standards.

Understandably, educators have grown tired of "upsetting the apple cart" by constantly reinvesting their effort to revamp student instruction based on what could turn out to be only the latest educational fad—unequivocally praised at first, adopted without question or introspection, implemented without necessary supports or opportunity for collegiate conversations, executed without confidence or understanding of the original purpose or intent, and ultimately rejected and replaced by a new trend—and so the never-ending, exhausting cycle continues. However, as the writers in this volume suggest, the Common Core standards, despite their limitations, hold the promise of a positive new direction in America's literacy instruction—if they are approached thoughtfully and executed in meaningful ways that align with the intent and goals that set them apart from methods of the past.

This book, with its critical approach, honest guidance, and abundance of examples and resources, will help educators and administrators embark on the journey to successful and lasting incorporation of the standards throughout all facets of classroom instruction. *Teaching with the Common Core Standards for English Language Arts, PreK–2*, marks the beginning of a roadmap for understanding and applying these standards in the classroom to foster meaningful literacy learning for all students and for inspiring teachers across the country to build upon this initial collection of interpretations and examples for the shared benefit of all. Let the conversation continue.

Contents

Teaching with the Common Core Standards for English Language Arts, PreK–2

CHAPTER 1

Understanding the Common Core State Standards

P. David Pearson
Elfrieda H. Hiebert

Standards have become a staple of the American school and curriculum since they first entered the reform scene in the early 1990s. They were conceived in the wake of the highly influential National Governors Association Conference of 1989, and have been endorsed by conservatives, liberals, and radicals alike (albeit for vastly different reasons) and reformulated many times since their inception. Schools, teachers, and students find their academic lives shaped by whatever standards hold court in their educational corner of the world. After the completely voluntary effort to produce national standards by the math community, the first major wave of standards was sponsored by federal and quasi-federal agencies, including the Office of Educational Research and Innovation and the National Academy of Sciences, with the goal of encouraging disciplinary professions (e.g., history, English language arts, and science) in the early 1990s to develop a clear statement of what students should know and be able to do at various developmental levels. The idea was that, with broad agreement on these curricular outlines of the typical progression of student performance, assessments and curricular schemes could be developed and implemented that would guarantee students would meet the benchmark performance standards along the journey to successful achievement and, eventually, participation in the world of work and higher education. Students would go on to college and into the workplace armed with the knowledge, skills, and dispositions needed to be successful in their postsecondary lives. That was the dream, the hope, and the expectation we began with in 1989. And it was still the dream in the late 1990s, when the Clinton administration undertook a valiant effort to ensure, via Title I (Improving America's Schools Act [IASA]), that all states had developed content standards and tests to measure their acquisition.

The Common Core State Standards (CCSS; National Governors Association [NGA] Center for Best Practices and Council of Chief State School Officers [CCSSO], 2010) represent the latest, and in many ways the most ambitious, version of that same vision of what standards could do for schools, teachers, and students. What is most significant about the CCSS is that, unlike the state action in response to IASA or No Child Left Behind (NCLB), the CCSS effort was driven by the states, not a federal agency or even a federally sponsored initiative. Initiated under the auspices of the NGA and the CCSSO, the CCSS are a bold attempt to ensure that at the end of the K–12 curricular journey students are prepared to enter either college or the workforce and take their place as knowledgeable, contributing members of the American economy, society, and polity. As a state-led initiative, the CCSS are intentionally designed to improve upon the current standards of individual states by creating clear, consistent, and rigorous standards to which all American students will be held, irrespective of the particular location of their residence. In short, opportunity to learn would not be an accident of a student's ZIP code.

There are many reasons for developing a common set of standards across American states, but the driving force is the potential for inequity created by the tremendous variability observed from state to state in policies and procedures related to curriculum, instruction, and assessment. Studies have shown considerable variability across states in the content and quality of state standards, state assessments used to measure student achievement, and the criteria used to gauge success on standards (Bandeira de Mello, 2011; Polikoff, Porter, & Smithson, 2011).

The CCSS were established by looking closely at standards and curriculum in sites where achievement is high. The designers of the CCSS looked carefully at standards of other countries (particularly those with high scores on international assessments) to ensure that all American students are prepared to succeed in a global economy and society. They have also been designed to reflect the knowledge and skills required to participate as workers and citizens in a digital–global world. The standard development process began with those goals required by high school graduates, proficiencies that would guarantee that students possessed college and career readiness (CCR). K–12 standards were developed to ensure learning progressions that would lead students to achieve CCR standards at the end of their K–12 school careers.

The title of the standards—*Common Core State Standards for English Language Arts & Literacy in History/Social Studies, Science, and Technical Subjects*—highlights the need for developing literacy and language proficiencies in the context of disciplinary knowledge—knowledge that extends to content-area courses rather than exclusively English language arts (ELA) courses. The CCSS aim for an integrated view of the components within the ELA at K–5: reading, writing, listening, and speaking, although there are separate (but highly similar) standards for literature and informational text. The grade 6–12 standards are first organized by discipline: ELA and then subject areas to distinguish which standards are the responsibility of the ELA curriculum (and teachers) and which are to be addressed by subject-area curricula and teachers. However, within ELA, history, or science and technology, the expectation is that reading, writing, speaking, and listening will be highly coordinated, if not fully integrated.

It is also worth noting that the CCSS are not intended to define all that can or should be taught; the standards are not intended to be a curriculum, as described within the standards: "By emphasizing required achievements, the *Standards* leave room for teachers, curriculum developers, and states to determine how those goals should be reached and what additional topics should be addressed" (NGA and CCSSO, 2010, p. 4). The intention of the standards is to provide guidance on core content of *any* curriculum, with the explicit expectation that districts, schools, and teachers will add specification and differentiation to their enactment of the core goals. Finally, they do not define the full range of support for English language learners and students with special needs. In short, the CCSS provide a core set of expectations and intentionally leave much to districts, schools, and teachers to figure out for themselves—to, if you will, put a local signature on their implementation of the core.

WHAT'S NEW AND DIFFERENT ABOUT THE CCSS?

In this section, we examine four aspects of the standards that set them apart from earlier iterations of state and/or national standards: close and critical reading, integration of language processes and disciplinary content, media/research literacy, and text complexity. We review these four in the order listed, as a way of acknowledging their progressive dissimilarity from earlier efforts. However poorly they have been implemented, neither close, critical reading nor integrated literacy is a new goal. Both have been around, in one form or another, at least since the days of John Dewey and progressive education and perhaps even earlier, in either Horace Mann's Common School Movement or Francis Parker's Quincy System (Cavanaugh, 1994). Then we move to two around which there has been considerable rhetoric but little action: disciplinary literacy and digital media as a new form of literacy. We end with the aspect that is as old as it is new and as controversial as it is commonplace: text complexity. Teachers and curriculum designers have been dealing with text complexity at least since the advent of the first readability formula (Lively & Pressey, 1923) and perhaps since the first "graded" reading series (McGuffey, 1836). However, text complexity is very new to standards documents, and this is the first set of standards that outlines specific expectations for increasing the level of challenge expected by students at each grade level.

We address each of the topics from two lenses: (1) a description of the topic that stays close to the text provided in the CCSS and (2) our "reading" of the implications for implementation inside classrooms and schools, with a special emphasis on implications that represent new rather than tried-and-true issues and practices. In the final section of the chapter, we address the dilemmas and conundrums that these standards, despite all of their advantages, bring to literacy education.

Close and Critical Reading

If there is a "first amongst equals" among the principles of the Common Core, it is surely close reading. Early on, the CCSS (2010) framers declare their commitment to this principle:

> Students who meet the Standards readily undertake the close, attentive reading that is at the heart of understanding and enjoying complex works of literature. They habitually perform the critical reading necessary to pick carefully through the staggering amount of information available today in print and digitally. They actively seek the wide, deep, and thoughtful engagement with high-quality literary and informational texts that builds knowledge, enlarges experience, and broadens worldviews. (p. 3)

The Perspective

The phrase "close reading" is used in the standards in much the way it entered the field of literary interpretation during the era of I. A. Richards and New Criticism in the mid-20th century (Richards, 1929/2008). In its canonical version, it can entail the explication and implication of every element (section, sentence, clause, phrase, word) in the text (although more often than not close readers "sample" sections of text for this sort of careful exegesis).

Appreciation of the structure of the text and the craft of the author are not the major outcomes of close reading; knowledge is. Students who read in a way that meets the standards gain strong disciplinary knowledge for their efforts, as they engage with texts in the disciplines of literature, history, science, and technical subjects. They know that different disciplines call for different types of evidence (e.g., documentary evidence in history, experimental evidence in science, textual clues in literature) and ways of formulating arguments to support claims about how the world works. Above all, students value evidence as the basic currency of academic discourse, and they are able to evaluate the claims made by the authors of texts and those that they make themselves in crafting arguments about the ideas they encounter in these texts.

One might anticipate that such a commitment to acquiring knowledge and constructing precise arguments achieves those goals at a cost; and the most likely candidate is an erosion of commitment to multicultural contributions and perspectives in literature, art, history, and science. Not so. The standards express clear commitments to cultural diversity. Early in the document, the standards announce this commitment clearly: "Students actively seek to understand other perspectives and cultures through reading and listening, and they are able to communicate effectively with people of varied backgrounds" (NGA and CCSSO, 2010, p. 4). Commitment to diversity does not imply unexamined acceptance of the ideas in the diverse array of texts students encounter. To the contrary, the same analytic and critical lenses that enable readers to critique and construct arguments are brought to bear on all texts they encounter. They evaluate other points of view critically and constructively.

Close reading is meant to occur both within and across texts, reflecting the general disposition of the standards that students are always trying to connect the ideas they encounter in a given text with other ideas from a range of sources, including previously read texts, their prior experiences, and other media (e.g., digital content).

Implications for Implementation

In our discussion of implications for close reading, one might expect us to focus on the first cluster (Standards 1–3) of Key Ideas and Details. After all, isn't a clear exposition of what the text *says* the natural result of close reading? While this might be true in a very narrow sense of what it means to read closely, this perspective misses the point of close reading. We read closely to acquire knowledge, but we cannot acquire that knowledge except in relation to what we already know; hence the significance of the third cluster of standards: Integration of Knowledge and Ideas (Standards 7–9). We also read closely to critique and evaluate the validity of the claims made by authors or the tools they use to engage and persuade readers; hence critique—the stuff of Standard 7 entails close reading in a very direct way. We are not suggesting that the other two clusters of standards—Key Ideas and Details (Standards 1–3) and Craft and Structure (Standards 4–6)—are not fundamental to integrating and using knowledge. The integration of knowledge depends on understanding the generation of key ideas and details and, when appropriate, analyses of how aspects of craft and structure influence the presentation and positioning of those key ideas and details. However, the ultimate goal of reading is (1) the integration of knowledge and ideas from text; (2) the delineation, evaluation, and critique of arguments and specific claims in a text; and (3) the analysis of ideas encountered across multiple texts and experiences to build knowledge. Put differently, close reading entails all of the standards. We privilege the last cluster because we fear that if we begin our instructional journey with the first cluster, we may become mired there and never get to the knowledge building and integration facets of the reading curriculum that is the core goal of the standards.

In order to keep students' eyes on the prize of gaining knowledge and insight from reading, we would emphasize two particular curricular and pedagogical moves:

- Teachers should give students—better yet, help students set—purposes for reading as well as promote connections to previously read texts and experiences. Such scaffolding of content does not require vast amounts of time. A simple reference to memorials or to the loss of life that results from wars may be sufficient to place Lincoln's Gettysburg Address or Winston Churchill's *Blood, Toil, Sweat, and Tears* into perspective for students.
- Students benefit from opportunities to review key ideas and themes from literature and also disciplinary areas. If knowledge is viewed to be cumulative, opportunities to review and revisit are essential. This means helping students extract common themes, topics, insights, and problems from sets of texts. The essential questions are, what's new in the text we just read, and how does it jive with what we already know about this issue?

Helping students watch their knowledge grow, change, and deepen is the ultimate goal of close reading. That is a principle not to be forgotten when one encounters a heavy dose of low-level literal comprehension questions in a well-meaning but misguided teachers' manual.

Integration of Language Processes and Disciplinary Content

The essence of reading is text complexity and the growth of comprehension. For writing, it is text types, responding to reading, and research. For speaking and listening: flexible communication and collaboration, and for language: conventions, effective use, and vocabulary. . . . By reading texts in history/social studies, science, and other disciplines, students build foundation of knowledge in these fields that will also give them the background to be better readers in all content areas. Students can only gain this foundation when the curriculum is intentionally and coherently structured to develop rich content knowledge within and across grades. (NGA and CCSSO, 2010, pp. 8, 10)

The Perspective

Integration is implicated in two assumptions about learning and content that underlie the CCSS/ELA: (1) Receptive (reading and listening) and productive (writing and speaking) language processes are integrated in learning and (2) content is viewed as the source and site of language use. That is, content acquisition requires, rationalizes, and enhances language use. The integrated view within the language arts and of the language arts with disciplinary knowledge presented by the CCSS contrasts sharply with the heavy emphasis that has been placed on reading as an encapsulated, independent subject in the years of NCLB.

In previous scholarship, the integration among the language arts and the integration of language processes and disciplinary content have often been treated separately (or not at all). In a summary of the research on integration, Gavelek, Raphael, Biondo, and Wang (2000) identified two perspectives on the integration of language arts: process driven and text driven. In the former, text selection tends to be incidental, and what matters is staying true to the processes and activities; subject matter texts, a single literary text, or a text set related by theme or topic serve equally well in the service of language process development. In the text-driven approach, processes are taken up to the degree that they promote a clear exposition of the ideas and themes in a given text, but content acquisition trumps the practice of any given language process.

Integration of language processes around literature makes good sense, but when disciplinary content is added to the mix, the nature of instruction takes quite a different form. A disciplinary view of literacy recognizes that literacy is an essential part of any disciplinary practice and that different skills, knowledge, and reasoning processes hold sway as one moves from one discipline to the next (Heller & Greenleaf, 2007; Shanahan & Shanahan, 2008).

One of the most obvious ways in which literacy demands differ across disciplines is in the nature of the text (van den Broek, 2010). Texts that students encounter in history are quite different from those they encounter in chemistry. An obvious difference is in vocabulary, but syntax is also different, as evident in a mathematical equation and a historical document (e.g., Bill of Rights). Disciplines also vary in the uses of language and the relationships between texts and ways of developing knowledge (Moje, 2008). Shanahan and Shanahan (2008) found that the experts in different disciplinary areas approached texts in unique ways. These differences, Shanahan and Shanahan suggested, reflect variation in the values, norms, and methods of scholarship within disciplines. Historians, for example, read to ascertain the author's perspective since the heavy reliance within historical scholarship on retrospective analyses of source documents can mean selective analysis and biased interpretation.

Examples of how literacy processes can be developed with disciplinary content, even in the early elementary years, are most readily available for science instruction. The works of Cervetti and Barber (2008), Magnusson and Palincsar (2005), and Varelas, Pappas, Barry, and O'Neill (2001) provide clear examples of the attempt to embed literacy practices within a science learning framework with younger learners. In the work of Cervetti and Barber (2008), students read to deepen their knowledge for science inquiry activities. For example, a text might give detailed information of a real-world example of a scientific phenomenon (e.g., an oil spill) or a text might depict and describe different kinds of specimens that might not be available for students to examine firsthand (e.g., a close-up of sand particles depicting their size, shape, and color). Discussions and writing/documentation activities are also a prominent part of the science inquiry process in these efforts. In comparison to more "encapsulated" instruction, students from grades 2 through 5 have shown consistent advantages in their growth in science content, vocabulary, and writing (Cervetti, Barber, Dorph, Pearson, & Goldschmidt, 2009; Wang & Herman, 2005) but less consistent growth in reading comprehension.

The Reading Apprenticeship program (Greenleaf et al., 2011) provides frames for high school teachers to use in integrating disciplinary literacy practices into high school science teaching. (They also provide examples in history but science is the most carefully examined discipline.) Teachers are guided in engaging in conversations with their students in which they model and discuss how to read science texts, why people read science texts in these ways, and how to unearth, come to terms with, and summarize the content of the texts. The students use complex science texts as they engage in the intellectual work of science inquiry. High school students in Reading Apprenticeship classrooms have been found to make greater gains on standardized tests in reading and biology than students in control classrooms (Greenleaf et al., 2011).

The conceptual foundation for disciplinary knowledge as a context for supporting language learning is equally as strong within social studies as it is in science, although the real-world implementations in classrooms are much rarer; even rarer is research evaluating the impact of integrating literacy activities directly into social studies content. This discrepancy reflects the disparity in federal funding in social studies versus science; some argue that as a nation we avoid research about social studies content because of fears that it will lead to instruction and inculcation of humanistic values (Evans, 2004).

Several small-scale projects at the elementary school level illustrate the manner in which literacy processes can be developed through and used in the service of content in social studies. Williams and colleagues (2007) describe a project in which low-income second-grade students were placed in one of three instruction conditions: (1) typical social studies content but with a comprehension treatment (instruction in text structure as well as an emphasis on questioning and graphic organizers), (2) a social studies content-only program, or (3) no instruction. The students who received the comprehension plus content treatment performed as well on the social studies as those in the content-only treatment with the additional benefits of increased performances in reading comprehension.

More projects have been conducted at the high school level, such as the instruction of historical reasoning strategies for 11th graders by De La Paz and Felton (2010), with the aim of supporting students' writing of argumentative texts on historical topics. One strategy, for example, was described as "Consider the Author," with questions such as "How does the author's viewpoint have an effect on his argument?" Students who participated in this instruction produced better elaborated and more persuasive historical arguments than comparison students.

The humanities tell a somewhat different tale, largely through the literature curriculum. The central themes of literature have been identified within philosophy, literary theory, and even psychology, but typically the themes of core reading programs are scattershot, some dealing with genres (e.g., puzzles and mysteries, fables) and others with potentially powerful themes of literature (e.g., survival, turning points) that often crumble through surface-level, almost trivial, treatment in commercial programs. The content of literature is more than a simple topic, however. Literature is the context in which writers and readers explore the human experience (Probst, 1986). Some text may not have the most profound themes, especially the texts of beginning reading. True literature, even in picture books, grapples with the great themes of human experience—for example, the relationship of the individual to family, community, and even morality. Despite its emphasis on disciplinary knowledge, the CCSS have not necessarily done a better job of identifying the content of literature than previous standards documents or, for that matter, literature anthologies available in the marketplace. In emphasizing disciplinary knowledge, however, the CCSS open the way for educators to attend to the critical content that is part of the disciplines, including the humanities.

Implications for Implementation

For true integration of disciplinary and language processes, actions need to occur outside the classroom: in state departments, in district offices, and at departmental and school levels. Granted, there are things that teachers can do on their own and even in local sites, but the critical point is that collective teacher action is required to move this agenda forward. For example:

- Educational units are going to need to achieve clarity on major curricular themes. There is some guidance on how educators can go about identifying these themes (Lipson, Valencia, Wixson, & Peters, 1993; Valencia & Lipson, 1998) and convincing peers to adopt them over more conventional approaches to curriculum.

- In literature (as in other disciplines), teachers need to make selections of texts and tasks with a clear view of the larger themes and understandings of human experience that these texts and tasks could promote. Themes are big ideas or enduring questions that have relevance for the people of a diverse society in many aspects of their lives, both in and out of school and that possess enough gravitas to sustain inquiry over time (e.g., "Culture and life experience influence how people respond to challenges they face"). This is quite different from a statement such as "Friends must learn to get along." Getting serious about the knowledge dimensions of literature teaching is essential; otherwise, literary themes may be easily trivialized into fluff that fails to build knowledge and insight.

- Science is a good place to start, not only because there is more work on the science–literacy integration agenda but also because the emerging national science standards (National Research Council, 2012) take on literacy and language as an essential part of learning science. Learning the oral and written discourses of science is as prominent in these new standards as is the acquisition of content and engagement of inquiry processes.

Research and Media

> Students cite specific evidence when offering an oral or written interpretation of a text. They use relevant evidence when supporting their own points in writing and speaking, making their reasoning clear to the reader or listener, and they constructively evaluate others' use of evidence. (NGA and CCSSO, 2010, p. 7)

The Perspective

No book, no library, no learning environment in human history has had the capacity to make available to students the volume of information, the variety of forms of information, and the connections within and across information sources that digital environments allow (Cavanaugh & Blomeyer, 2007). The digital–global age makes knowledge available in ways not experienced by previous generations. To be ready for college, the workforce, and life in this digital–global world, students need the ability to gather, comprehend, evaluate, synthesize, and report on information and ideas from an extensive volume and range of print and nonprint media. They also need to be able to evaluate, create, and contribute to information on topics and, in doing so, use the full range of media. Students' ability to use and contribute to knowledge using a range of media is embedded throughout other standards in the CCSS.

Educators, community members, and legislators all agree with the essential role of students' acquisition of high levels of proficiency in using technologies to gain, organize, critique, and share knowledge. How to reach this goal with large numbers of students in a world where new technologies and new stores of knowledge proliferate by the hour is the challenge. The research and media goal of the CCSS is known as informational literacy among the professional group that has traditionally been responsible for archiving and organizing knowledge: librarians (Rader, 2002). From the perspective of informational literacy, a distinction needs to be made between using multiple resources for acquiring knowledge and for organizing and sharing knowledge. A variety of skills and strategies are involved in using resources on the Internet to research a question or to solve a problem. As Labbo and Reinking (1999) have described it, individuals need to become their own librarians, adept at locating and evaluating sources of information. When the task involves sharing information that has been gained from research, regardless of whether it is first- or secondhand, individuals need to be able to organize their information in ways that communicate to others. To do this requires skill at selecting the appropriate media for communicating and, within any given medium, the appropriate ways to organize information.

A distinction between knowledge acquisition and knowledge communication is not articulated within the CCSS. Nor will educators find a wealth of information on how knowledge acquisition and knowledge communication with digital environments can be developed. In particular, we know of no large-scale projects, over the K–12 span, that illustrate how teachers can guide students in either the gaining knowledge or the organizing/sharing knowledge dimension. Writers from the field of information literacy frequently recommend the use of projects to develop both knowledge acquisition and knowledge communication proficiencies. Project-based learning has a long history (Darling-Hammond et al., 2008), dating back at least to Dewey within American education, and is most evident in several decades of work in science education, such as the examples described earlier.

For most teachers, project-based learning will be a challenging venture. When coupled with the demands for integration of various technologies, its widespread use, at least in the immediate future, is dim. Keeler and Langhorst (2008) have suggested that teachers be supported in ways of moving from simple integration of technology (e.g., using a particular kind of software) to more complex forms (e.g., students' contributions to a book blog) in a series of small steps. However, this progression does not address developmental issues. Developmental issues can be viewed from both the perspective of children of different ages and in terms of the cultivation of particular proficiencies in students of any age. In terms of the first concern, two critical questions must be addressed: At what age should children become involved with a variety of technologies, and how much time should be devoted? For example, how much time should kindergartners be spending with digital devices? With regard to the second face of developmental progression, the manner in which the "critical reading" of resources available on digital devices progresses has yet to be documented. The manner in which graphics, animation, and gaming components influence students' critical stance, in particular, requires examination.

There is a substantial amount of work left to be done regarding the acquisition of knowledge and the sharing/organization of knowledge by students that might ultimately guide any large-scale effort to infuse this digital perspective into American classrooms. Even a short tour of websites indicates that there is considerable teacher activity and many powerful reports on how students' acquisition of knowledge and their communication of knowledge are enhanced through technology. The movement in this domain is so rapid that documentation and evaluation lag far behind the implementations in real classrooms. The knowledge resources in a variety of media are many. The work to understand how students can be supported in powerfully using the technological resources currently available—both to acquire knowledge and communicate their own knowledge—requires documentation, evaluation, and substantial collaboration among teachers, industry, and researchers.

Implications for Implementation

Ways to support media and research proficiencies include:

- Teachers should support students, even in the primary grades, to use a variety of resources to find answers to compelling questions.
- Teachers should support students, beginning in the primary grades, to organize information that has been learned and to develop means for sharing that information.

Text Complexity

> The Reading standards place equal emphasis on the sophistication of what students read and the skill with which they read. Standard 10 defines a grade-by-grade "staircase" of increasing text complexity that rises from beginning reading to the college and career readiness level. (NGA and CCSSO, 2010, p. 31)

The Perspective

The 10th and final reading standard of the CCSS calls for students to have the capacity to read, compared with their grade-level counterparts from earlier eras, more complex texts for their own grade level. The hope, and expectation, is that by upping the ante at every grade level beginning in grade 2, within 5 or 6 years high school graduates will actually be able to read the complex texts expected of them in college and the workplace. This focus on text complexity derives from concerns that today's high school graduates are not prepared to read the materials of college or the workplace (ACT, 2006). The CCSS is the first standards document, either at the state or national level, to include a standard devoted solely to students' capacity to read increasingly complex text over the grades. In previous standards documents, student reading proficiencies were described in relation to "grade-level text," but grade-level text was assumed rather than defined.

The CCSS writers provided two sources of guidance for educators (and test makers) to determine the progression in text complexity: (1) a tripartite model of text complexity and (2) exemplars for steps along the grade-by-grade staircase. The dimensions of the tripartite model are *qualitative* (i.e., levels of meaning or purpose, structure, language conventionality and clarity, and knowledge demands), *reader and task dimensions* (i.e., elements of instruction that teachers address in assignments, lesson planning, and moment by moment scaffolding); and *quantitative* (e.g., readability formulas that address word familiarity/frequency and syntactic complexity as well as newer measures that report on referential or deep cohesion).

In Appendix A of the CCSS document, the writers indicated that further guidance on qualitative dimensions would be forthcoming, but within the standards document only one quantitative system was presented: the Lexile Framework (MetaMetrics, 2000). Lexiles for grade-level bands, starting with grades 2–3, were recalibrated to ensure that the final point on the staircase—grade 11 CCR—would match the Lexiles of college and career texts. A second form of guidance is in Appendix B, which provides text exemplars that illustrate the nature of complex and high-quality texts at different grade bands.

The specification of a grade-by-grade staircase with quantitative levels and the provision of exemplar texts for different grade bands are the features that distinguish this standards document from its predecessors. A standard that addresses the complexity of the text makes eminent sense (one can only wonder why this standard has been overlooked in previous documents). However, the underlying theory and research on text complexity that would support creation of state and district curricula and programs are in short supply.

Evidence for particular assumptions regarding text complexity within the CCSS is sparse and, in some cases, nonexistent. Two telling examples of assumptions lacking a substantive evidence base are (1) the ramp-up trajectory and (2) expectations about struggling readers. There is no basis, at least that we can determine, for beginning the ramp-up process in grade 2 to ensure that high school students are at CCR levels (Hiebert, 2012); one could make an even more plausible argument for beginning the ramp-up at, say, grade 6. Regarding the plight of struggling readers, what makes us think that the current population of struggling readers, for whom the goal of grade-level texts is elusive, will suddenly master texts that far outstrip their reading level (Hiebert & Van Sluys, in press) just because we have asked them to try harder? We do not see how we can begin to enact higher standards for increased text complexity unless we also up the ante on the availability of strategies for scaffolding students' attempts to cope with texts that far exceed their reading current capacities. And we do not see how that can happen without a dramatic increase in teachers' knowledge about text and pedagogy.

One other concern centers on complete disregard for two key ideas that have been part of the rhetoric of individualized instruction for decades: (1) that there exists an optimal trajectory of difficulty for each child and (2) that students make the most progress in mastering increasingly difficult text when they are working squarely in their "zone of comfort"—not too easy but not too hard. There is no room for between-student accommodations of this sort when the ramp-up is in play.

Our concerns aside, amidst many unanswered questions, educators in states and districts need to press on to identify texts that align with the standards. In the next section, we identify how educators can respond in responsible ways. We do underscore the need for answers to questions about text complexity from the research community. We have yet to develop the research base that could help teachers and administrators stand up to this challenge.

Implications for Implementation

We offer guidelines to three groups of educators: leaders at district and state levels, leaders at school sites (principals, literacy coaches), and classroom teachers.

At the State or District Level. In many contexts, teachers do not have the prerogative of choosing the primary texts of instruction. Often these choices are determined on a district level or by state committees (e.g., California, Texas, Florida). Decisions at these levels will likely be highly influential in the interpretation of the CCSS text complexity standard. We offer the following implementation suggestions for those involved in text selection:

• Educators need to make qualitative criteria clear for the selection of texts selected for use in states and/or districts. The four qualitative dimensions (derived from ACT,

2006) identified by the CCSS writers (levels of meaning, structure, language convention-ality and clarity, and knowledge demands) have already been presented. One instantia-tion of this system that is currently popular describes each of these dimensions on a scale of "little" to "much" and an overall score is given to a text, irrespective of differences on the four dimensions (Copeland, Lakin, & Shaw, 2012). Two questions need to the answered: (1) whether these four dimensions capture the critical traits that matter in comprehension and (2) whether different traits would not be expected to have different manifestations or different effects at particular developmental points. That is, a number that summarizes the qualitative features fails to capture the very elements of texts that should be the growing edge for students.

At the School Level. The CCSS provided exemplars of complex texts at different levels but failed to describe what made these texts complex for students at particular grade bands (they also neglected to ensure that texts fit the Lexile parameters set for grade bands). What the CCSS writers failed to do is what teachers in schools (and in pro-fessional development venues) need to do to understand how text features influence their students' understanding of texts.

• Teachers within and across grade levels need to select texts that are anchors for different points for a grade or grade band. In the case of the primary levels, where growth in reading is substantial, benchmark texts should be identified for different periods in the school year (e.g., trimesters or semesters). The texts are not the ones that are taught but, rather, provide a "North Star" for reading instruction and evaluation.

At the Classroom Level. Even when teachers are required to use to the particular texts assigned to them, their instruction can either facilitate or hinder their students' growth in learning from complex texts. Positive actions include:

• Helping students understand and appreciate the differences in vocabulary of nar-ratives and informational texts. The unique words of narratives are typically synonyms or nuanced meanings for concepts that, at their core, students know (*timid/full of fear*). The unique words of informational texts, by contrast, often represent concepts that stu-dents do not know *and* are core to understanding the content (e.g., *photosynthesis, con-vection, nonrenewable resource, inflation rate*). A reader may be able to slide by *timid* but not *photosynthesis*.

• Giving students opportunities to pursue topics of personal interest. In interna-tional comparisons, American students have adequate reading performance but their interest in reading is among the lowest in the world (Mullis, Martin, Gonzalez, & Ken-nedy, 2003). Until American students are invited to explore their interests with text, they are unlikely to read extensively unless "they have to." Even the chance to select from among two or three texts can increase students' engagement as readers (Guthrie et al., 2006). The real benefit of offering students choice is increased engagement with reading more text for longer periods of time, thus building both knowledge and stamina for read-ing on their own.

• Ensuring that students read sufficient amounts of text (*volume*) and also read increasingly longer selections (*stamina*). The amounts of time devoted to reading in class-rooms and the amount of text that students are expected to read and use in tasks appear to be less than optimal in many American classrooms (Brenner, Hiebert, & Tompkins,

2009; Hiebert, Wilson, & Trainin, 2010). If students are to be prepared for the complex texts and tasks of college and careers, increasing the amount of text they are given and the size of chunks that draw on this knowledge needs to be a priority at the elementary school level. Opportunity, volume, and stamina should be the goals for these personal reading programs.

CONUNDRUMS, DILEMMAS, AND UNANSWERED QUESTIONS

As well intentioned as standards seem (who can oppose the goal of high achievement on rigorous standards for all students irrespective of demographic circumstances?), they have a checkered history in closing the achievement gap between educational haves and have-nots. In this section, we address what might be construed as the potential dark side of the CCSS. Unsurprisingly, most of our concerns are future oriented because they depend largely on how the standards will be implemented. The validity and efficacy of the CCSS, as with all previous standards efforts, will depend not so much on the goals they promote but on the degree to which they are implemented in a way that *supports* and *defines* excellence, so that they actually *do* promote more equitable achievement rather than just provide another opportunity for us to demonstrate to ourselves what we have known for all too long: that we, as a profession and a nation, are much better at advancing the achievement of those students least in need of our help. (See Lagana-Riordan & Aguilar, 2009, for an account of how the last decade has seen children of the wealthiest Americans make the greatest gains in achievement.) In this section, we address several of these potential unintended consequences, with the goal of maximizing the likelihood that we do not fall victim to them as these promising standards are translated into curriculum, pedagogy, and assessment in schools.

Our experience in working with the standards since their adoption in June 2010 in a variety of settings has brought several of these troubling possibilities to the surface. We share them here not so much to discourage educators from adopting and adapting the standards as to ensure that educators use them with a complete awareness of their constraints and affordances.

Upping the Ante on Text Complexity

An explicit goal of the CCSS is to increase the challenge level of the texts that students read in grades 3–12. The stated purpose of this move is to close, or at least narrow, the gap in text complexity of approximately 200 Lexiles (roughly two grade levels) that exists between the average grade 12 text and the average college freshman text. The expectation is that if the profession can gradually increase text challenge over the grades, in a few years students will leave high school ready to meet the challenge of college freshman-level texts. The further hope is that this process will eventually reduce our reliance on remedial courses—about 40% of entering freshman take them—in community colleges and universities.

This is a noble goal, but it is not at all clear how it can be achieved. Merely raising the bar on the complexity of texts that students are required to read at any grade level will not make it happen. Right now, educators struggle to help students meet the challenge of the texts that fall short of the mark for college readiness at the high school level. What makes us think that by raising the expectations and exhorting teachers and students to try harder we will all meet the challenge? It reminds us of the early days of the first standards movement in the 1990s, when the theory of action was that by raising the bar all the players in the system—administrators, teachers, and students—would be motivated to try harder to meet higher expectations. That is, standards/assessment/ accountability would lead to clear expectations and motivation, leading to higher levels of performance. It didn't work! By the mid-1990s, reformers had learned that they had to add professional development and teacher knowledge and practices to their theories of action as mediating variables to help meet the challenge.

Without infusing major changes in professional development for teachers and curriculum designers (so that those who design and deliver challenging texts understand the critical features of texts), increasing text complexity will be little more than a cruel hoax visited upon teachers and students. Increased text challenge will not lead to increased capacity for students to deal with complexity without increased teacher scaffolding and knowledge of the nature of text and language (see Fillmore & Snow, 2000) and how to scaffold conversations around text (see Murphy, Wilkinson, Soter, Hennessey, & Alexander, 2009) in order to manage complexity. It is not at all clear to us how anything short of a major investment in the development of teacher knowledge about text at all levels and in all disciplines will allow that to happen.

Keeping Our Word on Models of Complexity

The standards document promises to assess text complexity in the three ways described earlier: quantitatively, qualitatively, and by matching reader to text and task. Our fear is that both the qualitative and reader–text dimensions will either drop out when the standards are implemented at the state level or, equally as problematic, they will be given only token lip service. In short, states and districts will monitor the quantitative indices, leaving the other two categories to "fend for themselves." Thus, when all is said and done, only the quantitative indices will have any "teeth" and bear any consequences in shaping curricular expectations. It this happens, it will be a great loss to the teaching profession because teachers have much to learn about the nature of text complexity and ways of responding to it in collaborative examinations of a particular text and how to manage its tough patches when attempting to make it accessible to their students.

Some educators, ourselves included, were expecting the CCSS sponsors to create resources, such as a share website, where teachers can contribute their plans or successful accounts of how they had engaged their students in reading and responding to particular texts. Imagine what a resource that might be—where any teacher could find 5, 10, 20, 50, or even 100 accounts of how other teachers in specific settings with particular groups of students had negotiated their way through commonly used texts. The teachers' editions of basals and literature anthologies would pale in comparison to such highly contextualized stories of classroom implementation.

Our skeptical nature compels us to predict that the qualitative and reader–text dimensions will never see the light of day as the standards are implemented. Nothing would please us more than to be chided a decade from now for having been so pessimistic now.

We Already Do That!

In any organization, a major strategy for dealing with the novelty of change is to assimilate it by asserting prior ownership, expressed in the often-heard response, "That's nothing new! I've been doing that for years!" The implication is that if we are already doing it, then there is no reason to change what we are doing. So business as usual prevails! Reform accommodated! Next?

The degree to which this sort of assimilation of the CCSS is possible depends entirely on the "grain size" at which the match between past and future practice is made. If a state committee lines up the CCSS with their current ELA standards and asks, "Where in our current standards do we have language that maps onto the CCSS?", then they will be able to easily dismiss the CCSS as "same old, same old." However, if they take a more careful, deliberate approach to examining the CCSS ELA—where they examine the entire "logic" of the standards, complete with the appendices that define tasks, exemplars, and common texts that might be used—then there will be little overlap between the old and the new. For starters, few, if any, state standards we know of ground the standards within genre and disciplinary contexts in the same way and at the same level of detail of the CCSS. Likewise, few state standards documents invite an integrated view of the ELA *and* support an analysis of the synergies between ELA and disciplinary learning in the way the CCSS do. In short, only a shallow reading and mapping will support pigeonholing the CCSS as nothing new; dipping even slightly below the surface of both existing and new standards demands a call to action for a new way of thinking about the relationship between ELA and disciplinary learning.

Bait and Switch

We chose this highly pejorative metaphor of bait and switch intentionally as the title for this section not because we believe that the designers of the standards and its implementation documents had any malevolent intentions in mind when they shaped this effort, but because that's what things look like from the perspective of the consumers of the standards—the educators at the local level who will have to live with the consequences of their implementation. If we only had to deal with the standards, this might never have become a concern. However, the recent publication of "Publishers' Criteria" (Coleman & Pimentel, 2011) on the Common Core standards website alarms us greatly and leads us to wonder whether the letter and spirit of the standards document have been sacrificed at the altar of shaping published programs and materials. We will unpack passages from the publishers' guidelines and compare them with statements from the original standards documents to allow readers to decide for themselves whether the bait and switch label is appropriate.

Language from the Standards

Earlier, we suggested that the standards are noteworthy (and a refreshing change from the "mandate" frenzy of NCLB) for the degrees of freedom that they cede to the local level, even classroom teachers, with our citation from the introduction (p. 2) that the standards "leave room for teachers, curriculum developers, and states to determine how those goals should be reached and what additional topics should be addressed."

This statements sounds similar to the logic of standards in the first wave (early 1990s): Standards specify the goals of instruction, leaving the means of achieving them to teachers, schools, and districts. For the first several years of the standards movement, this logic prevailed. Then NCLB came along and mandated schools to use curricula that were based on "scientifically-based reading research" (SBRR), which was interpreted to be whatever was in the National Reading Panel (National Institute of Child Health and Human Development, 2000) report. Once this was done, both the ends (the standards) and the means (the set of curriculum programs that met the SBRR standard) of reading curriculum were set, leaving no room for teacher prerogative or local signature. Could something like this happen with the CCSS?

We provide a sequence of verbatim passages from the "Publishers' Criteria" (Coleman & Pimentel, 2011) to illustrate how they undermine the promise of teacher choice in the standards themselves:

Regarding the Nature of Texts

A significant percentage of tasks and questions are text dependent. . . . Rigorous text-dependent questions require students to demonstrate that they not only can follow the details of what is explicitly stated but also are able to make valid claims that square with all the evidence in the text. Text-dependent questions do not require information or evidence from outside the text or texts; they establish what follows and what does not follow from the text itself. (p. 6)

Regarding Questions and Tasks

The Common Core State Standards call for students to demonstrate a careful understanding of what they read before engaging their opinions, appraisals, or interpretations. Aligned materials should therefore require students to demonstrate that they have followed the details and logic of an author's argument before they are asked to evaluate the thesis or compare the thesis to others. (p. 9)

Staying Close to the Text

Materials make the text the focus of instruction by avoiding features that distract from the text. Teachers' guides or students' editions of curriculum materials should highlight the reading selections. . . . Given the focus of the Common Core State Standards, publishers should be extremely sparing in offering activities that are not text based. (p. 10)

These directives to publishers directly contradict the commitment to teacher prerogative promised in the standards (setting aside for another essay the fact that they reveal a professionally suspect and long-abandoned text-centric perspective on the topic of close reading). The biblical reference "The Lord giveth, the Lord hath taketh away" seems apt here: Promise teachers some professional choice in the standards and then direct publishers to write teacher guides with scripts that remove all the choice! Bait and switch? You decide.

Assessment

It comes as a surprise to absolutely no one who has lived through the last 20 years of educational reform that the assessments developed to measure progress in meeting curriculum standards matter more than the standards themselves (National Research Council, 1999; Pearson, 2007; Shepard, Hannaway, & Baker, 2009). The very logic of accountability systems demands that assessments play this lynchpin role. And the tighter we make the link between standards and assessment, and the finer the grain size at which we measure progress (e.g., a subtest for every letter sound rather than a subtest for letter sounds as a group), the greater the likelihood that assessments will drive instructional activities in the classroom (Paris, 2005; Pearson, 2007). If this practice is followed to its logical conclusion, then the assessment system becomes the default curriculum, shaping virtually all aspects of instruction as schools "teach to the test" through test preparation activities that can last for weeks, even months, in anticipation of the state standards test.

This puts a great burden on the tests we use to monitor progress—for individual students, teachers, and schools. What if the tests are not up to the task? What if they do not really measure the knowledge or the process they are designed to measure? Then students will have practiced, and teachers will have taught, material or skills that do not actually lead to increases in what is supposed to be measured. Haladyna, Nolen, and Hass (1991) have aptly labeled this shortcoming "test score pollution," which refers to an increase or decrease in a score on a test without an accompanying increase or decrease in the construct being measured. In short, students might get better (or worse) reading test scores without reading any better (or worse) than before.

Pollution is a concern for all assessments. Complex performance assessments and even portfolio systems can fall victim to the malady just as easily as multiple-choice standardized tests. When the stakes attached to an assessment are high, the temptation to seek higher scores without greater learning is always there, and it must be monitored with vigilance. Surely we want students to achieve higher scores on assessments, but because they learned more about the content or practice assessed and not because they practiced the test format and content more assiduously and more often. In the early 1990s, when the first standards movement was born, there was a widespread call for complex performance tasks to replace what most scholars regarded as the more easily corruptible standardized tests. To paraphrase Resnick and Resnick (1992) and Wiggins (1999), if schools are going to teach to the test, then let's have tests worth teaching to—a noble goal that is still quite elusive in our educational system. Why? We believe that it is the stakes that are attached to a test, not its content or format, that propel the counterproductive teaching-to-the-test syndrome that we all complain about but continue to enact annually in our schools.

As Pearson (2007) has pointed out, this situation makes a mockery of the age-old tradition of transfer as the gold standard for assessing learning. If what is "on the test" is highly consequential, what well-meaning teacher would encourage students to eschew what is right in front of them and instead study and apply what they are learning to novel (and risky, in terms of test scores) tasks and formats? Practicing what is on the test is an age-old tradition, spawning the phrase "the tradition of past exams" as a way of characterizing what students did (and do) to prepare for tests of consequence for either themselves or their schools. It doesn't seem to matter whether it is a low-level high school exit exam or an advanced placement exam (or a bar exam for that matter): Teaching to the test is a pervasive practice, one that discourages extending one's knowledge or skill far beyond the boundaries of the anticipated test.

Stakes aside, we believe that more complex assessment tasks—tasks that require the orchestration of many skills, strategies, and concepts—stand a much better chance of promoting productive, engaging pedagogy than do multiple-choice assessments of componential skills, particularly in reading and writing assessments—and so apparently do the developers in the two large consortia that have been funded to build world-class assessments of the Common Core standards. Both Partnership Assessment for Readiness for College and Careers (PARCC; 2011) and Smarter Balanced Assessment Consortium (SBAC; 2012) are developing hybrid assessments that balance the use of multiple-choice tests to maximize coverage of lower-level skills and concepts with extended constructed response (short essays of 100–300 words) and genuine performance tasks (activities that might take 2 or 3 hours to complete over more than 1 day) to measure deeper learning or transfer of skills and knowledge to new scenarios.

It remains to be seen whether these consortia will be successful in building exams that rely on complex performance for task completion and employ human judgment in scoring. The major question is whether these assessments will pass the tests of feasibility, affordability, and psychometric rigor when they are put to use in wide-scale assessment systems across the entire grade span. We recall the burst of enthusiasm that accompanied the performance assessment efforts of the early 1990s (Pearson, Spalding, & Myers, 1998; Valencia, Hiebert, & Afflerbach, 1994), as well as the bitter disappointment that ensued when these assessments did not stand up to the financial (who can afford to score them?), political ("Don't be evaluating my kid's values and thoughts—just whether he mastered the facts of the curriculum"), and psychometric (the assessments cannot demonstrate intertask generalizability—the scores of individuals might well be an accident of the particular task they were asked to complete). And it wasn't that there were no success stories. There were. For example, the assessments in states like Maryland, Kentucky, Vermont, and Washington survived for years with some combination of performance tasks and portfolios. Eventually, by the time NCLB was in place, however, all but a few pockets of these traditions had been replaced with conventional multiple-choice assessments. As we look toward the future, we wonder: In schools where financial resources are scarce, where political will is weak, and where stakes for individuals are high, can this new batch of constructed response and performance tasks meet the daunting challenge that lies ahead of them?

In one sense, there is no choice. The challenge must be met, primarily because mastery of the CCSS for the ELA cannot be measured easily (if at all) with simple, skill-by-skill multiple-choice tests. Perhaps some of the standards in Cluster 1, Key Ideas and Details, could be measured with simpler tests, and maybe even some of the structural aspects of text invited by Cluster 2—Craft and Structure. But few if any of the standards in Cluster 3—Integration of Knowledge and Ideas—lend themselves to anything less than constructed responses and, even more appropriately, performance examinations. So the challenge is there. The assessment players in PARCC and SBAC seem to be prepared to try to develop these sorts of measures and make them work, even as a part of large-scale assessment. It remains to be seen whether we, as a profession, will succeed in meeting a challenge that our predecessors have consistently failed to meet.

CODA

Our goal in this opening chapter is modest: to emphasize what the standards are really about, to discern what is new and different about them (and their implications when trying to implement them), and to heighten awareness of some of the vexing issues that require resolution as we move toward implementation (or decide what's worth implementing and what isn't).

In truth, our modest introduction is little more than a prelude to the remainder of this volume. In the chapters that follow, you will reencounter the themes and issues of which we have only scratched the surface here, plus many more that space did not permit us to touch upon. With greater awareness of these issues, readers will develop a clearer sense of how to manage local efforts to implement, accept, and/or reject the CCSS—what to emphasize, what to downplay, what to tackle first, what later, what never. We wish you well in the process and on the journey. It certainly won't be boring. And with a little luck it will be both interesting and worthwhile.

REFERENCES

ACT. (2006). *Reading between the lines: What the ACT reveals about college readiness in reading.* Iowa City, IA: Author.

Bandeira de Mello, V. (2011). *Mapping state proficiency standards onto the NAEP scales: Variation and change in state standards for reading and mathematics, 2005–2009* (NCES 2011-458). Washington, DC: U.S. Government Printing Office.

Brenner, D., Hiebert, E. H., & Tompkins, R. (2009). How much and what are third graders reading?: Reading in core programs. In E. H. Hiebert (Ed.), *Reading more, reading better* (pp. 118–140). New York: Guilford Press.

Cavanaugh, C., & Blomeyer, R. (Eds.). (2007). *What works in K–12 online learning.* Washington, DC: International Society for Technology in Education.

Cavanaugh, M. P. (1994). *A history of holistic literacy: Five major educators.* Westport, CT: Praeger.

Cervetti, G. N., & Barber, J. (2008). Text in hands-on science. In E. H. Hiebert & M. Sailors (Eds.), *Finding the right texts: What works for beginning and struggling readers* (pp. 89–108). New York: Guilford Press.

Cervetti, G. N., Barber, J., Dorph, R., Pearson, P. D., & Goldschmidt, P. G. (2009, April). *Integrating science and literacy: A value proposition?* Symposium paper presented at the annual meeting of the American Educational Research Association, San Diego, CA.

Coleman, D., & Pimentel, S. (2011). *Publishers' criteria for the Common Core State Standards in English language arts and literacy, grades 3–12.* Washington, DC: Council of the Chief State School Officers and National Association of State Boards of Education.

Copeland, M., Lakin, J., & Shaw, K. (2012, January 26). Text complexity and the Kansas Common Core standards for English language arts and literacy in history/social studies, science, and technical subjects. Retrieved from *www.ccsso.org/Resources/Digital_Resources/The_Common_Core_State_Standards_Supporting_Districts_and_Teachers_with_Text_Complexity.html.*

Darling-Hammond, L., Barron, B., Pearson, P. D., Schoenfeld, A. S., Stage, E., Zimmerman, T. D., et al. (2008). *Powerful learning: What we know about teaching for understanding.* San Francisco: Jossey-Bass.

De La Paz, S., & Felton, M. K. (2010). Reading and writing from multiple source documents in history: Effects of strategy instruction with low to average high school writers. *Contemporary Educational Psychology, 35,* 174–192.

Evans, R. W. (2004). *The social studies wars: What should we teach the children?* New York: Teachers College Press.

Fillmore, L. W., & Snow, C. E. (2000). *What teachers need to know about language.* Washington, DC: Center for Applied Linguistics.

Gavelek, J. R., Raphael, T.E ., Biondo, S. M., & Wang, D. (2000). Integrated literacy instruction. In M. L. Kamil, P. B. Mosenthal, P. D. Pearson, & R. Barr (Eds.), *Handbook of reading research* (Vol. III, pp. 587–607). Mahwah, NJ: Erlbaum.

Greenleaf, C. L., Litman, C., Handon, T. L., Rosen, R., Boscardin, C. K., Herman, J., et al. (2011). Integrating literacy and science in biology: Teaching and learning impacts of Reading Apprenticeship professional development. *American Educational Research Journal, 48,* 647–717.

Guthrie, J. T., Wigfield, A., Humenick, N. M., Perencevich, K. C., Taboada, A., & Barbosa, P.

(2006). Influences of stimulating tasks on reading motivation and comprehension. *Journal of Educational Research, 99*, 232–245.

Haladyna, T. M., Nolen, S. B., & Haas, N. S. (1991). Raising standardized achievement test scores and the origins of test score pollution. *Educational Researcher, 20*(5), 2–7.

Heller, R., & Greenleaf, C. L. (2007). *Literacy instruction in the content areas: Getting to the core of middle and high school improvement.* Washington, DC: Alliance for Excellent Education.

Hiebert, E. H. (2012). The Common Core's staircase of text complexity: Getting the size of the first step right. *Reading Today, 29*(3), 26–27.

Hiebert, E. H., & Van Sluys, K. (in press). Standard 10 of the Common Core State Standards: Examining three assumptions about text complexity. In K. Goodman & R. C. Calfee (Eds.), *Using knowledge from the past to create the future: Perspectives from the Reading Hall of Fame.* Washington, DC: Council of Chief State School Officers.

Hiebert, E. H., Wilson, K. M., & Trainin, G. (2010). Are students really reading in independent reading contexts? An examination of comprehension-based silent reading rate. In E. H. Hiebert & D. R. Reutzel (Eds.), *Revisiting silent reading: New directions for teachers and researchers* (pp. 151–167). Newark, DE: International Reading Association.

Keeler, C. G., & Langhorst, E. (2008). From PowerPoint to podcasts: Integrating technology into the social studies. *Social Studies Research and Practice, 3*(1), 164–175.

Labbo, L. D., & Reinking, D. (1999). Negotiating the multiple realities of technology in literacy research and instruction. *Reading Research Quarterly, 34*, 478–492.

Lagana-Riordan, C., & Aguilar, J. (2009). What's missing from No Child Left Behind? *Children & Schools, 31*(3), 135–142.

Lipson, M. Y., Valencia, S. W., Wixson, K. K., & Peters, C. W. (1993). Integration and thematic teaching: Integration to improve teaching and learning. *Language Arts, 70*, 252–262.

Lively, B. A., & Pressey, S. L. (1923). A method for measuring the vocabulary burden of textbooks. *Educational Administration and Supervision, 9*, 389–398.

Magnusson, S. J., & Palincsar, A. S. (2005). Teaching to promote the development of scientific knowledge and reasoning about light at the elementary school level. In M. S. Donovan & J. D. Bransford (Eds.), *How students learn: Science in the classroom* (pp. 421–474). Washington, DC: National Academies Press.

McGuffey, W. H. (1836). McGuffey's first eclectic reader. Cincinnati, OH: Truman & Smith. Retrieved March 14, 2011, from *www.gutenberg.org/files/14640/14640-pdf.pdf.*

MetaMetrics. (2000). *The Lexile framework for reading.* Durham, NC: Author.

Moje, E. B. (2008). Foregrounding the disciplines in secondary literacy teaching and learning: A call for change. *Journal of Adolescent and Adult Literacy, 52*(2), 96–107.

Mullis, I. V. S., Martin, M. O., Gonzalez, E. J., & Kennedy, A. M. (2003). *PIRLS 2001 international report: IEA's study of reading literacy achievement in primary school in 35 countries.* Chestnut Hill, MA: International Study Center, Boston College.

Murphy, P. K., Wilkinson, I. A. G., Soter, A. O., Hennessey, M. N., & Alexander, J. F. (2009). Examining the effects of classroom discussion on students' high-level comprehension of text: A meta-analysis. *Journal of Educational Psychology, 101*, 740–764.

National Governors Association Center for Best Practices and Council of the Chief State School Officers. (2010). *Common Core State Standards for English language arts & literacy in history/social studies, science, and technical subjects.* Washington, DC: Author.

National Institute of Child Health and Human Development. (2000). *Report of the National Reading Panel. Teaching children to read: An evidence-based assessment of the scientific research literature on reading and its implications for reading instruction* (NIH Publication No. 00-4769). Washington, DC: U.S. Government Printing Office.

National Research Council. (1999). *Testing, teaching, and learning: A guide for states and school districts.* Washington, DC: National Academies Press.

National Research Council. (2012). *A framework for K–12 science education: Practices, crosscutting concepts, and core ideas.* Washington, DC: National Academies Press.

Paris, S. G. (2005). Reinterpreting the development of reading skills. *Reading Research Quarterly*, *40*(2), 184–202.

Partnership for Assessment of Readiness for College and Careers. (2011, November). PARCC model content frameworks: English language arts/literacy (Grades 3–11). Retrieved March 18, 2012, from *www.parcconline.org/sites/parcc/files/PARCC%20MCF%20for%20 ELA%20Literacy_Fall%202011%20Release%20(rev)pdf*.

Pearson, P. D. (2007). An endangered species act for literacy education. *Journal of Literacy Research*, *39*(2), 145–162.

Pearson, P. D., Spalding, E., & Myers, M. (1998). Literacy assessment in the New Standards Project. In M. Coles & R. Jenkins (Eds.), *Assessing reading 2: Changing practice in classrooms* (pp. 54–97). London: Routledge.

Polikoff, M. S., Porter, A. C., & Smithson, J. (2011). How well aligned are state assessments of student achievement with state content standards? *American Educational Research Journal*, *48*(4), 965–995.

Probst, R. E. (1986). Three relationships in the teaching of literature. *English Journal*, *75*(1), 60–68.

Rader, H. B. (2002). Information literacy 1973–2002: A selected literature review. *Library Trends*, *51*, 242–259.

Resnick, L. B., & Resnick, D. (1992). Assessing the thinking curriculum: New tools for educational reform. In B. R. Gifford & M. C. O'Connor (Eds.), *Changing assessments: Alternative views of aptitude, achievement and instruction* (pp. 37–75). Boston: Kluwer.

Richards, I. A. (2008). *Practical criticism: A study of literary judgment*. Warrington, UK: Myers Press. (Original work published 1929)

Shanahan, T., & Shanahan, C. (2008). Teaching disciplinary literacy to adolescents: Rethinking content-area literacy. *Harvard Educational Review*, *78*, 40–59.

Shepard, L., Hannaway, J., & Baker, E. (2009). *Standards, assessment and accountability*. Washington, DC: National Academy of Education.

Smarter Balance Assessment Consortium. (2012, January 6). Content specifications for the summative assessment of the Common Core State Standards for English language arts and literacy in history/social studies, and technical subjects. Retrieved March 18, 2012, from *www. smarterbalanced.org/wordpress/wp-content/uploads/2011/12/ELA-Literacy-Content-Specifications_010612.pdf*.

Valencia, S. W., Hiebert, E. H., & Afflerbach, P. (Eds.). (1994). *Authentic reading assessment: Practices and possibilities* (pp. 218–227). Newark DE: International Reading Association.

Valencia, S. W., & Lipson, M. Y. (1998). Thematic instruction: A quest for challenging ideas and meaningful learning. In T. E. Raphael & K. H. Au (Eds.), *Literature-based instruction: Reshaping the curriculum* (pp. 95–123). Norwood, MA: Christopher Gordon.

van den Broek, P. (2010). Using texts in science education: Cognitive processes and knowledge representation. *Science*, *328*, 453–456.

Varelas, M., Pappas, C., Barry, A., & O'Neill, A. (2001). Examining language to capture scientific understandings: The case of the water cycle. *Science and Children*, *38*(7), 26–29.

Wang, J., & Herman, J. (2005). *Evaluation of Seeds of Science/Roots of Reading Project: Shoreline science and terrarium investigations*. Los Angeles: CRESST/University of California, Los Angeles.

Wiggins, G. P. (1999). *Assessing student performance: Exploring the purpose and limits of testing*. San Francisco: Jossey-Bass.

Williams, J. P., Nubla-Kung, A. M., Pollini, S., Stafford, K. B., Garcia, A., & Snyder, A. E. (2007). Teaching cause–effect text structure through social studies content to at-risk second graders. *Journal of Learning Disabilities*, *40*(2), 111–120.

CHAPTER 2

Reading Standards for Literature
Developing Comprehension

Lesley Mandel Morrow
Diane H. Tracey
Kellyanne M. Healey

Children's literature has become an increasingly important and prevalent dimension of high-quality literacy instruction (Galda, 2010; Martinez & McGee, 2000; Morrow & Gambrell, 2000). Such texts are used for a variety of educational reasons and in a variety of instructional approaches and are associated with many beneficial outcomes.

There are multiple reasons for including children's literature in literacy instruction. First and foremost is the belief that literacy development occurs as a consequence of meaningful interactions with texts (Morrow, 2012; Morrow & Gambrell, 2011; Rosenblatt, 1978, 1994; Sipe, 2008). Children learn by listening to literature, reading it themselves, thinking about it, talking about it, relating it to their own lives, and responding to it in a variety of ways (Bryan, Tunnell, & Jacobs, 2007). Children's literature is the authentic context in which these cognitive, social, and emotional interactions take place. High-quality children's books are also motivating; they encourage children to want to read more, which is associated with overall literacy achievement gains (Guthrie, 2011; Pressley et al., 2003). Children's literature builds background knowledge about people, places, and things. It also builds intangible concepts, which are useful for all students but especially those from disadvantaged backgrounds (Moore, Alvermann, & Hinchman, 2000). Children's literature is used to teach vocabulary, comprehension, text structure, text genre, and author and illustrator style (Beck & McKeown, 2001; Gunning, 2010; Leung, 2008). Perhaps most importantly, it is through the use of real children's literature that the love and appreciation for reading can be cultivated (Galda, 2010; Galda & Cullinan, 2003).

Children's literature is used in myriad instructional approaches in the classroom, including teacher read-alouds and independent reading and as a component of content-based thematic instruction. Classroom research on teacher read-alouds shows that reading literature aloud to students is associated with gains in vocabulary acquisition, comprehension development, background knowledge, listening skills, and attitudes toward reading (Baker, Chard, & Edwards, 2002; Beck & McKeown, 2001; Fisher, Flood, Lapp, & Frey, 2004; Leung, 2008; Martinez & McGee, 2000). Independent reading of children's literature has been found to be effective when children are given a goal to account for what is read (Gunning, 2010). Finally, children's literature should be embedded in content-based thematic instruction to bring content-area concepts (e.g., the science of weather using the book *The Mitten*; the history of the Civil War using *The Red Badge of Courage*) to life (Fisher & Frey, 2011; Guthrie, 2011). According to research, the use of children's literature in the classroom in guided instruction and independent and partner reading is associated with a variety of beneficial outcomes in reading (Edmunds & Bauserman, 2006; Neuman, 1997, 1999; Neuman & Celano, 2001; Pachtman & Wilson, 2006). It is also clear that reading more frequently positively correlates with literacy achievement (Guthrie, 2011; Lau, 2009). As a result of the tremendous importance of infusing literature into literacy instruction, a significant portion of the Common Core State Standards (CCSS) is dedicated to its use.

According to the website for the CCSS Initiative, the key features of the reading standards for literature are to support students' ability to read and comprehend increasingly complex text with deep understanding. This standard focuses on narrative literature, which includes folktales, fairy tales, fables, picture storybooks, and novels. To accomplish this goal at the PreK–2 level, four subareas of standards are addressed: (1) Key Ideas and Details, (2) Craft and Structure, (3) Integration of Knowledge and Ideas, and (4) Range of Reading and Level of Text Complexity. The content addressed in Key Ideas and Details refers to helping students learn how to identify key details in a text, retell familiar stories, and identify the characters, settings, and major events in a story. The content addressed in Craft and Structure refers to helping students learn unknown words, types of texts, and information about authors and illustrators. The content from Integration of Knowledge and Ideas refers to helping students understand the relationships between illustrations and print and compare and contrast the adventures and experiences of characters within stories. The content from Range of Reading and Level of Text Complexity refers to helping students read and comprehend grade-level literature, including stories and poetry. As students progress through the grades, the content for each of these standards spirals in difficulty.

THEORETICAL BACKGROUND FOR READING STANDARDS FOR LITERATURE

Schema theory (Anderson & Pearson, 1984; Bartlett, 1932) can be used to frame an understanding of the relationships between the stated goal of the reading standards for literature (to support students' ability to read and comprehend increasingly complex text) and the standards identified to reach that goal. In general, schema theory strives to explain how knowledge is created and used by learners. According to the theory, people organize everything they know into schemas, or knowledge structures (Gunning, 2010). Central characteristics of schema theory are that everyone's schemas are individualized (Cobb & Kallus, 2011) and that these differences greatly influence learning. Schema theory suggests that the more elaborated an individual's schema and background knowledge for any topic (e.g., zoos, beaches, cooking), the more easily he or she will be able to learn new information about it. Individuals have schemas for content (e.g., people, places, things), reading processes (e.g., decoding, skimming, inferencing, summarizing), and different types of text structures (e.g., narrative texts, expository texts). As children build multiple schemas, reading achievement will grow.

RESEARCH SUPPORT FOR READING STANDARDS FOR LITERATURE

While theories provide explanations for relationships within education, research studies provide data that support, refute, or inform the existence and quality of those relationships. Major research findings verify that the CCSS goals will enhance students' ability to comprehend both simple and complex text appropriate for their grade level.

The standards within the category of Key Ideas and Details refer to helping students learn to identify key details in a text, retell familiar stories, and identify the characters, settings, and major events. Much existing research documents the importance of these skills in successful reading comprehension. For example, in their work on best practices in comprehension instruction, Almasi and Hart (2011) state that the ability to summarize (which entails recognizing main ideas and important details) and identify story grammar components such as characters, settings, and major events in a story are among the most important strategies that can be taught to readers. Almasi and Hart's research also validates the positive relationships between the development of these skills and successful reading comprehension. Similarly, Gunning (2010) supports the importance of these skills for readers and provides instructional ideas for skills development. Morrow (2012) elaborates on the concept and value of having students retell familiar stories. She also reviews the connection between retelling and comprehension: "Retelling, whether it is oral or written, engages children in holistic comprehension and organization of thought" (p. 230). Thus, identifying key details in a text, identifying characters, settings, and major events in a story, and retelling familiar stories all help readers comprehend texts by helping them focus on the central aspects of what they are reading.

The standards within Craft and Structure refer to helping students learn unknown words, types of texts, and author and illustrator information. Knowing the meaning of words is a critical component of successful reading comprehension. Without word knowledge, sentence, paragraph, and full text comprehension may suffer or even completely fail because students will be unable to successfully construct the meaning of what they are reading. Blachowicz and Fisher (2011), Beck, McKeown, and Kucan (2008), and Bear, Invernizzi, Templeton, and Johnston (2008) share guidelines for best practices regarding vocabulary instruction. Knowing about different types of text structure also enhances comprehension. Familiarity with text structures, such as genres of narrative literature and poems (as well as expository text structures such as compare and contrast, explanation–process, and time sequence), helps readers organize the information they are processing, thus enhancing understanding. Knowledge of authors and illustrators falls under the umbrella of concepts about books and assists young readers in deepening their appreciation for reading and writing processes. Comprehension is facilitated when readers can identify the styles of different authors and illustrators.

The standards within Integration of Knowledge and Ideas refer to helping students understand the relationships between illustrations and print and compare and contrast the adventures and experiences of characters within stories. Often very young children "pretend read" by looking at story illustrations (Sulzby, 1985). Gradually, as they mature, they turn their attention from the pictures to the print in order to make meaning of what they are reading (Sulzby, 1985). Furthermore, as readers continue to develop, they learn not only that pictures and print are related but that pictures can also be used to assist in word identification and, ultimately, comprehension.

Just as comparing, contrasting, and understanding the relationship of print and pictures to each other eventually aid comprehension, so do the comparing and contrasting of the adventures and experiences of story characters, which is ideally taught with the use of graphic organizers such as Venn diagrams (Pearson & Duke, 2002).

Finally, the standards within Range of Reading and Level of Text Complexity refer to helping students read and comprehend grade-level literature, including stories and poetry. There are several types of text complexity to consider. Quantitative text complexity is measured by several factors such as (1) the proportion of words with phonically regular relationships between letters and sounds, (2) the degree of match between letter–sound relationships represented in the text, (3) the difficulty of vocabulary, (4) the length of sentences, (5) the number of words in a sentence, (6) the number of different words, and (7) the complexity of sentence structure. There are several readability formulas to determine text level of difficulty to match a student's reading achievement, such as the Fry Readability Formula (1968) and the Dale–Chall Readability Formula (1948). Software tools are available also, including the Lexile Framework for Reading (Meta Metrics). Each of these techniques have their strengths and weaknesses. Another way to determine text complexity has to do with the reader, the text, and the task. This takes into account the background knowledge and interest that readers have about the topic, which can influence their motivation for reading. Finally, there are the qualitative dimensions of text complexity, including (1) levels of meaning, (2) structure of text, (3) language conventions and clarity, (4) and knowledge demands.

1. *Levels of meaning:* Text can range from single to multiple levels of meaning, correlating with level of difficulty.
2. *Structure:* How the text is presented, ranging from simple (e.g., material is presented in sequential order) to a more difficult (use of time flashbacks and flashforwards).
3. *Language conventions and clarity:* the vocabulary in the book. In simpler text, the language is easier; the text is conversational, literal, and clear. More complex texts contain less common words and language that is ironic, figurative, and unfamiliar.
4. *Knowledge demands:* Text does not make assumptions about the readers' prior knowledge and is less complex than text that makes these assumptions (Heibert, 2009; Malloy & Gambrell, in press).

According to the CCSS, key features of the narrative literature standards are to build comprehension. The standards are to support students' ability to read and comprehend increasingly complex text. We now discuss the CCSS for grades K–2.

PUTTING K–2 READING STANDARDS FOR LITERATURE INTO PRACTICE

The spiral effect of the CCSS is unique and important. These are less specific standards than those we have seen in the past, but each one is repeated from one grade to the next, with increasing difficulty. Therefore, children learn to read with more depth and understanding.

Key Ideas and Details

The first major category is Key Ideas and Details (see Table 2.1). Standard 1 in this category for kindergarten is: "With prompting and support, ask and answer questions about key details in a text." In grade 1, the skill is the same but worded differently so that the response needs to be more in depth: Simply, "Ask and answer questions about key details in a text." Notice there is no support provided for the children in grade 1. In grade 2, the same standard becomes more complex: "Ask and answer such questions as *who, what, where, when, why*, and *how* to demonstrate understanding of the key details in a text." The activities for these standards in the different grades will have similarities and differences since the achievement levels of the children will vary.

In kindergarten, children still have trouble listening in whole groups. Most children are not yet reading so books will have to be read aloud. In first grade, there will be some very beginning readers early in the year and those who are on grade level or above as the year continues. Books can be read aloud by the teacher or in small groups with discussion. The same is true for second grade, where students should have mastered decoding skills and are moving toward fluent automatic reading with prosody. The teacher can decide to read and discuss a complex book to the group, or children can read on their own in material appropriate for them and have small-group discussions. The standards also talk about the inclusion of literacy instruction in content areas. Thus, these skills should be a part of explicit reading instruction and also a part of content-area subjects such as science, social studies, art, music, play, and even physical education.

In the following classroom example, Ms. Lynch has been focusing on Key Ideas and Details and the three standards in that category for grade 1. The first standard deals with promoting and supporting a child when asked questions about key details in a text, then providing no support, and then specifically dealing with questions such as *who, what, where, when, why*, and *how*.

TABLE 2.1. Reading Standards for Literature K–2: Key Ideas and Details (Anchor Standards 1–3)

Kindergartners	Grade 1 students	Grade 2 students
1. With prompting and support, ask and answer questions about key details in a text.	1. Ask and answer questions about key details in a text.	1. Ask and answer such questions as *who, what, where, when, why*, and *how* to demonstrate understanding of the key details in a text.
2. With prompting and support, retell familiar stories, including key details.	2. Retell stories, including key details, and demonstrate understanding of their central message or lesson.	2. Recount stories, including fables and folktales from diverse cultures, and determine their central message, lesson, or moral.
3. With prompts and support, identify settings, characters, and major events in a story.	3. Describe characters, settings, and major events in a story, using key details.	3. Describe how characters in a story respond to major events and challenges.

**READING LITERATURE STANDARDS IN ACTION:
KEY IDEAS AND DETAILS**

Ms. Lynch likes working with storytelling and having the children retell to demonstrate the details in a story. She has a literacy center filled with puppets, props, a felt board with story characters, and more. She tells stories using these materials and after modeling their use, these materials are placed in the center to use at a designated time. The class has explicit whole-class lessons when they discuss details in stories—specifically, what happened, who did what, where did it happen, when, how, and why. During center time, the children can use the materials for the purpose of the stated standard. An observer on any given day can see the following:

Tesha and Tiffany are on the floor with a felt board and character cutouts from *The Gingerbread Man*, alternately reading and manipulating the figures. Tesha and Tiffany chant, "Run, run as fast as you can! You can't catch me, I'm the Gingerbread Man!" As they chant this phrase from the story, Tiffany holds the Gingerbread Man and moves him up and down and around the board to make him look like he is running.

Tyrone has a big book of *The Little Red Hen* and gives several copies of the same story to a group of children who have gathered together. Sitting in the classroom rocking chair, he role-plays a teacher: "Now, boys and girls, let's read the title and the name of the author together," which they do. He occasionally stops and asks a question, such as "Who is in the story?", "What does the Little Red Hen want help with?", and at the end "Why didn't the hen give the animals any of the bread she baked?"

Rosa and Jovanna are doing a chalk talk of *Harold and the Purple Crayon*. One draws as the other tells the story. When they finish, they revisit the book to be sure they included all of the details. They find that they had missed two, which they then add to their project.

Another group is acting out the story *Caps for Sale*. There are caps in the center for role-playing as well as monkey puppets to re-create the story. One person is the storyteller and uses the book to help him narrate as the others act out the story.

In all these cases, children are demonstrating knowledge of details and literal comprehension of the story they chose. Without the teacher asking a single question, they illustrate that they know general and specific details.

In Standard 2 of Key Ideas and Details, the teacher helps the children to learn to retell stories, include key details, and demonstrate understanding of the central message or the main ideas. The skill also includes being able to do this with different types of children's literature such as fables, folktales, and picture storybooks.

Story Retelling and Rewriting: Key Ideas and Details—Standard 2

Letting a listener or reader retell or rewrite a story offers active participation in a literacy experience that helps develop language structures, comprehension, and sense of story structure (Paris & Paris, 2007). Retelling, whether oral or written, engages children in holistic comprehension and organization of thought. It also allows for original thinking as children mesh their own life experiences into their retelling. With practice in retelling, children come to assimilate the concept of narrative or expository text structure. They learn to introduce a narrative story with its beginning and its setting. They recount its theme, plot episodes, and resolution. In retelling stories, children demonstrate their comprehension of story details and sequence and their ability to organize them coherently. They also infer and interpret the sounds and expressions of characters' voices.

Retelling is not an easy task for children, but with practice they learn the skill. To help children to retell, let them know before they read or listen to a story that they will be asked to retell or rewrite it (Morrow, 1996). Guidance depends on the teacher's purpose in the retelling. If the intent is to teach or test sequence, instruct children to concentrate on what happened first, next, and so on. If the goal is to teach the ability to integrate information and make inferences from text, instruct children to recall their own experiences that are similar to those that happen in the selection. If the purpose is to remember details, ask the children to remember: Who is in the story? What happens to them? When? Where? Why? Props such as felt board characters or the pictures in the book can be used to help students retell. Pre- and postreading discussions of text helps to improve retelling, as does the teacher's modeling a retelling for children.

Retellings can develop many types of comprehension and provides teachers with an opportunity to evaluate children's progress. During the evaluative retellings, offer only general prompts, such as "Then what happened?" or "Can you think of anything else about the selection?" Retellings of narrative text can reveal a child's sense of story structure, focusing mostly on literal recall, but they also reflect a child's inferential and critical thinking ability. To assess the child's retelling for sense of story structure, first parse (divide) the events of the story into four categories: setting, theme, plot episodes, and resolution. Use a guide sheet and the outline of the parsed text to record the number of ideas and details the child includes within each category in the retelling, regardless of

---

SCAFFOLDING STORY RETELLING

1. Ask the child to retell the story: "A little while ago, I read the story [name the story]. Would you retell the story as though you were telling it to a friend who has never heard it before?"

2. Use the following prompts only if needed:
   a. If the child has difficulty beginning the retelling, suggest beginning with "Once upon a time" or "Once there was . . ."
   b. If the child stops retelling before the end of the story, encourage continuation by asking "What comes next?" or "Then what happened?"
   c. If the child stops retelling and cannot continue with general prompts, ask a question that is relevant at the point in the story where the child has paused. For example, "What was Jenny's problem in the story?"

3. When a child is unable to retell the story or if the retelling lacks sequence and detail, prompt the retelling step by step. For example:
   a. "Once upon a time or "Once there was . . ."
   b. "Who was the story about?"
   c. "When did the story happen?" (Daytime? At night? In the summer or winter?)
   d. "Where did the story happen?"
   e. "What was [the main character's] problem in the story?"
   f. "How did [he or she] try to solve the problem? What did [he or she] do first [second, next]?"
   g. "How was the problem solved?"
   h. "How did the story end?" (Morrow, 1996)

order. Credit the child for partial recall or for recounting the gist of an event (Wasik & Bond, 2001; Whitehurst & Lonigan, 2001). Evaluate the child's sequencing ability by comparing the order of events in the retelling with the proper order of setting, theme, plot episodes, and resolution. The analysis demonstrates which elements the child includes or omits and how well he or she sequences, thus indicating where instruction might be focused. Comparing retellings over the school year will indicate the child's progress, as seen in the following vignette. Retellings can be used throughout all grades, starting with kindergarten.

READING LITERATURE STANDARDS IN ACTION: KEY IDEAS AND DETAILS

This vignette begins with a summary of the story *Jenny Learns a Lesson* (Fujikawa, 1980), followed by 5-year-old Beth's first retelling early in the school year (Morrow, 1996).

Story Summary

A little girl named Jenny liked to play. She played with her friends Nicholas, Sam, Mei Su, and Shags, her dog. Every time Jenny played with her friends, she bossed them. Jenny decided to pretend to be a queen. She called her friends. They came to play. Jenny told them all what to do and was bossy. The friends became angry and left. Jenny decided to play dancer. She called her friends and they came to play. Jenny told them all what to do. The friends became angry and left. Jenny decided to play pirate. She called her friends and they came to play. Jenny told them all what to do. The friends became angry and left. Jenny decided to play duchess. She called her friends and they came to play. Jenny told them all what to do. The friends became angry and left. Jenny's friends refused to play with her because she was so bossy. Jenny became lonely and apologized to them for being bossy. The friends all played together, and each person did what he or she wanted. They all had a wonderful day and were tired at the end of the day.

Verbatim Transcription of Beth's Retelling

Once upon a time there's a girl named Jenny and she called her friends over and they played queen and went to the palace. They had to do what she said and they didn't like it, so then they went home and said that was boring. It's not fun playing queen and doing what she says you have to. So they didn't play with her for 7 days and she had an idea that she was being selfish, so she went to find her friends and said, I'm sorry I was so mean. And said, let's play pirate, and they played pirate and they went onto the ropes. Then they played that she was a fancy lady playing house. And they have tea. And they played what they wanted and they were happy. The end.

This retelling by 5-year-old Beth was transcribed when she was in the first part of her kindergarten year. With practice and over time, Beth's retellings become more sophisticated, with many more story details included. Following is another retelling by Beth at the end of kindergarten. The story is called *Under the Lemon Tree* (Hurd, 1980).

Story Summary

A donkey lives under a lemon tree on the farm and watches out for all the other animals. A fox comes in the night to steal a chicken and duck, and the donkey hee-haws loudly to protect them. He scares the fox away, but wakes the farmer and his wife, who never see the fox. This happens frequently until the farmer can no longer take the noise and moves the donkey to a tree far from the farmhouse where he is very unhappy. The fox comes back and steals the farmer's prize red rooster. The other animals quack and cluck and wake up the farmer, who chases after the fox. When the fox passes him, the donkey makes his loud noises again, frightening the fox, who drops the red rooster. The farmer realizes that the donkey has been protecting his animals and moves him back to the lemon tree where he is happy again.

Verbatim Transcription of Beth's Retelling

Once upon a time there was a donkey, and he was in a farm. He lived under a lemon tree close to the animals on the farm. In the morning, all the bees buzzed in the flowers under the lemon tree. He was next to the ducks, the chickens, and the roosters. It was nighttime. The red fox came into the farm to get something to eat. The donkey went "hee-haw, hee-haw" and then the chickens went "cluck, cluck" and the ducks went "quack-quack." Then the farmer and his wife waked up and looked out the window and saw nothing. They didn't know what came into their farm that night. They said, "What a noisy donkey we have. When it gets dark we will bring him far away." So when it get darker and darker they brang the donkey over to a fig tree. And he had to stay there. He couldn't go to sleep alone. That night the red fox came into the farm again to try and get something to eat. All the ducks went quack-quack and the turkeys went gobble-gobble. The farmer and his wife woke up and said, "Is that noisy donkey back again?" They rushed to the window and saw the fox with their red rooster in his mouth and yelled, "Stop thief, come back." The fox passed the donkey and shouted "hee-haw, hee-haw." The red fox heard it and dropped the rooster and ran away. The farmer and his wife said, "Aren't we lucky to have the noisiest donkey in the whole world?" And they picked up the rooster and put one hand around the donkey and they all went home together and tied the donkey under the lemon tree.

Retellings can be evaluated for many different comprehension tasks. The directions to students prior to retelling and the method of analysis should match the goal. Figure 2.1 provides a form for evaluating oral retellings in which checks are used for a general sense of the elements a child includes. The form is useful to determine progress over time.

In Standard 3, children are to describe characters and how they respond to the major events and challenges in the story. In the following vignette, Ms. Bushell has her children demonstrate the ability to do this.

READING LITERATURE STANDARDS IN ACTION: KEY IDEAS AND DETAILS

In Ms. Bushell's first-grade class, students are focusing on details in stories, with a particular emphasis on the characters in the stories. They have discussed the main character in *Madeline*, and since there are a lot of books about her, they could get a good sense of who she

```
QUALITATIVE ANALYSIS OF STORY RETELLING
```

Child's name _____ **Date** _____

Name of story _____

	Yes	No
Setting		
a. Begins story with an introduction	☐	☐
b. Names main character	☐	☐
c. List other characters named here: _____		
_____		
d. Includes statement about time and place	☐	☐
Theme		
a. Refers to main character's primary goal or problem to be solved	☐	☐
Plot Episodes		
a. Episodes are recalled	☐	☐
b. List episodes recalled	☐	☐
Resolution		
a. Includes the solution to the problem or the attainment of the goal	☐	☐
b. Puts an ending on the story	☐	☐
Sequence		
a. Story is told in sequential order	☐	☐

FIGURE 2.1. A sample form for qualitative analysis of story retelling.

was. They discuss *Amelia Bedelia*, the main character in *Arthur*, and others. They talk about what they looked like and how they acted. They make a Venn diagram to list similarities and differences in the characters. Ms. Bushell asks each child to select a character from one of the books they had read. The assignment is to dress up like the character using dress-ups and props from the classroom. The teacher confers with each child to help them select a book, a character, and how they might dress. They also have to act like their character and say some things they think the character would say. Ms. Bushell asks Natalie to begin the presentations by acting like her character. Natalie walks to the front of the room and says, "I have on a pink ruffled tutu skirt, and have butterfly wings on my back. I have a diamond tiara on my head and a neckless that is bright and glitters. I am wearing sparkly pink shoes from my Halloween costume when I was Dorothy from *The Wizard of Oz* and I have on lots of bracelets I made that I brought from home. I dress like this all the time and I speak fancy like I dress. I say things like I look fantastic in my fabulous clothes. Who am I?"

One child suggests, "Dorothy in *The Wizard of Oz*?" and Natalie says, "No, not Dorothy." Someone else offers, "Pinkalicious!" "No, that's not right either." Then one little girl shouts out, "I know! You are Fancy Nancy." And Natalie says, "That's right! I am Fancy Nancy. I am very fancy. I wear fancy clothes and I say big, fancy words. Fancy Nancy would say to you that you are spectacular to figure out who I am." Natalie holds up her *Fancy Nancy* book and shows a few pages to the class, and everyone applauds.

Craft and Structure

The standards for Craft and Structure (see Table 2.2) deal with children learning about genres of children's literature and how they differ from each other. It deals with vocabulary in the books; differences in types of books and their structures, such as poetry and informational books; dialogue; and, when dealing with a story, the character's point of view. In the course of the school year, teachers need to use a variety of literature with children. The following describes some of the genres to explore.

Picture Storybooks

Picture storybooks are those in which the story and the illustrations are closely associated and one can't do without the other. Picture storybooks are available on a wide range of topics. Quality picture storybooks will include a setting, a well-defined theme, episodes closely tied to the theme, and a resolution of the story.

Informational Books

As adults we read material that is mostly nonfiction; Children thus need exposure to this type of text. Informational text—for example, about the solar system, other countries, or dinosaurs—broaden children's background knowledge, introduce them to new

TABLE 2.2. Reading Standards for Literature K–2: Craft and Structure (Anchor Standards 4–6)

Kindergartners	Grade 1 students	Grade 2 students
4. Ask and answer questions about unknown words in a text.	4. Identify words and phrases in stories or poems that suggest feelings or appeal to the senses.	4. Describe how words and phrases (e.g., regular beats, alliteration, rhymes, repeated lines) supply rhythm and meaning in a story, poem, or song.
5. Recognize common types of texts (e.g., storybooks, poems).	5. Explain major differences between books that tell stories and books that give information, drawing on a wide reading of a range of text types.	5. Describe the overall structure of a story, including describing how the beginning introduces the story and the ending concludes the action.
6. With prompting and support, name the author and illustrator of a story and define the role of each in telling a story.	6. Identify who is telling the story at various points in a text.	6. Acknowledge differences in the points of view of characters, including by speaking in a different voice for each character when reading dialogue aloud.

vocabulary, and stimulate interest in new topics. Well-written expository text will include description, sequence, compare–contrast, cause–effect, and problem–solution.

Traditional Literature

Traditional literature includes nursery rhymes, fairy tales, and familiar stories that are part of our heritage and originated in the oral tradition of storytelling. We assume that children are familiar with *Goldilocks and the Three Bears* (Daley & Russell, 1999) and *The Three Little Pigs* (Zemach, 1991), yet many youngsters have not been exposed to these traditional stories. Traditional literature also includes fables and folktales.

Realistic Literature

Realistic literature is a category within picture storybooks that deals with real-life problems. *Tight Times* (1983) by Barbara Hazen, for example, describes how a family handles the problems that arise when the father loses his job. The father tries to explain the situation to his son so he will understand when he calls it "tight times." Books in this category deal with issues that children face (e.g., bedtime fears, a new baby in the family) and can touch on very sensitive areas, such as divorce, drugs, alcohol, and death. Some can be read to the entire class if they address issues that all share. Teachers should use discretion as to what to read to the whole class. Specific titles can be recommended to families of children who face difficult issues.

Poetry

Poetry is often forgotten in collections of children's literature. Many themed poetry anthologies have been compiled for children. Be sure you have them in your literacy center.

Novels

Novels are longer books with chapters. We can begin reading novels to young children to expose them to the genre. They are attracted to them since they know they are for older children. Children call novels *chapter books*.

Biography

Biography is another genre appropriate for young children. There are simple biographies of historical figures, popular figures in sports, and television performers.

Big Books

Big books are usually large versions of smaller picture storybooks. They are oversized books that rest on an easel in order to be read. The purpose of the big book is for children to be able to see the print and pictures during reading, to make the association between oral and written language, and to see how the print is read from left to right across the page.

Digital Texts

Digital texts include any text that students read on the computer, a cell phone, a Kindle, or an iPad. These might include digital stories, e-mails, websites, and computer games. Since digital and global texts are now being used as well as print and paper-based books, it is critical that we introduce and incorporate digital texts in the early childhood classroom.

In addition to these categories of books, young children enjoy "nontraditional texts" such as joke and riddle books, craft books, graphic novels, comic books, cookbooks, participation books (which involve them in touching, smelling, and manipulating), book series built around a single character, and books related to television programs and pop culture, appropriate for their age. Magazines and newspapers should also be choices for reading in the library corner. They provide a nonthreatening format, different topics, and reading matter for diverse ability levels. Menus, directions, and maps can be read as well.

Children enjoy literature that is predictable because it helps them to understand the story and they learn different patterns in stories, which makes them easy to comprehend and to use as a model in their own writing. Predictable literature contains rhyme, repetition, catchphrases, conversation, familiar sequences (e.g., days of the week or numbers), cumulative patterns (in which events are repeated or added as the story continues), stories about familiar topics, uncluttered illustrations that match the text, and stories that have well-developed structures.

The Craft and Structure standards help children learn new vocabulary and be able to acknowledge differences in the points of view of character by using different voices and expression. A strategy that will help with almost any skill is a directed listening/reading and thinking activity (DLTA/DRTA). In this activity, a purpose is set for reading and that purpose is carried through to the end of the lesson. In this DLTA, the objective is to enhance vocabulary and to acknowledge characters' different points of view by demonstrating expression when reading and changing one's reading voice to fit the character.

The DLTA/DRTA for Narrative and Expository Text

The format of the DLTA and the DRTA sets a purpose for reading, thus helping to direct thought. This strategy, when internalized as a result of frequent use by the teacher, will be transferred and used by students when new material is read or listened to (Morrow, Gambrell, & Freitag, 2009; Roskos, Tabor, & Lenhart, 2009). Whatever the DLTA- or DRTA-specific objectives may be, its framework offers the listener or reader a strategy for organizing and retrieving information from the text. In the following DRTA–DLTA for the story *Swimmy* (Lionni, 1973), children are asked to participate in two main strategies:

1. Developing vocabulary.
2. Recognizing the points of view of characters, in this case by reciting conversation as the character would.

When children internalize the DLTA–DRTA format, they will be able to decide their own purpose for reading. In the vignette that follows, children are listening to the story as the teacher, Ms. Kinzer, reads to them.

READING LITERATURE STANDARDS IN ACTION:
CRAFT AND STRUCTURE

Lesson with Pre-questions and Discussion

"Today I'm going to read a story entitled *Swimmy*," says Ms. Kinzer. "I selected this book since it is about fish and the sea and we have been talking about this in our theme. Let's look at the pictures together to see if you can tell what the story is going to be about." Ms. Kinzer presents a PowerPoint slide show of the book. As she does so, the children comment. Jim says, "There are a lot of fish in the book." Julia says, "On this page there is a scary fish and the little fish are swimming away." "On this page there is only one left, a little black fish," says Jonah. Jovanah says, "On the next few pages it looks like the black fish sees lots of things under the sea. One is a lobster."

After some conversation Ms. Kinzer says, "You have very good ideas and you are right about your ideas. But I will read it and we will find out the ending. There are also some interesting words in the book. I'll put them up on the board, and when I say the word you can repeat it after me. Listen to this: 'One bad day a tuna fish *swift, fierce*, and very hungry came *darting* through the waves.'" Ms. Kinzer puts a circle to make a web on the board and puts the words *tuna fish* in the middle. She then makes four lines and at the end writes, "Fierce," "Swift," "Darting," and "Gulp" at the end of each. She makes the words she wants to explain bold and underlined on the PowerPoint slide. To help with the meaning of *swift*, she asks one child to run quickly in circles and the other to walk slowly. She asks the class how those demonstrators are moving. Everyone says "slowly" for the one child and "fast" for the other. "You are right," she says, "but there is another word for *fast* in the book." She resumes reading, "One bad day a tuna fish *swift, fierce*, and very hungry came *darting* through the waves. In one *gulp* he swallowed all the little fish." As she points to the word *swift*, she asks if that reminds them of the slow or the fast child. Most of the children say "fast" and they repeat "swift" again. The teacher whispers to another child to run in circles and to make himself look like a monster with his mouth open wide. She also asks the children to look in the book on the page with the big black fish. She reads again *swift, fierce*, and very hungry came *darting* through the waves. Then she says, "How does the fish look? Listen: *swift, fierce*." Everyone says "fierce." Finally, she says, "Came *darting* through the waves." She asks, "Did the fish come slowly through the waves?" The children say, "No, he came fast through the waves." The book says "darting through the waves," says the teacher. The children say, "Darting means fast." Ms. Kinzer reads it again, "One bad day a tuna fish swift, fierce, and very hungry came darting through the waves" and asks "Can someone tell me what 'swift' means?" They all say "Fast." She asks, "What does 'fierce' mean?" They respond, "Scary." Then, "What does 'darting' mean?" and they answer, "Fast." Ms. Kinzer has one more word. She reads from the book: "In one *gulp* he swallowed all the little fish." "What does the word 'gulp' mean?" The children say, "Eat." Ms. Kinzer says, "Yes, but it is eating a whole bunch in one swallow. Let's review our web." She reads from the book and points to the web, "One bad day a tuna fish *swift, fierce*, and very hungry came *darting* through the waves. In one *gulp* he swallowed up all the little fish." The children say the words as she points to them.

Ms. Kinzer reads the entire story without interruption. Toward the end, when Swimmy has a conversation with the little red fish, Ms. Kinzer makes her voice high when she reads Swimmy's dialogue and then low when she pretends to be all of the other fish. This helps to establish the different voices in conversation. Then she finishes the book.

Discussion after Reading

The postdiscussion should be guided by the objectives or purpose set for listening and reading:

1. Developing vocabulary.
2. Recognizing the points of view of characters, in this case by reciting conversation as the character would.
3. Children eventually decide on their own purpose for reading and the strategies to retrieve the information to use when reading or listening.

Ms. Kinzer reviews the new words and puts them up on the word wall. She tells the children to use the words in a story they would write about fish in the sea.

She also reads the last few pages of the book where there was conversation and the children echo-read the conversation using different voices for Swimmy and the little red fish.

A DLTA or DRTA can have many different objectives. The framework, however, is always basically the same: (1) preparation for listening or reading—pre-questions and discussion; (2) reading the story with few interruptions; and (3) discussion after reading. Whatever the objective is for the DLTA or DRTA, it should be focused on during discussion (Baumann, 1992; Pearson, Roehler, Dole, & Duffy, 1992).

Integration of Knowledge and Ideas

Standards 7, 8, and 9 fall under Integration of Knowledge and Ideas (see Table 2.3). These standards have students discussing the text and illustrations and comparing how they support each other. They also compare and contrast different texts and illustrations by different authors.

TABLE 2.3. Reading Standards for Literature K–2: Integration of Knowledge and Ideas (Anchor Standards 7–9)

Kindergartners	Grade 1 students	Grade 2 students
7. With prompting and support, describe the relationship between illustrations and the story in which they appear (e.g., what moment in a story an illustration depicts).	7. Use illustrations and details in a story to describe its characters, setting, or events.	7. Use information gained from the illustrations and words in a print or digital text to demonstrate understanding of its characters, setting, or plot.
8. (Not applicable to literature.)	8. (Not applicable to literature.)	8. (Not applicable to literature.)
9. With prompting and support, compare and contrast the adventures and experiences of characters in familiar stories.	9. Compare and contrast the adventures and experiences of characters in stories.	9. Compare and contrast two or more versions of the same story (e.g., Cinderella stories) by different authors or from different cultures.

Ms. Win, a first-grade teacher, works on these standards in the following vignette.

READING LITERATURE STANDARDS IN ACTION: INTEGRATION OF KNOWLEDGE AND IDEAS

For several months, Ms. Win has been discussing different authors and illustrators with her first-grade students. She has their favorites on a chart in her classroom. Today Ms. Win asks the children to add names to the list because they had recently read stories by authors and illustrators who were new to them. She had asked the librarian to help her find additional copies of books by the authors they were studying. First, she asks students to identify authors, and the following names were mentioned: Ezra Jack Keats, Tomie dePaola, Leo Lionni, and Arnold Lobel. Next, she asks the students to name some illustrators. They offer the following: Dr. Seuss, Eric Carle, and Maurice Sendak. Jamie raises her hand: "Hey, something weird just happened. I noticed that all of the authors named are also illustrators and all of the illustrators are all authors too." Christopher raises his hand and says, "That's not so weird. I know a bunch of people who are authors and illustrators. There's me, and Josh, Jennifer, and Patrick." Christopher was looking around the room and naming all the children in the class. "We're all authors and illustrators. We all write books and illustrate them. We publish them and they are in our classroom library. How could we forget that?"

Ms. Win projects two T-charts on the electronic white board (see Figure 2.2). One side of a chart has two columns for authors: "Dr. Seuss" and on one side, "Ezra Jack Keats" on the other. The other T-chart has the same format for illustrators: "Dr. Seuss" on one side and "Ezra Jack Keats" on the other. Ms. Win explains to the children that the T-chart was a strategy to help organize and understand information read. The T-chart would help them to compare and contrast the characteristics of the authors and illustrators, to find out what they had in common and how they were different. She then guides the children by modeling how to use the T-chart. She asks them to think of the characteristics of each author's illustrations first and types their ideas under each author's name. Then she asks the children to talk about the author's stories and lists the characteristics they mentioned. When they finish, they look for shared and different characteristics. Ms. Win then mixes up all the words compiled on the T-chart. She selects two pairs of children to rearrange the words back onto the T-chart in the proper places. On another day, Ms. Win does this activity with the whole class again using two new author-illustrators. She then pairs children together to work on their own paper T-charts and walks around the room to help. Finally, the T-chart activity is put into the

AUTHORS		ILLUSTRATORS	
Dr. Seuss	Ezra Jack Keats	Dr. Seuss	Ezra Jack Keats
Rhymes	No rhymes	Bold colors	Bright colors
Cartoon characters	Real characters	Watercolor	Collage
Imaginary	Real-life story	Cartoon characters	Realistic
Made-up words	Real words		

FIGURE 2.2. T-charts.

literacy center for independent center time. For completing this task, the children are encouraged to use the books of the author-illustrators to help with the characteristics lists. In addition to the T-chart, Ms. Win asks the children to write a sentence about how these authors and illustrators are the same and how they are different. She shares the lesson with the art teacher, who creates a lesson in which the children draw two pictures, one in the style of one of the authors and one in the style of the other.

The steps for instruction include (1) explaining the purpose of the strategy, (2) modeling the use of the strategy, (3) having the students practice the strategy with her guidance, and (4) having the children use the strategy in a cooperative setting with a partner.

At a later date, Ms. Win consults with the librarian again for several different versions of the story *Cinderella* so the children can compare and contrast the similarities and differences of the fairy tale by different authors from different cultures.

Range of Reading and Level of Text Complexity

The final standard for grades K, 1, and 2, Range of Reading and Level of Text Complexity (see Table 2.4), encourages wide and varied reading in whole groups when children listen to complex texts and read in collaboration with each other. This standard suggests that the reading be integrated into content areas as well. Teachers need to fill their rooms with books that deal with all types of texts and genres for children to eventually read with critical comprehension. The types of text are mentioned earlier in the chapter.

USING THE CCSS IN CONTENT AREAS THROUGHOUT THE SCHOOL DAY

The CCSS attempt to coordinate the education of the children in the United States. Families move often; therefore, we need to have continuity in the teaching of reading in schools throughout the country. The standards ask teachers to expose children to equal amounts of informational and narrative literature. The standards want children to read magazines, poetry, novels, newspapers, and new literacy media. The CCSS want children exposed to information to increase vocabulary. When we integrate literacy strategies into content areas such as social studies and science, we can accomplish the goals discussed.

TABLE 2.4. Reading Standards for Literature K–2: Range of Reading and Level of Text Complexity (Anchor Standard 10)

Kindergartners	Grade 1 students	Grade 2 students
10. Actively engage in group reading activities with purpose and understanding.	10. With prompting and support, read prose and poetry of appropriate complexity for grade 1.	10. By the end of the year, read and comprehend literature, including stories and poetry, in the grades 2–3 text complexity band proficiently, with scaffolding as needed at the high end of the range.

The CCSS are not designed to replace small-group, differentiated explicit literacy instruction but rather to supplement it. Teachers have used themes in the past, but not with the intention of teaching and reinforcing literacy skills. With CCSS, literacy is intentionally taught within content areas. Following are CCSS and activities for a part of a mini-thematic unit in science on healthy food written for children in grades K–2. Literacy is intentionally integrated throughout. Although this chapter is on narrative literature, the CCSS suggest that children need to read both narrative and informational texts. There are several informational pieces included in the following unit.

The *factual information* children will learn in the following science unit is that to remain healthy we need to eat healthy food. Healthy food supplies our bodies with nutrients and vitamins, which give us energy and strength to work, play, and grow. People need to have about three servings a day of the following healthy foods:

1. Vegetables: Broccoli, carrots, spinach, and squash for their vitamins.
2. Fruit: Apples, oranges, pears, and bananas for vitamins and nutrients.
3. Grains/cereal: Bread or pasta or rice and oat cereals. These have carbohydrates and fiber that give us energy.
4. Meat, beans, poultry, fish, nuts, and eggs: These provide minerals and protein, which promote growth and build muscles.
5. Milk, cheeses, and yogurt: These contain protein, calcium, and nutrients that build bones and teeth.

Prepare classroom environments with materials to enrich the Healthy Food unit. Enhance the *science center* by adding seeds, plastic foods to categorize, and journals to record progress of growing plants. *Social studies* materials can include cookbooks from other countries to compare food from different cultures. For *music*, find songs that are about food with written lyrics to read, for example, "Food, Glorious Food," from the Broadway musical *Oliver.* Include in the *art* center magazines with pictures of food, recipes, and books with famous historical food paintings. In the *library corner*, add health, fitness, and cooking magazines, pamphlets about good food, and books pertaining to the unit from all genres. The *author's spot* contains a box of index cards to fill with recipes, blank books for writing narrative and expository text about food, and journals for new vocabulary, for charting foods eaten daily, and for charting growth of plants.

Unit Activities and CCSS: Healthy Food

Following are a few activities in this mini-science unit about healthy food. Each activity begins with the Common Core standards it is accomplishing.

RL 3.2: Describe how characters in a story respond to major events and challenges.

Begin the unit by reading *Mr. Rabbit and the Lovely Present.* Before reading, show the pictures in the book to predict what children think the rabbit and the girl will do in the story. Read the story, and have a basket beside you. As the girl in the book selects apples, bananas, grapes, and pears for her mother's birthday present, put this fruit in the basket. After reading, discuss the healthy present the girl and the rabbit created. Ask if they created a good birthday present and why.

IT 2.4: Determine the meaning of words and phrases in text relevant to a grade 2
topic or subject area.

IT 2.10: Compare and contrast the most important points presented by two texts on
the same topic.

At the Morning Meeting, read *Fruit Is a Suitcase of Seeds* and at another time *How a Seed Grows*. Discuss and write down the new words and phrases in the books. Then choral read the following Morning Message:

"We are learning about good foods to eat to stay healthy. Fruit is good for us since it has vitamins and nutrients. I will give some of you an apple and some a banana. Observe and describe the properties of these fruits as you cut them open, smell them, look at, touch, and taste them.

"Write banana words and apple words on separate Post-it notes. Put banana word Post-its on the banana web and apple word Post-its on the apple web. Discuss what apples are like and what bananas are like."

W 2.3: Write a narrative in which you recount a well-elaborated event or short
sequence of events. Include details to describe actions, thoughts, and feelings; use
temporal words to signal event order; and provide a sense of closure.

After the Morning Message activity, ask the children to select either an apple or a banana as the focus of a story they are to write. Begin with the following sentence: "One day my family and I bought some fruit from a farm. I took an apple [or banana] to eat." Using the words generated based on characteristics of an apple and a banana, students write about a fictional experience that happens to them when biting into the fruit. They write three events that happened after they bit into the apple or banana, including what took place and how it felt. Finally, there will be a resolution and an ending to the story.

SL 2.4: Tell a story or recount an experience with appropriate facts and relevant
descriptive details, speaking audibly in coherent sentences.

RL 2.5: Describe the overall structure of story, including how the beginning introduces the story and the ending concludes the action.

Read *The Tiny Seed* and have children retell the story in sequential order and talk about the introduction of the story and the ending action.

Learn more about the growth of seeds by wrapping a wet paper towel on the inside walls of a clear plastic cup. Put a seed between the wet paper towel and the wall of the cup so you can see the plant grow. Put your cup in a bright, warm place. Watch and chart the growth of the two beans.

RL 2.1: Ask and answer such questions as *who*, *what*, *where*, *when*, *why*, and *how*
to demonstrate understanding of key details in a text.

Discuss a program for parents to share what was learned in the Healthy Food unit. Prepare healthy snacks, such as a fruit salad, and vegetable platter. Read *Good Enough to Eat: A Kid's Guide to Food and Nutrition* to help prepare the food.

RF 2.4: Read with sufficient accuracy and fluency to support comprehension. a. Read on level with purpose and understanding. b. Read on-level prose and poetry orally with accuracy, appropriate rate, and expression on successive readings. c. Use context to confirm or self-correct word recognition and understanding, rereading as necessary

- The teacher reads the story *The Carrot Seed*. Five children repeat the phrase "It won't come up." Each time this phrase appears, the children sign those words.
- Three children retell the story *Mr. Rabbit and the Lovely Present*. They use props as the teacher did: a basket, an apple, a pear, grapes, a banana, and a stuffed animal rabbit. One child is the rabbit, one is the girl, and one is the narrator.
- Two children present persuasive book talks, one on *Bread and Jam for Frances* and another on *Gregory, the Terrible Eater*.
- To end the program, the class choral reads poems from *Munching: Poems about Eating*.

CHILDREN'S BOOKS FOR HEALTHY FOOD UNIT

Narrative Books

Carle, E. (1969). *The very hungry caterpillar*. New York: Philomel.
Carle, E. (1987). *The tiny seed*. New York: Simon & Schuster.
Demuth, P. (1996). *Johnny Appleseed*. New York: Grosset & Dunlap.
Hoban, R. (1976). *Bread and jam for Frances*. New York: Harper & Row.
Krauss, R. (1945). *The carrot seed*. New York: Scholastic.
McCloskey, R. (1948). *Blueberries for Sal*. New York: Penguin.
Shartmat, M. (1984). *Gregory, the terrible eater*. New York: Macmillan
Zolotow, C. (1962). *Mr. Rabbit and the lovely present*. New York: Harper & Row.

Poetry

Freese, S. M. (2008). *Carrots to cupcakes: Reading, writing, and reciting poems about food*. Minneapolis, MN: Super Sandcastle.
Hopkins, L. B. (1985). *Munching: Poems about eating*. Boston: Little, Brown.

Informational Books

Jordon, H. (1992). *How a seed grows*. New York: HarperCollins.
Rockwell, L. (1999). *Good enough to eat: A kid's guide to food and nutrition*. New York: HarperCollins.

Technology to Use during the Unit

Children's games about nutrition: *www.mypyramid.gov/kids*.
Games, presentations, and material for teachers about nutrition: *www.facs.pppst.com/food-pyramid.html*.

CONCLUSION

Children's literature has become an increasingly important and visible dimension of high-quality literacy instruction. As a result of the tremendous importance of infusing literature into literacy instruction, a significant portion of the Common Core standards is dedicated to its use. This chapter has presented a review of the key elements of the Reading Standards for Literature (K–2), including a theory that can be used to frame these standards (schema theory), research that supports the standards, and discussion of the ways in which teachers can use the standards to frame and strengthen their classroom practice.

The Common Core standards have been agreed upon and are in the process of being implemented in most of the 50 states in the country. There is an intense emphasis on reading a lot of literature as well as many different kinds and on discussing literature through analysis, synthesis, and deep understanding. It is hoped that these standards will assist educators in strengthening their instruction, thereby enabling children to succeed.

ACTIVITIES AND QUESTIONS

Activities

1. Select a theme study for such as authors of picture storybooks. Select three or four well-known authors and compare and contrast their styles of writing and illustrations. Then write a story using the authors' writing and illustration style.

2. Assume you are studying the four seasons in your first- or second-grade class. Collect poems, songs, and online activities that you can use with that unit.

3. Create a unit of your choice for an early childhood class. Prepare five activities and match them with appropriate Common Core standards. Focus on those in reading literature.

4. Create a workshop for parents and teachers about the Common Core standards. Include their purpose, their characteristics, how they are meant to be used, and how they are different from other standards we have used.

5. As a schoolwide activity, have each grade level—in this case kindergarten and first and second grades—select the themes for the year. Figure out how long you want them to last and the standards to include in each. Create activities in the theme that include art, music, physical education, science, social studies, and, of course, the language arts. Include in your themes an abundance of reading narrative literature, but also include this throughout the units all the standards for K–grade 2.

6. Review your language arts program. Review the CCSS, especially in narrative literature. Be sure that all of the standards in this category for each of the grade levels are explicitly dealt with when teaching reading, writing, listening, speaking, and viewing.

Questions

1. Take an inventory of the books in your classroom. How many are in genres such as folk tales, fairy tales, poetry, picture storybooks, and others mentioned in this chapter? Try to fill in the gaps for genres that are missing or need to be improved.

2. Review the activities you do in science, social studies, art, music, play, and math. Are you using the standards for narrative literature in these areas? Could a narrative literature standard be added where there isn't any?

3. What scaffolds will you use when reading aloud to young children with texts that are complex for them?

4. Pose the following question in a study group and take notes on the discussion: Assuming learning to read fluently is the ultimate goal for instruction in PreK–grade 2, how would you change what you do with children?

REFERENCES

Almasi, J. F., & Hart, S. J. (2011). Best practices in comprehension instruction. In L. M. Morrow & L. B. Gambrell (Eds.), *Best practices in literacy instruction* (4th ed., pp. 250–275). New York: Guilford Press.

Anderson, R. C., & Pearson, P. D. (1984). A schema-theoretic view of basic processes in reading. In P. D. Pearson (Ed.), *Handbook of reading research* (Vol. 1, pp. 185–224). New York: Longman.

Baker, S., Chard, D. J., & Edwards, L. (2002). *The Story Read-Aloud Project: The development of an innovative instructional approach to promote comprehension and vocabulary in first grade classrooms.* Washington, DC: U.S. Department of Education, Institute of Education Sciences.

Bartlett, F. C. (1932). *Remembering: A study in experimental and social psychology.* Cambridge, UK: Cambridge University Press.

Baumann, J. F. (1992). Effect of think aloud instruction on elementary students' comprehension monitoring abilities. *Journal of Reading Behavior, 24*(2), 143–172.

Bear, D. R., Invernizzi, M., Templeton, S., & Johnston, F. (2008). *Words their way: Word study for phonics, vocabulary, and spelling instruction* (4th ed.). Upper Saddle River, NJ: Prentice Hall.

Beck, I. L., & McKeown, M. G. (2001). Text talk: Capturing the benefits of read-aloud experiences for young children. *The Reading Teacher, 55*(1), 10–20.

Beck, I. L., McKeown, M. G., & Kucan, L. (2008). *Creating robust vocabulary: Frequently asked questions and extended examples.* New York: Guilford Press.

Blachowicz, C. L. Z., & Fisher, P. J. (2011). Best practices in vocabulary instruction revisited. In L. M. Morrow & L. B. Gambrell (Eds.), *Best practices in literacy instruction* (4th ed., pp. 224–249). New York: Guilford Press.

Bryan, G., Tunnell, M., & Jacobs, J. (2007). A most valuable player: The place of books in teaching children to read. *Canadian Children, 32*(2), 25–33.

Cobb, J. B., & Kallus, M. K. (Eds.). (2011). *Historical, theoretical, and sociological foundations of reading in the United States.* Boston: Pearson.

Dale, E., & Chall, S. (1948). A formula for predicting readability. *Education Research Bulletin, 27,* 11–20, 37–54.

Edmunds, K. M., & Bauserman, K. L. (2006). What teachers can learn about reading motivation through conversations with children. *The Reading Teacher, 59,* 414–424.

Fisher, D., Flood, J., Lapp, D., & Frey, N. (2004). Interactive read-alouds: Is there a common set of implementation practices. *The Reading Teacher, 58,* 8–17.

Fisher, D., & Frey, N. (2011). Best practices in content-area literacy. In L. M. Morrow & L. B. Gambrell (Eds.), *Best practices in literacy instruction* (4th ed., pp. 343–360). New York: Guilford Press.

Fry, E. (1968). A readability formula that saves time. *Journal of Reading, 11*(7), 513–526, 575–578.

Galda, L. (2010). First things first: Why good books and time to respond to them matter. *New England Reading Association Journal, 46*(1), 1–7.

Galda, L., & Cullinan, B. E. (2003). Literature for literacy: What research says about the benefits of using trade books in the classroom. In J. Flood, D. Lapp, J. R. Squire, & J. M. Jensen (Eds.), *Handbook of research on teaching the English language arts* (2nd ed., pp. 640–648). Mahwah, NJ: Erlbaum.

Gunning, T. G. (2010). *Creating literacy instruction for all children* (7th ed.). Boston: Allyn & Bacon.

Guthrie, J. T. (2011). Best practices in motivating students to read. In L. M. Morrow & L. B. Gambrell (Eds.), *Best practices in literacy instruction* (4th ed., pp. 177–198). New York: Guilford Press.

Heibert, E. H. (Ed.). (2009). *Reading more, reading better.* New York: Guilford Press.

Lau, K. (2009). Reading motivation, perceptions of reading instruction and reading amount: A comparison of junior and secondary students in Hong Kong. *Journal of Research in Reading, 32,* 366–382.

Leung, C. B. (2008). Preschoolers' acquisition of scientific vocabulary through repeated read-aloud events, retellings, and hands-on scientific activities. *Reading Psychology, 29,* 165–193.

Malloy, J. A., & Gambrell, L. B. (2013). Reading standards for literature. In L. M. Morrow, K. K. Wixson, & T. Shanahan (Eds.), *Teaching with the Common Core Standards for English Language Arts, Grades 3–5* (pp. 22–49). New York: Guilford Press.

Martinez, M., & McGee, L. (2000). Children's literature and reading instruction: Past, present, and future. *Reading Research Quarterly, 35*(1), 154–169.

Moore, D. W., Alvermann, D. E., & Hinchman, K. A. (Eds.). (2000). *Struggling adolescent readers: A collection of teaching strategies.* Newark, DE: International Reading Association.

Morrow, L. M. (1996). Story retelling: A discussion strategy to develop and assess comprehension. In L. B. Gambrell & J. F. Almasi (Eds.), *Lively discussions: Fostering engaged reading* (pp. 265–285). Newark, DE: International Reading Association.

Morrow, L. M. (2012). *Literacy development in the early years* (7th ed.). Boston: Pearson.

Morrow, L. M., & Gambrell, L. B. (2000). Literature-based reading instruction. In M. L. Kamil, P. B. Mosenthal, P. D. Pearson, & R. Barr (Eds.), *Handbook of reading research* (Vol. III, pp. 563–586). Mahwah, NJ: Erlbaum.

Morrow, L. M., & Gambrell, L. B. (2011). *Best practices in literacy instruction* (4th ed.). New York: Guilford Press.

Morrow, L. M., Gambrell, L. B., & Freitag, E. (2009). *Using children's literature in preschool to develop comprehension: Understanding and enjoying books.* Newark, DE: International Reading Association.

Neuman, S. B. (1997). *Getting books in children's hands: The book flood of '96. Final report to the William Penn Foundation.* Philadelphia: Temple University.

Neuman, S. B. (1999). Books make a difference: A study of access to literacy. *Reading Research Quarterly, 34,* 286–311.

Neuman, S. B., & Celano, D. (2001). Books Aloud: A campaign to "put books in children's hands." *The Reading Teacher, 54,* 550–557.

Pachtman, A. B., & Wilson, K. A. (2006). What do the kids think? *The Reading Teacher, 59,* 680–684.

Paris, A. H., & Paris, S. G. (2007). Teaching narrative comprehension strategies to first graders. *Cognition and Instruction, 25*(1), 1–44.

Pearson, O. D., Roehler, L. R., Dole, J. A., & Duffy, G. G. (1992). Developing expertise in reading comprehension. In S. J. Samuels & A. E. Farsturp (Eds.), *What research has to say about reading instruction* (2nd ed., pp. 145–199). Newark, DE: International Reading Association.

Pearson, P. D., & Duke, N. K. (2002). Comprehension instruction in the primary grades. In C. C. Block & M. Pressley (Eds.), *Comprehension instruction: Research-based best practices* (pp. 247–258). New York: Guilford Press.

Pressley, M., Dolezal, S. E., Raphael, L. M., Mohan, L., Roehrig, A. D., & Bogner, K. (2003). *Motivating primary-grade students.* New York: Guilford Press.

Rosenblatt, L. M. (1978). *The reader, the text, the poem: The transactional theory of literacy work.* Carbondale: Southern Illinois University Press.

Rosenblatt, L. M. (1994). The transactional theory of reading and writing. In R. B. Ruddell, M. R. Ruddell, & H. Singer (Eds.), *Theoretical models and processes of reading* (4th ed., pp. 1057–1092). Newark, DE: International Reading Association.

Roskos, K. A., Tabor, P., & Lenhart, L. (2009). *Oral language and early literacy in preschool: Talking, reading and writing.* Newark, DE: International Reading Association.

Sipe, L. R. (2008). *Storytime! Young children's literary understanding in the classroom.* New York: Teachers College Press.

Sulzby, E. (1985). Children's emergent reading of favorite storybooks. *Reading Research Quarterly, 20,* 458–481.

Wasik, B. A., & Bond, M. A. (2001). Beyond the pages of a book: Interactive book reading and language development in preschool classrooms. *Journal of Educational Psychology, 93*(2), 243–250.

Whitehurst, G. J., & Lonigan, C. J. (2001). Emergent literacy: Development from prereaders to readers. In S. B. Neuman & D. K. Dickinson (Eds.), *Handbook of early literacy research* (Vol. 1, pp. 11–29). New York: Guilford Press.

CHILDREN'S BOOKS CITED

Brett, J. (1989). *The mitten.* New York: Putnam Juvenile.

Carle, E. (1969). *The very hungry caterpillar.* New York: Philomel.

Carle, E. (1987). *The tiny seed.* New York: Simon & Schuster.

Crane, S. (2005). *The red badge of courage.* New York: Simon & Schuster.

Daley, A., & Russell, C. (1999). *Goldilocks and the three bears.* London: Ladybird Books.

Demuth, P. (1996). *Johnny Appleseed.* New York: Grosset & Dunlap.

Fujikawa, A. (1980). *Jenny learns a lesson.* New York: Harcourt.

Freese, S. M. (2008). *Carrots to cupcakes: Reading, writing, and reciting poems about food.* Minneapolis, MN: Super Sandcastle.

Hazen, B. S. (1983). *Tight times.* New York: Picture Puffins.

Hoban, R. (1976). *Bread and jam for Frances.* New York: Harper & Row.

Hopkins, L. B. (1985). *Munching: Poems about eating.* Boston: Little, Brown.

Hurd, E. (1980). *Under the lemon tree.* Boston: Little, Brown.

Johnson, C. (1998). *Harold and the purple crayon.* New York: HarperCollins.

Jordon, H. (1992). *How a seed grows.* New York: HarperCollins.

Krauss, R. (1945). *The carrot seed.* New York: Scholastic.

Lionni, L. (1973). *Swimmy.* New York: Dragonfly Books.

McCloskey, R. (1948). *Blueberries for Sal.* New York: Penguin.

Richards, J. (2006). *A fruit is a suitcase for seeds.* Minneapolis, MN: First Avenue Editions.

Rockwell, L. (1999). *Good enough to eat: A kid's guide to food and nutrition.* New York: HarperCollins.

Shartmat, M. (1984) *Gregory, the terrible eater.* New York: Macmillan.

Slobodkina, E. (2011). *Caps for sale.* New York: HarperCollins.

Zemach, M. (1991). *The three little pigs.* New York: Tandem Library.

Zolotow, C. (1962). *Mr. Rabbit and the lovely present.* New York: Harper & Row.

CHAPTER 3

Reading Standards
for Informational Text

Nell K. Duke
Juliet L. Halladay
Kathryn L. Roberts

DEFINING STANDARDS FOR READING INFORMATIONAL TEXT

Informational text plays a prominent role in the Common Core State Standards (CCSS). Standards involving informational text are found in all four major strands of the English language arts standards (reading, writing, language, and speaking and listening), and informational text is implicitly or explicitly entailed in many of the standards for literacy in history/social studies, science, and technical subjects. In fact, the overall approach to literacy in the standards was driven in part by concern about informational text: "Part of the motivation behind the interdisciplinary approach to literacy promulgated by the Standards is extensive research establishing the need for college and career ready students to be proficient in reading complex informational text independently in a variety of content areas" (National Governors Association Center for Best Practices and Council of Chief State School Officers, 2010, p. 5). The CCSS recognize that literacy extends well beyond English class to mediate learning in all content areas and ultimately in college and career.

If the CCSS followed a traditional approach, standards involving informational text would begin in fourth grade, when children are conventionally expected to shift from learning to read to reading to learn (Chall, 1983, 1996). However, in the CCSS, standards for informational text begin in kindergarten. Can kindergarten-age children really learn from and about informational text? Research strongly suggests that they can (Duke, Bennett-Armistead, & Roberts, 2003). For example, kindergarten children can learn to approximate the typical language of informational text if it is read aloud to them (Duke & Kays, 1998; Pappas, 1993).

The CCSS ask for a 50/50 split of literature and informational text in grades K–5 (p. 5). This is quite a bit more use of informational text than is likely to be found in K–5 classrooms presently (Duke, 2000; Jeong, Gaffney, & Choi, 2010; Wright, 2011). However, we have no indication that such an increase would have negative consequences for children. For example, an intervention in which grade 1 teachers aimed for one-third informational text (defined more narrowly than in the CCSS), one-third narrative text, and one-third other genres (including biography, which the CCSS categorize as informational text) throughout the school day showed no negative impacts on children compared with a comparison group. Children made equivalent progress in decoding and encoding (in fact, children in classrooms with relatively low initial alphabet knowledge did better when more informational text was employed) and in narrative writing. Their informational writing and attitudes toward reading were actually higher than those of children in the comparison group (Duke, Martineau, Frank, Rowe, & Bennett-Armistead, 2012). There is also some evidence that young children can develop content knowledge, vocabulary, and fluency through informational text (Fingeret, 2008; Hiebert, 2008; Santoro, Chard, Howard, & Baker, 2008).

As we would expect given only two categories—literature and informational text—the term *informational text* is used quite broadly in the CCSS to include, in grades K–5, "biographies and autobiographies; books about history, social studies, science, and the arts; technical texts, including directions, forms, and information displayed in graphs, charts, or maps; and digital sources on a range of topics." We strongly urge the field to plan exposure and instruction not just for the broad category of informational text but for more specific categories of text within that. For example, it will be important to provide children with exposure to and instruction in directions (what we call procedural or how-to text) and exposure to what is often called expository text, such as text that teaches—for example, about panda bears or Mexico. This exposure to a range of texts is important because different kinds of text have varied purposes: The primary purpose of procedural text is to tell someone how to do something, whereas the goal of expository text (what we have called "informational text" in past writings, defining it more narrowly than the CCSS) is to convey information about the natural or social world (Purcell-Gates, Duke, & Martineau, 2007). These texts also have markedly different features. For example, common procedural text features include having a materials section, having a set of ordered steps, and using imperative verbs (e.g., *cut, arrange*). In contrast, common expository text features include opening with a general statement or classification, having a series of paragraphs organized topically, and using timeless verbs (e.g., "Pandas *walk* on four legs"). Furthermore, different strategies or processes are likely to be used to read procedural versus expository text. For example, whereas procedural text must be read (and steps carried out) from beginning to end in order, expository text often need not be read in its entirety or in order: One might turn first to the index of the text, then to the middle of the text, where the desired information is expected to be found, and so on. There is growing evidence that proficiency with one type of text does not necessarily mean proficiency with another (Duke & Roberts, 2010); thus, we need to provide exposure to and instruction with each type of informational text we want children to learn to read and write.

PUTTING THE INFORMATIONAL TEXT STANDARDS INTO PRACTICE

As noted earlier, standards involving informational text are found in all four major strands of the English language arts standards, not only reading but also writing, language, and speaking and listening. For example, the language standards for second grade include a call to have children use reference materials, including beginning dictionaries, and the speaking and listening standards for kindergarten expect children to "confirm understanding of a text read aloud or information presented orally or through other media. . . ." However, the bulk of the standards involving informational text reading in K–2 come from the reading standards for informational text, K–5, and those are the standards on which we focus in this chapter. Those standards are divided into four categories:

1. Key Ideas and Details
2. Craft and Structure
3. Integration of Knowledge and Ideas
4. Range of Reading and Level of Text Complexity

In this section, we describe instruction appropriate for each of these categories. We draw heavily on the What Works Clearinghouse (WWC) practice guide *Improving Comprehension in Kindergarten through Third Grade* (Shanahan et al., 2010) to articulate effective comprehension instructional practices and on *Reading and Writing Genre with Purpose in K–8 Classrooms* (Duke, Caughlan, Juzwik, & Martin, 2012) for how to tailor comprehension instruction to informational text specifically.

Key Ideas and Details

The Key Ideas and Details standards focus on children identifying, asking, and answering questions about the main topic and key details of a text and making connections among pieces of a text. See Table 3.1 for grade-by-grade detail.

TABLE 3.1. Reading Standards for Informational Text K–2: Key Ideas and Details (Anchor Standards 1–3)

Kindergartners	Grade 1 students	Grade 2 students
1. With prompting support, ask and answer questions about key details in a text.	1. Ask and answer questions about key details in a text.	1. Ask and answer such questions as who, what, where, when, why, and how to demonstrate understanding of key details in a text.
2. With prompting and support, identify the main topic and retell key details of a text.	2. Identify the main topic and retell key details of a text.	2. Identify the main topic of a multiparagraph text as well as the focus of specific paragraphs within the text.
3. With prompting and support, describe the connection between two individuals, events, ideas, or pieces of information in a text.	3. Describe the connection between two individuals, events, ideas, or pieces of information in a text.	3. Describe the connection between a series of historical events, scientific ideas or concepts, or steps in technical procedures in a text.

Foster Children's Motivation

The tasks in Table 3.1 are hard cognitive work for young children. Even older children can struggle with them (e.g., Taylor, 1986; Yussen, Rembold, & Mazor, 1989). For this reason, we highly recommend doing all that is possible to foster children's motivation—to help them want to do this hard work. Research has identified many teacher practices associated with higher levels of student motivation, including (from Brophy, 1987):

- Model interest in learning.
- Induce curiosity and suspense.
- Make abstract materials more concrete and understandable.
- Make learning objectives clear.
- Provide informative feedback.
- Adapt academic tasks to student interests and provide novel content as much as possible.
- Give students choices between alternative tasks.
- Allow students as much autonomy as possible in doing tasks.
- Provide tasks with an appropriate level of challenge/difficulty.

In the primary grades specifically, Pressley and colleagues (2003), in their observational study of eight third-grade teachers, found that the two teachers whose students were rated as most highly engaged used 63 and 74 different practices, respectively, that support motivation! It is for good reason that the WWC Panel on Improving Comprehension in Kindergarten through Third Grade had as one of its five recommendations "Establish an engaging and motivating context in which to teach reading comprehension."

With informational text, selecting engaging texts on engaging topics is likely to be very important (e.g., Guthrie, McRae, & Klauda, 2007; Jiménez & Duke, 2011). Even as early as preschool, topics that some children find engaging other children may find disengaging (Renninger & Wozniak, 1985), so sometimes grouping children for reading instruction by common interests is advised (Guthrie & McCann, 1996). We also recommend keeping individual children's interests in mind when identifying books and other texts they can choose among for independent or home reading. Indeed, choice itself fosters motivation. Thus, rather than approach a reading group with "the book we are going to read today," consider offering two or three titles from which the children can choose through a vote or by rotating who gets to select the text.

Also important to fostering motivation to comprehend informational text is providing some reason to read it beyond being told or asked to do so (Guthrie et al., 2007). It appears that children's informational text comprehension develops better when they are regularly reading informational text for the same reasons people read this kind of text outside of school: because they want or need to know information (Duke, Purcell-Gates, Hall, & Tower, 2006/2007; Purcell-Gates et al., 2007). For example, children might read (or listen to) informational text to inform a letter the class is writing to the mayor about an issue in their community, or to answer questions from their pen pals about a topic they are studying in school, or to figure out what they should feed a ladybug they caught on the playground. They have some larger purpose for engaging in the hard work of grappling with key ideas and details in informational text.

Teach Comprehension Strategies

It is not enough to simply motivate children to grasp main idea and details in text; we also need to teach them *how* to do it. The WWC practice guide panel referenced earlier identifies teaching comprehension strategies as one of their five recommendations and the one with the strongest evidence. A full description of how to teach comprehension strategies is well beyond the scope of this chapter, but briefly teaching comprehension strategies should involve the following:

- Explicitly explaining the strategy, including when and how to use it.
- Modeling the strategy by "thinking aloud" as you use it while reading aloud to children.
- Collaboratively practicing use of the strategy, with you and the children working together to apply it.
- Guided practice in which children are primarily responsible for applying the strategy but you are available to provide prompting, coaching, and support as needed.
- Independent practice in which children work to apply the strategy on their own as they read or are being read to.

(See Duke & Pearson, 2002; Shanahan et al., 2010; and the Doing What Works website [*http://dww.ed.gov/Reading-Comprehension/topic/?T_ID=36*] for more information.)

Many specific strategies are deserving of instruction, such as activating background knowledge; predicting; questioning; visualizing; monitoring, clarifying, and fixing up; drawing inferences (often making connections); and summarizing. Summarizing, both for sections of the text and the text as the whole, is perhaps most closely related to the CCSS listed in Table 3.1. The vignette that follows provides one example of how a teacher might teach this strategy and do so in a motivating context as described earlier.[1]

> **INFORMATIONAL TEXT STANDARDS IN ACTION:**
> **KEY IDEAS AND DETAILS**
>
> Ms. Jones starts off Morning Meeting with her second-grade students with an announcement. Mr. Williams, the other second-grade teacher in the building, is concerned because his students have been picking out a lot of information books that they don't end up liking. He thinks Ms. Jones's class might be able to help by sending over reviews—good and bad—of information books they have been reading. Ms. Jones asks the children whether they would like to help out and gets a resounding "Yes!" in response.
>
> Over the next several days, Ms. Jones shares a variety of book reviews with the children, including some by and for adults (e.g., from the *New York Times Review of Books*) and some by and for children (e.g., from the Spaghetti Book Club [*www.spaghettibookclub.org/about. html*] and Scholastic's Share What You're Reading [*http://teacher.scholastic.com/activities/ swyar/*]), and she teaches a common format/template for a review:

---

[1]This and other vignettes in the chapter are amalgamated from several observations and sources and should not be viewed as representing the practice of any specific teacher.

- Title and author of the book
- Name of the reviewer
- Engaging opening (e.g., "Did you know that . . . ?") about interesting facts from the book
- Summary of the book
- Evaluation of the book (e.g., "I liked this book because . . . ")

(Notice how this format draws children's attention to notable details and key ideas, as required by the CCSS.) Ms. Jones reads two information books aloud and works collaboratively with the children to write whole-class reviews of each. From there she supports individual children in writing their own reviews of information books from read-alouds and guided and independent reading (making sure that each child reviews a different book).

To support children's review writing, Ms. Jones teaches a series of lessons on summarizing, with particular focus on identifying the main topic of a text. She provides lessons involving explicit explanation, modeling, collaborative practice, and guided practice. For example, she explains and models and then guides children in small groups to look at the title and to notice repeated words in text to help figure out the text topic. In one of her favorite lessons, Ms. Jones pretends to be mistaken about the main topic of a book she'd read to children. She claims that a particular detail in the book was the main topic. The children protest. Ms. Jones argues, "But that part is so interesting!" The children giggle as they explain to Ms. Jones that the main topic is not the most interesting part, it's what the book is mostly about! Then Ms. Jones says, "OK, here's my summary of the book: It's about dogs." The children giggle again, explaining that Ms. Jones needs to say more than that. Together, the children help Ms. Jones construct a better summary of the book. Throughout lessons and their independent work, the children work hard to apply the strategies they are learning, eager to provide quality reviews for Mr. Williams's second graders.

Craft and Structure

The Craft and Structure standards engage children in meta-textuality—in thinking about text as text. In Standard 4, children are expected to think about the words and phrases they know and do not know in informational text. In Standard 5, they are expected to think about specific parts and features of text, particularly in grades 2 and 3, those that allow one to navigate the text. In Standard 6, they think about the creation of text—the author and the illustrator, the words and the pictures, and the purposes for which text is written. See Table 3.2 for grade-by-grade detail.

There is remarkably little research on the impact of instruction for K–2 children in the areas named in the Craft and Structure standards. One thing we can be fairly sure of is that children will vary considerably in these areas even in the earliest years of school depending on their home and preschool experiences with written text. It appears that children will also vary a great deal in their ability to navigate text. In one recent study, 78% of K–2 children were able to navigate within a website while 22% of children in that same grade range were not (Dodge, Husain, & Duke, 2011). Twenty-four percent were able to use a search engine and navigation to find information on a specific topic (panda bears), and 76% were not. As in so many areas, teachers will be faced with the challenge of bringing some children a long way to reach the standards while also stimulating those who have already met them.

TABLE 3.2. Reading Standards for Informational Text K–2: Craft and Structure (Anchor Standards 4–6)

Kindergartners	Grade 1 students	Grade 2 students
4. With prompting support, ask and answer questions about unknown words in a text.	4. Ask and answer questions to help determine or clarify the meaning of words and phrases in a text.	4. Determine the meaning of words and phrases in a text relevant to a grade 2 topic or subject area.
5. Identify the front cover, back cover, and title page of a book.	5. Know and use various text features (e.g., headings, tables of contents, glossaries, electronic menus, icons) to locate key facts or information in a text.	5. Know and use various text features (e.g., captions, bold print, subheadings, glossaries, indexes, electronic menus, icons) to locate key facts or information in text efficiently.
6. Name the author and illustrator of a text and define the role of each in presenting the ideas or information in text.	6. Distinguish between information provided by pictures or other illustrations and information provided by the words in a text.	6. Identify the main purpose of a text, including what the author wants to answer, explain, or describe.

INFORMATIONAL TEXT STANDARDS IN ACTION: CRAFT AND STRUCTURE

Ms. Grifaldi leads a shared reading of *Rainforest Colors* (Canizares & Chessen, 1998) with her first graders and then begins reading aloud the information contained in the back of the book. As she reads the section on the yellow flower and frog featured in the book, she finds herself flipping back trying to find those pages to show the children. She notes to the children, "This is tricky. You know what would really help?" Having seen Ms. Grifaldi model use of an index several times, some children chime in, "An index!" Ms. Grifaldi reminds the rest of the group what an index is and what it is for. She shows them that this book does not have an index and then talks about why it would be helpful to have one.

Following this, the children work independently and in small groups to develop an index for each classroom copy of the book. They realize that this also involves making page numbers for the book. When they finish, the children are proud of their indexes (see Figure 3.1 for an example), which Ms. Grifaldi attaches to each book using correction tape. She notices many children looking closely at the indexes during free-choice time and sometimes actually using them—for example, to find the plant and frog of their favorite color.

Improve-a-Text

The activity described in the vignette uses a technique we call "Improve-a-Text." In Improve-a-Text, children are engaged in adding to a published text to make it better. They might add an explanation of a word likely to be unfamiliar to readers or add an entire glossary for a text, experiences that will help move them toward meeting Standards 4 and 5 for informational reading. They might add navigational devices, such as

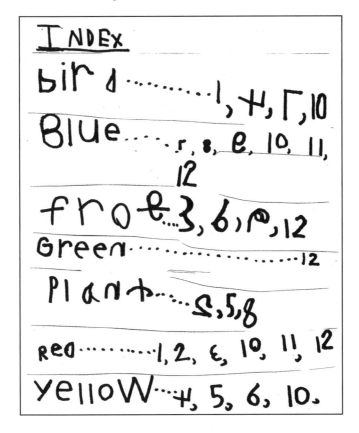

FIGURE 3.1. A child's index for *Rainforest Colors* (Canizares & Chessen, 1998).

an index or a table of contents, headings, and subheadings, which will help move them toward meeting Standard 5. They might add captions to photos or illustrations or a back cover blurb articulating the purpose of the text, addressing Standard 6. This activity can include a range of types of informational text; for example, numbers could be added to the steps included in directions/procedural/how-to text, or headings could be added to sections of a biography.

In our experience, creating text features from scratch or improving upon existing features pushes children to take a close look at the characteristics and purposes of each feature, more so, even, than when they are just reading or using them. For example, if children create a glossary for a text, they have to think about what which words might be unfamiliar to readers, which words are important enough to be in a glossary, what makes words important enough to be in the glossary, how the glossary is organized, and what types of things belong in a definition or explanation of a word. (For more about vocabulary instruction, see Chapter 7.) The activity may also encourage children to read with a "reviser's eye," meaning that they are not just trying to understand the text but also actively working to make it understandable (Beck, McKeown, Sandora, Kucan, & Worthy, 1996).

In addition, text feature creation, as it is described in the vignette, meets the criterion discussed earlier of having a purpose in children's minds beyond just learning to read or satisfy a teacher: The books actually *need* these features for readers to be able to access or learn information more easily. As noted earlier, these kinds of purposeful tasks are associated with greater growth in comprehension (and writing skill) (Purcell-Gates et al., 2007). They can also serve as a motivator for many children (Guthrie et al., 2004).

Carrying Out Improving a Text. To get started using Improve-a-Text, choose a book that is relevant to what your students are currently learning. You will want this text to be of good quality and only in need of a few additions so it is not too overwhelming for the children to modify. Then:

- If you know an obvious feature is missing (e.g., table of contents, index, glossary), you may choose to preview the book and ask children whether they notice any text features that could be added to make the text more user-friendly.
- Better yet, in order to underscore the authentic need for the feature, you could begin reading the book, attempt to use a feature at an appropriate moment (e.g., if a child asked what bears eat, you could attempt to use the table of contents or index) and "discover" with your class that it is missing.
- If the feature is more subtle (e.g., a picture that would be more comprehensible if labeled like a diagram), the suggestion for improvement may come from you or the children during the course of reading.
- To facilitate child-initiated changes, you may want to get them into the habit of using a particular phrase such as, "This text would be better if . . . "

From this point, you can move into creating or modifying the feature as a class, in small groups, or individually. Finally, be sure that the "improved" texts are available to children in the classroom library or elsewhere in the room so that they can admire, and use, their handiwork at a later date.

Integration of Knowledge and Ideas

To better understand the K–2 standards for integration of knowledge and ideas, it is especially helpful to look to the original anchor standards:

7. Integrate and evaluate content presented in diverse media and formats, including visually and quantitatively, as well as in words.
8. Delineate and evaluate the argument and specific claims in a text, including the validity of the reasoning as well as the relevance and sufficiency of the evidence.
9. Analyze how two or more texts address similar themes or topics in order to build knowledge or to compare the approaches the authors take.

In the K–2 standards, the diverse media and formats referenced in Anchor Standard 7 are simply illustrations and the larger text (including written words) in which they appear. The K–2 standards for Anchor Standard 8 focus children on the points or argument the author is making and the reasons given to support them. The K–2 standards for Anchor Standard 9 consist of comparing and contrasting two and more texts. See Table 3.3 for grade-by-grade detail.

TABLE 3.3. Reading Standards for Informational Text K–2: Integration of Knowledge and Ideas (Anchor Standards 7–9)

Kindergartners	Grade 1 students	Grade 2 students
7. With prompting and support, describe the relationship between illustrations and the text in which they appear (e.g., what person, place, thing, or idea in the text an illustration depicts).	7. Use the illustrations and details in a text to describe its key ideas.	7. Explain how specific images (e.g., diagram showing how a machine works) contribute to and clarify a text.
8. With prompting and support, identify the reasons an author gives to support points in a text.	8. Identify the reasons an author gives to support points in a text.	8. Describe how reasons support specific points the author makes in a text.
9. With prompting and support, identify basic similarities and differences between two texts on the same topic (e.g., in illustrations, descriptions, or procedures).	9. Identify basic similarities in and differences between two texts on the same topic (e.g., in illustrations, descriptions, or procedures).	9. Compare and contrast the most important points presented by two texts on the same topic.

Discussion

As with any of the K–2 standards, discussion can play a critical role in helping children attain Standards 7–9. Not surprisingly, "Guide students through focused, high-quality discussion on the meaning of text" was one of the five recommendations of the WWC panel (Shanahan et al., 2010). Specifically, the panel recommended that educators:

- Structure the discussion to complement the text, the instructional purpose, and the readers' ability and grade level.
- Develop discussion questions that require children to think deeply about text.
- Ask follow-up questions to encourage and facilitate discussion.
- Have children lead structured small-group discussions.

While the evidence for this recommendation in the K–3 grade range received only a "minimal" rating, in research with older children quality discussion has clearly been shown to be a tool that can improve comprehension of text (Murphy, Wilkinson, Sotor, Hennessey, & Alexander, 2009).

Critical to high-quality discussion are open-ended, no-single-answer questions that encourage higher-order thought processes. Here are some examples of such questions for Standard 7:

- "What can we learn from this picture that the words did not tell us?"
- "Why did the author/illustrator choose to put this picture here?"
- "How does this picture help us understand the words better?"

- "What could we do to make this picture better?" (See prior Improve-a-Text discussion.)
- "What pictures could be added to help explain the words I just read?"

With these and any big questions, it is very helpful to ask follow-up questions (from Shanahan et al., 2010, p. 27), such as:

- "What makes you say that?"
- "Can you explain what you meant when you said _____?"
- "Do you agree with what _____ said? Why or why not?"
- "How does what you said connect with what _____ already said?"

Follow-up questions can push children's thinking and improve their ability to articulate text–picture relationships, helping them to meet Standard 7 and other reading standards for informational text.

Graphic Organizers

Another instructional strategy that will be helpful in addressing the Integration of Knowledge and Ideas standards in K–2 is the use of graphic organizers. Graphic organizers, including concept maps, Venn diagrams, fishbone charts, and sequence diagrams or flowcharts, are suggested by the WWC panel (Shanahan et al., 2010) for developing comprehension of the structure of individual texts (and indeed there is research to support doing so), but they can also be used to develop the ability to comprehend across texts. For example, to address Standard 9, a Venn diagram could be used to compare and contrast two texts about dinosaurs. To begin with, it may be useful to compare two quite different texts, such as a fantasy story about dinosaurs and a dinosaur encyclopedia. Over time, more similar texts can be compared, such as two informational websites about dinosaurs. It can be an especially rich learning opportunity when the texts differ on the same questions or issue—for example, when the texts provide different explanations for why dinosaurs became extinct. Such experiences can help children begin to understand that not everything they read in informational text is necessarily true and that text must always be read with a critical eye. Establishing a purpose for comparing and contrasting the texts—for example, to provide advice for a kindergarten teacher who had asked the children which they think she should read—is likely to further encourage careful and critical reading and analysis.

In the vignette for this strand, we provide another example of the use of a graphic organizer to develop children's ability to integrate knowledge and ideas, this time in the service of Standard 8.

INFORMATIONAL TEXT STANDARDS IN ACTION: INTEGRATION OF KNOWLEDGE AND IDEAS

Mr. Rajiv found the perfect book to help him begin work with his kindergartners on identifying the reasons an author gives to support points in a text. The book *Lend a Hand* (Graves, 2005) is a persuasive text aimed at kindergartners addressing the question "Why should you lend a hand?" After each reason for lending a hand is communicated in the main body of the text and a supporting photograph, it is added to a recurring box in the upper right-hand side of each spread, which ultimately reads:

Why You Should Lend a Hand
☺ To help someone
☺ To learn new things
☺ To feel grown up

Mr. Rajiv explicitly explains that the author is giving reasons to try to support her argument—to convince us—that children should lend a hand. He explains that figuring out the reasons or points the author is making to support her argument can help us decide whether we want to agree with the argument and can help us make better arguments ourselves. Over the next few days, he elicits examples from the children's own lives and the classroom—for example, all the reasons the children gave for why they should be allowed to play on the "big kids' playground" and listing them on chart paper.

Once the children seem to have a handle on the basic idea, Mr. Rajiv turns to reading aloud texts with somewhat more complex arguments. As he reads, he and the children complete a graphic organizer, similar to that in Figure 3.2. To encourage the children to do the hard mental work of identifying an author's argument and reasons, Mr. Rajiv provides a larger purpose for the analysis: to write a letter to the book's author as a class indicating whether they agreed or disagreed with him or her. He notices that the children began importing the argument-and-reasons analysis into their own activities, chuckling when one child says, "I have three reasons for my argument that we should get extra recess . . . "

Range of Reading and Level of Text Complexity

Anchor Standard 10 deals with the types of informational texts to be used in classrooms. The goal is to engage children in reading experiences that will help them become independent and proficient in their reading of complex informational texts. As children progress from kindergarten through grade 2, the standards suggest a shift from working with texts in group activities to reading complex texts independently. See Table 3.4 for grade-by-grade detail.

Classroom texts vary in a range of ways, including content, format, genre, and readability. This variation contributes to a text's complexity and to its appropriateness for given children and situations. The CCSS offer a three-part framework for determining text complexity: (1) qualitative evaluation of the text; (2) quantitative evaluation of the text; and (3) matching reader to text and task. The first factor deals with text characteristics, including level of meaning, supportiveness of graphic elements, and print format. The second factor deals with quantitative measures of readability, typically calculated with formulas such as the Lexile Framework for Reading and the Dale–Chall Readability Formula. In addition to these traditional readability measures, Coh-Metrix is a newer formula that measures text cohesion by accounting for additional text- and sentence-level variables (Graesser, McNamara, & Kulikowich, 2011). The third factor deals with reader characteristics (e.g., motivation and background knowledge) and task characteristics (e.g., purpose for engaging with the text). Taken together, the three parts of the framework are intended to help teachers think about multiple factors that can affect a particular reader's proficiency with a particular text.

Argument and Reasons

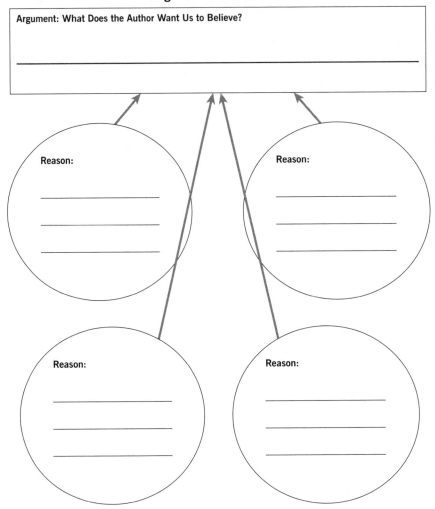

FIGURE 3.2. A graphic organizer for a basic analysis of argument and reasons.

TABLE 3.4. Reading Standards for Informational Text K–2: Range of Reading and Level of Text Complexity (Anchor Standard 10)

Kindergartners	Grade 1 students	Grade 2 students
10. Actively engage in group-reading activities with purpose and understanding.	10. With prompting and support, read informational texts appropriately complex for grade 1.	10. By the end of year, read and comprehend informational texts, including history/ social studies, science, and technical texts, in the grades 2–3 text complexity band proficiently, with scaffolding as needed at the high end of the range.

The standards also demand a focus on both *what* and *how* children read. They require children to read progressively more complex texts, and they outline some of the requisite component skills and strategies for reading and comprehending complex texts. Regarding informational texts in particular, comprehension of complex texts demands (among other things) knowledge of genre-specific text features (e.g., diagrams, headings, tables) and integration of text content with prior knowledge. The role of the teacher is to provide children with a range of appropriately complex texts, help children set purposes for reading, and supply scaffolded instruction as needed.

In kindergarten classrooms, Anchor Standard 10 calls for children to be given opportunities to engage purposefully with informational texts. This same approach can be applied in prekindergarten classrooms. For example, a preschool teacher might help her children prepare for a trip to the local fire station by reading aloud to the class the informational text *Fire Fighter!* (Royston, 2011). The teacher is scaffolding her children to meet this standard when she sets a purpose for reading and helps children activate background knowledge in a way that facilitates comprehension of the text. As with the examples earlier in this chapter, students are motivated to participate in an engaging reading task that serves a clear, authentic purpose.

In first-grade classrooms, children are given opportunities to engage more independently with informational texts, while teachers play an important role in selecting texts and providing instructional supports. For example, as part of their study of habitats, a teacher might use the text *Life in the Ocean* (Huxley, 2005) with a guided reading group to teach children how to use an index to find information about ocean animals.

By second grade, children are expected to read and comprehend a range of complex informational texts more independently, using their reading skills to access information and build knowledge across subject areas. For example, children might conduct a local history project by working with a variety of informational texts (e.g., newspaper articles, biographies, trade books, time lines), with the teacher providing support as needed. The following vignette illustrates the way this type of instruction might be implemented in a prekindergarten classroom.

INFORMATIONAL TEXT STANDARDS IN ACTION: RANGE OF READING AND LEVEL OF TEXT COMPLEXITY

Ms. Washington gathers her prekindergarten students in a circle on the carpet to continue their work on a month-long study of Arctic and Antarctic animals. She begins by showing them the book she had read aloud the day before: *North Pole, South Pole* (Levinson, 2002). She asks for volunteers to share something they remembered from the book, and the children eagerly raise their hands to contribute. As the children offer their ideas, Ms. Washington turns to the relevant pages in the book so that the children can see the pictures and reread the text as needed. She prompts the children to check their prior knowledge by asking, "Was there anything in the book that you already knew?" She encourages them to extend their learning by asking, "Was there anything in the book that surprised you?" and "Are there any things that this book makes you wonder about?" She then reads a new book—*A Penguin's Life* (Dickmann, 2011)—and encourages students to look for connections to the previous book. The children enjoy learning new information from the second text, and the variety of informational text features (e.g., diagram, picture glossary, index) offers additional learning opportunities.

Over the next few days, Ms. Washington and the children continue to build their knowledge of Arctic and Antarctic animals through similar read-alouds and discussions. During center time, the children explore books on their own, listen to books on tape, play with plastic animal toys, and create classroom murals. At the writing center, they use a set of labeled pictures to help them label their artwork. After consulting a world map, the class decides to hang the Arctic mural on the north wall of the classroom and the Antarctic mural on the south wall. Each student picks a favorite animal and works with Ms. Washington to make a page for a classroom book. She provides support as needed, depending on the individual child's level of writing skill.

Throughout their study of the topic, Ms. Washington works to expose the children to a variety of rich and engaging informational texts, including books, maps, audio recordings, and digital texts. She helps students integrate information from pictures and from the text, and she engages students in thinking across texts.

USING THE STANDARDS THROUGHOUT THE SCHOOL DAY

There are many opportunities for embedding the standards for reading informational text throughout the school day. For example, a typical daily schedule in a primary-grade classroom includes time for independent reading, whole-class instruction, small-group guided reading, read-alouds, and content-area learning. All of these instructional components of the school day offer opportunities for children to engage with informational texts of increasing complexity over time, whether as a whole class, in small groups, or individually.

During independent reading, teachers set the stage for quality time with informational texts by making sure that the classroom environment contains a variety of informational texts that are engaging and accessible. Arranging texts thematically helps children make connections across texts. For example, a first-grade teacher could supplement a science unit on the solar system by adding a display of texts about space exploration to the classroom library. The teacher could also give children access to digital texts by bookmarking related websites on the classroom computers or linking classroom iPads to a visual tour of the solar system.

Whole-class lessons are a great part of the day for using informational texts to teach all students about text structure and features while building content knowledge. Teachers can lead students in shared reading of rich informational texts, whether by reading from a big book on an easel or using a document camera and projector to make a standard-size book visible to all. For example, a second-grade teacher could use excerpts from the book *Earth's Resources* (Barraclough, 2008) to teach a lesson that builds content vocabulary and instructs students about the use of boldface type in informational texts.

During small-group, guided-reading instruction, teachers can provided targeted instruction and support as children work in small groups to read informational texts. For instance, a guided-reading lesson could focus on using headings and subheadings to identify key ideas and details in a text. Teachers can use this instructional time to observe individual children closely, monitor their progress toward standards, and offer instructional support as needed.

Whole-class read-alouds offer another opportunity for teachers to engage their children with informational texts in very intentional ways. For example, a kindergarten teacher could choose to read *Let's Eat!: What Children Eat Around the World* (Hollyer, 2004) during daily read-aloud time as part of a larger study of cultures around the world. During the read-aloud, the teacher can focus on building content knowledge and learning how to use a glossary to support vocabulary learning.

While there is often separate time allocated to content-area learning, this component of the school day offers rich opportunities for engagement with informational text and integration of content areas and literacy skills. For example, a first-grade teacher could use the informational text *Monarch Butterfly* (Gibbons, 1991) as a supplement to hands-on science lessons about butterflies and life cycles.

Through all of these components of the school day, teachers can use informational texts to build content knowledge, support reading and writing skill development, encourage interdisciplinary connections, and engage children with text. To help children meet the standards related to informational text, teachers must be intentional about selecting texts and providing scaffolding that will help all children move toward independent comprehension of complex informational texts.

EXAMPLE INFORMATIONAL TEXTS
FOR PreK–GRADE 2 (USING CCSS TERMINOLOGY)

PreK

Book about science: *Wonderful Worms* by L. Glaser (Scholastic, 1992).

> This book provides opportunities to teach vocabulary, the notion of cross-section, and sequential text structure. It ends with the answers to many questions young children commonly ask about worms and thus is a great book for teaching children to ask questions as they read.

Technical text (specifically, procedural): *Pretend Soup and Other Real Recipes: A Cookbook for Preschoolers and Up* by M. Katzen & A. L. Henderson (Tricycle Press, 2004).

> This text is great for exposing young children to directions or how-to text. Children can learn to read the simple recipes with informative graphics.

Digital source: *http://pbskids.org/sid/videoplayer.html*.

> Sid the Science Kid provides explanations and demonstrations of many science concepts appropriate for preschool-age children. The site offers a lot of exposure to oral and, with the captioning feature enabled, written informational text.

Kindergarten

Book about social studies: *Two Eyes, a Nose, and a Mouth* by R. G. Intrater (Scholastic, 2000).

> This unique book offers an important message about diversity. It presents opportunities to talk about ways photographs can help convey information and messages to the reader.

(cont.)

Technical text (specifically, procedural): *What Is It?* by L. Kimmelman (Pearson Education, 2005).

> This simple procedural text guides children in creating a guessing game in which players try to identify an object by its feel. It would work well in a unit on senses and for teaching common characteristics of procedural text.

Digital source: *http://pbskids.org/dinosaurtrain/games/fieldguide.html.*

> This site provides a great introduction to field guides; each entry offers key information about a dinosaur (e.g., a quadruped or biped; the time period in which it lived). There are a lot of opportunities to teach about icons as well.

First Grade

Book about social studies and science: *Good Enough to Eat: A Kid's Guide to Food and Nutrition* by L. Rockwell (HarperCollins, 1999).

> Packed with fascinating facts and big ideas, this book makes the topic of nutrition interesting and accessible for children. There are many informational text features, including diagrams, labels, and speech bubbles.

Technical text (specifically, procedural): *Hairy Harry* by B. Perez (National Geographic Society, 2001).

> This book provides directions for making a "chia pet"–like craft. There are opportunities to teach many common features of procedural text, and the end product makes a great Father's Day or Mother's Day gift.

Digital source: *http://kids.nationalgeographic.com/kids/animals.*

> The sloth video is fabulous, as is so much on this site. Children's interest will keep them coming back, resulting in wide exposure to informational language and images.

Second Grade

Book about science (read-aloud): *You're Tall in the Morning but Shorter at Night and Other Amazing Facts about the Human Body* by M. Berger (Scholastic, 2003).

> One of our favorite books about the human body, this text conveys important and interesting information and provides opportunities to teach about many common informational text features.

Technical text (specifically, procedural): *Let's Play: Games Around the World* by T. B. Morton (Pearson Education, 2005).

> This book includes several procedural texts children can follow in order to play a series of simple yet engaging games. Conventional features of procedural text, such as materials and procedures, are included.

Digital source: *http://photojournal.jpl.nasa.gov.*

> Children can click on a diagram to unlock thousands of images from space. Information about the images is provided in table form, making this a great tool for teaching about tables.

CONCLUSION

If supported in appropriate ways, learning to read and interact with informational text can be at once challenging and pleasurable for young children. Motivation is a key component to success with challenging material, and we believe that, among other things, providing students with texts that meet their interests and skill levels, presenting authentic purposes for engagement, allowing for choice, and carefully planning activities in which children can exert as much autonomy as possible are important steps toward building and maintaining that motivation. Carefully designed instruction—particularly teaching comprehension strategies, drawing attention to craft and structure, and engaging children in discussion—is also critical, as is incorporating a broad range of text throughout the classroom environment and throughout the school day. The CCSS advocate for literacy skills to cross the borders of English classrooms and language arts instructional blocks into other content areas, and informational text is the perfect medium with which to build those bridges.

ACTIVITIES AND QUESTIONS

Activities

The following are additional activities designed to support children's development toward meeting the CCSS for informational text.

1. *Key Ideas and Details.* During a read-aloud or structured lesson with an informational text, point out the headings and subheadings in the text. On chart paper, work with children to use the headings and create a concept map that indicates key ideas and supporting details. For more independent readings, provide the beginnings of a concept map they can add to on their own. As children become more sophisticated in their use of informational texts, attention can shift from identifying key ideas and details for their maps to focusing on the nature of the connections among ideas and concepts.

2. *Craft and Structure.* During a read-aloud or structured lesson with an informational text, point out text features common to informational texts. Focus on how readers can use the features to learn from informational texts. Children can apply their knowledge by identifying text features in texts they read independently or during guided reading. Children can extend their knowledge of text features through the Improve-a-Text method, described earlier, of creating text features and adding them to existing informational texts. For example, if a child finds an informational text that doesn't contain captions, he or she can write captions and add them to the text with sticky notes.

3. *Integration of Knowledge and Ideas.* Teachers can help children develop their knowledge of informational texts by writing their own informational texts using text structures they are investigating during reading. For example, if a class is studying the compare–contrast text structure, children might create their own texts with a compare–contrast structure. Again, these texts should mirror real-world texts and have purpose beyond just learning to read and

write. Similarly, teachers can help develop children's understanding of how graphics in text can support comprehension and learning by engaging children in creating visuals for texts they are reading. Similarly, they can present children with a visual display (e.g., an illustration or a diagram) and ask them to write text that complements the graphic.

4. *Range of Reading and Level of Text Complexity.* It's important to take an inventory of the classroom library to ensure that children have access to many informational texts, of different types, on different topics, and with a variety of text structures and features. Nonbook texts, such as magazines, newspapers, brochures, maps, posters, charts, and digital media, should definitely be included. Teachers can scaffold children's reading of complex texts by frontloading their vocabulary and content knowledge on a topic. For example, a teacher can choose to use some hands-on activities to give children information about a science topic like erosion before extending their knowledge through the reading of several complex texts on the topic. Teachers can also provide instruction in key vocabulary words while reading a challenging text.

Questions

1. What are some opportunities for integrating instruction in reading skills and strategies into content-area learning? For example, how might a teacher use informational texts to teach comprehension strategies in the context of science and social studies instruction?

2. What are some scaffolds or supports than can help all children gain access to interesting and essential content through reading complex informational texts?

3. What kinds of challenges and opportunities do informational texts present compared with literary texts? How might teachers help children understand the similarities and differences in reading texts of different genres?

4. How can teachers determine whether an informational text is appropriate for a specific child and/or a specific task? What role should quantitative and qualitative measures play in making these determinations? What other factors are important to consider?

REFERENCES

Beck, I. L., McKeown, M. G., Sandora, C., Kucan, L., & Worthy, J. (1996). Questioning the author: A yearlong classroom implementation to engage students with text. *Elementary School Journal, 96*(4), 385–414.

Brophy, J. (1987). Synthesis of research on strategies for motivating students to learn. *Educational Leadership, 45*, 40–48.

Chall, J. S. (1983). *Stages of reading development.* New York: McGraw-Hill.

Chall, J. S. (1996). *Stages of reading development* (2nd ed.). Fort Worth, TX: Harcourt Brace.

Dodge, A. M., Husain, N., & Duke, N. K. (2011). Connected kids?: K–2 children's use and understanding of the Internet. *Language Arts, 89*, 86–98.

Duke, N. K. (2000). 3.6 minutes per day: The scarcity of informational texts in first grade. *Reading Research Quarterly, 35*, 202–224.

Duke, N. K., Bennett-Armistead, V. S., & Roberts, E. M. (2003). Filling the great void: Why we should bring nonfiction into the early-grade classroom. *American Educator, 27*(1), 30–35.

Duke, N. K., Caughlan, S., Juzwik, M. M., & Martin, N. M. (2012). *Reading and writing genre with purpose in K–8 classrooms.* Portsmouth, NH: Heinemann.

Duke, N. K., & Kays, J. (1998). "Can I say 'Once upon a time'?": Kindergarten children developing knowledge of information book language. *Early Childhood Research Quarterly, 13,* 295–318.

Duke, N. K., Martineau, J. A., Frank, K. A., Stebbe, S. M., & Bennett-Armistead, V. S. (2012). *The impact of including more informational text in first-grade classrooms.* Unpublished manuscript, Michigan State University.

Duke, N. K., & Pearson, P. D. (2002). Effective practices for developing reading comprehension. In A. E. Farstrup & S. J. Samuels (Eds.), *What research has to say about reading instruction* (3rd ed., pp. 205–242). Newark, DE: International Reading Association.

Duke, N. K., Purcell-Gates, V., Hall, L. A., & Tower, C. (2006/2007). Authentic literacy activities for developing comprehension and writing. *The Reading Teacher, 60,* 344–355.

Duke, N. K., & Roberts, K. M. (2010). The genre-specific nature of reading comprehension. In D. Wyse, R. Andrews, & J. Hoffman (Eds.), *The Routledge international handbook of English, language and literacy teaching* (pp. 74–86). London: Routledge.

Fingeret, L. (2008). "March of the Penguins": Building knowledge in a kindergarten classroom. *The Reading Teacher, 62,* 96–103.

Graesser, A. C., McNamara, D. S., & Kulikowich, J. M. (2011). Coh-Metrix: Providing multilevel analyses of text characteristics. *Educational Researcher, 40,* 223–234.

Guthrie, J. T., & McCann, A. D. (1996). Idea circles: Peer collaborations for conceptual learning. In L. Gambrell & J. Almasi (Eds.), *Lively discussions!* (pp. 87–105). Newark, DE: International Reading Association.

Guthrie, J. T., McRae, A., & Klauda, S. L. (2007). Contributions of concept-oriented reading instruction to knowledge about interventions for motivations in reading. *Educational Psychologist, 42,* 237–250.

Guthrie, J. T., Wigfield, A., Barbosa, P., Perencevich, K. C., Taboada, A., Davis, M., et al. (2004). Increasing reading comprehension and engagement through concept-oriented reading instruction. *Journal of Educational Psychology, 96,* 403–423.

Hiebert, E. H. (2008). The word zone fluency curriculum: An alternative approach. In M. R. Kuhn & P. J. Schwanenflugel (Eds.), *Fluency in the classroom* (pp. 154–170). New York: Guilford Press.

Jeong, J. S., Gaffney, J. S., & Choi, J. O. (2010). Availability and use of informational text in second, third, and fourth grades. *Research in the Teaching of English, 44,* 435–456.

Jiménez, L. M., & Duke, N. K. (2011). *The effect of high and low interest on multiple text reading comprehension in elementary-age readers.* Unpublished manuscript.

Murphy, P. K., Wilkinson, I. A. G., Sotor, A. O., Hennessey, M. N., & Alexander, J. F. (2009). Examining the effects of classroom discussion on students' comprehension of text: A meta-analysis. *Journal of Educational Psychology, 101,* 740–764.

National Governors Association Center for Best Practices and Council of Chief State School Officers. (2011). *Common core state standards for English language arts and literacy to history/social studies, science, and technical subjects.* Washington, DC: Author.

Pappas, C. (1993). Is narrative "primary"?: Some insights from kindergarteners' pretend readings of stories and information books. *Journal of Reading Behavior, 25,* 97–129.

Pressley, M., Dolezal, S. E., Raphael, L. M., Mohan, L., Roehrig, A. D., & Bogner, K. (2003). *Motivating primary-grade students.* New York: Guilford Press.

Purcell-Gates, V., Duke, N. K., & Martineau, J. A. (2007). Learning to read and write genre-specific text: Roles of authentic experience and explicit teaching. *Reading Research Quarterly, 42,* 8–45.

Renninger, K. A., & Wozniak, R. H. (1985). Effect of interest on attentional shift, recognition, and recall in young children. *Developmental Psychology, 21,* 624–632.

Santoro, L., Chard, D. J., Howard, L., & Baker, S. K. (2008). Making the very most of classroom read-alouds to promote comprehension and vocabulary. *The Reading Teacher, 61*, 396–408.

Shanahan, T., Callison, K., Carriere, C., Duke, N. K., Pearson, P. D., Schatschneider, C., et al. (2010). *Improving reading comprehension in kindergarten through 3rd grade: A practice guide* (NCEE 2010-4038). Washington, DC: National Center for Education Evaluation and Regional Assistance, Institute of Education Sciences, U.S. Department of Education. Retrieved from *whatworks.ed.gov/publications/practiceguides*.

Taylor, K. K. (1986). Summary writing by young children. *Reading Research Quarterly, 21*, 193–208.

Wright, T. S. (2011). *What classroom observations reveal about oral vocabulary instruction in kindergarten*. Unpublished doctoral dissertation, University of Michigan, Ann Arbor.

Yussen, S. R., Rembold, K. L., & Mazor, A. (1989). Identifying main ideas in picture stories and written narratives. *Journal of Applied Developmental Psychology, 10*, 313–335.

CHILDREN'S BOOKS CITED

Barraclough, S. (2008). *Earth's resources*. Chicago: Heinemann Library.

Canizares, S., & Chessen, B. (1998). *Rainforest colors*. New York: Scholastic.

Dickmann, N. (2011). *A penguin's life*. Chicago: Heinemann Library.

Gibbons, G. (1991). *Monarch butterfly*. New York: Holiday House.

Graves, S. (2005). *Lend a hand*. London: Dorling Kindersley.

Hollyer, B. (2004). *Let's eat!: What children eat around the world*. New York: Holt.

Huxley, G. (2005). *Life in the ocean*. Monterey, CA: National Geographic School Publishing.

Levinson, N. S. (2002). *North Pole, South Pole*. New York: Holiday House.

Royston, A. (2011). *Fire fighter!* London: Dorling Kindersley.

CHAPTER 4

Reading Standards
Foundational Skills

Kristin M. Gehsmann
Shane Templeton

In the Common Core State Standards (CCSS; National Governors Association Center for Best Practices and Council of Chief State School Officers, 2010), the introduction to the foundational skills reading standards appropriately describes the role of these skills in the broader context of meaningful literacy instruction:

> These standards are directed toward fostering students' understanding and working knowledge of concepts of print, the alphabetic principle, and other basic conventions of the English writing system. These foundational skills are not an end in and of themselves; rather, they are necessary and important components of an effective, comprehensive reading program designed to develop proficient readers with the capacity to comprehend texts across a range of types and disciplines. (p. 15)

Students' efficient, fluent, and meaningful engagements with text depend on their understanding of and efficient access to the ways in which letters in printed words represent information about language—its sounds, its structure, and its meanings. As we describe in this chapter, developing this knowledge depends on the depth and breadth of developmentally grounded word study. This study is systematic, explicit, *and* embedded in the reading and writing in which students are engaged, reflecting the Common Core's emphasis on "an integrated model of literacy" (p. 4).

In the CCSS the signpost phonics and word analysis skills at each grade level are applied to spelling patterns. It is no accident that phonics and word recognition skills are discussed in conjunction with spelling. In this chapter, we address spelling as a reflection and indicator of students' underlying word knowledge—not only their ability to write words but their ability to read words—what they attend to when they encounter familiar words and decode unfamiliar words in connected text (Perfetti, 2007; Rapp & Lipka, 2011; Templeton, 2011).

We ground foundational skills instruction in a developmental model of literacy (Chall, 1995; Ehri, 2005; Templeton & Bear, 2011). The model to which we refer here derives from the research investigating the development of word knowledge in children—how learners come to understand, over time, the relationships between the printed word and sound and meaning.

Most children in the preschool years fall within the emergent literacy stage, as do many kindergartners. Emergent learners draw, scribble, and eventually incorporate features of print into their written efforts. While they are not reading in the conventional sense, they "pretend read" using the illustrations and their knowledge of storybook language (e.g., "Once upon a time . . . ") to guide their efforts (Sulzby, 1985). As learners continue to be engaged in explicit instruction and meaningful reading and writing activities, they learn about letters and their names and gradually develop the critical understanding of the *alphabetic principle*—phonemes or individual sounds correspond to letters, arranged left to right on the page. This fundamental insight is the onset of beginning reading in the conventional sense, which many children move into during the kindergarten year.

When beginning readers write, they try to match sounds to the letters whose names they have learned. This is why this stage is also referred to as "letter name"—the name of a letter usually contains the sound that the child is trying to spell (e.g., *drive* is often spelled JRIF; *chicken* may be spelled HEKN). As these children interact with conventional spellings, with the teacher's support and instruction, their spellings come to reflect this interaction (DRIV, CHIKN).

When children begin to include the features of long-vowel spellings in their writing, this is an important benchmark that suggests they are moving beyond the strict left-to-right processing of and thinking about printed words. They are becoming transitional readers, "chunking" two or three letters together and learning about how such groups of letters correspond to sound (*drive* may now be spelled DRIEV, *float* spelled FLOTE). The fact that they are "using but confusing" these spellings (Invernizzi, Abouzeid, & Gill, 1994) tells us they are ready to systematically explore these within-word patterns. Many children in first grade move into the transitional stage during the year; most children in second grade are in the transitional stage.

The key to appreciating the power of a well-grounded developmental model lies in its instructional applications. The importance of teaching students at their instructional level is compelling. It is simply the case that when we teach students where they are rather than where they are not, their learning will advance more quickly and efficiently and students' gains are more likely to be maintained over time (Harré & Moghaddam, 2003; Morris, Blanton, Blanton, Nowacek, & Perney, 1995; Morris & Perney, 1984). When we turn our attention back to grade-level standards and expectations this is important to bear in mind, particularly for those students who are performing well below those expectations.

PUTTING THE FOUNDATIONAL SKILLS STANDARDS INTO PRACTICE

In this section, we describe each of the four foundational skills noted in the standards—print concepts, phonological awareness, phonics and word recognition, and fluency—and suggest some possible ways to teach these skills to young children across the early stages of literacy development. Early and effective teaching of these foundational skills will enable children to engage, experience, and independently read more complex texts over time, a central goal of the Common Core. However, we must also be vigilant that the Common Core's focus on sophisticated interactions with complex text not eclipse the critical importance of teaching these foundational skills in the early stages of development. In the vignettes that follow, you will see how effective teachers teach these skills both explicitly and within the context of meaningful reading and writing activities.

Print Concepts

Table 4.1 highlights the anchor standards for children's early understanding of print concepts (K–1), and related prekindergarten standards are also noted.

As the CCSS emphasize, much of our teaching with emergent learners involves modeling how print works: (1) its directionality—in English, left to right and top to bottom, and (2) its forms and functions (Justice & Piasta, 2011). Young children's understanding of how spoken words are represented in print—a concept of word in text—will take time (Flanigan, 2007; Morris, Bloodgood, Lomax, & Perney, 2003). This understanding will develop from your explicit teaching of letters, letter names, and some of the sounds for which letters stand as well as modeling how to apply this knowledge in shared reading and writing activities. We begin this exploration of the alphabet and letter–sound relationships in preschool and kindergarten.

In our teaching of the alphabet, we use the alphabet song (sung to the tune of *Twinkle, Twinkle Little Star*) to help children learn the letters in sequential order, pointing to each letter as we sing. It's especially helpful for children to have their own alphabet strip to follow along. With guidance and practice, children will learn the song by heart and improve their voice–print match; soon they'll come to understand that "ellemenopee" is not one letter! The *function* of letters is emphasized right from the start: Using children's names to talk about letters is a unique motivator (Cunningham, 2005; Krech, 2000): *L* is Latisha's letter, *T* is Tanya and Terrence's letter. A "name of the day" activity allows the

---

TABLE 4.1. Standards for Foundational Skills: Print Concepts (Anchor Standards for K–1)

Kindergartners	Grade 1 students

1. Demonstrate understanding of the organization and basic features of print.
  a. Follow words from left to right, top to bottom, and page by page.
  b. Recognize that spoken words are represented in written language by specific sequences of letters.
  c. Understand that words are separated by spaces in print.
  d. Recognize and name all upper- and lowercase letters of the alphabet.
	1. Demonstrate understanding of the organization and basic features of print.
	  a. Recognize the distinguishing features of a sentence (e.g., first word, capitalization, ending punctuation).

Related PreK Standards:
- Knows that alphabet letters are a special category of visual graphics that can be individually named.
- Knows that it is print that is read in stories.
- Understands that different forms are used for different functions of print (e.g., grocery list).
- Can identify 10 alphabet letters, especially those in own name (Snow, Burns, & Griffin, 1998, p. 61).

introduction of more letters than is possible in traditional "letter of the day" instruction (Bear, Invernizzi, Johnston, & Templeton, 2010).

In teaching beginning sound–letter correspondences, we follow a sequence that contrasts not only the names of the consonant letters, but their shapes (upper- and lowercase forms), sounds, and point of articulation. With these criteria in mind, for example, over a couple of weeks the consonants *m* and *s* may first be explored and then *b* and *r* added, compared, and contrasted. Alphabet knowledge is taught explicitly, as described here, and as part of children's developing concepts about print, as illustrated in the following vignette.

FOUNDATIONAL SKILLS STANDARDS IN ACTION: PRINT CONCEPTS

Developing a concept of word in text requires children to orchestrate knowledge of letters and sounds, oral language, memory, and written text. Here we see Ms. Scott use a familiar song, "Row, Row, Row Your Boat," to teach her kindergarten children various aspects of the standards for print concepts:

Row, Row, Row Your Boat
Row, row, row, your boat
Gently down the stream.
Merrily, merrily, merrily, merrily,
Life is but a dream.

"Let's start our morning with a favorite song. The title of this song is 'Row, Row, Row Your Boat.'" Ms. Scott points to each word as she reads the title. "What is the title of our song?" The children reply in unison: "Row, Row, Row Your Boat." "That's right! And each word in our title begins with a capital letter. *Row* starts with a letter we've been learning about—this is a capital *R*." (As she says this, she frames the letter.) "What letter does *Row* start with? Yes, a capital *R*. *Row* begins with the letter *R* and it sounds like /r/. Get your mouths ready to make the sound of *R*—/r/. Nice! Let's read this word together." As the children read in unison, Ms. Scott elongates the sounds in the word as she runs her finger underneath the letters and then repeats the word: "Row." After reading the word, she contextualizes it by repeating the title while pointing to each word as she reads. She repeats this process by exploring the word *boat* and the initial consonant *B*, also found in the title. Ms. Scott invites the children to help her fingerpoint read the memorized line. If they get off track, as some will, she gently brings them back to noticing the initial letter in the words and even invites one child to "ride along with her" as they point together. The pacing of this introduction is lively, the tone is positive, and the learning integrates so many important aspects of the print concepts standards: letters, sounds, words and even capitalization!

After exploring the title, Ms. Scott sings the song aloud, pointing to each word, and then the children join her in singing the memorized text. After enjoying the song a couple of times, she brings the children back to exploring words that begin with letters they're learning (*m, b, r*). She also helps them see and hear how some words have more than one syllable, and the children clap the syllables with great enthusiasm (e.g., *gent-ly, mer-ri-ly*). She focuses the children's attention on the initial consonant in these words and emphasizes that words sometimes have more than one syllable or part, and she connects this idea to some children's names in the class (e.g., *Ad-am; Sil-vi-a*). She then repeats the line of text and the children take turns leading the fingerpoint reading. After a couple of minutes, Ms. Scott invites them to find words they've talked about (e.g., *row*, *boat*, *merrily*) and when they do, she asks, "How did you know that says . . . *merrily*?"—a question that encourages the children to reflect on their understanding of letters, sounds, words, and context.

In the days that follow, Ms. Scott provides each child a copy of the song for their personal readers, folders that contain collections of familiar texts for children to reread and interact with during center and independent reading times (Bear, Casserta-Henry, & Venner, 2004). Later in the day during word study, the children sort pictures that begin with the initial letters they're studying that week (*r*, *m*, *b*), and they may return to this text to highlight words that begin with these initial consonants. They also draw and label pictures of objects that begin with these letters in their own ABC books—writing the words with "phonic spelling" (Invernizzi & Hayes, 2004), which reinforces their growing awareness of letter–sound correspondence and concept of word.

As you can see, Ms. Scott's teaching of print concepts is both explicit and connected to authentic reading and writing tasks, the goal of the CCSS and the practice of highly effective teachers (Taylor, Pearson, Clark, & Walpole, 2000).

Phonological Awareness

Phonological awareness is a skill that requires children to slow down speech to identify and manipulate its "pieces" and "parts," beginning with large units of sound—spoken words and syllables—and moving to smaller speech units—onsets and rimes and finally phonemes, the smallest unit of sound (Ziegler & Goswami, 2005). Table 4.2 highlights the anchor standards for phonological awareness (K–1) and also notes related prekindergarten standards.

TABLE 4.2 Standards for Foundational Skills: Phonological Awareness (Anchor Standards for K–1)

Kindergartners	Grade 1 students
2. Demonstrate understanding of spoken words, syllables, and sounds (phonemes).	2. Demonstrate understanding of spoken words, syllables, and sounds (phonemes).
a. Recognize and produce rhyming words.	a. Distinguish long- from short-vowel sounds in spoken single-syllable words.
b. Count, pronounce, blend, and segment syllables in spoken words.	b. Orally produce single-syllable words by blending sounds (phonemes), including consonant blends.
c. Blend and segment onsets and rimes of single-syllable spoken words.	c. Isolate and pronounce initial, medial vowel, and final sounds (phonemes) in spoken single-syllable words.
d. Isolate and pronounce the initial, medial vowel, and final sounds (phonemes) in three-phoneme (consonant–vowel–consonant [CVC]) words. (This does not include CVCs ending with /l/, /r/, or /x/.)	d. Segment spoken single-syllable words.
e. Add or substitute individual sounds (phonemes) in simple, one-syllable words to make new words.	
Related PreK Standards: Pays attention to separable and repeating sounds in language (e.g., Peter, Peter, Pumpkin Eater, Peter Eater) (Snow et al., 1998)	

Becoming "phonologically aware" means children are able to think explicitly about spoken language. Nurturing this ability begins in the preschool years, when children are exposed to nursery rhymes and rhythmic texts such as poetry, fingerplays, chants, songs, and jingles. As the CCSS indicate, we capitalize on this interest by playing rhyming games with children's names in preschool and kindergarten classrooms: "Tiffany Miffany" "Letisha Bonisha" (McGee & Richgels, 1990) and other games such as rhyming concentration with pictures of rhyming words or sorting pictures by their rhyming sounds (Bear et al., 2010).

Phonemic awareness, a subset of phonological awareness, refers to children's ability to recognize, identify, and manipulate phonemes, the smallest units of sound. Phonemic awareness, like phonological awareness, is an oral language activity; however, children's phonemic awareness and phonological awareness develop in concert with alphabet knowledge—each reinforcing the other—and so we teach them concurrently, both explicitly and in the context of reading and writing activities. Figure 4.1 outlines the typical scope and sequence for phonemic awareness instruction beginning in preschool through first grade (Armbruster, Lehr, & Osborn, 2006).

In the following vignette, we see how teachers can explicitly teach the phonological standards of the CCSS and extend children's practice to authentic reading and writing activities:

> ### FOUNDATIONAL SKILLS STANDARDS IN ACTION: PHONOLOGICAL AWARENESS
>
> Ms. Pepin, a first-grade teacher, gathers a small group of on-level readers—at the beginning of the transitional stage—at the Smart Board for their daily word study lesson. The focus of today's lesson is from the first-grade phonological awareness standards: distinguishing long- from short-vowel sounds in spoken single-syllable words.
>
> "Good morning, readers. Today we're going to focus our attention on hearing and sorting the vowel sounds in words." Pointing to images on the screen, Ms. Pepin says, "Let's review

Phoneme isolation	What's the first sound in *boat*?
Phoneme identification	What sound is the same in the words *cake, cup, cook*?
Phoneme categorization	Which word doesn't belong: *run, ring, rope, tub*?
Phoneme blending	What is this word: /p/-/ă/-/t/?
Phoneme segmentation	How many sounds are in the word *pin*? Let's push and say these sounds: /p/-/ĭ/-/n/. How many sounds are in the word *pin*?
Phoneme deletion	What is *jeep* without the /j/?
Phoneme addition	What do you have when you add /s/ to the beginning of the word *nap*? (*snap*)
Phoneme substitution	The word is *kit*. Change the /k/ to /f/. What's the new word? (*fit*)

FIGURE 4.1 Scope and sequence of phonemic awareness instruction.

the pictures in today's sort." As she names each of the pictures, she briefly talks about some of the words' meanings, particularly words that a few students may not know: "A crab is a little creature that lives in the sand at the beach." She then turns her attention to the sort: "Readers, today we have two key pictures in our sort: a cat and a cake." She slides the pictures to the top of the screen. "This is a picture of a cat: c-ăăă-t. Listen to the vowel in the middle and help me say it: c-ăăă-t. *Cat* has the short *a* sound in the middle." She writes ă next to the image. "This is a picture of a cake: c-āāā-k. I hear the letter *A* say its name in the middle of this word. Say it with me: c-āāā-k. When a vowel says its name, we call it a long vowel. *Cake* has a long *a* in the middle." She writes ā next to the image.

"Let's see if we can sort our pictures by long and short *a* today." Choosing the images one by one, Ms. Pepin compares and contrasts the medial vowel sound of each image with the key picture: "This is a picture of a game. What vowel sound do you hear in g-āāā-m? Is it like *cat* or *cake*?" As she asks, she moves the picture up to show that she's comparing it with each of the key pictures. "Yes, it's a long vowel like *cake*." With that, she places the image under the picture of the cake. After some additional modeling, the children each come up to the Smart Board and sort the remaining pictures following the same procedure. When they're done, they check the sort by reading down the column of pictures and discuss any pictures that may be confusing or misplaced. Ms. Pepin prompts the children to reflect on what they learned by sorting the pictures: "What's the big idea in today's sort? Turn to your partner and discuss what you noticed." Ms. Pepin reinforces the idea that vowels can be long as in the words *cake*, *rain*, and *game* or short as in the words *cat*, *grass*, and *flag*.

In the days that follow, the children in Ms. Pepin's group receive their own copy of the pictures to practice sorting in school and at home, and she draws their attention to words with long and short *a* sounds in them during guided reading. During center time, they use old magazines to find pictures of other words with long and short *a* sounds, and they add them to their word study notebooks (Bear, Invernizzi, Johnston, & Templeton, 2012) and label them too, reinforcing both their alphabet knowledge and phonemic awareness. Later in the week, the children may play matching games using the pictures from the week's sort or practice phoneme segmentation and counting phonemes by pushing and saying the sounds in each of the words. (See Invernizzi, Johnston, Bear, & Templeton, 2009, for more suggestions.)

Phonics and Word Recognition

Table 4.3 highlights the anchor standards for children's understanding of phonics and word recognition (K–2). For beginning readers, the phonics or letter–sound standards of grades K–1 are pretty straightforward: predictable consonant and primarily short-vowel correspondences that match their expectation of a linear, sequential left-to-right matchup. As these children encounter more words that contain long-vowel spelling patterns, this information comes to be incorporated within their developing orthographic knowledge as they move into the transitional stage of literacy. Teachers are able to scaffold children's understanding patterns *within* words based on this underlying orthographic knowledge.

Transitional readers have accumulated in their sight vocabularies quite a number of words that contain long-vowel spelling patterns. Understanding the logic underlying these patterns strengthens the connections among sound, spelling, and meaning in children's lexicons, or "dictionaries in the head." The stronger these connections, the more rapid and efficient word identification during reading will be. Just as beginning readers with alphabetic-level orthographic knowledge can learn to read and remember words

TABLE 4.3. Standards for Foundational Skills: Phonics and Word Recognition (Anchor Standards for K–2)

Kindergartners	Grade 1 students	Grade 2 students
3. Know and apply grade-level phonics and word analysis skills in decoding words. a. Demonstrate basic knowledge of one-to-one letter–sound correspondences by producing the primary or many of the most frequent sounds for each consonant. b. Associate the long and short sounds with common spellings (graphemes) for the five major vowels. c. Read common high-frequency words by sight (e.g., *the, of, to, you, she, my, is, are, do, does*). d. Distinguish between similarly spelled words by identifying the sounds of the letters that differ.	3. Know and apply grade-level phonics and word analysis skills in decoding words. a. Know the spelling–sound correspondences for common consonant digraphs. b. Decode regularly spelled one-syllable words. c. Know final -*e* and common vowel team conventions for representing long-vowel sounds. d. Use knowledge that every syllable must have a vowel sound to determine the number of syllables in a printed word. e. Decode two-syllable words following basic patterns by breaking the words into syllables. f. Read words with inflectional endings. g. Recognize and read grade-appropriate irregularly spelled words.	3. Know and apply grade-level phonics and word analysis skills in decoding words. a. Distinguish long and short vowels when reading regularly spelled one-syllable words. b. Know spelling–sound correspondences for additional common vowel teams. c. Decode regularly spelled two-syllable words with long vowels. d. Decode words with common prefixes and suffixes. e. Identify words with inconsistent but common spelling–sound correspondences. f. Recognize and read grade-appropriate irregularly spelled words.

that have long-vowel spellings, so can transitional readers with pattern-level orthographic knowledge learn to read and remember words of two or more syllables. In other words, the orthographic knowledge at each developmental stage supports the decoding of words whose spelling children won't fully master until the following stage.

The two word-sort activities in the following vignette develop two fundamental understandings about the letters that represent sounds within single syllables:

1. How sounds are spelled very often depends on where they occur within a word.
2. How sounds are spelled very often depends on other sounds they are close to.

These two critical insights are nurtured throughout the transitional stage of reading.

FOUNDATIONAL SKILLS STANDARDS IN ACTION: PHONICS AND WORD RECOGNITION

On a January morning, Ms. McClelland meets with her group of early transitional readers. She is planning a word study activity that addresses phonics and word recognition Anchor Standard 3c: Know final -*e* and common vowel team conventions for representing long-vowel sounds. She is planning a word-sort activity using words that the children have learned as sight words. Because the words are familiar, it will be easier for them to analyze spelling patterns and derive phonic generalizations. She passes out a packet of small word cards to each pair of students. Each packet contains the following words:

sail	*clay*	*mane*	*mail*	*pane*	*male*
play	*main*	*sale*	*may*	*pain*	*away*

"Girls and boys, here are some words that we've picked up the last few weeks in our reading. Read through them with your partner—if there are any that you do not know, put them in a separate pile."

After the cards have all been read, Ms. McClelland says, "Turn to your partner and discuss: What do you notice about these words?" She often uses this question to begin a word categorization activity. After a minute, Ms. McClelland asks the children to share out; they comment that all the words have a long *a* sound. "Good! Did you notice anything else?" The children mention different spellings for long *a*; if they hadn't made this observation, Ms. McClelland would have helped them reach it. She builds upon their observations: "So if you run into a word in your reading that you don't know, and it has one of these spelling patterns, you know to try the long *a* sound first in order to sound it out to see if it sounds like a word you know. Let's explore these words a little more closely. With your partner, sort the words by their spelling pattern: Those in which long *a* is spelled *ai* in one column, those in which it is spelled *a*-consonant-*e* in a second column, and those in which it's spelled *-ay* in a third column:"

sale	*sail*	*play*
pane	*pain*	*clay*
mane	*main*	*away*
male	*mail*	*may*

When the children finish, Ms. McClelland asks them to share their observations of the role position plays when spelling the long *a* pattern. If necessary, she helps facilitate their understanding of the big idea in today's sort: "When long *a* comes in the middle of a word, what do you think: Is it ever spelled *-ay*? How about at the end of a word? Is it ever spelled *ai*?" The children come to the realization that where sounds occur usually determines their spelling, and for words such as *pane* and *pain* often they are homophones: "We need a different spelling, boys and girls, because these words need to look different because they *mean* different things."

When the children return to their seats, they each sort the words again, then copy the sort in their word study notebooks, and include a brief reflection on what they learned from the sorting activity. On successive days of the week, they work with the words and the patterns they represent through different activities, including sorting them according to different criteria, writing them in different categories, and looking for and recording other words that contain the same patterns in texts they have read.

*   *   *

On a morning in March, Ms. McClelland introduces a new sort with the same group of students who have been working on long-vowel patterns for many weeks. This time the sort reinforces phonic knowledge and addresses an anchor language standard (see Chapter 7):

"Generalize learned spelling patterns when writing words." The following words are included in the sort:

page   bridge   edge   stage   lodge   badge   huge   cage

"Boys and girls, read through the words in your sort, then let's sort them by *spelling pattern*: those in which the /j/ sound is spelled *dge* and those in which it is just spelled *ge*":

edge   page
badge   huge
bridge   stage
lodge   cage

"Turn to your partner and talk: When do you think the /j/ sound is spelled *dge* and when is it spelled just *ge*?" This can be a challenging question at first, and when Ms. McClelland has conducted this sort with groups in the past, she's often found that one or two children may see the patterns—they can share with the others. In this case, these words reveal that the /j/ sound is usually spelled *dge* when it follows a short vowel and *ge* when it follows a long vowel. Ms. McClelland uses this insight to share with the children that how sounds are spelled very often depends on other sounds they are close to. This understanding will help these transitional readers not only decode words with these patterns but spell them accurately as well.

Fluency

The goal of the foundational skills of the CCSS is to "develop proficient readers with the capacity to comprehend texts across a range of types and disciplines" (p. 15). To achieve this goal, children must be *fluent* readers, meaning they must be able to process words both *accurately* and *efficiently* and read with appropriate expression (Duke & Carlisle, 2011; Rasinski, Reutzel, Chard, & Linan-Thompson, 2011). The anchor standards for fluency (K–2) are highlighted in Table 4.4.

TABLE 4.4. Standards for Foundational Skills: Fluency (Anchor Standards for K–2)

Kindergartners	Grade 1 students	Grade 2 students
4. Read emergent-reader texts with purpose and understanding.	4. Read with sufficient accuracy and fluency to support comprehension. a. Read on-level text with purpose and understanding. b. Read on-level text orally with accuracy, appropriate rate, and expression on successive readings. c. Use context to confirm or self-correct word recognition and understanding, rereading as necessary.	4. Read with sufficient accuracy and fluency to support comprehension. a. Read on-level text with purpose and understanding. b. Read on-level text orally with accuracy, appropriate rate, and expression on successive readings. c. Use context to confirm or self-correct word recognition and understanding, rereading as necessary.

Beginning readers are "glued to print" (Chall, 1995). As they bring their knowledge of letter–sound correspondence to bear, they read aloud in a word-by-word manner and their reading is often quite labored. Transitional readers are more efficient at recognizing the patterns within words. They also recognize considerably more words by sight—upward of 250–400 words. This increased accuracy and efficiency alleviates the need for more discrete letter–sound analysis, thereby freeing up cognitive resources to focus on syntactic and semantic knowledge; this leads to their improved ability to self-monitor, read with expression, and comprehend text (Perfetti, 2007).

In addition to time simply spent reading independent-level text, repeated oral readings are a common means of developing fluency in the primary grades (Rasinski et al., 2011). Repeated oral readings allow children the opportunity to practice their automatic processing of words through repeated exposure to both the phonological and orthographic representations of these words (Ehri, 2005). Importantly, repeated readings also increase children's sensitivity to syntactic and prosodic features of language (Schreiber, 1991; Schreiber & Read, 1980), and this facilitates both fluency and comprehension. The text box below highlights several different methods of repeated oral reading.

METHODS OF REPEATED ORAL READING

Shared Reading—An instructional technique in which the teacher shares a piece of text, often an enlarged text, with a small group of children. While the protocols can vary, the basic lesson format includes a strong book introduction and the teacher guiding the group's reading of the text, much like Mr. Hajdun does in the following vignette. After reading the book, the teacher engages the children in a discussion of the book's plot or main idea(s), followed by the children rereading the text in pairs and independently.

Paired Reading—Two children, or a child and an adult, reading a piece of text together multiple times. As the stronger reader reads, the less skilled reader reads along, and they flexibly switch roles, with the more skilled reader helping out only as needed. Paired reading is most effective when children have some choice in the selection of an appropriately difficult text and of the partner with whom they work (Meisinger, Schwanenflugel, Bradley, & Stahl, 2004; Stahl, Heubach, & Holcomb, 2005).

Technology-Assisted Reading—Students' reading practice can be effectively supported with technology. By listening to prerecorded fluent reading of passages and texts, children follow along in appropriately challenging texts (Fisher, Frey, & Lapp, 2012). With repeated practice, researchers have found results similar to paired reading: improvements in word recognition, fluency, and comprehension.

Fluency-Oriented Reading Instruction (FORI)—A 5-day repeated-reading protocol designed to support children's reading of on-grade level basal stories with high levels of support (Stahl et al., 2005). On Day 1 the teacher reads the text to the students while children follow along in their own copies. The teacher supports children's comprehension of the text by discussing it after the initial reading. In subsequent days, the children reread the text several different ways using a mix of choral reading, echo reading, and partner reading. Students are also encouraged to read the text at home for an additional 15–30 minutes per day.

Fluency instruction, like the other foundational skills, is optimized when taught within the broader goals of an integrated model of literacy, as illustrated in the following vignette.

FOUNDATIONAL SKILLS STANDARDS IN ACTION: FLUENCY

Mr. Hajdun, a second-grade teacher at Lakeside Elementary, plans his next guided-reading lesson for his below-level readers. These students are a mix of English language learners (ELLs) and native English speakers and they're in the beginning reading stage. The group reads at text level 8–10, which means that they have a stable concept of word and a growing bank of sight words, and they're beginning to look across words, particularly taking in the graphophonic information in the middle of words, but this is a new skill for them and it needs considerable support. The texts these children are reading now contain a bit more plot than the more predictable pattern books they've been reading in recent months, and Mr. Hajdun recognizes that beginning readers, particularly ELLs, need to get oriented to the gist of a story before reading it, and he thinks about how he'll have to introduce new vocabulary and words that are beyond their decoding ability too. He's amazed at how complex texts can be for beginning readers (Hiebert, 2005).

As he looks over his collection of guided-reading books, he comes across a beloved story: *Mrs. Wishy-Washy* (Cowley, 1990). Previewing the text, he notices strong picture support, repeated phrases, alliteration, important sight vocabulary, and a little dialogue. He thinks this book may be perfect to support his students' word recognition and fluency because it's so supportive of beginning readers' needs: It's an engaging text and they will be able to read it with high levels of accuracy, which will allow them to focus on expressive reading and comprehension. He begins to plan his lesson:

"Readers, in recent weeks we've been learning to look across words to make our voice match the letters, and we've been thinking about the story as we read. Today we'll do both of these things in this new book. It's called *Mrs. Wishy-Washy* by Joy Cowley—we know many books by her, don't we?" (He points to Joy Cowley's name as he reads it and they talk about this favorite author.) "'Mrs. Wishy-Washy' is a funny name for a person. She got this name because she likes to keep her farm animals very clean!" Taking a scrub brush and a stuffed toy, he shows the children how she cleans her farm animals and repeats, "Wishy-washy, wishy-washy," to the children's delight. "Let's listen to her name: 'Mrs. Wishy-Washy.' *Wishy* and *washy* sound a lot alike, but there's one part that's different. Can you hear it?" Through this conversation, Mr. Hajdun focuses the children's attention to the importance of the middle part of words as well as reinforcing their letter–sound knowledge.

As Mr. Hajdun introduces the gist of the story, he turns his attention to reading and talking about the first pages of the story. He helps the children orchestrate their print knowledge, phonological awareness, word recognition, and phonics skills by prompting them to find words: "Where would you expect it to say *cow*? Are you right? How do you know?" On the page with a duck, a child exclaims, "It's a chicken!" Mr. Hajdun suggests that they read the text to see if it is a chicken. As they chorally read the text and come to the word *duck*, the child smiles and says, "It's not a chicken; *chicken* doesn't start with the letter *d*!" Together, they sound out the word while thinking about the story—Mr. Hajdun's two recent teaching points. When the pattern of the text changes, Mr. Hajdun reads with great expression and even a little drama and the children giggle. When it's their turn to echo the line back, some imitate his expressive reading. Along the way, Mr. Hajdun points out words the children know from their word banks too: *and, she, went, the, house, to,* and *in.*

After sharing the text a couple of times through, Mr. Hajdun invites partners to read the text one of three ways: by taking turns, by reading it chorally, or by echo reading (one partner reads a page and the other echoes it back). As they practice reading, he takes notes of their strengths and their challenges. As needed, he coaches the children in their phonics and word recognition skills: "Hmm . . . I think something confused you on that page. Can you find the tricky part? Let's look at it together. What can you try to fix that up?" Or "Wow! *Paddled* is a new word! How did you know that said *paddled*?" After several rounds of reading this short text, the children take it back to their reading nooks to continue practicing and sharing with their friends.

Later in the week, Mr. Hajdun takes several lines of this text and copies them onto sentence strips. After some practice reading the lines of text with the children, he cuts the sentences into words, and the children enjoy reading each word and then scrambling them up only to reconstruct the sentence again. As the children read the words both in and out of context, they solidify both their phonological and orthographic representations of these words, thereby increasing the speed and accuracy of their reading. As Mr. Hajdun notices this improvement, he also notes that they're reading the story with improved expression and even a little improvisational drama. With this, he knows they're ready for the next new text.

USING THE K–2 FOUNDATIONAL SKILLS STANDARDS THROUGHOUT THE DAY

When teaching the foundational skills throughout the day, we consider the learning opportunities that are best presented to the whole class and those that are more appropriate for smaller developmentally grounded groups. Whole-class instruction is effective when teaching skills that the vast majority of students have yet to acquire and use independently—skills such as concepts about print with preschoolers or the concept of word with kindergarteners—while other skills such as phonological awareness or phonics and word recognition might be better taught in developmentally grounded small groups. The authors of the CCSS emphasize this point in the introduction to the foundational skills when they note that "instruction should be *differentiated*" (p. 15; emphasis added).

In preschool, kindergarten, and first grade, teachers help scaffold children's understanding of print concepts though shared reading (Holdaway, 1979) and interactive writing experiences (McCarrier, Pinnell, & Fountas, 1999; Stauffer, 1970). As texts are read and composed together, teachers integrate oral language development with children's developing awareness of letter–sound knowledge, concepts about print, and concept of word. By contextualizing these foundational skills, teachers observe and encourage children's growing sense of accomplishment as they apply their developing print knowledge to authentic reading and writing activities, and not just during literacy block but in other subjects and activities throughout the day.

Most of your instruction in the foundational skills will happen in smaller, developmentally grounded guided-reading, guided-writing, and word study groups. In these settings, we explicitly teach these foundational skills and help children apply their growing knowledge about print, letters, sounds, and spelling in meaningful, authentic, and developmentally appropriate literacy tasks. Importantly, young children need ample practice applying these skills in independent and guided-reading and writing activities throughout the day.

CHILDREN'S BOOKS
FOR TEACHING THE CCSS FOUNDATIONAL SKILLS PreK–GRADE 2

Title	Author	Publisher
Eating the Alphabet	Lois Ehlert	Sandpiper
David McPhail's Animals A to Z	David McPhail	Cartwheel
Read Aloud Rhymes for the Very Young	Jack Prelutsky	Knopf
Sheep in a Jeep	Nancy Shaw	Sandpiper
The Arnold Lobel Book of Mother Goose: A Treasury of More Than 300 Classic Nursery Rhymes	Arnold Lobel	Knopf
Take Me Out of the Bathtub	Alan Katz	Margaret K. McElderry Books
The Wheels on the Bus	Paul Zelinsky	Dutton
Anna Banana 101 Jump Rope Rhymes	Joanna Cole	HarperCollins
Diez Deditos and Other Play Rhymes and Action Songs from South America	Jose-Luis Orozco	Puffin

CONCLUSION

For many students, the grade-level expectations and their developmental level will coincide. But for many others, they will not. Teachers who understand the significance of their students' level of literacy development are in a better position to teach print concepts, phonological awareness, phonics and word recognition, and fluency in a developmentally responsive way. As highlighted in the CCSS, "Good readers will need much less practice with these concepts than struggling readers will. The point is to teach students what they need to learn and not what they already know" (p. 15).

ACTIVITIES AND QUESTIONS

Activities

1. *Foundational Standards: Print Concepts.* Copy several lines of familiar text onto sentence strips. Match the print features and line breaks to the original text. Place these strips in a pocket chart; compare and contrast them with the original text. Read the new text several times and invite children to participate in fingerpoint reading. Then ask children to find particular letters and words on the sentence strip: "Who can find the letter *m* at the beginning of a word? Yes, that word is *merrily.* Who can find the letter *m* at the end of a word?" Or "Who can find the word *stream*? Are you right? How did you know that said *stream*?" This kind of print referencing reinforces children's understanding of the relationship among letters, sounds, and words.

2. *Foundational Standards: Phonological Awareness.* After children develop an explicit awareness of rhyme, they can play with it in a variety of ways. Using pictures from the rhyming picture sorts you have done with the students, support children in creating new lyrics to familiar songs or lines of text like "Down by the Bay":

> Down by the bay
> Where the watermelons grow . . .
> "Did you ever see a _____
> Kissing a _____?"
> Down by the bay

You can also encourage children to generate their own rhymes and they'll likely find this great fun: "Have you ever seen a frog kissing a dog? Down by the bay."

3. *Foundational Standards: Phonics and Word Recognition.* With first- or second-grade transitional readers, conduct a word sort, comparing and contrasting certain long-vowel patterns—for example, long *a* (*rain*, *blade*) or long *o* (*rope*, *boat*). Then share with students that, based on what they know about these patterns in one-syllable words, they can decode longer words. On the white board, frame certain sentences in a text, and pointing to words such as *contain* and *floater*, ask students to turn to their partner and explain how they might figure out those words. Afterward, encourage children to share their word-solving strategies and reinforce their understandings of sound, pattern, and meaning.

4. *Foundational Standards: Fluency.* Select one of the methods for repeated reading in Table 4.4. These methods may be used to "stretch" students' reading beyond their current independent level. Next, select a book that you believe would be at the upper range for a group of students. Explain that over the next week they will be reading and talking about the text with you and each other, and while the book may feel a bit challenging now, by the end of the week they will be reading it independently in a way that sounds like talking! As you work with the children throughout the week, affirm the importance of reading words accurately and efficiently and in a way that makes sense and sounds like talking. It's important to reinforce the critical relationship between comprehension and fluent reading in this way.

Questions

1. If becoming aware of the sounds of language is such a critical ability, why is there such an emphasis on *print* in developing this awareness?

2. Children's writing provides great insight into their developing foundational literacy skills. Collect several samples of children's writing; analyze them with peers. Discuss and plan instruction that would be developmentally responsive and scaffold children's phonological awareness and/or phonics/word recognition skills.

3. Select one of the two following online position statements about early literacy. Compare and contrast the recommendations with your current practices and the

practices recommended in this chapter. What are the strengths of your program? What are the opportunities for improvement?

- National Early Literacy Panel Report: Developing Early Literacy: Report of the National Early Literacy Panel: *http://lincs.ed.gov/publications/pdf/NELPReport09.pdf*
- Joint Position Statement of the International Reading Association and the National Association of Young Children: Learning to Read and Write: Developmentally Appropriate Practices for Young Children: *www.reading.org/General/AboutIRA/PositionStatements/ DevelopmentallyAppropriatePosition.aspx*

REFERENCES

Armbruster, B., Lehr, F., & Osborn, J. (2006). *Put reading first: The research building blocks for teaching children to read*. Washington, DC: National Institute for Literacy.

Bear, D. R., Invernizzi, M., Johnston, F., & Templeton, S. (2010). *Words their way: Letter and picture sorts for emergent spellers*. Boston: Pearson/Allyn & Bacon.

Bear, D. R., Invernizzi, M., Templeton, S., & Johnston, F. (2012). *Words their way: Word study for phonics, vocabulary, and spelling instruction* (5th ed.). Boston: Pearson/Allyn & Bacon.

Chall, J. (1995). *Stages of reading development*. Belmont, CA: Wadsworth.

Cunningham, P. (2005). *Phonics they use: Words for reading and writing*. Boston: Allyn & Bacon.

Duke, N., & Carlisle, J. (2011). The development of comprehension. In M. Kamil, P. D. Pearson, E. Birr Moje, & P. P. Afflerbach (Eds.), *Handbook of reading research* (Vol. IV, pp. 199–228). New York: Routledge.

Ehri, L. C. (2005). Learning to read words: Theory, findings, and issues. *Scientific Studies of Reading, 9*(2), 167–188.

Fisher, D., Frey, N., & Lapp, D. (2012). *Text complexity: Raising rigor in reading*. Newark, DE: International Reading Association.

Flanigan, K. (2007). A concept of word in text: A pivotal event in early reading acquisition. *Journal of Literacy Research, 39*(1), 37–70.

Harré, R., & Moghaddam, F. (Eds.). (2003). *The self and others: Positioning individuals and groups in personal, political, and cultural contexts*. Westport, CT: Praeger.

Hiebert, E. H. (2005). State reform policies and the reading task for first graders. *Elementary School Journal, 105*, 245–266.

Holdaway, D. (1979). *The foundations of literacy*. Sydney: Ashton Scholastic.

Invernizzi, M., Abouzeid, M., & Gill, T. (1994). Using students' invented spellings as a guide for spelling instruction that emphasizes word study. *Elementary School Journal, 95*(2), 155–167.

Invernizzi, M., & Hayes, L. (2004). Developmental-spelling research: A systematic imperative. *Reading Research Quarterly, 39*, 216–228.

Invernizzi, M., Johnston, F., Bear, D., & Templeton, S. (2009). *Words their way: Word sorts for within word pattern spellers*. Boston: Pearson/Allyn & Bacon.

Justice, L. M., & Piasta, S. (2011). Developing children's print knowledge though adult–child storybook reading interactions: Print referencing as an instructional practice. In S. B. Neuman & D. K. Dickinson (Eds.), *Handbook of early literacy research* (Vol. 3, pp. 200–213). New York: Guilford Press.

Krech, B. (2000). *Fresh and fun: Teaching with kids' names*. New York: Scholastic.

McCarrier, A., Pinnell, G., & Fountas, I. (2000). *Interactive writing: How language and literacy come together, K–2.* Portsmouth, NH: Heinemann.

McGee, L., & Richgels, D. (1990). *Literacy's beginnings: Supporting young readers and writers.* Boston: Pearson.

Meisinger, E. B., Schwanenflugel, P. J., Bradley, B., & Stahl, S. (2004). Interaction quality during partner reading, *Journal of Literacy Research, 36*(2), 111–140.

Morris, D., Blanton, L., Blanton, W. E., Nowacek, J., & Perney, J. (1995). Teaching low-achieving spellers at their "instructional level." *Elementary School Journal, 96,* 163–178.

Morris, D., Bloodgood, J. W., Lomax, R. G., & Perney, J. (2003). Developmental steps in learning to read: A longitudinal study in kindergarten and first grade. *Reading Research Quarterly, 38,* 302–328.

Morris, D., & Perney, J. (1984). Developmental spelling as a predictor of first grade reading achievement. *Elementary School Journal, 84,* 441–457.

National Early Literacy Panel. (2008). *Developing early literacy.* Washington, DC: National Institute for Literacy.

National Governors Association Center for Best Practices and Council of Chief School Officers. (2010). Common core state standards for English language arts and literacy in history/social studies, science, and technical subjects. Washington, DC: Author. Retrieved from *www.corestandards.org.*

Perfetti, C. (2007). Reading ability: Lexical quality to comprehension. *Scientific Studies of Reading, 11,* 357–383.

Rapp, B., & Lipka, K. (2011). The literate brain: The relationship between spelling and reading. *Journal of Cognitive Neuroscience, 23*(5), 1180–1197.

Rasinski, T. V., Reutzel, D. R., Chard, D., & Linan-Thompson, S. (2011). Reading fluency. In M. L. Kamil, P. D. Pearson, E. Birr Moje, & P. Afflerbach (Eds.), *Handbook of reading research* (Vol. IV, pp. 286–319). New York: Routledge.

Schreiber, P. A. (1991). Understanding prosody's role in reading acquisition. *Theory into Practice, 30,* 158–164.

Schreiber, P. A., & Read, C. (1980). Children's use of phonetic cues in spelling, parsing and—maybe—reading. *Bulletin of the Orton Society, 20,* 209–224.

Snow, C. E., Burns, M. S., & Griffin, P. (Eds.). (1998). *Preventing reading difficulties in young children.* Washington, DC: National Academy Press.

Stahl, S. A., Heubach, K., & Holcomb, A. (2005). Fluency-oriented reading instruction. *Journal of Literacy Research, 37,* 25–60.

Stauffer, R. (1970). *The language-experience approach to the teaching of reading.* New York: Harper & Row.

Sulzby, E. (1985). Children's emergent reading of favorite storybooks. *Reading Research Quarterly, 20,* 458–481.

Taylor, B. M., Pearson, P. D., Clark, K., & Walpole, S. (2000). Effective schools and accomplished teachers: Lessons about primary-grade reading instruction in low-income schools. *Elementary School Journal, 101*(2), 121–165.

Templeton, S. (2011). Teaching spelling in the English/language arts classroom. In D. Lapp & D. Fisher (Eds.), *The handbook of research on teaching the English language arts* (3rd ed., pp. 247–251). New York: Routledge.

Templeton, S., & Bear, D. R. (2011). Phonemic awareness, word recognition, and spelling. In T. Rasinski (Ed.), *Developing reading instruction that works* (pp. 153–178). Bloomington, IN: Solution Tree Press.

Ziegler, J. C., & Goswami, U. (2005). Reading acquisition, developmental dyslexia, and skilled reading across languages: A psycholinguistic grain size theory. *Psychological Bulletin, 13*(1), 3–29.

CHILDREN'S BOOKS CITED

Cole, J. (1991). *Anna Banana 101 jump rope rhymes*. New York: Scholastic.

Cole, J., & Calmenson, S. (1990). *Miss Mary Mack and other children's street rhymes*. New York: Morrow Junior Books.

Cowley, J. (1999). *Mrs. Wishy-Washy*. New York: Philomel.

Ehlert, L. (1989). *Eating the alphabet: Fruits & vegetables from A to Z*. San Diego, CA: Harcourt Brace Jovanovich.

Katz, A. (2001). *Take me out of the bathtub*. New York: Scholastic.

Lobel, A. (1986). *The Arnold Lobel book of Mother Goose: A treasury of more than 300 classic nursery rhymes*. New York: Random House.

Orozco, J. (2002). *Diez deditos and other play rhymes and action songs from South America*. New York: Puffin.

Prelutsky, J, (1986). *Read aloud rhymes for the very young*. New York: Knopf.

Shaw, N. E. (1986). *Sheep in a jeep*. Boston: Houghton Mifflin.

Zelinsky, P. (1990). *The wheels on the bus*. New York: Dutton Children's Books.

CHAPTER 5

Writing Standards

Jane Hansen

Writing fascinates young children. When they hold their first marker and stroke it across a piece of paper or the hallway wall, they know they can make their mark on the world. Our task as teachers is to celebrate that accomplishment and support the writers as they try to finesse what they want to say.

Emig (1971), although she studied high school students, probably started our profession on the idea of seeing students as writers—real writers. What students do when they write counts. Importantly, what young writers do is often the same as what professionals do—regardless of age: They can make decisions about what to write about and how to put that idea into an effective format.

Along the way, their teachers provide them with ideas, and then confer with the writers to find out which ideas they have chosen to use and why. The importance of the teacher in this process seems to have arrived with Murray (1968), a writer who taught writing and advocated that all writing teachers should be writers. Thus, he maintained, students will not be taught artificial, school-created, nonauthentic means by which to produce texts. Real writers will not engage students in fruitless exercises.

In order to provide authentic instruction, teacher-writers spend time amidst their writers, while the children are writing, engaging them in conversations about their work. In so doing, adults attend, first and foremost, to what the young writers want to say; children must know that others are interested in what they are trying to say. Plus, their teachers confer (Calkins, Hartman, & White, 2005) with the young writers about the authentic decisions the children may make as they figure out how to design their vibrant thoughts on a flat sheet of paper. In addition, these quick conferences often provide the teachers with ideas for all-class instruction.

Often those lessons include the study of children's literature, from which the teacher and children learn a great deal about writing. Various current educators write about the importance of mentor texts, with Ray (1999) perhaps bringing the usefulness of literature—within the lives of young writers and their teachers—to our attention. Then Ray and Cleaveland (2004) studied the children in Cleaveland's kindergarten classroom, and we all saw the importance of young writers creating books—just as their mentors do.

Dorfman and Cappelli (2007, 2009) provided specific ideas for possible texts to use when we teach certain craft techniques, and Fletcher (2011) started to question. He worried that the mentor texts idea is in danger of losing its authenticity. In other words, we must be wary of regular, frequent situations where teachers provide a mentor text on a certain day for all writers to use on that day. Instead, we must remember that when writers read they absorb words, they read with their own writing in mind, and they don't know what they'll find, but when they hear it, they use it—that day, or on a future day, when they write. Thus, in a classroom where young writers are engaged in various drafts on various topics, in different genres, for different purposes, they study mentor texts with the open minds of writers and readers on the prowl.

Another important feature of writing instruction for young children is the broad scope, especially the social nature of children's lives in and out of the classroom. Dyson (1993, 2008) records children's interactions while they write and, in so doing, documents the importance of their comments, questions, and teasing as they compose. These interactions bring the children's lives and relationships into the others' lives as writers, energize the children, and promote their growth as language users (Horn & Giacobbe, 2007).

Mermelstein (2007) specifically focuses on the instructional importance of the talk children engage in when they read their work aloud for response from their classmates—and for response in later lessons when their teacher uses information from these share sessions to guide lessons. Overall, various oral opportunities influence the children's abundance of ideas for what to write about, how to place their ideas on the page, and why to engage at all.

Table 5.1 shows all the Common Core State Standards (CCSS) for writers in kindergarten through grade 2. Overall, there are three categories of standards, with subdivisions, for a total of seven standards. The first group of standards refers to Text Types and Purposes, and is divided into three types: opinion, informative/explanatory, and narrative. Within each of the types, you will see a progression from kindergarten through grade 2 as the expectations become increasingly complex.

The second group of standards is Production and Distribution of Writing, with two divisions. The first standard in this section (Standard 5) focuses on the addition of details and becomes, by grade 2, the ability to strengthen writing via revision and editing. The second of these standards (Standard 6) requires the use of digital tools to produce and publish writing.

The third group of standards is Research to Build and Present Knowledge and comprises Standards 7 and 8. The first of these requires that children participate in shared research and writing projects, and Standard 8 focuses on the recall of information gained from experiences, or the gathering of information to answer a question. From PreK to grade 2, children are to move from the use of guidance and support to the ability to engage independently in research-related tasks.

PUTTING THE WRITING STANDARDS INTO PRACTICE

In this section for all seven standards I present examples of writing by a student at one of the three (PreK–K, 1, 2) grade levels, surround it with context, and explain how it serves as an example for all three grade levels across that standard. As I progress through the standards, you will notice that I include, at various times, one example from PreK,

TABLE 5.1. Writing Standards for K–2

Kindergartners	Grade 1 students	Grade 2 students
Text Types and Purposes		
1. Use a combination of drawing, dictating, and writing to compose opinion pieces in which they tell a reader the topic or the name of the book they are writing about and state an opinion or preference about the topic or book (e.g., *My favorite book is . . .*).	1. Write opinion pieces in which they introduce the topic or name the book they are writing about, state an opinion, supply a reason for the opinion, and provide some sense of closure.	1. Write opinion pieces in which they introduce the topic or book they are writing about, state an opinion, supply reasons that support the opinion, use linking words (e.g., *because, and, also*) to connect opinion and reasons, and provide a concluding statement or section.
2. Use a combination of drawing, dictating, and writing to compose informative/explanatory texts in which they name what they are writing about and supply some information about the topic.	2. Write informative/explanatory texts in which they name a topic, supply some facts about the topic, and provide some sense of closure.	2. Write informative/explanatory texts in which they introduce a topic, use facts and definitions to develop points, and provide a concluding statement or section.
3. Use a combination of drawing, dictating, and writing to narrate a single event or several loosely linked events, tell about the events in the order in which they occurred, and provide a reaction to what happened.	3. Write narratives in which they recount two or more appropriately sequenced events, include some details regarding what happened, use temporal words to signal event order, and provide some sense of closure.	3. Write narratives in which they recount a well-elaborated event or short sequence of events, include details to describe actions, thoughts, and feelings, use temporal words to signal event order, and provide a sense of closure.
Production and Distribution of Writing		
4. (Begins in grade 3)	4. (Begins in grade 3)	4. (Begins in grade 3)
5. With guidance and support from adults, respond to questions and suggestions from peers and add details to strengthen writing as needed.	5. With guidance and support from adults, focus on a topic, respond to questions and suggestions from peers, and add details to strengthen writing as needed.	5. With guidance and support from adults and peers, focus on a topic and strengthen writing as needed by revising and editing.
6. With guidance and support from adults, explore a variety of digital tools to produce and publish writing, including in collaboration with peers.	6. With guidance and support from adults, use a variety of digital tools to produce and publish writing, including in collaboration with peers.	6. With guidance and support from adults, use a variety of digital tools to produce and publish writing, including in collaboration with peers.

(cont.)

TABLE 5.1. *(cont.)*

Kindergartners	Grade 1 students	Grade 2 students
	Research to Build and Present Knowledge	
7. Participate in shared research and writing projects (e.g., explore a number of books by a favorite author and express opinions about them).	7. Participate in shared research and writing projects (e.g., explore a number of how-to books on a given topic and use them to write a sequence of instructions).	7. Participate in shared research and writing projects (e.g., read a number of books on a single topic to produce a report; record science observations).
8. With guidance and support from adults, recall information from experiences or gather information from provided sources to answer a question.	8. With guidance and support from adults, recall information from experiences or gather information from provided sources to answer a question.	8. Recall information from experiences or gather information from provided sources to answer a question.

two from kindergarten, two from grade 1, and two from grade 2, for a total of seven vignettes.

Text Types and Purposes

This category includes three text types, and Standard 1, in particular, focuses on students composing opinion pieces (see Table 5.2), followed, in an unintended order, by informative/explanatory and narrative texts. These three writing types are not intended as units of study; the younger writers will engage in them throughout the year. Children are known for strong opinions; they started expressing them before they could talk! Thus, they will write about those opinions throughout each grade. Similarly, narratives are stories—and children tell and hear stories every day. Thus, they will write them throughout the year. Finally, informative/explanatory text is what we use throughout the year when we study, for example, reptiles (Sill, 1999), builders (Johnson, 2001), and skeletons (Jenkins, 2010). This text type, as with the others, is engaged in by young writers from the beginning of the year until the end (Glover, 2009).

TABLE 5.2. Writing Standards for K–2: Text Types and Purposes (Standard 1)

Kindergartners	Grade 1 students	Grade 2 students
1. Use a combination of drawing, dictating, and writing to compose opinion pieces in which they tell a reader the topic or the name of the book they are writing about and state an opinion or preference about the topic or book (e.g., *My favorite book is . . .*).	1. Write opinion pieces in which they introduce the topic or name the book they are writing about, state an opinion, supply a reason for the opinion, and provide some sense of closure.	1. Write opinion pieces in which they introduce the topic or book they are writing about, state an opinion, supply reasons that support the opinion, use linking words (e.g., *because, and, also*) to connect opinion and reasons, and provide a concluding statement or section.

Opinion Pieces

Standard 1 highlights the importance of the concept of voice, a vital aspect of all writing, and the focus of opinion pieces. Each child's writing should sound like no other. We do not give them forms to follow; all pieces of writing do not begin with the same phrase. Children have opinions about very different ideas, and they use words that vary from those used by the children who sit on either side of them (Kissel, 2009). Over time children learn to create increasingly effective reasons to support their opinions. By grade 2 they are to be able to use linking words to connect their opinion with reasons. Solley (2005) shows the importance, especially for children of poverty, to frequently write about their unsettling lives so they do not hide their worries. By engaging in the writing of opinion pieces—on topics that are important to the individual child—throughout PreK–2, the children will satisfy this standard.

The following vignette shows an opinion piece written by a public school PreK student. All the children in this class live in a low socioeconomic status environment, and all are writers (Solley, 2005). The vignette shows the strong—and in this case positive—opinion of a young child toward her family. For the children in this class, their families are their base, their foundation, their security (or not). Whereas these 4-year-olds have strong opinions about many topics, the note this girl writes represents one of the most common forms of opinion writing engaged in by very young writers when their classroom focuses on the creation of writing that is important to them. To write notes when they choose, and to take them home—or wherever, depending on the note—is an important way for young children to gain confidence in expressing themselves on paper.

WRITING STANDARDS IN ACTION: TEXT TYPES AND PURPOSES (OPINION PIECES)

Ms. Ronda opens this lesson, as she does each of the children's daily writing sessions, by reading children's literature to them, and then she writes. On her large tablet, mounted on an easel, she writes whatever she wants. Maybe it is about a content area they are studying, which may have been the topic of the book she read. Maybe she writes about an experience with one of her daughters. Today she writes an opinion piece—a note to one of the girls in the class (see Figure 5.1)!

FIGURE 5.1.

Then the children go to their tables to write. Some of them write something similar to what Ms. Ronda wrote, and many of them don't—they have other, more important, agendas to pursue. As they write, Ms. Ronda moves among them, clipboard in hand, asking the one question she always asks and, yes, the children come to expect it and answer as soon as she pauses beside them, before she can open her mouth to say, "Please tell me what you are writing about today." She asks a question or two to learn more about each young writer's agenda, notes this conference, and moves on.

On this day, a few of the children do write notes—and include opinions, such as the one shown in Figure 5.2, written by one of the girls.

FIGURE 5.2.

Notice, at the beginning of this vignette, that the teacher writes. Over the course of the year, Ms. Ronda writes repeatedly in all genres, and over time the children do as well. Specifically, in some way, they tell their intended readers what they are writing about, and they state their opinion. This very young writer, of course, does not say, "I am writing to tell you how I feel about you," but what she is writing about and her opinion will be clear to her mother, which is what is required at the PreK–K level.

For grades 1 and 2, teachers and children will write opinions on various topics and in various subject areas. Stating their opinions on paper is something the children and teacher will do regularly and frequently. The children and teacher are not afraid to say, nor to write, what they think. And they learn to do so with increasing care and reason.

Next is Standard 2 (see Table 5.3). Standard 2 addresses informative/explanatory texts. Young writers are to name what they are writing about and supply information. Over the years they learn to include more complex information and develop a sense of closure. Writing about information is often appealing to young children, as they tend to be fascinated by their world, frequently wondering about events, people, and creatures that puzzle them. Engaging in this text type helps to value and keep alive children's seemingly innate curiosity.

The vignette on the next page takes us into the world of science, an area ripe with possibilities for writing (Heuser, 2002; Saul, Reardon, Pearce, Dieckman, & Neutze, 2002). In particular, we see a book written by a kindergarten child while his class was in the midst of a study of insects.

TABLE 5.3. Writing Standards for K–2: Text Types and Purposes (Standard 2)

Kindergartners	Grade 1 students	Grade 2 students
2. Use a combination of drawing, dictating, and writing to compose informative/explanatory texts in which they name what they are writing about and supply some information about the topic.	2. Write informative/explanatory texts in which they name a topic, supply some facts about the topic, and provide some sense of closure.	2. Write informative/explanatory texts in which they introduce a topic, use facts and definitions to develop points, and provide a concluding statement or section.

WRITING STANDARDS IN ACTION: TEXT TYPES AND PURPOSES (INFORMATIVE/EXPLANATORY TEXTS)

The teacher opens their writing time by introducing the children to a new insect: bees. The children cluster around her, their classroom document projector, and Smart Board. She starts with two children's informational books (Hartley & Macro, 2006; Unstead, 2006) in which she has tabbed four pieces of information that they talk about briefly. Plus, she points out the different formats in the books—sometimes the illustrations and words are on adjacent pages and at other times the words are below the photos.

Then, in a blank book with a yellow construction paper cover and a few sheets of white paper—all folded in half to fit inside the cover—she quickly sketches a flower and a bee on the first page. Then she writes: *My bee is collecting pollen.* As she turns to the next blank page, she decides to use the entire double spread and creates a large bee. She writes *Buzzzzzzzzz* across the two pages. She does not have time, during this minilesson, to finish her book, and worries whether the children's books will just stop or if they will create endings.

The children leave their cluster one by one as they tell her what they plan to write about. Even though she demonstrated with bees, she does not require the children to do so but they intend to. They each walk to a table, blank book in hand, and soon all start to write.

Their teacher circulates, stopping beside several children, among them Alden (pseudonym), who is having a hard time drawing a beehive with hexagons, one of the pieces of information the teacher had showed them. She shows Alden, in her notebook, how to draw a beehive with circles, and he seems pleased. He resumes his writing, and she moves on, overhearing many little conversations among the children as they excitedly share and ask each other questions while they work. These young writers are used to writing every day and are engaged!

The teacher confers with Mohammed, who is writing about a BLFyh (butterfly). When he reads, he says, "Bullaflyuh," which is exactly what he wrote!

When it is time to share, the teacher asks for hands and lots fly! One is Narden, who reads the book shown in Figure 5.3 to his classmates, gathered before him. The children clap with glee at his great ending, and Narden smiles bashfully. His friends ask him questions, such as, "Is your ladybug making honey?" and he shakes his head "no." We do see that his drawing on that page does not match his text, but no one, including his teacher, pursues this. This young writer needs and receives support.

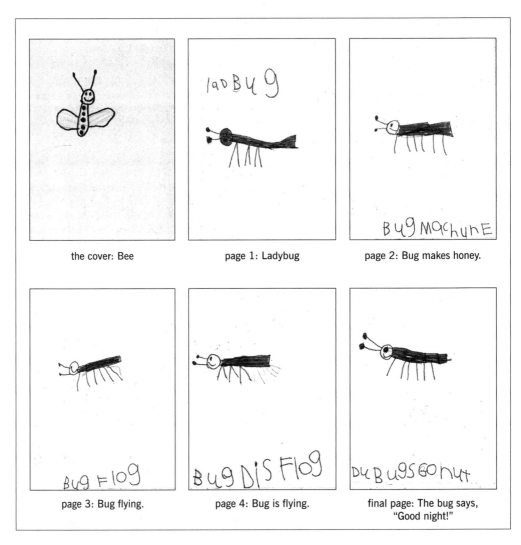

the cover: Bee   page 1: Ladybug   page 2: Bug makes honey.

page 3: Bug flying.   page 4: Bug is flying.   final page: The bug says, "Good night!"

FIGURE 5.3.

Narden came from East Africa at the beginning of the year without knowing a word of English. For a long time, he did not speak or volunteer, but on this day in April he raised his hand to share! Narden was not forthcoming with information in the Author's Chair, but his never-ending smile showed everyone that he loved sharing the new information he was learning.

Throughout the writing time on this day, Narden had written without asking his teacher for any help; his teacher had carefully taught the children to draw, sound out words, spell some words (bug), and write thoughts. While doing so, they could interact with the other children at their table (Fay & Whaley, 2004), as the teacher circulated, conferring with her students as necessary.

In regard to the expectations of the CCSS, Narden does "name what he is writing about and supplies some information about the topic." At the same time, we see his confusion. The children had studied ladybugs, and he is confusing them with bees, but he will understand the difference over the next several days as they continue to study.

Importantly, as his class has studied ways that books often end, Narden has accomplished a grade 1 standard as well: He provided a sense of closure. Equally as significant, his classroom is a great place for Narden to learn (Sumida & Meyer, 2006). There is no reason to be afraid in this safe space. Narden fearlessly learns English, finds new information fascinating, writes, and puts himself forward.

Overall, Narden's teacher is excited by his progress. This kindergarten English language learner is studying English, learning about bugs, writing information books (Cervetti & Barber, 2009), and creating excellent endings!

By the time he is in second grade (Read, 2005), we are reasonably confident Narden will be able to "write informative/explanatory texts in which he introduces a topic, uses facts and definitions to develop points, and provides a concluding statement or section."

Standard 3 (see Table 5.4) will move us into narrative texts. Narratives may be true or fiction stories, and a preference is not stated in this standard. In general, in the field of composition, it is advocated that student writers engage in the writing of nonfiction narratives before they attempt fiction, as it is often difficult to create a focus in fiction. The creation of personal narratives by young writers gained a foothold with Graves (1983/2003), and their prevalence has continued, even though writing instruction has become much more varied.

The following vignette, written by a first grader, almost sounds like a personal narrative, but it is fiction (Hansen, 2009). The young writer "recounts two or more appropriately sequenced events, includes details regarding what happened, uses temporal words to signal event order, and provides a sense of closure."

WRITING STANDARDS IN ACTION: TEXT TYPES AND PURPOSES (NARRATIVE TEXTS)

Before this young writer created this narrative, Ms. Meaney, her teacher, had read many stories (e.g., *Henry Climbs a Mountain* [Johnson, 2003]; *Oh, No, Toto!* [Tchana & Pami, 1997]) to the children and, since the beginning of the school year, they had written every day, often composing narratives, both truthful and inventive, if they chose to do so. While reading to the children, Ms. Meaney and her class had talked about various features the book authors used to be sure their meaning was as clear as possible. One feature they had noticed was ellipses,

TABLE 5.4. Writing Standards for K–2: Text Types and Purposes (Standard 3)

Kindergartners	Grade 1 students	Grade 2 students
3. Use a combination of drawing, dictating, and writing to narrate a single event or several loosely linked events, tell about the events in the order in which they occurred, and provide a reaction to what happened.	3. Write narratives in which they recount two or more appropriately sequenced events, include some details regarding what happened, use temporal words to signal event order, and provide some sense of closure.	3. Write narratives in which they recount a well-elaborated event or short sequence of events, include details to describe actions, thoughts, and feelings, use temporal words to signal event order, and provide a sense of closure.

which this young author tried . . . successfully (see Figure 5.4). This young writer devoted more than one work period to this narrative, and when she finished she read her snowboard story aloud to her class. Typically, in Ms. Meaney's classroom, a writer ends a reading with this request: "Comments and questions, please." On this day, however, the author paused, turned her text toward them, and pointed out her "dot, dot, dots." Then she requested, "Comments and questions, please."

I will ride my snowboard with my mom and my dad. And my brother just rides right in front of us and then . . . my sister just got right in front of my brother and he was mad so . . . me and my mom and dad went right in front of them so me and my mom and dad won the race and me and my mom and dad won a trophy.

FIGURE 5.4

This vignette shows a young writer who wanted to create an effective narrative, worked hard at it, and displayed pride in her work. When children accomplish a feat, they proudly share, and others may try the same technique. With further instruction, continued study of literature (Laminack & Wadsworth, 2006), and much practice, these young writers will be able, in second grade, to write with more elaboration as is prescribed in this standard.

Production and Distribution of Writing

Standard 5 (see Table 5.5) addresses the addition of information to strengthen a text— the ability to focus on a topic, revise, and edit, all of which are processes young writers gradually become adept at with daily writing practice and instruction over the course of their first years.

In the following vignette, we see a kindergarten writer who has historically experienced difficulty as a writer. Midyear, the faculty determined this student to be on the road to failing, and they decided to provide him with intense literacy instruction for the spring semester. For 90 minutes each day, his small group of culturally diverse children (Pransky, 2008) received 45 minutes of writing instruction carefully coordinated with 45 minutes of reading instruction. By the end of the year, all the children in the group moved on to first grade.

WRITING STANDARDS IN ACTION:
PRODUCTION AND DISTRIBUTION OF WRITING

We begin with the group gathered around a table, where they have already chanted a poem, engaged with Ms. Gaffney while she read a children's literature book about animals (Loufane, 2005), interacted with her while she created her writing for the day (not about animals), and opened their handmade writing books, which consisted of several sheets of stapled blank paper. It is now time for each writer to make his or her first writer's decision of the day: Do I want to continue to work on something I started yesterday, or do I want to start something new?

Judd decides to start something new and draws himself amidst several animals. Then he writes: *I saw a turtle. Done.* At this point, Ms. Gaffney, constantly interacting with the tableful, excitedly says, "Oh, Judd! What did you write?" He reads his brief text to her, emphasizing the end: "Done!" Tired of Judd's inclination to write only a small amount, Ms. Gaffney comments and presses, "Your turtle is so colorful, Judd. He's beautiful. And what

---

TABLE 5.5. Writing Standards for K–2: Production and Distribution of Writing (Standard 5)

Kindergartners	Grade 1 students	Grade 2 students
5. With guidance and support from adults, respond to questions and suggestions from peers and add details to strengthen writing as needed.	5. With guidance and support from adults, focus on a topic, respond to questions and suggestions from peers, and add details to strengthen writing as needed.	5. With guidance and support from adults and peers, focus on a topic and strengthen writing as needed by revising and editing.

are all these other animals?" Judd names all of them. Then the clincher—"Judd, I'm sure you can write about one more animal. Which is your favorite?" Judd then is prompted to admit that his favorite is the pig. Ms. Gaffney simply says, "I love your pig also! Now, I am going to listen to Mari, and you are going to write about your pig. I'll be back in a minute for you to read to me." Judd picks up his pencil, and when she returns her attention to him, she sees his addition (see Figure 5.5).

Judd reads, "And I see a pig too. Now, done!" Ms. Gaffney smiles, "You added information about the pig, Judd. Yes, you are done now!"

Soon, when the children read their writing to the group, all see, hear, and learn of the importance of adding information to strengthen their writing.

FIGURE 5.5.

Notice how Ms. Gaffney interacted with this child. First, she expressed specific interest in what he had done. Then, given that she is well versed in children's development as writers (Shagoury, 2009), she decided to lead him toward the addition of information. Specifically, she had become aware of Judd's typical, short pieces of writing, and determined, with all the animals in his illustration, that this was the day to push him. In a positive manner, she engaged him in a brief conversation, in which he mentioned the pig. Thus, she knew he had something else to say; it was legitimate for her to expect him to write more. Furthermore, she knew he did not need her when he placed his words on the page, as he had written his first sentence on his own, so she moved her attention elsewhere. She trusted him to write more, and he did.

In general, revising begins with the adding of information, although adding, rearranging, and/or deleting information all play important roles in revision. To foster revision with young writers, we encourage them to write long drafts, which enables their fluency. One way to encourage length is to typically begin writing class by giving young writers the opportunity to make this decision: *Do I want to continue on a piece of writing I started previously, or do I want to start something new?* It is quite difficult to become fluent if you start a new piece of writing every day.

Importantly, while children are in the process of creating a draft, conferences with them are short, just a bit of interaction to help them think of what to write next—nothing about the conventions of spelling or word choice. When writers draft, they just get it down, adding as much as they can. Eventually, as writers become fluent, they add too much and must learn to focus, which brings in the revision processes of rearranging and deleting information.

Every now and then children choose a draft they especially like and edit it for publication—a chosen audience/the "public" will read it. Importantly, we expect children to edit on their own! We do not write on their papers—they are the writers. We teach them the conventions they need by showing them in our own writing, in theirs, and in literature. Often a series of several lessons on one little type of editing is necessary. So when a child chooses a draft to edit, the writer, depending on grade level, may check a list of skills to edit. Then she may meet with a classmate and later with the teacher, who will point out (literally—we do not write on the child's paper) one or two edits; the child fixes them; and the draft is a finished final version. It will not be perfect, but it will be the best for this child at this time.

Importantly, young writers bring only a portion of their drafts to the point of being final, and they may never do this in PreK. They are gaining fluency. They will do this only a very few times in kindergarten, as they are continuing to gain fluency, so they write and write every day! In first grade, they will mature a great deal, but at the beginning they may edit less frequently than later in the year. Overall, the editing time lines will vary per child, as they write various lengths of drafts and work on them for different numbers of days. Maybe by the end of the year all the children will edit approximately one-third of their drafts, and they may maintain that rate throughout second grade.

Standard 6 moves our young writers into the use of digital tools to create and publish their work (see Table 5.6). As they mature from PreK to second grade, they learn to use a variety of tools with guidance and support from adults and in collaboration with their peers.

TABLE 5.6. Writing Standards for K–2: Production and Distribution of Writing (Standard 6)

Kindergartners	Grade 1 students	Grade 2 students
6. With guidance and support from adults, explore a variety of digital tools to produce and publish writing, including in collaboration with peers.	6. With guidance and support from adults, use a variety of digital tools to produce and publish writing, including in collaboration with peers.	6. With guidance and support from adults, use a variety of digital tools to produce and publish writing, including in collaboration with peers.

In the following vignette, we hear two second-grade children in their iMovie production of a book trailer about *Town Mouse, Country Mouse* (Brett, 1994). Viewers see the video frames, hear background music, see the children's words on each frame, and hear them reading alternating frames.

WRITING STANDARDS IN ACTION:
PRODUCTION AND DISTRIBUTION OF WRITING

After reading children's literature classics, the second-grade class breaks up into groups of two and three to create book trailers about their favorites. Alvord and Marista spend a few days learning to upload scanned pages from the book, and they import photos of a great eagle and a fierce cat from the Internet. They find music, write the text, and learn to print them on their chosen images. They record their own voices and the flourishes for the ending, when each of their names appears. The sequence of their work follows.

Image from the book: the two mice meet
    Words: *The town mouse goes to visit the country mouse.*
Image from the book: the two mice are eating bread
    Words: *They start to eat,*
Image from the Internet: eagle swooping down for a catch
    Words: *but an eagle tries to catch them.*
Image from the book: a town
    Words: *So they go to the town.*
Image from the book: the mice are eating cheese
    Words: *They start to eat,*
Image from the Internet: a fierce cat reaching for a mouse
    Words: *but a cat chases them.*
Image: book cover
    Words: *If you want to know more, read Town Mouse, Country Mouse.*
Image: boy's name zooms into the frame
    Words: *by Alvord*
Image: girl's name sparkles onto the frame
    Words: *and Marista*

Note how the children wrote their own words and learned several digital skills within the iMovie application. With guidance and support from their teacher, they have certainly gained expertise in this digital tool, and have produced and published a CD of their work. They did this in the fall, and will learn other digital skills (Miller, 2010) this year and as they progress through second grade.

Research to Build and Present Knowledge

The final group of standards engages young students in research and presentation of their knowledge. We begin with Standard 7—to participate in shared research and writing projects (see Table 5.7). Throughout this standard, children will be given opportunities to "participate in shared research and writing projects," and over the course of these years,

TABLE 5.7. Writing Standards for K–2: Research to Build and Present Knowledge (Standard 7)

Kindergartners	Grade 1 students	Grade 2 students
7. Participate in shared research and writing projects (e.g., explore a number of books by a favorite author and express opinions about them).	7. Participate in shared research and writing projects (e.g., explore a number of how-to books on a given topic and use them to write a sequence of instructions).	7. Participate in shared research and writing projects (e.g., read a number of books on a single topic to produce a report; record science observations).

they will "express an opinion" about their research and, ultimately, "produce a report." Research is something young children love. They have been curious about almost everything since their very early years, and their teachers foster their interests by engaging the children in projects that immerse them in studies of the world around them (Rogovin, 2001).

The following vignette takes us to first grade again, but this time in the classroom of Ms. James. Her students are studying icons of the United States, among them the American flag, Monticello (which is 15 miles from the school), and the Statue of Liberty. On this day, the children work in groups, and each group chooses a feature. As a researcher in the classroom that day, I follow Devon, whose group chooses the Statue of Liberty.

**WRITING STANDARDS IN ACTION:
RESEARCH TO BUILD AND PRESENT KNOWLEDGE**

I join the children as they choose books from the classroom collection and gather on the floor in a nook by their classroom doorway. A girl volunteers to read one of the books (Maestro, 1989) to the group; it has attractive illustrations and sparse words, and the students have never heard it. When she reads the page about France giving the statue to the United States as a thank-you gift, Devon says, "That was very nice of them." Throughout the reading, the children interact, as they have been taught to do during all read-alouds in their classroom.

The children in each group are to decide whether they want to create a piece of writing as a group or if they each want to create their own. This group decides on the latter option, and I follow Devon as he goes for paper, choosing plain white. He starts to sketch the statue and is dissatisfied, gets another sheet and tries again; goes for a third sheet, tries to use a book illustration as a guide, is not pleased, and walks slowly for a fourth sheet.

Then clearly a light bulb goes on in his head! "I'm going to look it up on the computer!" He knows how to do this and with a bit of my help finds several renditions of the statue. Devon chooses one to draw. Then he writes, with Figure 5.6 as his finished draft.

Devon, a talkative child, narrates as he works: "Look at these hands. Good, right?" "It is a long way up. I've walked it more than once. The first time I did, I was young, and my baby legs were sooooo tired!" His labels on the drawing reflect the features of the informational children's literature his teacher has been reading to the class, and the particular labels Devon chooses are those with which he identifies.

His text, which he writes across the top of his drawing, reflects the portion of his classmates' read-aloud that stood out for him (Moss, 2005).

Overall, Devon's work reflects what his class has been doing, what happened in his group, what his family has done, and the computer knowledge he possesses as a result of both his family and school experiences. He knows what to do to create an effective piece of writing.

Devon works in the midst of writing/social studies time, during which all the students are busy writing, talking, drawing, and creating. We see Ms. James among them, offering support and encouragement, but this is the spring of first grade and very few of the children actually have questions for her. They have a great deal of experience; they have been writing every day for months and know how to pursue this research task.

The Statue of Liberty is a good thing that France gave to us for friendship.
He was a monument to America. I think we say the Pledge of Allegiance to say
thank you.

FIGURE 5.6.

In reflecting on this case, we realize that Ms. James taught the children, over the course of the preceding months, to portray what they know in what they think is the most effective format. She has read to them from many formats and has given them opportunities to try them.

According to the CCSS, the children are on track. They know how to "participate in shared research and writing projects." Plus, they can write about facts, with consequences. When they are in second grade, they will be able to produce longer reports.

Standard 8 (see Table 5.8) moves us beyond the skill set of Standard 7 to the ability to "recall information from experiences or gather information from provided sources to answer a question." It is possible for many young children to find their own sources when

TABLE 5.8. Writing Standards for K–2: Research to Build and Present Knowledge (Standard 8)

Kindergartners	Grade 1 students	Grade 2 students
8. With guidance and support from adults, recall information from experiences or gather information from provided sources to answer a question.	8. With guidance and support from adults, recall information from experiences or gather information from provided sources to answer a question.	8. Recall information from experiences or gather information from provided sources to answer a question.

they want to find the answer to a question, as they search the Internet and find books in the library. They know exactly where the sources are for their favorite topics.

In our next vignette, Ms. Akers's second-grade students have studied a topic they all enjoy: magnets. Now they are to write about what they have learned using any type of writing they prefer. We enter the classroom, and focus on a female scientist.

WRITING STANDARDS IN ACTION: RESEARCH TO BUILD AND PRESENT KNOWLEDGE

Carlista remembers a lot, and starts with what is to become her third page. After creating it, she decides to create another page that is only about what she sees as the outstanding feature of magnets. It becomes page 2. Finally, she decides to fasten these together as a science report with a cover (see Figure 5.7 on page 102).

While Carlista creates this, we see the other children interacting a bit within their clusters of desks. Two or three of them are usually clustered around Ms. Akers, who sits in a chair at the center of their desks, ready to help the children generate options and choose among alternatives when they come to her with questions. Yes, she tries to guide them so they, in time, learn to answer their own questions.

This vignette, chosen as an example of what children can write when asked to show what they have learned about a topic of study, illustrates one young writer's ability to retell considerable information about magnets using various types of writing within one document. Importantly, she includes a diagram and a list, types of writing she has seen frequently in children's literature on scientific topics. She also adds a paragraph that includes a statement bringing her own voice into her work: *The neat part is opposites attract.* Finally, she creates an attractive title.

Overall, we see a creative, young scientist; scientists, she has learned, are imaginative persons—as are young writers.

USING THE PreK–2 WRITING STANDARDS THROUGHOUT THE SCHOOL DAY

The writing in these seven vignettes was created at various times during the children's school day. Three occurred during what was known as writers' workshop—the Dear Mommy opinion piece (PreK), the snowboard narrative (grade 1), and the book trailers

repel **M**attract
repel **A**attract
repel **G**attract
repel **N**attract
repel **E**attract
repel **T**attract
repel **S**attract

These are some things that do not attact and that attact.

A metel ball attacts,

A ring attacts.

A siser attracts.

A ruler dose not attact,

Stapels attact,

A nife dose not attact,

A South and a South Pole do not attact. A North and a Noth do not attact. A south and a Noth attrat. When the Noth is agenst a Noth it repels. The same gose fer South and South. The next part is that Opposits attract

I will gire you one egzampel. of a magnetic fild

↓ magnet

they form a magnet ican feild

paper going over the magnet

put tiny Pesesof Irn over the paper

FIGURE 5.7.

(grade 2). One piece of writing was created during the kindergarten children's literacy block: "I see a pig too. Now, done!"

The two science examples, the kindergarten bug book and the grade 2 magnets piece, were created during scientists' workshops—a way these teachers efficiently created time for both science and writing on days they wanted their children to write in science. Similarly, the social studies example (grade 1, Statue of Liberty) was created during what was usually the writers' workshop, but was used as a social studies period on days when Ms. James wanted the children to write about that content.

In general, writing is writing. It happens whenever and wherever it fits on given days. Importantly, it happens. Every day. Well, nearly every day! Writing is always scheduled and it occurs as regularly as anything happens in schools—where interruptions are one thing teachers and children know for sure will occur.

CONCLUSION

The CCSS provide a background against which PreK and kindergarten children can become excited writers. With opportunities every day to hold some markers, crayons, and pencils or touch keys on the computer keyboard, they will begin to create their paper selves, to figure out who they want to be as writers. To enable their engagement, it is important, most of the time, for them to choose their paper, what they write about, and in which format. In addition, their teachers occasionally provide time for them to write on specific assignments. In no particular order, these young writers can engage in shared research, conduct their own research, create narratives, write informational text, add information to their work, and show their opinions on paper. Some of our young children come to school having never held a marking tool—the sooner they get started, the better!

Already writers, these children will arrive in first grade ready to go! They will jump right in to informational/explanatory texts, write their research, search for new information with their classmates, use the classroom computers, feel free to state their opinions on paper, create stories to read aloud, and add information when they realize their drafts are insufficient. I have been in classrooms where first graders do all of these things. It is wise to immerse them in the busyness of writing every day so the production of information—from the serious to the frivolous—becomes a part of their lives.

By second grade, the children are at least in their third year of daily writing. This is the year, typically, when young writers become fluent. They can't stop—and don't know when to stop! They write for quantity. Their teachers love their volumes of words and, with great care, suggest a bit of honing. These young writers start to learn how to focus their writing, regardless of whether it is a narrative, research, or an opinion piece.

It is exciting to picture classroom after classroom, school after school, in which children write. Every day. Their teachers, as writers, understand the complexity of writing, the history of it, and the scariness of it (Boldt, Gilman, Kang, Olan, & Olcese, 2011). As a teacher of adults, I always have some in my classes who find writing daunting. So it is for children. Writing happens when writers—of any age—know they are safe (Hansen et al., 2010), and that they are expected to intentionally try new ways with words in order to grow as writers. They break through imaginary boundaries. Great writers, regardless of age, surprise us.

I found the examples in the vignettes just presented in my bank of children's writing, and I have many, many more. None of these teachers teach to a test (Wohlwend, 2009). They provide frequent, regular opportunities in which they and their young writers become immersed in the precious words of children's literature, their own talk, their various cultures, and the illustrations and words they use to create themselves. These teachers treasure the wonderful twists of language that only our youngest writers can create.

ACTIVITIES AND QUESTIONS

Activities: Additional Writing Experiences

1. *Text Types and Purposes.* PreK–2 writers can write opinion essays about various prominent figures in U.S. history, comments about science controversies, and thoughts about children's literature. We are careful, however, in our requests of them to write about what they read. Sometimes children become bogged down by this task, and we don't want writing to ever interfere with children's love of reading.

   For informational texts, young children can compare and contrast ideas, people, and objects, and may do so via Venn diagrams or conversations conveyed via speech bubbles in comic form. Various comic formats are available online.

   For narratives, children can learn to include dialogue. A study of this feature in the children's literature can help young writers learn where and how to add talk to their stories. Even PreK children can include dialogue in their writing. Often young writers draw before they write and, for the very young, months may transpire before they write words. Sometimes their first written word will be one spoken by a person in a drawing. Spoken language fascinates children, and they love to create it.

2. *Production and Distribution of Writing.* As the children become older, the idea of revision is for them to learn to focus their writing—as a primary way to decide what goes in their draft and what does not belong. One first-grade girl, in response to a question from her teacher, realized that the main event on her day of fishing with her dad was not the number of fish caught—it was when he consoled her after a hook scratched her. Her teacher's minilessons had been about that: When writing a narrative about an experience, think about the one main thing that made this experience important.

   There are many digital tools available for children to use. Maybe the most effective use of the computer, however, is for composing (Van Leeuwen & Gabriel, 2007). It has been typical for us to expect children to compose on paper and then, when a draft is ready for publication, move to a computer. It is within the composing process, however, when it is so easy to move words, letters, and ideas, that the computer may be the most useful as a writing tool.

3. *Research to Build and Present Knowledge.* As a way to learn about a place, young writers can make maps. Map reading can be difficult, and the ability to create maps improves students' map-reading skills (Ekiss, Trapido-Lurie, Phillips, & Hinde, 2007). As with various kinds of reading, the reader who can create a text type has an inside track when it comes to understanding, comprehending, and reading that text genre.

   We saw the recall a second-grade girl wrote when her class had studied magnets. Importantly, her recall was a piece of writing—instead of a test. As teachers of writing, we do not always determine what our children know by giving them tests.

Questions

1. In order for young children to know their thoughts are heard, to whom will they address and distribute their opinion pieces so they receive responses?

2. Given the proliferation of information online, what resources can the children access in order to be able to answer the multitude of questions they raise?

3. When children write narratives, how can we honor the different narrative formats used in various cultures?

4. While children are drafting, and we are circulating to confer with them, what do we say so we are not tempted to jump in too soon with editing concerns?

5. What links in other parts of the world can our young writers use when they distribute their writing?

6. In what ways can young children work in small groups to conduct research that is unique to their group?

7. What kinds of research can young children conduct that engages them in the collection of interview data?

REFERENCES

Boldt, G., Gilman, S., Kang, S., Olan, E., & Olcese, N. (2011). Having words: Contrasting perspectives on children's writing through the history of *Language Arts*. *Language Arts*, 88(6), 439–448.

Calkins, L., Hartman, A., & White, Z. (2005). *One to one: The art of conferring with young writers*. Portsmouth, NH: Heinemann.

Cervetti, G., & Barber, J. (2009). Bringing back books. *Science & Children*, 47(3), 36–39.

Dorfman, L. R., & Cappelli, R. (2007). *Mentor texts: Teaching writing through children's literature, K–6*. Portland, ME: Stenhouse.

Dorfman, L. R., & Cappelli, R. (2009). *Nonfiction mentor texts: Teaching information writing through children's literature, K–8*. Portland, ME: Stenhouse.

Dyson, A. H. (1993). *Social worlds of children learning to write in an urban primary school*. New York: Teachers College Press.

Dyson, A. H. (2008). Staying in the (curricular) lines: Practice constraints and possibilities in childhood writing. *Written Communication*, 25, 119–159.

Ekiss, G. O., Trapido-Lurie, B., Phillips, J., & Hinde, E. (2007). The world in spatial terms: Mapmaking and map reading. *Social Studies and the Young Learner*, 20(2), 7–9.

Emig, J. (1971). *The composing processes of twelfth graders*. Urbana, IL: National Council of Teachers of English.

Fay, K., & Whaley, S. (2004). *Becoming one community: Reading and writing with English language learners*. Portland, ME: Stenhouse.

Fletcher, R. (2011). *Mentor author, mentor texts: Short texts, craft notes, and practical classroom uses*. Portsmouth, NH: Heinemann.

Glover, M. (2009). *Engaging young writers: Preschool–grade 1*. Portsmouth, NH: Heinemann.

Graves, D. (2003). *Writing: Teachers and children at work*. Portsmouth, NH: Heinemann. (Original work published 1983)

Hansen, J. (2009). Young writers use mentor texts. In B. Cullinan & D. Wooten (Eds.), *Children's literature in the reading program: An invitation to read* (3rd ed., pp. 88–98). Newark, DE: International Reading Association.

Hansen, J., Davis, R., Evertson, J., Freeman, T., Suskind, D., & Tower, H. (2010). *The PreK–2 writing classroom: Growing confident writers*. New York: Scholastic.

Heuser, D. (2002). *Reworking the workshop: Math and science reform in the primary grades*. Portsmouth, NH: Heinemann.

Horn, M., & Giacobbe, M. E. (2007). *Talking, drawing, writing: Lessons for our youngest writers*. Portland, ME: Stenhouse.

Kissel, B. (2009). Beyond the page: Peers influence pre-kindergarten writing through talk, image, and movement. *Childhood Education, 85*(3), 160–166.

Laminack, L. L., & Wadsworth, R. M. (2006). *Learning under the influence of language and literature: Making the most of read-alouds across the day* (pp. 131–149). Portsmouth, NH: Heinemann.

Mermelstein, L. (2007). *Don't forget to share: The crucial last step in the writing workshop.* Portsmouth, NH: Heinemann.

Miller, L. (2010). *Make me a story: Teaching writing through digital storytelling.* York, ME: Stenhouse.

Moss, B. (2005). Making a case and a place for effective content area literacy instruction in the elementary grades. *The Reading Teacher, 59*(1), 46–55.

Murray, D. (1968). *A writer teaches writing: A practical method of teaching composition.* Boston: Houghton Mifflin.

Pransky, K. (2008). *Beneath the surface: The hidden realities of teaching culturally and linguistically diverse young learners.* Portsmouth, NH: Heinemann.

Ray, K. W. (1999). *Wondrous words: Writers and writing in the elementary classroom.* Urbana, IL: National Council of Teachers of English.

Ray, K. W., & Cleaveland, L. (2004). *About the authors: Writing workshop with our youngest writers.* Portsmouth, NH: Heinemann.

Read, S. (2005). First and second graders writing informational text. *The Reading Teacher, 59*(1), 36–44.

Rogovin, P. (2001). *The research workshop: Bringing the world into your classroom.* Portsmouth, NH: Heinemann.

Saul, W., Reardon, J., Pearce, C., Dieckman, D., & Neutze, D. (2002). *Science workshop: Reading, writing, and thinking like a scientist.* Portsmouth, NH: Heinemann.

Shagoury, R. E. (2009). *Raising writers: Understanding and nurturing young children's writing development.* Boston: Pearson.

Solley, B. A. (2005). *When poverty's children write: Celebrating strengths, transforming lives.* Portsmouth, NH: Heinemann.

Sumida, A., & Meyer, M. (2006). Teaching to the fourth power: Transformative inquiry and the stirring of cultural waters. *Language Arts, 83*(5), 437–449.

Van Leeuwen, C., & Gabriel, M. (2007). Beginning to write with word processing: Integrating writing process and technology in a primary classroom. *The Reading Teacher, 60*(5), 420–429.

Wohlwend, K. (2009). Dilemmas and discourses of learning to write: Assessment as a contested site. *Language Arts, 86*(5), 341–351.

CHILDREN'S BOOKS CITED

Brett, J. (1994). *Town mouse, country mouse.* New York: Putnam's.

Hartley, K., & Macro, C. (2006). *Bee.* Portsmouth, NH: Heinemann.

Jenkins, S. (2010). *Bones.* New York: Scholastic.

Johnson, A. (2001). *Those building men.* New York: Blue Sky Press.

Johnson, D. B. (2003). *Henry climbs a mountain.* New York: Houghton Mifflin.

Loufane, G. (2005). *Lola.* Wheaton, IL: me+mi publishing.

Maestro, B. (1989). *The story of the Statue of Liberty.* New York: HarperChildren.

Sill, C. (1999). *About reptiles: A guide for children.* Atlanta, GA: Peachtree.

Tchana, K., & Pami, L. T. (1997). *Oh, no, Toto!* New York: Scholastic.

Unstead, S. (2006). *The beautiful bee book.* Columbus, OH: School Specialty Publishing.

CHAPTER 6

Speaking and Listening Standards

Sandra L. Gillam
D. Ray Reutzel

Oral language—speaking and listening—provides the foundation for young children's later learning, reading, and academic success in early childhood (Dickinson & Tabors, 2001; Roskos, Tabors, & Leinhart, 2009; Snow, 1983; Strickland, 2001; Tabors & Snow, 2001; Whitehurst & Lonigan, 2001). Past studies of infants' and toddlers' electrophysical responses to language stimulation demonstrate a clear and strong relationship between oral language input and output and children's later reading abilities, especially reading comprehension (Scarborough, 2001; Watson, 2011). We illustrate in Figure 6.1 the developmental path from the early acquisition of preschool oral language and literacy skills to later reading comprehension ability.

Similarly, proficiency, or the lack thereof, in comprehending and expressing one's thoughts in oral language is both related to and predictive of difficulties in academic achievement, specifically reading comprehension for monolingual children developing typically, children with language impairment (Bishop & Edmundson 1987; Fazio, Naremore, & Connell, 1996), and Spanish-speaking bilingual students (Miller et al., 2006). Many children with language impairments also experience problems with decoding as well as reading comprehension (Bishop & Adams, 1990; Catts, Fey, & Proctor-Williams, 2000; Catts, Fey, Tomblin, & Zhang, 2002).

Proficiency in speaking and listening to oral language involves ability to acquire, practice, and integrate linguistic, symbolic, and practical knowledge across the domains of (sound units), semantics (vocabulary), morphology (grammatical morphemes), syntax (grammar), and pragmatics (social use). Even with evidence-based instruction, the benefits to academic and reading outcomes, specifically as related to comprehension performance, will be limited if children do not receive adequate instruction in the foundational skills of speaking and listening using a rich variety of vocabulary and language patterns (Rand Reading Study Group, 2002, p. 64).

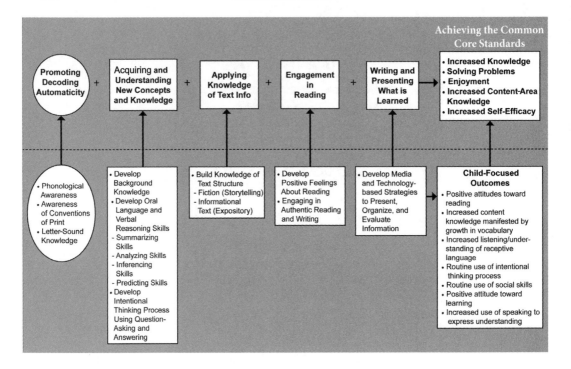

FIGURE 6.1. Framework for reading comprehension development in the early years.

During the PreK and kindergarten years, children learn the pragmatic (social use) conventions that govern how conversations are co-constructed by communication partners. Children must also learn to identify when a conversational breakdown has occurred and how to repair it. Young children typically violate many of the rules of conversation as they navigate these first few years of formal schooling. For example, a typically developing 5-year-old may introduce into a single 15-minute conversation as many as 50 different topics. In grades 1 and 2, students expand their use of more complex sentence structures and discourse patterns as well as increase the breadth and depth of their oral speaking vocabularies (Biemiller, 2006; Fernald & Weisleder, 2011; Gee, 2001; Harris, Golinkoff, & Hirsh-Pasek, 2011; Scarborough, 2001; Vasilyeva & Waterfall, 2011). Similarly, grade 1 and 2 students need to develop the ability to listen to increasingly complex orally presented speech and text discourse patterns through read-aloud and remember what they hear, seeking to clarify their oral language comprehension when it breaks downs (Blair, 2002). Research shows that children learn best the words and language patterns they hear the most (Christie, Enz, & Vukelich, 2007; Dickinson & Tabors, 2001; Fernald & Weisleder, 2011; Harris, Golinkoff, & Hirsh-Pasek, 2011; Hart & Risley, 1995; Vasilyeva & Waterfall, 2011). As a consequence, it is imperative that young children become immersed in rich language use in classrooms and receive carefully crafted explicit instruction in oral word vocabulary meanings and complex orally expressed sentence and discourse patterns (Dickinson & Tabors, 2001).

The K–2 Common Core State Standards (CCSS; National Governors Association Center for Best Practices and Council of Chief State School Officers, 2010) for speaking and listening are divided into two categories: comprehension and collaboration and presentation of knowledge and ideas. In PreK–K, comprehension and collaboration broadly refers to students' ability to participate in and contribute to ongoing discussions on a variety of topics introduced in the classroom, on the playground, in the lunchroom, or other educational contexts in which students interact with their peers, the classroom teacher, or with other adults and specifically to students' skill in the area of language called "pragmatics." Children with appropriate pragmatic language skill know "when" to say "what" and "how much" to "whom." In addition, children must acquire skill in listening, attending to, and monitoring the comprehensibility of information presented orally or through other media. Children must be able to ask and answer questions about oral or textual discourse to confirm their understanding and to clarify when understanding is not achieved. Some comprehension questions asked of children relate to explicit information stated in the oral discourse or written text, and others require children to generate inferences. In both instances, children must attend carefully to information, remember it, and access their own world knowledge to answer the questions. When children do not understand, they must formulate a clarifying response by asking a relevant question.

Presentation of knowledge and ideas refers to students' ability to talk about people, places, thoughts, ideas, feelings, and events in their life audibly, clearly, and with sufficient detail. These six speaking and listening anchor standards for K–2 demonstrate a spiral of increasing listening and speaking complexity and flexibility expectations from one grade to the next, as shown in Table 6.1. Common Core standards on speaking and listening focus on developing young students' expressive oral language complexity and flexibility. From kindergarten to grade 2, these standards expect students to speak audibly using complete sentences and a variety of discourse patterns, including conversations, descriptions, explanations, storytelling, and asking or answering questions requiring clarification or requesting additional information.

PUTTING THE SPEAKING AND LISTENING STANDARDS INTO PRACTICE

In the second section of this chapter, it is our intent to give teachers a sense of the types of experiences young students should have in PreK, kindergarten, and primary grades to learn, practice, and achieve the expectations associated with each of the six anchor CCSS in speaking and listening at each grade level. To organize the content of this section for readers' ease of use, we list the relevant CCSS anchor standard for each grade level followed by an expanded description of the standard in classroom terms and a classroom vignette demonstrating the use of the standard in the classroom. We then offer brief comments about how the vignette satisfies the specific expectations of the grade-level anchor speaking and listening standard. Once again, we want to draw attention to the spiraling nature of the anchor standards. As these standards evolve through the grades, students are expected to demonstrate increasingly more complex linguistic, cognitive, and pragmatic skills over time.

Comprehension and Collaboration

Standard 1 deals with the pragmatic conventions that govern how conversations are co-constructed by communication partners (see Table 6.2). A conversation involves a number of skills such as initiating or establishing a topic, maintaining focus and making

TABLE 6.1. Six Speaking and Listening Anchor Standards for K–2

Kindergartners	Grade 1 students	Grade 2 students
Comprehension and Collaboration		
1. Participate in collaborative conversations with diverse partners about PreK and kindergarten topics and texts with peers and adults in small and larger groups.	1. Participate in collaborative conversations about grade 1 topics and texts with peers and adults in small and larger groups.	1. Converse about grade 2 topics.
2. Confirm understanding of a text read aloud or information presented orally or through other media by asking and answering questions about key details and requesting clarification if something is not understood.	2. Ask and answer questions about key details in a text read aloud or information presented orally or through other media.	2. Describe details or key ideas instead of asking or answering questions.
3. Ask and answer questions in order to seek help, get information, or clarify something that is not understood.	3. Ask and answer questions about what a speaker says in order to gather additional information or clarify something that is not understood.	3. Ask questions to clarify comprehension or to deepen understanding of a topic or issue.
Presentation of Knowledge and Ideas		
4. Describe familiar people, places, things, and events and, with prompting and support, provide additional detail.	4. Describe people, places, things, and events with relevant details, expressing ideas and feelings.	4. Tell a story or recount an experience with appropriate facts and relevant, descriptive details, speaking audibly in coherent sentences.
5. Add drawings or other visual displays to descriptions as desired to provide additional detail.	5. Add drawings or other visual displays to descriptions when appropriate to clarify ideas, thoughts, and feelings.	5. Create audio recordings of stories or poems.
6. Speak audibly and express thoughts, feelings, and ideas clearly.	6. Produce complete sentences when appropriate to task and situation.	6. Provide details or clarifications as needed.

relevant contributions to the topic, and ultimately terminating the topic. In addition, children must learn to recognize when a conversational breakdown has occurred and how to repair it. Conversations are ruled by the "cooperation principle" (Grice, 1975), which states participants must provide relevant, sufficient, truthful, and clear information to one another. Not only do children have to learn these conversational rules, they must also learn rules related to "direct and indirect" speech and the expected roles of speakers and listeners in different contexts. Direct speech acts involve direct orders or requests to do something, such as "Get me a snack." An indirect speech act is a request

TABLE 6.2. Standards for Speaking and Listening: Comprehension and Collaboration (Anchor Standard 1)

Kindergartners	Grade 1 students	Grade 2 students
1. Participate in collaborative conversations with diverse partners about *kindergarten topics and texts* with peers and adults in small and larger groups. a. Follow agreed-upon rules for discussions (e.g., listening to others with care, taking turns speaking about the topics and texts under discussion). b. Continue a conversation through multiple exchanges. c. Ask questions to help comprehension of the topics and texts under discussion.	1. Participate in collaborative conversations with diverse partners about *grade 1 topics and texts* with peers and adults in small and larger groups. a. Follow agreed-upon rules for discussions (e.g., listening to others with care, speaking one at a time about the topics and texts under discussion). b. Build on others' talk in conversations by responding to the comments of others through multiple exchanges. c. Ask questions to clear up any confusion about the topics and texts under discussion.	1. Participate in collaborative conversations with diverse partners about *grade 2 topics and texts* with peers and adults in small and larger groups. a. Follow agreed-upon rules for discussions (e.g., gaining the floor in respectful ways, listening to others with care, speaking one at a time about the topics and texts under discussion). b. Build on others' talk in conversations by linking their comments to the remarks of others. c. Ask questions to clear up any confusion about the topics and texts under discussion.

made in a polite way that is intended to achieve the same result as the direct speech act, such as, "Boy, I sure would like a snack." Children must also understand that one's "role" in the conversation determines the choice of vocabulary that is used and the manner in which the information is presented. For example, a child must learn that casual, familiar language may be used with a peer at recess (e.g., What's up?) but not with a teacher in the classroom (e.g., How are you?).

Conversational rules take time to learn. Young children, particularly those in PreK and kindergarten, typically violate many of the rules of conversation as they navigate those first few years of formal schooling. Children learn the rules of pragmatics within conversational contexts as adults carry the responsibility of modeling the rules, conventions, and roles of conversational partners. Predictable contexts and routines provide children with opportunities to practice their emerging pragmatic skills. In these contexts, teachers may scaffold children's developing communicative attempts. Teachers must understand that young children make more coherent contributions to a conversation when they are talking about an activity they are currently participating in.

The following vignette is intended to exemplify a conversational exchange between two first-grade girls who had just listened to their teacher read aloud a text set of two books: Tomie DePaola's *Pancakes for Breakfast* and Jim Belosic's *OMG Pancakes!: 75 Cool Creations Your Kids Will Love to Eat*. Following the reading of these two books, the students were invited to turn to a neighbor and share their thoughts about the two books on pancakes. With the help of their teacher, Ms. Paska, the children immediately focus their attention on the topic of pancakes and their own experiences making and eating pancakes.

SPEAKING AND LISTENING STANDARDS IN ACTION: COMPREHENSION AND COLLABORATION

"Boys and girls, turn to your elbow partner and tell them whether you like or dislike pancakes and why. You can also tell an experience you've had with pancakes," instructs Ms. Paska. Roshanda and Michelle turn to each other as elbow partners.

"Pancakes are my favorite food to eat for breakfast, lunch, and dinner," says Roshanda. "I'd eat them every day if I could!"

"My grandma makes the best chocolate chip pancakes," replies Michelle.

"Well, my dad makes Mickey Mouse pancakes every Saturday morning," answers Roshanda.

Ms. Paska overhears these two girls talking. She leans down to Michelle and whispers in her ear, "Ask Roshanda how her dad makes Mickey Mouse pancakes."

"How does he do it?" Michelle quickly queries.

"Oh, first he pours a big pancake for the face. Then he pours two little pancakes on top of the big pancake head to make the ears," explains Roshanda.

Ms. Paska helps Michelle keep the conversation going by suggesting to Michelle that she ask Roshanda how her daddy makes the face on the Mickey Mouse pancakes.

"Well, how does he make the face?" inquires Michelle.

"Hmm," Roshanda thinks for a minute. "Well, he uses banana slices for the eyes, a slice of strawberry for the nose, and some blueberries for the mouth!" Roshanda says proudly.

"Wow, and I thought my grandma's chocolate chip pancakes were good," says Michelle. "I think I'll tell my grandma about how your dad makes Mickey Mouse pancakes. Maybe she'll make some for me!"

Ms. Paska commends the two girls for their conversation. She tells the girls that she will put the *OMG Pancakes!: 75 Cool Creations Your Kids Will Love to Eat* book in the back of the room at the writing center. Later they can look through the book and find other interesting pancake recipes they might want to copy onto recipe cards to take home and share with their families.

Note how Ms. Paska listened in and suggested ways for the girls to keep their conversation going. She helped Michelle build upon Roshanda's comments about her dad's Mickey Mouse pancakes and ask about how her dad made them. In so doing, Ms. Paska scaffolded their conversation so they could practice the conversational skills embedded in CCSS Speaking and Listening Anchor Standard 1 for First Grade. The girls evidenced care in listening to one another by speaking one at a time and remaining focused on the topic of the read-alouds: pancakes. They built on one another's comments through multiple exchanges of questions and answers about the types of pancakes they ate and processes for making Mickey Mouse–shaped pancakes.

Standard 2 (see Table 6.3) deals with the pragmatic conventions that govern how understanding of a message can be clarified or enhanced through questions and requests for additional information. Children do not master the ability to clarify or "reformulate" an insufficient message until middle elementary school age. Similarly, preschool and kindergarten children have great difficulty pinpointing exactly what in a conversation was not understood. Teachers must be diligent in asking these young children to clarify and then assisting them to do so. In most instances, preschool and kindergarten children will

TABLE 6.3. Standards for Speaking and Listening: Comprehension and Collaboration (Anchor Standard 2)

Kindergartners	Grade 1 students	Grade 2 students
2. Confirm understanding of a text read aloud or information presented orally or through other media by asking and answering questions about key details and requesting clarification if something is not understood.	2. Confirm understanding of a text read aloud or information presented orally or through other media by asking and answering questions about key details and requesting clarification if something is not understood.	2. Recount or describe key ideas or details from a text read aloud or information presented orally or through other media.

choose to "repeat" the information rather than rephrase or add information necessary to help the listener understand the message. Teachers will need to help children understand that simply repeating the same information does not constitute a clarification.

The following vignette is an example of how a teacher might model and then scaffold children in the process of monitoring listening comprehension and asking for clarification when listening comprehension breakdowns occur during a science lesson. In this example, the teacher, Mrs. Stackler, is reading aloud *Air Is All Around You* by Franklyn M. Branley. The teacher is using a think-aloud procedure to model the comprehension monitoring process during listening and to facilitate the use of age-appropriate clarification strategies. Mrs. Stackler discovers that a child does not understand the concept of "valley" and proceeds to assist him in identifying and repairing a listening comprehension breakdown.

SPEAKING AND LISTENING STANDARDS IN ACTION: COMPREHENSION AND COLLABORATION

After reading the book *Air Is All Around You*, Mrs. Stackler turns to Tyler and says, "Air is all around you. What do you know about air now?"

"That air is around your body?" questions Tyler.

" That's right, Tyler. Air is all around your body. Can you feel it?"

"Yeah, when it's blowing on you, like the wind," Tyler says with excitement.

"Exactly. OK. Listen to the next part of the book. There is air down in a deep valley. What do you know about air now?"

Tyler pauses to think and says, "Um, it is in something."

"What is it in?"

"Well," says Tyler, "Something. I'm not sure what it is."

Mrs. Stackler continues to probe. "Can you tell me what the something is?"

"Nope!" replies Tyler.

"Tyler, when you say something over and over again, it is hard for me to know what it is you do not understand. When you do not understand something I've read, you can ask me to repeat it. Would you like me to repeat what I just read about air?"

"Yes, please," Tyler answers.

"OK, Tyler. You listen for the part that you did not understand so you can tell me what it was, OK? Try not to say 'something.' Here goes. There is air down in a deep valley. What part did you have trouble understanding?"

"The last part about a deep va . . . ," Tyler struggles to respond.

"Oh, I see. The word you are having trouble with is *valley*. Can you say 'valley'?

"Valley," Tyler repeats.

"That's right. When you hear a word you don't know, remember that you can ask me to tell you what it means. You can say, 'What does that word mean?' or 'What does *valley* mean?' Try that," instructs Mrs. Stackler.

"What is a valley?" Tyler asks.

"It is a place at the bottom between two mountains," Mrs. Stackler explains. Next, she takes a white piece of paper and draws quickly two mountains with a valley in between. She points to the valley in the drawing and says, "See? This is a valley.[1] OK. Let's go over that part one more time. There is air down in a deep valley. What do you know about air now?" quizzes Mrs. Stackler.

"That it is in the valley at the bottom between two mountains," Tyler answers confidently.

"Excellent, Tyler. You are learning how to listen for times when you don't understand something and then ask a good question to find out the answer!"

---

[1]The teacher may then take a series of actions to be sure the child understands the concept, but should return discussion to identifying and clarifying listening comprehension breakdowns.

In this vignette, Mrs. Stackler facilitated the acquisition of the speaking and listening PreK–K anchor Standard 2 during a science lesson by guiding Tyler through the processes of identifying when information was not understood and modeling ways to resolve comprehension breakdowns when they occurred.

In reference to Standard 3 (see Table 6.4), young children may gain practice in asking and answering questions in any number of classroom-based activities. In the following vignette, Ms. Gomez supports young children in learning how to ask relevant questions in a science lesson on insects using *The Icky Bug Book* by Jerry Pallotta. Ms. Gomez seats the children on the rug at the front of the classroom for a read-aloud.

TABLE 6.4. Standards for Speaking and Listening: Comprehension and Collaboration (Anchor Standard 3)

Kindergartners	Grade 1 students	Grade 2 students
3. Ask and answer questions in order to seek help, get information, or clarify something that is not understood.	3. Ask and answer questions about what a speaker says in order to gather additional information or clarify something that is not understood.	3. Ask and answer questions about what a speaker says in order to clarify comprehension, gather additional information, or deepen understanding of a topic or issue.

SPEAKING AND LISTENING STANDARDS IN ACTION: COMPREHENSION AND COLLABORATION

"Boys and girls, there are many different kinds of bugs in our world. Another name for 'bug' is 'insect.' In this book, we will learn all kinds of things about insects. One way we can learn and remember what we learn about new things is to ask questions. Sometimes it's hard to know what questions to ask. I'm going to read you some interesting things about an insect and then I will model how I think about a question to ask. After I have shown you how to think about which question to ask, it will be your turn to ask questions about what we have read. Ready? Let's learn first about the tarantula!" Ms. Gomez smiles. She begins reading from the book: "The tarantula is a big furry spider. It can grow to be as large as your hand. Tarantulas and scorpions are found in warm climates." "OK, I am going to stop there. An easy way to make questions is to think about what I have read in the book. For example, the tarantula is a big furry spider. I can make this statement in the book into a question by using a *w* or *h* word such as *what, who, where, when,* or *how.* So I could ask, What is a tarantula? Answer: It is a big furry spider! The question and the answer use the same words from the statement in the book," she points out. "Let me try one more: 'It, the tarantula, can grow to be as large as your hand.' Using this statement, I could ask, How big is a tarantula?" The children all shout out in unison, "As big as your hand!" "That's right," Ms. Gomez responds. "Good answer! Tarantulas can grow to be as big as your hand. Now it is your turn to make a question from what we have read in the book. Here is another statement in the book: 'Tarantulas and scorpions are found in warm climates.' Now you try to make a question like I did using a *w* or *h* word. Turn to your neighbor and talk about the statement and how you could use a *w* or *h* word to make it a question." The children talk and begin to raise their hands. "OK, Ian, what is the question you would ask about this statement?" "Well, I would ask, Where do tarantulas and scorpions live?" "Excellent job," Ms. Gomez intones. "Children, what is the answer?" They respond in choral unison, "Tarantulas and scorpions live in warm places!" "Mrs. Gomez, what is a climate?" queries Jackie. "Oh, Jackie, thank you for asking that clarification question. Did you notice that Jackie didn't know what the word *climate* means and asked a question to find out? Nice thinking, Jackie! Give yourself a kiss on the forehead, like this," as Ms. Gomez demonstrates. "A *climate*, boys and girls, means the temperature, or how hot or cold, a place is where things live. A climate is about a place and how hot or cold it is in that place. Now I'm going to read about another insect and *you* get to ask more questions. Ready?" Ms. Gomez reads: "The water spider makes its home underwater. It weaves a special web, which allows it to bring air under the water. It catches and eats things that swim or float nearby." "Now, everybody, talk to your neighbor again and think of a good question to ask about the water spider. Remember, you can think about what we have read and turn the statements into questions." Ms. Gomez lets the children talk for about 30 seconds. "James, you have your hand up. You go first. What is your question about the water spider?" "Where does the water spider live?" The children call out spontaneously, "In the water!" "How did you know that answer?" Ms. Gomez asks. She calls on Bianca, who has her hand raised. "It said so in the book. It said the water spider makes its home underwater." "Wow, Bianca, that's great!" Melanie raises her hand. "Can I ask the class a question?" "Sure, go ahead," says Ms. Gomez. "What does the water spider eat?" The children start to buzz with their peers. Hands shoot into the air with excitement. "Cody, what do water spiders eat?" "They eat bugs, flies, fish, dirt, and other stuff." "Melanie, did Cody get the answer?"

"Yeah, kinda. Water spiders eat stuff that floats by it, but probably not flies." "Why not flies?" "Because they don't live under water," Melanie replies. "Good. The water spider lives under the water so it probably only eats things that are under the water. Cody answered that the water spider might eat a fish. What do you think of that answer?" "No, fish are too big for a spider to eat, unless it was a really little baby fish." "Great! Give yourselves a kiss on the forehead for such good thinking today!"

Notice how Ms. Gomez made it a point to model how to take statements from the book and turn them into questions. She also identified that she was "asking a question" or that a student had "asked a question." In this way, the children were explicitly directed to attend to the specific instruction provided on framing or asking questions. If the teacher had not done this, the children may have missed this crucial element of the lesson. Throughout the classroom interaction, the teacher makes a point to balance teaching content (e.g., information about insects) with opportunities for children to practice asking and answering questions.

Presentation of Knowledge and Ideas

Standard 4 (see Table 6.5) deals with the pragmatic conventions of *representational* and *ideational* language that govern how one talks about, explains, or describes his or her ideas, feelings, and experiences with the natural and social world (Halliday, 1975; Smith, 1977). Children do not master the ability to describe events or objects in their world with rich details and precise vocabulary until the late elementary or early middle school years. Younger children often find themselves at a loss for adequate words to describe events and objects, even those with which they are familiar. Teachers must help these younger students develop the content knowledge and relevant vocabulary words through personal or virtual experiences in order to be able to represent to others familiar objects, ideas, and events in their immediate world. In many cases, preschool and kindergarten children and even primary-grade students are unable to do much more than label generally, use gestures and body language, point to a picture, or describe in very general terms familiar persons, objects, ideas, or events in their lives. In representing their knowledge of the world to others, younger students will often give a sequenced listing of events, objects, or ideas that they have experienced throughout their day in a sequential run-on like structure. Teachers will need to help younger children specifically identify the object, event, or idea they wish to describe. Then they will need to have teachers show them explicitly with sufficient practice and structure how to talk about the relevant characteristics of the event, idea, or object to be shared with others.

TABLE 6.5. Standards for Speaking and Listening: Presentation of Knowledge and Ideas (Anchor Standard 4)

Kindergartners	Grade 1 students	Grade 2 students
4. Describe familiar people, places, things, and events and, with prompting and support, provide additional detail.	4. Describe familiar people, places, things, and events with relevant details, expressing ideas and feelings clearly.	4. Tell a story or recount an experience with appropriate facts and relevant, descriptive details, speaking audibly in coherent sentences.

The following vignette exemplifies a first-grade child attempting to describe a picture of an insect from the book *Insects*, a part of the Newbridge Publishing Company's Go Facts Science series.

After read-alouds, Mr. Namer often engages his students in a guessing game activity, where a child gets to secretly select a picture from the book and describe the object to classmates and see if they can guess what it is. This time Mr. Namer selects Micha, who has an obvious interest in learning about bugs. Micha chooses a picture of a beetle. Mr. Namer instructs him to provide one clue at a time and then give his classmates a chance to guess.

SPEAKING AND LISTENING STANDARDS IN ACTION: PRESENTATION OF KNOWLEDGE AND IDEAS

"Boys and girls, Micha is looking at a picture of an insect in the book we just read about, *Insects*. He is going to give you some clues by describing the picture of the insect he is looking at. Your job is to listen carefully to the clues he gives. Then you can talk to your across-the-table partner about which insect in the book you think Micha is looking at. I will write each clue Micha gives us on the white board with a web around a question mark that stands for the unknown insect in the middle," instructs Mr. Namer. "OK, Micha, give us your first clue." Micha looks at the picture and thinks about his first clue.

"This insect has wings," says Micha. The students talk to their partners and hands shoot into the air. Mr. Namer calls on Brionne. "I think it is a bee," she says. "Great prediction! Bees do have wings." "Micha, is it a picture of a bee?" asks Mr. Namer. Micha responds, "No." Mr. Namer puts a line going out from the question mark in the middle of the white board and writes "wings."

"All right, Micha, what is your next clue for us?" Micha looks carefully at the picture. "It has six legs and two antennae," he blurts out. Kids immediately begin talking and hands are quickly waving in the air. Mr. Namer calls on Braxton. "I think it is a butterfly," he answers with confidence. "Another great prediction! Butterflies have wings and antennae." "Micha, is it a picture of a butterfly?" asks Mr. Namer. Micha responds, "No." The class groans with disappointment. Mr. Namer writes a line going out from the question mark in the middle of the white board and writes "six legs, two antennae."

"OK, Micha, give us another clue, like maybe its color." Micha instantly says, "It's black and red." The kids pause for a moment to process the clue and then the excited buzz of partners talking begins: "We know what it is! We know what it is!" "If you think you know which insect Micha is looking at, give me a thumbs-up," instructs Mr. Namer. Almost the entire class responds. Mr. Namer laughs, "Looks like you all think you know. So when I count to three and say 'Go', you can all shout it out together: One, two, three . . . go!" The children shout enthusiastically, "It's a ladybug!" "Is that right, Micha?" asks Mr. Namer. A smile sneaks across Micha's face as he responds, "Yes!" There is an audible cheer among the class. Mr. Namer writes another two lines out from the question mark at the middle of the white board and records "red and black." He then erases the question mark and asks the class, "What should I put here?" They call out in unison "Ladybug!" He writes "ladybug" in the middle of the web.

"So," says Mr. Namer, pointing to each clue around the web, "If I were going to describe an insect like a ladybug to a friend who had never seen a ladybug, I might say 'Ladybugs are red and black, they have six legs like all insects, and have wings to fly.' Is there anything else

I might describe about ladybugs?" Micha raises his hand. "They have black spots on their backs." "Good, Micha." Mr. Namer shows the picture of a ladybug in the book. "See the black spots on the wings?" he asks as he points. "Anything else we know?" Sasha raises her hand and says, "Ladybugs are a kind of beetle." "Great catch," Mr. Namer praises Sasha. He records this on the web as well.

"Now, boys and girls, I want you to pair up with your table partner. Partner 1 describes and partner 2 listens. When partner 1 is done, you switch, and partner 2 describes the ladybug and partner 1 listens. Your descriptions of the ladybug must have at least two sentences and no more than four sentences. Listeners, you count the sentences. Ready? Go."

Note how Mr. Namer guided and structured Micha's description of the insect in the picture. Also note how his approach heightened student motivation and language interaction around these descriptive characteristics. Mr. Namer recorded each clue in a web at the board and kept the lesson moving quickly, with plenty of praise for responses. He modeled for the children how they could use the web to help them describe the insect and encouraged them to expand on its descriptive features. In so doing, Mr. Namer scaffolded the description of the familiar insect in the picture so that each pair of students could use these clues and characteristics to provide a focused description of the picture of a ladybug. This approach helps children to describe familiar people, places, things, and events with relevant details so that children can begin to acquire the abilities to describe embedded in CCSS speaking and listening anchor Standard 4 for First Grade. This teacher helped to guide, structure, and model how to look at an object, action, or idea and decompose it into its relevant parts with specific descriptive terms. This group learned how to describe a picture with scaffolds of a web of clues and modeled description by the teacher and then practice with a partner at their table.

Standard 5 (see Table 6.6) deals with adding semiotic or transmediational symbols to stories or poems that people can use to augment or clarify their message. As they develop, children learn early on to separate different symbol systems that can be used to represent and carry meaning such as writing, oral language, and drawing (Reutzel & Cooter, 2012). As their acquisition of language processes matures, children begin to recognize that these alternative sign or symbolic systems can be used separately or together. Used together, writing, oral language, and drawings (pictorial) can enhance and clarify intended meaning and messages, resulting in increased comprehensibility.

The following vignette illustrates a second-grade child's retelling of *Heckedy Peg* by Audrey Wood (1987). Mrs. Victor uses a variety of tools to help her students retell stories

TABLE 6.6. Standards for Speaking and Listening: Presentation of Knowledge and Ideas (Anchor Standard 5)

Kindergartners	Grade 1 students	Grade 2 students
5. Add drawings or other visual displays to descriptions as desired to provide additional detail.	5. Add drawings or other visual displays to descriptions when appropriate to clarify ideas, thoughts, and feelings.	5. Create audio recordings of stories or poems; add drawings or other visual displays to stories or recounts of experience when appropriate to clarify ideas, thoughts, and feelings.

using narrative text structure knowledge acquired from previous small-group reading lessons, including computers. Her students like technology and are learning to navigate digital equipment with confidence in the classroom. In this scenario, Mrs. Victor uses an iPad and a recording application to teach her students about story structure and to foster their oral and written story retelling skills.

SPEAKING AND LISTENING STANDARDS IN ACTION: PRESENTATION OF KNOWLEDGE AND IDEAS

"Samantha, it is your turn to come and tell me the story of *Heckedy Peg*," Mrs. Victor calls. "Can you come back to this center?" Samantha seats herself next to Mrs. Victor at a small table where an iPad is set up for use in story retelling. "Samantha, turn on the iPad and select the app called Dragon Dictation." Samantha quickly accesses the desired application.

"Now, using this story map, which we have used before in class, I want you to retell the story of *Heckedy Peg*, speaking clearly and loudly enough to make a good recording. The app will record your oral retelling of the story. When you are done, push 'Stop' and the app will convert your spoken words into a written story retell," says Mrs. Victor.

As soon as Samantha is finished, Mrs. Victor says, "Now, I'll transfer this written retelling on the iPad wirelessly to the computer at our computer center. I want you to go over to the computer and, using our story map, double-check that your written retelling has all of the necessary story structure components. Also, check your written retelling and correct any errors or problems like missing periods, commas, or spellings. Do you understand?" Mrs. Victor asks. Samantha nods affirmatively.

Later, Samantha returns with her printed story retell in hand. "I'm done," she says proudly. "Wonderful, Samantha! Now I want you to fill in the blank story map on the computer by copying and pasting parts of your retelling into it. Illustrate your story map with pictures from our clip art file from the Heckedy Peg DVD in the Scholastic Book Collection. When you are done, we'll print this illustrated story map out as a poster to be displayed in our independent reading area, OK?" Samantha nods once again and heads to the computer to finish making her illustrated story map retelling of *Heckedy Peg*.

Mrs. Victor had taught Samantha about story structure and provided her with a visual scaffold to help her render a complete, well-structured oral retelling of the story. She made it easy for Samantha to have her oral language converted into a written file for her to read, correct, paste into a story map, and illustrate for a poster to be displayed in the classroom. In this single lesson, Mrs. Victor assisted Samantha in retelling a story, making an audio recording and a visual diagram of the retelling using a story map, and illustrating the critical parts of the story retelling. It is clear that Mrs. Victor was guiding Samantha in a way the met the requirements outlined in anchor Standard 5 for speaking and listening as well as extending this into printed text and writing.

Anchor Standard 6 (see Table 6.7) specifies that children should be able to speak audibly and express thoughts, feelings, and ideas clearly using complete sentences. In the next vignette, Mr. Silva implements a language facilitation technique called "vertical structuring" to teach his students to use complete, complex sentences containing the subordinating conjunction *because*. The vertical structuring is used during a succession

TABLE 6.7. Standards for Speaking and Listening: Presentation of Knowledge and Ideas (Anchor Standard 6)

Kindergartners	Grade 1 students	Grade 2 students
6. Speak audibly and express thoughts, feelings, and ideas clearly.	6. Produce complete sentences when appropriate to task and situation. (See grade 1 language Standards 1 and 3 for specific expectations.)	6. Produce complete sentences when appropriate to task and situation in order to provide requested detail or clarification. (See grade 2 language Standards 1 and 3 for specific expectations.)

of lessons focused on healthy eating and exercise habits. The children practice expanding simple utterances and sentences (subject + verb + object) into more complex sentences (subject + verb + object + *because* + subject + verb + object). The lesson begins with Mr. Silva reading *You Have Mail* by Anna Keyes to introduce the concept of how the mail system has changed throughout history. In subsequent lessons, children are given a wider range of vocabulary to use in talking about how mail is delivered historically and contemporarily. After children have a grasp of the concept of mail delivery, and a larger vocabulary base for thinking about and talking about getting mail, Mr. Silva conducts vertical structuring sessions to allow additional practice on the concepts and vocabulary students have learned to use in making complex sentences.

Mr. Silva begins this particular lesson by asking children which of two ways of delivering mail would be used today. Younger children may benefit from the use of real objects in the lesson rather than less concrete pictures of the nouns, verbs, and objects.

SPEAKING AND LISTENING STANDARDS IN ACTION: PRESENTATION OF KNOWLEDGE AND IDEAS

Mr. Silva begins the lesson by asking, "Which of these ways of getting mail would be used today? Stagecoach or e-mail? We choose _____?" The children respond spontaneously, "E-mail!" Mr. Silva restructures their response by asking them to respond again together by saying "We choose e-mail!"

"Why did you choose e-mail and not stagecoach?" inquires Mr. Silva. "Because e-mails are used to get mail today," the children answer. "OK, that's right," Mr. Silva responds. "Now let's say the answer to the question together, 'We choose e-mail because e-mail is used to get mail today.'" The children echo Mr. Silva, "We choose e-mail because e-mail is used to get mail today."

In this example of vertical structuring, Mr. Silva took two sentences that he elicited from the class—"We choose e-mail" and "e-mail is used to get mail today"—and put them together using the subordinated conjunction *because* to make a complex sentence: "We choose e-mail because e-mail is used to get mail today." It was important for Mr. Silva to put the sentences together into a complex sentence so that children hear the sentence produced in its entirety and say it.

USING THE K–2 SPEAKING AND LISTENING STANDARDS THROUGHOUT THE SCHOOL DAY

Few elementary schools hold teachers formally accountable for developing their students' abilities in listening and speaking even though we know that these form the foundation for launching and supporting students' later reading comprehension abilities. Consequently, primary-grade classroom teachers may totally overlook or give minimal attention to the work of increasing students' abilities to listen intently and purposefully and to speak clearly and audibly, using increasingly complex language constructions as they move through the early grades. Given all that is expected of primary-grade teachers to teach in language arts, mathematics, and other content areas, carving out time during the day to focus specifically on oral language development and listening may seem difficult. We want to be clear in this chapter that there is no need for the teacher to schedule a specific daily time for oral language and listening instruction. Addressing the K–2 listening and speaking CCSS anchor standards can be integrated easily and seamlessly into language arts, mathematics, and content instruction during the day. In fact, there is no particular need to isolate language arts instruction time from time devoted to content instruction either!

With younger students, teachers can integrate listening and speaking standards in reference to discussing story and information texts during daily read-aloud sessions. Moreover, teachers can also attend to listening and speaking CCSS anchor standards when engaging in shared reading with younger children using either a traditional print big book or a regular-size trade book projected onto a screen using a computer projector and a document camera. For example, in the first-grade science curriculum, students may be studying how to grow vegetables and plant a garden. The teacher selects *Growing Radishes and Carrots*, by Faye Bolton and Diane Snowball, to share with the children in a read-aloud. Afterward, the teacher shows students a YouTube video of how to start a vegetable garden (Clean Air Gardening, 2009). Students are then placed into groups of five and are instructed to number off from one to five in the group. Each group is given a game spinner with five sections numbered 1 to 5. Student number 1 in each group spins the spinner and waits to see whose number the spinner points to. For example, the spinner stops on the number 4. The number 4 student in the group is the one who gets to ask the others a question about what they heard in the read-aloud or the video presentation on YouTube. Student 4 might ask, "What are three things you need to start a vegetable garden?" Thinking back to the read-aloud and the video, students who know the answer give a thumbs-up signal. Student number 4 calls on each student one by one until a correct answer is given. The student with the correct answer then gets to spin the spinner to determine who gets to ask the next question. The last spin of the day determines who will get to read aloud the book *Growing Radishes and Carrots* with their group of five. This activity integrates speaking, listening, and reading of an information text and video presentation involving the students in asking and answering questions about key details in a text read aloud or information presented orally or through other media as found in CCSS speaking and listening anchor Standard 2 for first grade. In this way, students listen and talk about science content they need to learn and build their repertoire of speaking and listening skills as part of the language arts and science curriculum. To extend the complexity of the texts students listen to and discuss, the teacher selects a more difficult book on plants to read aloud the next day, called *From Seed to Plant* by Allan Fowler

(2001) in the Rookie Read-About Science collection by Children's Press. In this way the teacher scaffolds students' abilities to listen to and speak about more complex ideas and language structures found in more difficult books on the same or a similar content topic. In the text box below, we provide a listing of books that can be used to teach PreK–grade 2 CCSS listening and speaking anchor standards.

As the teacher moves around the groups of five observing and supervising the speaking activity, he or she can pick one or more students to observe and rate their oral language development using the Teacher Rating of Oral Language, and Literacy observation instrument (Dickinson, McCabe, & Sprague, 2003). It would be well for teachers to tie the grade-level-appropriate Common Core speaking and listening standards to individual items observed using this excellent classroom observation tool. In so doing, teachers also integrate a curriculum-embedded oral language assessment into the daily speaking and listening activities in their classrooms. This helps to close the evaluation cycle of assess–teach–reassess–reteach where necessary. Embedded assessment also helps teachers identify students who need additional support in a timely manner so that they can direct more instruction toward helping them master the Common Core K–2 speaking and listening standards.

CONCLUSION

The Common Core State Standards for English Language Arts (CCSS/ELA) dealing with listening and speaking are divided into two categories: (1) comprehension and collaboration and (2) presentation of knowledge and ideas. Each of these two categories include three anchor listening and speaking standards, for a total of six CCSS/ELA speaking and listening anchor standards in grades K–2. In this chapter, we have discussed the research evidence base supporting the inclusion of speaking and listening anchor standards in

CHILDREN'S INFORMATIONAL BOOKS FOR TEACHING THE CCSS SPEAKING AND LISTENING ANCHOR STANDARDS IN PreK–GRADE 2

Title	Author	Publisher
Looking at Worms	Cheryl Jakab	Rigby
Miss Nelson is Missing	James Marshall	Houghton-Mifflin
Martin Luther King, Jr.	Liz Ray	Sundance
King Bidgood's in the Bathtub	Audrey Wood	Harcourt Brace
The New Kid on the Block	Jack Prelutsky	Greenwillow Press
The Frog Prince Continued	Jon Scieszka	Viking Press
My Little Sister Ate One Hare	Bill Grossman	Crown
Old Black Fly	Jim Aylesworth	Henry Holt
Gregory, the Terrible Eater	Mitchell Sharmat	Simon & Shuster
The Icky Bug Book	Jerry Pallotta	Charlesbridge

grades K–2 as a part of the CCSS/ELA to support the later development of reading and writing skills. We asserted that speaking and listening are the very cognitive and linguistic foundations of early reading and writing development in schooling. As such, neglect of the development of oral language abilities, including speaking and listening, is likely to limit or undermine young students' acquisition of early reading and writing skill.

We then reviewed each of the six CCSS/ELA speaking and listening standards by grade level and provided an expanded description of the standard in classroom terms. We explained how each standard functions as a part of oral language acquisition among young children, whether these were primary language or English language learners. We richly described a specific grade-level classroom vignette intended as an exemplar to give classroom teachers insights into how to implement each of the six standards within the context of classroom content and English language arts instruction. Following each vignette, we discussed specifically how the teacher and children in the vignette addressed and attended to each of the six standards.

Finally, we offered suggestions of how preschool and primary-grade teachers can integrate the six CCSS/ELA anchor speaking and listening standards into daily classroom content-area instruction and within the ELA curriculum. We argued that there is no need to segment out a specific time during the school day for oral language development, speaking, and listening; rather, teachers can seamlessly integrate their attention to these standards throughout the school day in every subject or content area instructed. In this way, teachers can optimize students' acquisition of content knowledge, reading, writing, and language skills, and do so in collaborative ways that lead to better oral language comprehension and the ability to present and share this knowledge with others.

ACTIVITIES AND QUESTIONS

Activities

1. *Speaking and Listening Anchor Standard 1 (PreK–Grade 2).* Place students in pairs to engage in a Think–Pair–Share activity (Lyman & McTighe, 1988). This is a structured way to be sure that students think before they talk, discuss, and ask questions in preparation for sharing what they talked about with the whole class. It would be well if teachers created a simple wall poster showing the four steps of the process: (1) teacher asks a question; (2) students think; (3) pair students up and discuss, question, converse; and (4) share with the group. It is helpful to set a time limit for Step 3 so children sense an urgency in their conversations to produce something they can share.

2. *Speaking and Listening Anchor Standard 2 (PreK–Grade 2).* During circle time, the teacher may introduce two puppets to the group: one is the storyteller, Lizzie, and the other is a shy puppet named Alice. Tell the students that Alice wants to ask Lizzie questions. The problem is that Alice is so shy she needs help asking them. The teacher gives Alice to one of the students. The teacher models to the students the question that Alice wants to ask, and then the students provide Alice with the words to ask the question. The teacher may say, "Alice, ask Lizzie who the main character is." The children will offer suggestions to the student holding Alice. Then the teacher uses Lizzie to answer the questions asked by Alice. The questions may be tailored to the specific book, lesson, or activity

the teacher chooses for circle time. For example, if the teacher is conducting a lesson on story elements, questions may focus on *who, what, when, where,* and *how.* The teacher should continue the lesson until many students have an opportunity to be "Alice."

3. *Speaking and Listening Anchor Standard 3 (PreK–Grade 2).* A fun paradigm for working with children on requesting clarification is based on Creaghead's (1984) "Peanut Butter Protocol" and "environmental sabotage" techniques (Bricker & Cripe, 1992). The teacher may ask children questions during lessons or activities in which all or part of the information is unclear, necessitating that the students request clarification. For example, the teacher may ask children to "Open your (mumble) and (mumble) to page (mumble). The teacher would then wait expectantly for the student to do what has been asked. The teacher can then scaffold responses so that children learn to request for clarification. Similarly, the teacher may ask students to do something and fail to give them the necessary materials to do so. For example, the teacher may ask children to complete a math worksheet that she is holding in her hands. The teacher may stand in front of the class expectantly, and ask them, "Why are you waiting to do your math worksheet? I'd like you to get busy!" The teacher can scaffold responses to assist students in explaining that they can't do their math worksheet until it has been given to them. A variation on this activity is to ask students to perform a task using a material that is not present or out of reach. Children would need to tell the teacher why they could not perform the activity and request the necessary materials to do so. For example, the teacher may ask children to paint a picture of their favorite insect and give them only a sheet of paper to do so.

4. *Speaking and Listening Anchor Standard 4 (PreK–Grade 2).* Set up a table with a mirror to look into along with a digital tape recorder. Ask the children to look into the mirror and describe themselves on the digital recorder—for example, their eye color, hair color, gender, shape of eyes, lips, skin color, any particular facial characteristics, and ears—without using their name. Later, other children play back a random digital description and try to identify who it is by listening to the voice and the description.

5. *Speaking and Listening Anchor Standard 5 (PreK–Grade 2).* Create a retelling center in a relatively quiet part of the classroom using an iPad or iPod with Dragon Dictation installed (available free of charge at *www.nuance.com*). Have the children dictate a story, and the app will write it as the child dictates. Print stories out with a couple of lines per page and ask the children to illustrate them with their own artwork or clip art from the computer, printed out and pasted into the book.

6. *Speaking and Listening Anchor Standard 6 (PreK–Grade 2).* Sentence/not-a-sentence center-based activities can target children's skill in identifying and using complete sentences around curricular content. Sentence/not-a-sentence activity boxes or envelopes contain complete and incomplete sentences previously encountered in stories, science, math, and/or social studies lessons.

Children read the sentences and then sort them into "sentence" and "not-a-sentence" categories.

Questions

1. What are some of the skills and principles children need to learn to meet the expectations found in speaking and listening anchor Standard 1? Make a list of these for a poster to share with the children as you teach to this standard.

2. What can teachers do to assist children in monitoring their own comprehension in order to identify when breakdowns occur?

3. How can teachers help students pay attention to specific and pertinent attributes of people, places, ideas, or objects when they are asked to describe them in speaking and listening anchor Standard 3?

4. Design a generic "web of clues" graphic organizer that children can refer to during multiple activities to remember to provide sufficient detail in their descriptions of objects, concepts, and illustrations.

5. What are some scaffolds or support that will help younger children illustrate and create visuals, diagrams, or other displays to augment their stories, poems, or descriptions as required in speaking and listening anchor Standard 5?

6. How can teachers facilitate students' understanding and use of complete sentences during curricular instruction?

REFERENCES

Biemiller, A. (2006). Vocabulary development and instruction: A prerequisite for school learning. In D. K. Dickinson & S. B. Neuman (Eds.), *Handbook of early literacy research* (Vol. 2, pp. 41–51). New York: Guilford Press.

Bishop, D., & Adams, C. (1990). A prospective study of the relationship between specific language impairment, phonological disorders and reading retardation. *Journal of Child Psychology and Psychiatry, 31,* 1027–1050.

Bishop, D., & Edmundson, A. (1987). Language impaired four year olds: Distinguishing transient from persistent impairment. *Journal of Speech and Hearing Disorders, 52,* 156–173.

Blair, C. (2002). School readiness: Integrating cognition and emotion in a neurobiological conceptualization of children's functioning at school entry. *American Psychologist, 57,* 111–127.

Bricker, D., & Cripe, J. (1992). *An activity-based approach to early intervention.* Baltimore: Paul H. Brookes.

Catts, H., Fey, M., & Proctor-Williams, K. (2000). The relationship between language and reading. Preliminary results from a longitudinal investigation. *Logopedics, Phoniatric & Vocology, 25,* 3–11.

Catts, H., Fey, M., Tomblin, B., & Zhang, Z. (2002). A longitudinal investigation of reading outcomes in children with language impairments. *Journal of Speech, Language and Hearing Research, 45,* 1142–1157.

Christie, J. F., Enz, B. J., & Vukelich, C. (2007). *Teaching language and literacy: Preschool through the elementary grades.* Boston: Allyn & Bacon.

Clean Air Gardening. (2009, July 17). *Starting a vegetable garden* [Video file]. Retrieved from *www.youtube.com/watch?v=y-h259HURp8&feature=results_video&playnext=1&list=PL* CC98315941E8073F.

Creaghead, N. (1984). Strategies for evaluating and targeting pragmatic behaviors in young children. *Seminars in Speech and Language, 5,* 241–252.

Dickinson, D. K., McCabe, A., & Sprague, K. (2003). Teacher Rating of Oral Language and Literacy (TROLL): Individualizing early literacy instruction with a standards-based rating tool. *The Reading Teacher, 56*(6), 554–564.

Dickinson, D. K., & Tabors, P. O. (Eds.). (2001). *Young children learning at home and school: Beginning literacy with language.* Baltimore: Paul H. Brookes.

Fazio, B., Naremore, R., & Connell, P. (1996). Tracking children at risk for specific language impairment: A 3-year longitudinal study. *Journal of Speech and Hearing Research, 39,* 52–63.

Fernald, A., & Weisleder, A. (2011). Early language experience is vital to developing fluency. In S. B. Neuman & D. K. Dickinson (Eds.), *Handbook of early literacy research* (Vol. 3, pp. 3-19). New York: Guilford Press.

Gee, J. P. (2001). A sociocultural perspective on early literacy development. In S. B. Neuman & D. K. Dickinson (Eds.), *Handbook of early literacy research* (Vol. 1, pp. 30–42). New York: Guilford Press.

Grice, H. (1975). Logic and conversation. In P. Cole & J. Morgan (Eds.), *Syntax and semantics* (Vol. 3, pp. 41–58). New York: Academic Press.

Halliday, M. A. K. (1975). *Learning how to mean: Explorations in the development of language.* London: Edward Arnold.

Harris, J., Golinkoff, R. M., & Hirsh-Pasek, K. (2011). Lessons from the crib for the classroom: How children really learn vocabulary. In S. B. Neuman & D. K. Dickinson (Eds.), *Handbook of early literacy research* (Vol. 3, pp. 49–65). New York: Guilford Press.

Hart, B., & Risley, T. R. (1995). *Meaningful differences in the everyday experience of young American children.* Baltimore: Paul H. Brookes.

Lyman, F. T., & McTighe, J. (1988). Cueing thinking in the classroom: The promise of theory-embedded tools. *Educational Leadership, 45,* 18–24.

Miller, J., Hielmann, J., Iglesias, A., Fabiano, L., Nockerts, A., & Francis, D. (2006). Oral language and reading in bilingual children. *Learning Disabilities Research and Practice, 21,* 56–63.

National Governors Association Center for Best Practices, and Council of Chief State School Officers. (2010). *Common core state standards.* Washington, DC: Author.

RAND Reading Study Group. (2002). *Reading for understanding: Toward an R&D program in reading comprehension.* Santa Monica, CA: Science and Technology Policy Institute, RAND Education.

Reutzel, D. R., & Cooter, R. B. (2012). *Teaching children to read: The teacher makes the difference* (6th ed.). Boston: Pearson Education.

Roskos, K., Tabors, P. O., & Leinhart, L. A. (2009). *Oral language and early literacy in preschool: Talking, reading, and writing.* Newark, DE: International Reading Association.

Scarborough, H. S. (2001). Connecting early language and literacy to later reading (dis)abilities: Evidence, theory, and practice. In S. B. Neuman & D. K. Dickinson (Eds.), *Handbook of early literacy research* (Vol. 1, pp. 97–110). New York: Guilford Press.

Smith, F. (1977). The uses of language. *Language Arts, 54*(6), 638–644.

Snow, C. E. (1983). Literacy and language: Relationships during the preschool years. *Harvard Educational Review, 53*(2), 165–189.

Strickland, D. S. (2001). Early intervention for African American children considered to be at risk. In S. B. Neuman & D. K. Dickinson (Eds.), *Handbook of early literacy research* (Vol. 1, pp. 322–332). New York: Guilford Press.

Tabors, P. O., & Snow, C. E. (2001). Young bilingual children and early literacy development. In S. B. Neuman & D. K. Dickinson (Eds.), *Handbook of early literacy research* (Vol. 1, pp. 159–178). New York: Guilford Press.

Vasilyeva, M., & Waterfall, H. (2011). Variability in language development: Relation so socioeconomic status and environmental input. In S. B. Neuman & D. K. Dickinson (Eds.), *Handbook of early literacy research* (Vol. 3, pp. 36–48). New York: Guilford Press.

Watson, R. (2001). Literacy and oral language: Implication for early literacy acquisition. In S. B. Neuman & D. K. Dickinson (Eds.), *Handbook of early literacy research* (Vol. 1, pp. 43–53). New York: Guilford Press.

Whitehurst, G. J., & Lonigan, C. J. (2001). Emergent literacy: Development from prereaders to readers. In S. B. Neuman & D. K. Dickinson (Eds.), *Handbook of early literacy research* (Vol. 1, pp. 11–29). New York: Guilford Press.

CHILDREN'S BOOKS CITED

Belosic, J. (2011). *OMG pancakes!: 75 cool creations your kids will love to eat.* New York: Penguin.

Bolton, F., & Snowball, D. (1986). *Growing radishes and carrots.* New York: Scholastic.

Branley, F. (1986). *Air is all around you.* New York: HarperCollins.

DePaola, T. (1978). *Pancakes for breakfast.* Orlando, FL: Harcourt, Brace.

Ehlert, L. (2006). *Eating the alphabet.* San Diego, CA: Harcourt Brace.

Fowler, A. (2001). *From seed to plant.* New York: Grolier.

Keyes, A. (2004). *You have mail.* Northborough, MA: Sundance.

Pallotta, J. (1986). *The icky bug book.* Watertown; MA: Charlesbridge.

Pike, K. (2002). *Insects—go facts science.* Northborough, MA: Newbridge.

Wood, A. (1987). *Heckedy Peg.* Orlando, FL: Harcourt, Brace.

CHAPTER 7

Language Standards

Susan Watts-Taffe
Allison Breit-Smith

Young children's command of language is an important correlate of later reading and writing skills (e.g., Cutting & Scarborough, 2006; Rescorla, 2009; Scott, 2009). Bloom and Lahey's (1978) seminal work points to three major areas of language competence: content, form, and use. Content, or semantics, refers to the meaning the speaker or writer is attempting to convey to the listener or reader. Content relies heavily on understanding word meanings and the way words and concepts work together in a sentence. Form is related to phonology, morphology, and syntax or grammar, and includes elements such as word order and appropriate use of word endings and verb tenses. Use, also known as pragmatics, refers to the ability to use language in a variety of situations, such as school and home. It should be noted that any one of the many dialects and varieties of English (e.g., African American vernacular English) have mutually agreed-upon conventions for content, form, and use that are required for competence in that language variety. Since language and identify are intimately linked, it is critical to understand that these language varieties are not incorrect and that children bring legitimate language, of all varieties, to the classroom as a part of who they are (Delpit, 1995). The teacher plays an essential role in supporting children as they use language both to understand and to be understood.

The Common Core State Standards for language are concerned with understanding and using conventions of standard English and vocabulary required for college and career readiness. Children who struggle to learn the conventions of word and sentence combination as well as the various vocabularies used in school often experience reading and writing difficulties. In particular, children identified with learning disabilities and language impairments characteristically demonstrate weaknesses in the understanding and use of grammatical sentence structures and/or vocabulary knowledge (e.g., Montgomery & Evans, 2009; Scott & Windsor, 2000). Thus, it is enormously important to teach children at an early age how the components of language work together to convey information.

The K–2 Common Core standards for language consist of the following anchor standards, listed by category.

- Conventions of standard English
  - Demonstrate command of the conventions of standard English grammar and usage when writing or speaking.
  - Demonstrate command of the conventions of standard English capitalization, punctuation, and spelling when writing.
- Knowledge of language
  - Use knowledge of language and its conventions when writing, speaking, reading, or listening.
- Vocabulary acquisition and use
  - Determine or clarify the meaning of unknown and multiple-meaning words and phrases based on grade-level reading and content.
  - Explore and demonstrate understanding of word relationships and nuances in word meanings.
  - Use words and phrases acquired through conversations, reading and being read to, and responding to texts.

Conventions of standard English broadly refers to children's understanding and use of (1) the rules governing grammar and sentence combination and (2) the rules governing standard English writing forms, including capitalization, punctuation, and spelling when writing. Children who demonstrate command of standard English grammar know, for example, that in order to construct the plural from of the noun *dog* one must add /s/ to the end of the word (*dogs*). Additionally, they can speak and write in complete sentences using the appropriate word order of standard English, and can expand and rearrange sentences by manipulating grammatical structures (e.g., combine two simple sentences into a compound sentence by adding a conjunction such as *and*). Children in PreK to grade 2 who understand and use the rules of writing mechanics know when and what to capitalize, such as the first word in a sentence, the name of a person, or the name of a location. Furthermore, knowledge of writing mechanics includes using appropriate ending punctuation, commas, and apostrophes as well as drawing on letter–sound relationships, phonemic awareness, and common spelling patterns to spell words.

Knowledge of language consists of one competency, beginning in grade 2. This competency includes using knowledge of language conventions when writing, speaking, reading, or listening. Specifically, this competency refers to children's understanding that spoken and written language are two different forms; written language is not spoken language written down but rather includes different grammatical structures and vocabulary in relation to oral language. Children who demonstrate understanding of the use of language conventions also know that language can be used in both formal and informal ways in varying contexts.

Vocabulary acquisition and use consists of three competencies: (1) determine the meaning of unknown or multiple meanings words, (2) develop an understanding of how words are semantically related to one another through categorization, attributes, and world connections, and (3) produce vocabulary words learned in oral language. With respect to knowledge of specific words, children are expected to know words of many types, including words found in literature (e.g., *curious, horrible*), figurative expressions (e.g., *missed the boat*; *pulling your leg*), general academic words (e.g., *observe, explain*), and domain-specific, or content-based, terms (e.g., *number, add, subtract*). They are expected to be aware that many words have multiple meanings, and to be able to distinguish among meanings appropriate for a specific reading, writing, listening, or speaking tasks. Furthermore, they are expected to understand relationships among words and nuances in word meanings. Finally, this vocabulary knowledge reflects both receptive (reading and listening) as well as expressive (writing and speaking) modes, with expressive command of vocabulary representing the highest level of knowledge (Graves, 2006).

Knowledge of specific words, especially those occurring frequently in reading selections and those that are central to the acquisition of content knowledge, is a central component of vocabulary teaching and learning (Graves, 2006; Stahl & Nagy, 2006). However, not all words children need in order to be successful in school can possibly be taught directly (Nagy & Herman, 1987). Research suggests that most words are learned through exposure to words in rich contexts, both written and oral (Cunningham, 2005; Elley, 1989) and are enhanced through strategy instruction (Blachowicz & Fisher, 2010), such as using information from the context (i.e., context clues) and using information about the structure of the word itself (i.e., roots and affixes) to determine word meanings.

A broad view of the language standards reveals continuity and repetition as the standards spiral up the grades. For conventions of standard English, PreK–K children are expected to know the rules of grammar and sentence combination as well as writing mechanics. The same anchor standards repeat in grades 1 and 2, but include more grammatical categories and mechanics of writing. As mentioned earlier, the knowledge of language anchor standard begins in grade 2 and continues up through the elementary grades. For the vocabulary acquisition and use standard, PreK–K children are expected to determine the meaning of unknown words, explore word relationships with adult guidance, and use vocabulary words in conversations. In grade 1 children are expected to continue to define the meaning of unknown words, use strategies for determining word meanings and word relationships with adult guidance, and use acquired words when speaking and writing. In grade 2, children are expected to demonstrate more independence with defining the meanings of unknown words and use more sophisticated vocabulary word when speaking and writing.

PUTTING THE LANGUAGE STANDARDS INTO PRACTICE

The first set of standards for conventions of standard English (see Table 7.1) addresses grammatical complexity, which consists of the rules governing how words are organized into categories or parts of speech (e.g., nouns, verbs, prepositions, reflexive pronouns) and how parts of speech are sequenced, combined, and manipulated into phrases, clauses, and sentences. By the time children are of PreK to kindergarten age, they are able to produce and use complete sentences using simple grammatical structures (e.g., nouns, verbs, prepositions) and invert complete sentences into questions (e.g., *who, what, where, when, why, how*) and negative forms. Expectedly, children's oral language use develops before written language abilities, but experiences with written language assist oral language development.

In grades 1 and 2, children learn how to elaborate and embed grammatical structures in their sentences and begin to increase the complexity of their productions. During these primary grades, children also begin to refine their understanding of grammatical categories. Early in development, children know nouns and verbs as general classes, but in grades 1 and 2 they learn the distinctions between different types of nouns such as proper and collective nouns. In essence, during the early years of schooling, children are

TABLE 7.1. Conventions of Standard English Anchor Standards for K–2: Focus on Grammar and Usage

Kindergartners	Grade 1 students	Grade 2 students
1. Demonstrate command of the conventions of standard English grammar and usage when writing or speaking. a. Print many upper- and lowercase letters. b. Use frequently occurring nouns and verbs. c. Form regular plural nouns orally by adding /s/ or /es/ (e.g., *dog, dogs; wish, wishes*) d. Understand and use question words (interrogatives) (e.g., *who, what, where, when, why, how*) e. Use the most frequently occurring prepositions (e.g., *to, from, in, out, on, off, for, of, by, with*) f. Produce and expand complete sentences in shared language activities.	1. Demonstrate command of the conventions of standard English grammar and usage when writing or speaking. a. Print all upper- and lowercase letters. b. Use common, proper, and possessive nouns. c. Use singular and plural nouns with matching verbs in basic sentences (e.g., *He hops; We hop*). d. Use personal, possessive, and indefinite pronouns (e.g., *I, me, my; they, them, their; anyone, everything*). e. Use verbs to convey a sense of past, present, and future (e.g., *Yesterday I walked home; Today I walk home; Tomorrow I will walk home*). f. Use frequently occurring adjectives. g. Use frequently occurring conjunctions (e.g., *and, but, or, so, because*). h. Use determiners (e.g., *articles, demonstratives*). i. Use frequently occurring prepositions (e.g., *during, beyond, toward*). j. Produce and expand complete simple and compound declarative, interrogative, imperative, and exclamatory sentences in response to prompts.	1. Demonstrate command of the conventions of standard English grammar and usage when writing or speaking. a. Use collective nouns (e.g., *group*). b. Form and use frequently occurring irregular plural nouns (e.g., *feet, children, teeth, mice, fish*). c. Use reflexive pronouns (e.g., *myself, ourselves*). d. Form and use the past tense of frequently occurring irregular verbs (e.g., *sat, hid, told*). e. Use adjectives and adverbs, and choose between them depending on what is to be modified. f. Produce, expand, and rearrange complete simple and compound sentences (e.g., *The boy watched the movie; The little boy watched the movie; The action movie was watched by the little boy*).

learning how to construct language in grammatically acceptable ways. Given the vast array of language structures and combinations that characterize standard English, the process of acquiring grammatical complexity is essentially never ending.

The most effective teaching methods for helping children develop grammatical complexity have received a great deal of attention in the literature. A systematic review of the effect of teaching grammar on children's writing development, conducted by Andrews and colleagues (2006), revealed little evidence supporting drill-based, decontextualized grammar instruction for improving children's writing abilities. Rather, research suggests that the most effective way to target grammar and mechanics is through functional, context-based instruction (Andrews et al., 2006). The practice of providing context-based grammar instruction is further advocated by the National Council of Teachers of English (2008) in a policy brief that urges teachers to abandon grammar drills. Simply drilling children on the parts of speech in isolation does not teach them writing composition skills, including how to select a topic, develop an idea, organize information, or write for an audience—skills that are essential to the Common Core standards. Conversely, context-based instruction that focuses on sentence construction and combination activities (e.g., Saddler & Graham, 2005), process writing (Graves, 1983), or examining the child's own speaking or writing provide functional contexts for embedding instruction targeting key grammatical concepts (e.g., Blaauw-Hara, 2006; Fearn & Farnan, 2007). Integral to these activities, which also reflect best practice for English language learners (Helman, 2009), are conversations between the children and the teacher, which allow for explanations of grammatical concepts and help build understanding of how grammatical choices affect listeners, readers, and writers.

In the following vignette, Mrs. Rook, a PreK teacher, uses a language experience approach (Stauffer, 1970) in combination with shared writing (Strickland & Schickedanz, 2004) to explore and examine grammatical concepts. Prior to this conversation, Mrs. Rook took small groups of five to seven children on a science nature walk. She gave each child a paper bag along with instructions to collect an item found in nature (e.g., a rock) and to make special note of where the item was found (e.g., in the meadow).

LANGUAGE STANDARDS IN ACTION: CONVENTIONS OF STANDARD ENGLISH—GRAMMAR AND USAGE (PreK–K)

Mrs. Rook says, "Wow, that was a fun nature walk, wasn't it? I am so excited to talk about what you collected in your brown bags. And I want to know where you found your items. So, first we are going to make a list. Look at my big chart here. It has three columns. We are going to make a list of your names, what you found, and where you found it. Let's look at the first column. The first column is labeled 'WHO (Person): Who is the person that went on the nature walk?' The second column says 'WHAT (Thing): What thing did you find?' And the third column says 'WHERE (Place): Where or in what place did you find it?' Now I want you to open your bags and help me complete this list so we can know who found what and where you found it on our nature walk."

WHO (Person) Who is the person that went on the nature walk?	WHAT (Thing) What thing did you find?	WHERE (Place) Where or in what place did you find it?
Mrs. Rook	rock	by the stream
Jamal	stick	in the mud
Brooklyn	leaf	on the ground

After modeling what she expects the children to do, and filling out the first row of the chart, Mrs. Rook asks each child to help her complete the chart. Each child comes to the chart and writes his or her name, using upper- and lowercase letters appropriately. Then Mrs. Rook asks the child to open his or her bag and tell her what he or she found. She records this on the chart. Finally, she asks the child to tell her where he or she found the item.

Once each child has taken a turn in the small group and the chart is completed, Mrs. Rook says, "All of these words are called 'nouns.' Nouns are words that stand for people, places, or things. So you are a noun, a proper noun; a stick is a noun; and a stream is a noun. We could call this chart 'Nouns in Nature.' Here I'm going to write the title, 'Nouns in Nature,' at the top of the chart so that we can remember what type of words these are."

Once the list is complete, Mrs. Rook places the "Nouns in Nature" chart in the Art Center. Children are instructed to draw or paint a picture of what they found and where they found it during their time in the Art Center.

The next day, Mrs. Rook gathers the children, the list, and the illustrations. She says, "Now, each of you gave me this information about nouns in nature and we put it on a list, but I don't really know a lot about your experience on the nature walk. So let's write about everything we saw on the nature walk and where we saw it. Because we are writing this information down, it will help us remember all of the different things we saw in nature. I'm going to write on this piece of chart paper. I'm going to begin with a sentence that introduces our big idea: 'Today we went on a nature walk.' Now, let's tell about all of the things we collected and where we found them using our list. For me, I have these three nouns: *Mrs. Rook*, *rock*, *stream*. I am going to tell you more about my experience on the nature walk. To do that, I am going to make a complete sentence out of these words that tells you what I did: 'Mrs. Rook found a rock lying by the stream.' Now I'm going to write that sentence down." Mrs. Rook writes the sentence on the chart paper.

"Now, I'd like you to create sentences out of the nouns we listed here. Who is next? Whose name is listed here?" (She points to Jamal.)

Jamal says, "That's my name."

Mrs. Rook responds, "That's right, Jamal! Now let's look at the nouns you wrote: *Jamal*, *stick*, *mud*. Now let's look at your picture. Tell me about what you found on the nature walk and where you found it using the nouns *Jamal*, *stick*, and *mud*. As you tell me, I will write your words on the chart."

Jamal says, "Ummm . . . Jamal found a stick in the mud."

Mrs. Rook writes down exactly what Jamal says on the chart. As Mrs. Rook writes Jamal's sentence on the chart paper, she repeats each word aloud. Then she says, "Let's read what Jamal said together." Mrs. Rook points to each word Jamal said and reads it back to the group.

After all group members have created a sentence, Mrs. Rook says to the small group, "Let's read the whole description of our nature walk together."

This vignette illustrates how a shared writing experience helps young children make connections between oral and written language and learn to construct and expand sentences. By starting with a list, Mrs. Rook gives preschoolers at varying levels a chance to contribute. She also structures and focuses the shared writing on nouns and noun phrases. Using a three-column chart, she addresses many of the substandards of the conventions of standard English anchor standard, including upper- and lowercase letter writing and question forms (*who*, *what*, *where*). On the next nature walk, Mrs. Rook might target verbs and verb phrases by instructing the children to focus on actions in nature (e.g., leaves rustling, birds chirping).

The second set of standards for conventions of standard English (see Table 7.2) addresses elements of writing mechanics such as capitalization, punctuation, and spelling. Wide variability exists in the writing mechanics of beginning writers. For example, in

TABLE 7.2. Conventions of Standard English Anchor Standards for K–2: Focus on Writing Mechanics

Kindergartners	Grade 1 students	Grade 2 students

2. Demonstrate command of the conventions of standard English capitalization, punctuation, and spelling when writing.
  a. Capitalize the first word in a sentence and the pronoun *I*.
  b. Recognize and name end punctuation.
  c. Write a letter or letters for most consonant and short-vowel sounds (phonemes).
  d. Spell simple words phonetically, drawing on knowledge of sound–letter relationships.
	2. Demonstrate command of the conventions of standard English capitalization, punctuation, and spelling when writing.
	  a. Capitalize dates and names of people.
	  b. Use end punctuation for sentences.
	  c. Use commas in dates and to separate single words in a series.
	  d. Use conventional spelling for words with common spelling patterns and for frequently occurring irregular words.
	  e. Spell untaught words phonetically, drawing on phonemic awareness and spelling conventions.
		2. Demonstrate command of the conventions of standard English capitalization, punctuation, and spelling when writing.
		  a. Capitalize holidays, product names, and geographic names.
		  b. Use commas in greetings and closings of letters.
		  c. Use an apostrophe to form contractions and frequently occurring possessives.
		  d. Generalize learned spelling patterns when writing words (e.g., *cage–badge; boy–boil*).
		  e. Consult reference materials, including beginning dictionaries, as needed to check and correct spellings.

a study of writing samples of children at the end of their kindergarten year, the students wrote, on average, 16 words and produced four ideas in three sentences; yet 27–29% wrote no words, ideas, or sentences (Kim et al., 2011). In terms of punctuation, misplacing periods and commas in the primary grades tend to be the rule rather than the exception. Studies have shown that grade 1 children place periods between words, at the end of lines, and at the end of the page rather than at the end of sentences (Cordiero, 1988). In grade 2, children become more grammatically adept with ending punctuation, yet may still place periods at the end of phrase and clause boundaries or major sentence parts rather than at the end of complete sentences. Understanding the conventions of punctuation can be difficult for young children because oral speech is not bound by written conventions.

With regard to spelling, PreK children understand that there are various purposes for writing such as to inform, to describe, and to list (Bear, Invernizzi, Templeton, & Johnston, 2008). They also produce letter-like symbols, which are distinct from drawings (Ferreiro, 1984). In kindergarten, children learn that letters represent sounds, and they use this knowledge to produce letters in their writing (Ferreiro & Teberosky, 1982). In grades 1 and 2, children begin to memorize and recognize spelling patterns and produce these spelling patterns in their writing.

Similar to teaching the grammatical conventions of the language, writing mechanics are most effectively taught in functional, meaning-based contexts. Although content and composition should take center stage when writing, discussion of capitalization, punctuation, and spelling can and should be part of the reading and writing processes. One of the most effective ways of working on writing mechanics with young children is by discussing the mechanical features of their own writing. In the following vignette, Mrs. Thomas, a first-grade teacher, utilizes a short focus lesson in an adapted writer's workshop approach (Graves, 1983) to address various mechanical features of writing. She embeds her focus lesson in specialized journal writing, namely family message journals (Wollman-Bonilla, 2000). Mrs. Thomas's class has been exploring the concepts of past and present in social studies, so she read *The Keeping Quilt* (Polacco, 1988) to her students. In this story, the author relates her family's personal story of immigration to America from Russia and describes her family's "keeping quilt," a symbol of love her family passes down from generation to generation.

LANGUAGE STANDARDS IN ACTION: CONVENTIONS OF STANDARD ENGLISH—WRITING MECHANICS (GRADE 1)

After reading *The Keeping Quilt*, Mrs. Thomas tells her first graders that they will be exploring their own personal histories this year using a family message journal. She walks over to an easel holding chart paper, picks up a marker, and says, "One of the ways we will learn about our own history is through writing letters to our families about ideas in books we've read. In this book, we read about how a family immigrated from another country to America. That makes me wonder where my family came from and whether we immigrated from another country. So I am going to write a letter telling my family about *The Keeping Quilt*. I'm also going to ask my family some questions.

I'll start by putting the date up here in the right corner. When we write dates, we have to think about capital letters and little punctuation marks called commas. When we write a date, the first thing we do is write the name of the month. What is the name of the month?"

Francesca responds, "September."

Mrs. Thomas says, "Yes, it's September. Which letter do we capitalize? Steve, do you know?"

Steve answers, "The first letter?"

Mrs. Thomas says, "Yes, the first letter, *S*, is capitalized. The second part of the date is the actual number of the day in the month. What number is it today in September? Take a look at our calendar if you need a hint."

Crawford says, "Number *18*."

"That's right," says Mrs. Thomas. "It's the 18th of September, so I will write *18*. The last number I write for the date is the year. What is the year? Everybody, tell me."

A variety of children answer, "2012!"

Mrs. Thomas says, "Absolutely correct. It is 2012, so I will add that to my date. When I look at the date, though, there are a bunch of numbers here, *18* and *2012*. To separate the numbers, we put a comma between the *18* and the *2012*. Great! Now we have the date. The next part of the letter we need is called 'the greeting.' "

"We are writing to our family, so on the left side of the paper here, I am going to write, *Dear Mom*. Because this is the beginning of the greeting, I capitalize the *D* in *Dear*. What about *mom*? Do you think I capitalize *mom*? Yes, I do because that is the name of a person. I am writing this to my mother, and so we capitalize her name. And this is how letters look. They have a date and a greeting.

"Hmmm. Now I need to think about my first sentence. I know—how about I write, *'Today we read a book called "The Keeping Quilt"*? Notice these special marks I put around the title of the book. These are called quotation marks, and I'm using them to show that this is the actual name of the book. Now, what should I tell my mom the book was about?"

Marina says, "It was about, uhmmm . . . a family who came to America."

Mrs. Thomas says, "What else could I say the book is about? Frank?"

Frank answers, "About a girl."

Suzanne adds, "And a quilt! Don't forget about the quilt!"

Mrs. Thomas says, "OK, I will write, *It was about a family who came to America.* I am putting a period at the end of this sentence because it is telling my mom about the book. I am also going to make a list on a separate piece of chart paper of some of the other ideas I can write about—the girl, the quilt. What else?"

Mrs. Thomas continues to work with her students to brainstorm ideas and craft two more sentences describing the book. Then she says, "Now I want to ask some questions to my mom about my family and how they came to America. What are some questions I could ask?"

Returning to her second piece of chart paper, Mrs. Thomas records ideas brainstormed by the class. From this list, she writes the following questions in her letter: *How did we come to America? Where did we come from?* Then she says, "OK, let's look at my questions. What do they end with?"

Several children reply, "A question mark."

Mrs. Thomas says, "A question mark, yes—a question mark because I'm asking a question. Now, I want you to begin your own family message journal. Write the first parts of the letter, the date, and the greeting. Will you write *Dear Mom, Dear Grandma,* or *Dear Grandpa?* Who might read this message and know the most about your family history?"

As the children begin writing, Mrs. Thomas takes an active role in helping them. She stops and works with several children individually on the content and mechanics of their writing. She also makes note of what children are doing well and provides specific praise.

As children finish editing, they are encouraged to illustrate their message and share it with each other. The family message then goes home, and Mrs. Thomas instructs the children to read the journal to their family member. The family member then writes a response and is encouraged to return a photograph or artifact to accompany the response.

This vignette demonstrates how conventions of writing mechanics can be embedded into a literature activity with connections to social studies. Through book reading and journaling, students build a sense of time and place that will help them distinguish between the past and the present. Each week as students write and revise their journal entries, they examine and check their writing for proper capitalization, punctuation, and spelling. Through focus lessons and journaling, Mrs. Thomas can continue to address the conventions of writing standard English.

The knowledge of language anchor standard addresses the conventions of standard English for conveying information in various contexts (speaking, reading, writing) and for creating effect. This anchor standard, shown in Table 7.3, begins in grade 2 and includes only one substandard: compare formal and informal uses of English. Formal use of English occurs in particular contexts (e.g., academic and professional) and with particular communication partners (e.g., teachers, the principal), and is characterized by certain word choices and grammatical structures. For example, formal English involves greater use of the passive rather than the active voice. Conversely, informal use of English involves greater use of the active voice and vernacular expressions and occurs in more casual contexts with friends, siblings, or peers. Comprehension of these different language registers is important so that children understand how to toggle between formal

TABLE 7.3. Knowledge of Language Anchor Standards for K–2

Kindergartners	Grade 1 students	Grade 2 students
3. (Begins in grade 2)	3. (Begins in grade 2)	3. Use knowledge of language and its conventions when writing, speaking, reading, and listening. a. Compare formal and informal uses of English.

and informal English as they communicate with their peers and teachers and later with their coworkers and employers as they enter the career workforce.

By the time children reach grade 2, they likely code-switch between formal and informal English automatically but have yet to develop the metacognitive skills for talking about this toggling. Code-switching refers to the ability to alternate words and conversational style based on the context. Given the differences between language used at home and in the classroom, children need to know how to switch between formal and informal English to be successful in school. Therefore, teachers in grade 2 engage children in explicit discussions and explorations of differences between formal and informal language through reading literature, listening to others, and writing. Through these discussions, children begin to understand that there are different language registers, and that "correctness" of language depends on a variety factors such as communication context, audience, purpose, and desired impact on the listener or reader.

In the following vignette, Ms. Sanchez uses the book *Frank and Ernest* by Alexandra Day (1988) to discuss formal and informal use of language. The book is about Frank, a bear, and Ernest, an elephant, who answer an advertisement to run a local diner while the owner goes on vacation. To properly run the diner, Frank and Ernest must learn "diner slang." After customers order in formal language such as "A tuna sandwich on toast, please, and a Dr. Pepper with the ice left out," Frank calls the order to Ernest using diner/ informal talk: "Ernest, I need a radio sandwich down, and an M.D., hold the hail."

LANGUAGE STANDARDS IN ACTION: KNOWLEDGE OF LANGUAGE (GRADE 2)

Ms. Sanchez says, "Today we are going to read a book titled *Frank and Ernest* by Alexandra Day. This book is about two friends, a bear and an elephant, who help run a restaurant or a diner. In this book, you'll notice that Frank and Ernest speak to each other differently than they speak to the customers who come to the diner to eat. Before we read, let's talk about the different ways *we* talk when we are in different places. Let's start by thinking about some places where we talk to others. Where are some places you talk to others?"

Jenny raises her hand and answers, "At school."

Mrs. Sanchez probes: "Where at school do you talk to others? Can you think of two different places in school where you talk to others?"

Jenny responds, "On the playground and in the classroom."

"Great!" says Mrs. Sanchez. She writes this down on the Smart Board and encourages other ideas from the class, which she also records. "OK, now that we have some places written down, let's think about who we talk to in these places. Who do you talk to on the playground?"

Jenny raises her hand. "My friends," she says.

Mrs. Sanchez probes further: "And who do you talk to in the classroom?"

Jenny says with a giggle, "You!"

Mrs. Sanchez affirms, "That's right. You talk to me, your teacher. Now let's think about *how* we talk in these different places and with these different people. If you were talking to your friend and wanted to know how she was doing, and you were out on the playground, what would you say?"

Carl: "Umm, well I would say, 'Hey, what's up?'"

Mrs. Sanchez writes Carl's words on the Smart Board. "Great, Carl, and now how might you say this to me? If you wanted to know how I was doing, what would you say to me?"

Carl responds, "Hi, Mrs. Sanchez. How are you?"

Mrs. Sanchez writes Carl's words. "Yes, now let's look at these two questions. They both mean the same thing, right? But the words we chose to use are different. Sometimes we use language that is formal and sometimes we use language that is informal. The language you use with me is different than the language you use with your friends on the playground. When we're talking with our friends, we don't always use the rules of formal grammar. We have certain words, phrases, or slang that we use with our friends that we don't use with our teacher because it's just not appropriate. In this book, Frank and Ernest use some funny language to talk to each other about customers' food orders. I want you to listen for differences between the informal way that they talk to each other and the formal way they talk to their customers."

Mrs. Sanchez reads the book, stopping and discussing the informal language Frank and Ernest use with each other. When she finishes reading, the children discuss the funny language found in the book.

In this prereading discussion, Mrs. Sanchez activates children's prior knowledge and draws on their experiences using language in different contexts and with different people. She helps children understand, at a metacognitive level, that the type of language they use varies, and she further develops this concept through rich discussion as she reads *Frank and Ernest*. As an extension of this lesson, Mrs. Sanchez encourages students to be on the lookout for examples of formal and informal uses of language in their daily lives (e.g., in the lunchroom, in the principal's morning announcements, at home, and on TV). Periodically, over the next few weeks, time is set aside for sharing and recording these examples on a class chart.

The first set of vocabulary acquisition and use standards focuses on children's capacity for independent word learning, as shown in Table 7.4. Children can independently learn word meanings by (1) consulting resources such as the dictionary and glossary, (2) using information about word parts such as the meaning of a known root word, prefix, or suffix (known as structural or morphological analysis), and (3) using contextual information such as the general topic of the conversation or text and other words used in the conversation or text (known as contextual analysis). Instruction in strategies for determining word meanings independently is vital, since it would be impossible for teachers to teach the meanings of all of the words children need to know in order to

TABLE 7.4. Vocabulary Acquisition and Use Anchor Standards for K–2—Focus on Strategies for Independence

Kindergartners	Grade 1 students	Grade 2 students
4. Determine or clarify the meaning of unknown and multiple-meaning words and phrases based on *kindergarten reading and content.* a. Identify new meanings for familiar words and apply them accurately (e.g., knowing *duck* is a bird and learning the verb *to duck*). b. Use the most frequently occurring inflections and affixes (e.g., *-ed, -s, re-, un-, pre-, -ful, -less*) as a clue to the meaning of the unknown word.	4. Determine or clarify the meaning of unknown and multiple-meaning words and phrases based on *grade 1 reading and content,* choosing flexibly from an array of strategies. a. Use sentence-level context as a clue to the meaning of a word or phrase. b. Use frequently occurring affixes as a clue to the meaning of a word. c. Identify frequently occurring root words (e.g., *look*) and their inflectional forms (e.g., *looks, looked, looking*).	4. Determine or clarify the meaning of unknown and multiple-meaning words and phrases based on *grade 2 reading and content,* choosing flexibly from an array of strategies. a. Use sentence-level context as a clue to the meaning of a word or phrase. b. Determine the meaning of the new word formed when a known prefix is added to a known word (e.g., *happy/unhappy, tell/retell*). c. Use a known root word as a clue to the meaning of an unknown word with the same root (e.g., *addition, additional*). d. Use knowledge of the meaning of individual words to predict the meaning of compound words (e.g., *birdhouse, lighthouse, housefly, bookshelf, notebook, bookmark*). e. Use glossaries and beginning dictionaries, both print and digital, to determine or clarify the meaning of words and phrases.

comprehend what they hear and read and to adequately express themselves in speaking and writing (Stahl & Nagy, 2006).

It is noteworthy that this standard references both unknown and multiple-meaning words, since children encounter many words for which they have a meaning but not the meaning required for the particular context in which they appear. Consider the differences among a *piece* of cake, a *piece* of art, and a *piece* of writing. In the early grades, it is important for children to recognize that many words have more than one meaning, that they need to determine the meaning that makes sense in context, and that there are strategies they can use to determine word meanings on their own. In the following example, Mrs. Harrison uses the think-aloud strategy coupled with discussion to illustrate the use of context to determine the meaning of an unknown word. Her second graders are reading *Henry and Mudge and the Happy Cat* (Rylant, 1990). Prior to this conversation, the children have read the following from the book:

> Henry's father opened the door. Sitting on the steps was the shabbiest cat Henry had ever seen. It had a saggy belly, skinny legs, and fur that looked like mashed prunes. Henry and Henry's father and Henry's big dog Mudge stood in the door and looked at the shabby cat. (pp. 7–8)

LANGUAGE STANDARDS IN ACTION: VOCABULARY ACQUISITION AND USE—STRATEGIES FOR INDEPENDENCE (GRADE 2)

Mrs. Harrison points to a word, saying, "Let's take a look at the word *shabby*. It's used twice to describe the cat. Can you find the two times this word is used? It's used one way on page 7 and another way on page 8."

"Here and here," replies Jake, pointing to *shabbiest* and *shabby*.

"Well done, Jake," Mrs. Harrison commends. You found both forms of the word. Here on page 7 it says the cat was the shabbiest cat Henry had ever seen. Then again on page 8, it says that Henry and Henry's father and Henry's dog, Mudge, looked at the shabby cat. And guess what? This word will be used again when we get to page 9. Raise your hand if you've ever heard the word *shabby* before. Don't tell me what it means—just tell me if you've ever heard it before."

Jake raises his hand. Luther says, "I'm not sure. I think so." The rest of the children shake their heads.

Mrs. Harrison responds, "OK. Some of you are familiar with this word and some of you aren't. If this word is new to you, let's see if we can figure out what it might mean based on what else is written here. And if you have heard this word before, let's see if the definition we come up with is the same or different than what you've heard before about this word. As readers, we come across words that are new to us all the time. This is true for all readers, even adults. And when that happens, one of the things we can do is try to figure out what the word means by looking at the other words in the passage and also by thinking about what the author is trying to say. Let's start by thinking about what kind of word this is. The word comes right before the word *cat*, so it's an adjective. It describes the cat in some way."

Mrs. Harrison allows the children a moment to think and then asks, "Does the author use any other words that describe the cat? Because these words might give us an idea of what *shabby* means. George, can you find another adjective?"

George questions, "Skinny?"

Mrs. Harrison rewards his response: "Great! *Skinny*. The cat has skinny legs. What else?"

Lisa adds, "It says the cat has a saggy belly."

"Yes," the teacher responds, "A saggy belly. And also it says the cat's fur looks like mashed prunes! Does that sound like a good-looking cat?"

The entire class engages in an enthusiastic "No."

Mrs. Harrison says, "So it sounds like *shabby* has to do with not looking very good."

Luther adds a further thought: "And the picture too."

"That's exactly right, Luther," Mrs. Harrison says. "The picture provides us with another clue to let us know that this is *not* a good-looking cat! What else do you think *shabby* might mean based on what we've read so far?"

"Well," chirps Lisa, "It says he might be a stray, so he might be in bad condition. Like when we find stray animals they are usually hungry and if it's bad weather, they're cold. And they're also pretty dirty."

Mrs. Harrison agrees: "The fact that he's a stray may be giving us another clue. Based on the clues we have, what do you think *shabby* means?"

Keith responds, "I think it means in bad condition, kind of run down."

Addressing the class, Mrs. Harrison asks, "Would that make sense based on what we've read? What do the rest of you think?" Heads nod. "Those of you who have heard this word before—Annette and Maria, does that definition make sense based on your memory of the word? Is that how the word was used when you heard it or read it before?"

Annette replies, "Yes, because my mom always tells me that she looks shabby if she doesn't comb her hair."

Appreciating this response, Mrs. Harrison says, "OK, so this sounds like a pretty good guess at the word's meaning. What if our guess didn't make sense based on what we've read? Would you think we were right?"

"No," says Luther, "Reading should make sense."

Mrs. Harrison nods in agreement. "Absolutely. We always need to check that what we're reading makes sense. And if it doesn't, then we need to figure out why. Sometimes it's hard to figure out a word's meaning the way we did just now. Sometimes there aren't enough clues to help or the clues we find lead us in a totally different direction. That's why we always ask ourselves, 'Does this make sense?'"

In this example, Mrs. Harrison displays important characteristics of effective strategy instruction. First, she talks her students through her processing and also engages *them* in the cognitive processing required to determine the meaning of the word. Furthermore, she consistently refers to what the unknown word might mean rather than saying what it does mean. This is important because context is not always helpful, especially as texts become more complex—something she shares with her students when she says "sometimes there aren't enough clues." Finally, Mrs. Harrison returns her students to the overall meaning of the passage as a way of illustrating that vocabulary knowledge serves the overall meaning making process.

The second set of vocabulary acquisition and use standards, shown in Table 7.5, focuses on children's understanding of connections among word meanings, also known as semantic networks (Blachowicz & Fisher, 2010; Stahl & Nagy, 2006). Consider the words *walk*, *skip*, *jog*, *run*, and *charge*. A kindergartner may know the meaning of each of these words through rich and repeated experiences. Children are routinely reminded to walk rather than run; they often skip during outdoor play; they are familiar with parents and other adults who jog as a form of exercise; and they learn that animals often charge when attacking prey. In order to support depth of knowledge and to speed up the pace with which they can acquire new word meanings, it is helpful to draw students' attention to the relationships among the words they are learning. In this way, they will begin to understand, for example, how the meaning of *charge* is similar to and different from the meaning of *run*. In the following vignette, Ms. Cheng utilizes two easy and fun techniques for building semantic networks among word meanings. Both approaches are based on Beck, McKeown, and Kucan's (2002, 2008) stellar examples of ways to promote young children's cognitive engagement with word meanings.

TABLE 7.5. Vocabulary Acquisition and Use Anchor Standards for K–2—Focus on Word Relationships

Kindergartners	Grade 1 students	Grade 2 students

5. With guidance and support from adults, explore word relationships and nuances in word meanings.
  a. Sort common objects into categories (e.g., shapes, foods) to gain a sense of the concepts the categories represent.
  b. Demonstrate understanding of frequently occurring verbs and adjectives by relating them to their opposites (antonyms).
  c. Identify real-life connections between words and their use (e.g., note places at school that are *colorful*).
  d. Distinguish shades of meaning among verbs describing the same general action (e.g., *walk, march, strut, prance*) by acting out meanings.
	5. With guidance and support from adults, demonstrate understanding of word relationships and nuances in word meanings.
	  a. Sort words into categories (e.g., colors, clothing) to gain a sense of the concepts the categories represent.
	  b. Define words by category and by one or more key attributes (e.g., a *duck* is a bird that swims; a *tiger* is a large cat with stripes).
	  c. Identify real-life connections between words and their use (e.g., note places at home that are cozy).
	  d. Distinguish shades of meaning among verbs differing in manner (e.g., *look, peek, glance, stare, scowl*) and adjectives differing in intensity (e.g., *large, gigantic*) by defining or choosing them or by acting out the meanings.
		5. Demonstrate understanding of word relationships and nuances in word meanings.
		  a. Identify real-life connections between words and their use (e.g., describe foods that are *spicy* or *juicy*).
		  b. Distinguish shades of meaning among closely related verbs (e.g., *toss, throw, hurl*) and closely related adjectives (e.g., *thin, slender, skinny, scrawny*).

LANGUAGE STANDARDS IN ACTION: VOCABULARY ACQUISITION AND USE—WORD RELATIONSHIPS AND NUANCES IN MEANING (GRADE K)

Ms. Cheng lists the words *jog, walk, run, charge,* and *skip* on the board. To the right of her list, she draws a long line. Then she says, "Everyone, take a look at this list of words. The words are *jog, walk, run, charge,* and *skip*." She points to each word as she reads it and has her students read it back to her. "Now, a quiz question: What do all of these words have in common?"

Hands go up, and Mrs. Cheng calls on Alexis, who says, "They are all moving words."

"That's right. These are moving words, and we've talked about moving words, haven't we? These are words that describe a way of moving from one place to another. Now, what's different about these words? Is jogging the same as walking? Is walking the same as running?"

Aaron responds, "Walking is like running but not as fast."

Ms. Cheng confirms this, saying, "OK. So these words represent different speeds of movement, don't they? Anything else? Does walking look like running, just slower? Or do people look different when they walk compared with when they run?"

A group chimes in unison, "Different."

"Yes, they do look different, don't they?" says Ms. Cheng. "Let's take a look at this long line I've drawn. We're going to use this line to put these words in order from slowest to fastest." Ms. Cheng writes "Slowest" on the left end of the line and "Fastest" on the right end. "I've got the words on index cards with tape on the back, so we can stick them up there and then change them around until we get them in the right order."

After this activity, Ms. Cheng plays a game with the words called Thumbs Up, Thumbs Down. After hearing each word in a question, children give a thumbs-up if they believe the answer to the question is "yes" and a thumbs-down if they believe the answer is "no." She asks questions such as: Is it a good idea to run in the hallway? Is it a good idea to skip during recess? If a lion were chasing you, would you walk?

In this vignette, Ms. Cheng's students are actively engaged in figuring out how the set of words are alike and how they are different and, later, in determining where they belong on the continuum from slowest to fastest. As they experiment with placement of the words and talk about their thinking, Ms. Cheng provides focused instruction to address misunderstandings in meaning, something she would be unable to do if she simply placed the words on the continuum herself. By keeping the continuum up on the wall, she can encourage practice over time and extend her instruction to include other "moving words," such as *crawling, creeping, strolling,* and *marching.* The activity, Thumbs Up/Thumbs Down, provides meaningful practice and active engagement for all students.

The final vocabulary acquisition and use (see Table 7.6) standard focuses on children's ability to integrate and use vocabulary gleaned from a variety of sources. Specifically, this anchor standard involves children's expressive vocabulary, which represents the highest form of word knowledge, because children understand and have internalized words to the degree of using them in original oral and written expression. In order for children to meet this standard, they need many and varied opportunities to talk and experiment with new vocabulary. Research indicates that word learning is incremental, characterized by phases of partial word knowledge along a continuum from the unknown to the known (Nagy & Scott, 2000). Therefore, the classroom should be an environment where children take risks. Encouraging children to use their partial knowledge of new

TABLE 7.6. Vocabulary Acquisition and Use Anchor Standards for K–2—Focus on Expressive Vocabulary

Kindergartners	Grade 1 students	Grade 2 students
6. Use words and phrases acquired through conversations, reading and being read to, and responding to texts.	6. Use words and phrases acquired through conversations, reading and being read to, and responding to texts, including using frequently occurring conjunctions to signal simple relationships (e.g., *because*).	6. Use words and phrases acquired through conversations, reading and being read to, and responding to texts, including using adjectives and adverbs to describe (e.g., *When other kids are happy that makes me happy*).

words and concepts allows teachers to provide targeted feedback and support, which leads to mastery over time. In the following vignette, Mr. Cohen scaffolds his PreK students' use of language found in *The Rainbow Fish* (Pfister, 1992) as they discuss and respond to the book.

LANGUAGE STANDARDS IN ACTION: VOCABULARY ACQUISITION AND USE—EXPRESSIVE VOCABULARY (PreK)

Mr. Cohen starts the lesson by asking, "Who is this story about?"

Lisa says, "The shiny Rainbow Fish. I like how the book shines when you read it."

"Yes," says Mr. Cohen. "That word *shiny* is one of the words used in the story to describe the fish, so that's really good listening and remembering, Lisa. In the story, it says the fish had shiny scales in particular. The author used some other words to describe the fish's scales. Can anyone remember them?"

Beth Ann responds thoughtfully, "It said they were sparkly."

"Very good, Beth Ann!" praises Mr. Cohen. "*Sparkling* was another word used to describe the scales. Anybody else?"

Deirdre answers, "Pretty?"

Mr. Cohen suggests, "I'm not sure if the word *pretty* was used, but I remember the word *beautiful* and that's another way to say *pretty*, isn't it?" Deirdre nods. Mr. Cohen continues, "The scales are described as *sparkling, shimmering, beautiful, glimmering*, and *dazzling*. So these are some pretty amazing scales, aren't they?" Heads nod. "How did the Rainbow Fish feel about these incredible scales?"

Jonathan contributes, "He thought he looked good!"

Mr. Cohen responds, laughing, "Yes, he certainly did, Jonathan. He thought he looked very good. In fact, the author used a special word to describe how he felt. In the book, it says the Rainbow Fish felt *proud* of his shiny, shimmering scales. And why was he so proud of his scales? Did other fish have shiny, shimmering scales?"

Several students together chime, "No."

"No, they didn't." Mr. Cohen probes further: "What kind of scales did the other fish have?"

"Just regular," says Peter.

Mr. Cohen agrees: "Yes, they had regular, ordinary scales. The author makes a point of saying that the Rainbow Fish was not ordinary. He is special because of his scales. But he also had a problem. What was his problem?"

Geneva responds, "Didn't none of the other fish want to play with him."

Encouraging more discussion, Mr. Cohen adds, "None of the other fish wanted to play with him, that's right. So what did he do?"

Maria says, "He asked the octopus what to do, and he said he had to give his scales away."

Mr. Cohen continues the story retelling: "Yes. He went to the octopus with his problem and he asked the octopus for his advice, didn't he? And Maria just told us what the octopus told him to do. So did he do it?"

All respond, "yes," nodding their heads.

Mr. Cohen asks, "And did that turn out to be good advice?"

"Uh-huh," says Paul, " 'Cause when he gave his scales to the other fish, they liked him and they wanted to play with him."

Then Mr. Cohen offers, "So he solved his problem by giving something that he had to the other fish. This reminds me of a word we were talking about when we read *Cookies*. Remember when we read about sharing cookies with others? Can anyone remember the word that was used? It means to give something of yours away to someone else and it is the opposite of being greedy. If it's not greedy, it's what?"

Emma responds, "Generally."

"Very close, Emma," Mr. Cohen says encouragingly. "You're thinking of the word *generous*." Emma nods. "In the end, the Rainbow Fish was generous and he was no longer lonely."

In this vignette, Mr. Cohen models and scaffolds use of vocabulary found in the read-aloud as well as vocabulary used to respond to text. By revisiting words such as *shiny*, *sparkling*, *shimmering*, *beautiful*, *ordinary*, and *advice*, he reinforces these concepts. Rich conversation about words in read-alouds, coupled with repeated reading of these books, has been shown to significantly increase children's acquisition of words found in the text (Beck & McKeown, 2007; Collins, 2010). Mr. Cohen also makes connections to vocabulary in another text and models use of story grammar vocabulary (i.e., character, problem).

USING THE K–2 LANGUAGE STANDARDS THROUGHOUT THE DAY

In Mrs. Marcotte's mixed-level first- and second-grade classroom, children use purposeful talk to process ideas and make connections with prior experience. They manipulate concepts and vocabulary with teacher support and scaffolding, and are aware of themselves as competent language users. Mrs. Marcotte's approach is marked by curriculum integration, ongoing assessment, and an appreciation of the rich and varied cultural and linguistic experiences her students bring to the classroom. Her knowledge of best practice is evident in the following sample of a typical day's activities.

What's Going On in Your World?

Mrs. Marcotte starts the day with opportunities for scaffolded talk. With students gathered in a circle, she tosses her inflated beach ball globe to Marina and says, "Good morning, Marina! What's going on in your world today?" Marina shares a sentence about the tooth she lost last night and then tosses the ball to a classmate. Using Mrs. Marcotte's language frame, she says: "Good morning, Jack. What's going in on your world today?" Mrs. Marcotte is aware of the power of language frames for introducing all students, and especially English language learners, to a variety of language structures (Fisher & Frey, 2010) such as questions and summary statements. Furthermore, Mrs. Marcotte selects three to four students to observe each day, noting what they say on Vukelich, Christie, and Enz's (2012) Language Observation Recording Form. The recording form has four columns: Name (*Marina*); Context (*What's going on in your world?*); What Child Said (*"I lost a tooth last night and the tooth fairy came"*); Language Conventions (*compound sentence*). By paying careful attention to what her students know about language and under what conditions (Calfee & Miller, 2007), Mrs. Marcotte determines the most appropriate "next steps" for instruction.

Monarch Butterfly Notebook

Mrs. Marcotte's students are raising caterpillars and observing their growth and eventual transformation into monarch butterflies. Each Monday, Wednesday, and Friday, her students record the date, what they see (shapes, colors, textures), measurements, changes from their last observation, and any descriptive words that come to mind. Concepts and accompanying vocabulary the students are working with include general academic words (e.g., *observation, data, record*) and domain-specific words (e.g., *caterpillar, chrysalis, butterfly*).

Read-Aloud

After lunch and recess, Mrs. Marcotte reads aloud from the Caldecott Medal book *Officer Buckle and Gloria* (Rathman, 1995), a humorous book that ties into a thematic unit on safety and responsibility. Thus, several of the important words and concepts in this book, including *attention, commands, officer, safety,* and *accident,* will appear in other instructional contexts throughout the 2-week period of the unit. At the beginning of the unit, Mrs. Marcotte gives each child a list of the key vocabulary terms they will encounter. Each child rates his or her knowledge of each word ("I know it well"; "I know it a little bit"; "I don't know it at all") (Dale, 1965). Mrs. Marcotte uses this activity to foster metalinguistic knowledge about word learning (Nagy & Scott, 2000) and uses children's responses to identify words requiring the most instructional time. At the end of the unit, children re-rate their knowledge, allowing both Mrs. Marcotte and themselves to see their growth as word learners.

Integrating the language standards throughout the day includes consideration of the types of texts that provide an environment conducive to children's language and vocabulary acquisition. We want to stress the importance of a comprehensive classroom library that includes texts for read-alouds that use sophisticated vocabulary and increasingly complex language structures; texts for read-alouds and independent reading representing various text structures (e.g., narrative, procedural, and persuasive); texts for instruction and independent reading that are engaging and representative of a variety of cultural and linguistic experiences. A sample of books that lend themselves to the language standards are found in the text box on page 147. An excellent resource for locating children's books is the Children's Book Council website at *www.cbcbooks.org*.

CONCLUSION

Several years ago, a kindergarten teacher informed us that she was no longer permitted to read aloud to her students in order to devote more instructional time to meeting a set of standards. We hope this chapter has been imminently clear about the fact that read-alouds, thematic units, learning centers, dramatic play, writing workshop, word games, and rich conversations throughout the school day *are* the ways to maximize instruction. As children interact with high-quality literature, their peers, stimulating academic content, and the ideas they want to express, the language standards come alive.

CHILDREN'S BOOKS FOR TEACHING
THE CCSS LANGUAGE STANDARDS, PreK–GRADE 2

Title	Author	Publisher	Language skill
Animalia	Graeme Base	Abrams	Vocabulary
A Cache of Jewels and Other Collective Nouns	Ruth Heller	Puffin	Collective nouns
A Chocolate Moose for Dinner	Fred Gwynne	Aladdin	Vocabulary
School Bus	Donald Crews	Greenwillow	Plural nouns
Fortunately	Remy Charlip	Aladdin	Adverbs
I Wanna Iguana	Karen Kaufman Orloff	Putnam	Writing mechanics
Stars and Stripes: The Story of the American Flag	Sarah Thompson	HarperCollins	Past tense verbs
The Random House Book of Poetry	Jack Prelutsky	Random House	Adjectives
The True Story of the Three Little Pigs	John Scieszka	Puffin	Informal English
The Cat in the Hat	Dr. Seuss	Random House	Spelling patterns
Thesaurus Rex	Laya Steinberg	Barefoot Books	Vocabulary
Donavan's Word Jar	Monalisa DeGross	Harper	Vocabulary

ACTIVITIES AND QUESTIONS

Activities

1. *Conventions of Standard English Anchor Standards—Focus on Grammar and Usage.* Set up an Eye Spy basket modeled on the popular book series. In it, place items related to a current theme of study such as transportation. Items such as miniature buses, trains, airplanes, pilot, conductor, passengers, suitcases, fuel, and tires can be included in varying quantities. When two children play the game, they take turns asking the other an Eye Spy question: *"What do you spy in the basket?"* or *"Who do you spy in the basket?"* *"I spy one bus in the basket"* or *"I spy three passengers in the basket."* (PreK–kindergarten)

2. *Conventions of Standard English Anchor Standards—Focus on Writing Mechanics.* Use a daily morning message to greet your students and put them in the role of editor. Using previously taught conventions as your guide, intentionally misplace punctuation, misspell or misuse words, or omit capitalizations.

Remind your students that writers need "editors" and that you need them to edit your message. After reading the message aloud, open the floor for questions and allow the "editors" to do their work in community. (Grades 1–2)

3. *Knowledge of Language Anchor Standards.* Use peer coaching to support students' use of procedural language. Each week, choose a small group of students and teach them a classroom routine, such as how to gather a set of supplies or how to use a new learning center. Then charge these "coaches" with the task of teaching the rest of the class, two students per coach, throughout the course of the week. Language associated with gathering supplies for free art might be: "First, get a tray. Then put your supplies on the tray. You can collect one pair of scissors, one magazine, two pieces of construction paper, and one glue stick. Then take the tray to your desk. When you're finished, return the supplies and the tray." Use a wall chart with reminder words and pictures as a support both for the coach and those learning the routine. Watch for growth in procedural language, as children begin to own this particular type of language used for authentic purposes. (PreK–grade 2)

4. *Vocabulary Acquisition and Use Anchor Standard—Focus on Strategies for Independence.* Create a T-chart with the words *happy*, *fair*, and *safe* in the left column and *unhappy*, *unfair*, and *unsafe* in the right column. Tell students that they are about to be given a key to unlock the meaning of certain words. Explain that certain words have a few letters at the beginning, called prefixes, and that they will focus on one prefix: "un-." Explain how knowing the meaning of the word in the left column, combined with the meaning of the prefix, gives them the meaning of the word on the right. Discuss the examples and then work with children to come up with other examples such as *uneven* and *unreal*. Use any nonexamples suggested by your students (e.g., *under*) as an opportunity to explain that "un-" at the beginning of a word is only a prefix when it is attached to letters that make up a full word on their own. In small groups, have children draw pictures for each pair of words on the chart and then explain why they drew what they did for each pair (i.e., explaining *happy* vs. *unhappy*) (Kindergarten–grade 1)

5. *Vocabulary Acquisition and Use Anchor Standard—Focus on Word Relationships.* Read a book such as Van Fleet's *Fuzzy Yellow Ducklings* (1995). Using adjectives from the book (e.g., *furry*, *bumpy*, *scratchy*, *sticky*), create a large semantic map. Have students think of things that fit each concept category. For each item, write the word and attach a picture or drawing. Use this concept map to show relationships among words and how words and concepts can be classified. (PreK–kindergarten)

6. *Vocabulary Acquisition and Use Anchor Standard—Focus on Expressive Vocabulary.* Designate one day each week for word sightings (Beck et al., 2002). On this day, invite students to share instances when they've heard or seen key words discussed during instruction in other contexts. For a unit on safety, for example, students can share sightings of words such as *rules*, *safety*, and *obey*. Create a chart with one column per word and list the names of children who have sighted the word in the appropriate column. (Grades 1–2)

Questions

1. Consider the role of thematic instruction in preparing children to meet the language standards. Work with other teachers in your building to select one or more themes and, for each, brainstorm learning opportunities related to conventions of standard English, knowledge of language, and vocabulary acquisition and use.

2. This chapter has emphasized the importance of providing children with meaningful opportunities to use language; however, in many classrooms, there is far more teacher talk than student talk. Think through a recent day in your classroom. For each portion of the day, note the ways in which your students were engaged in talk. Next, note the ways in which you used *the context of their talk* to scaffold growth in their language knowledge and competence. Based on this self-analysis, think about ways you might improve your practice.

3. Think about the cultural and linguistic make-up of your classroom. Without taking a deficit perspective, what language strengths do your students bring to school? How can you affirm and build on these strengths in both words and in instructional action?

REFERENCES

Andrews, R., Torgeson, C., Beverton, S., Freeman, A., Locke, T., Low, G., et al. (2006). The effect of grammar teaching on writing development. *British Educational Research Journal, 32*, 39–55.

Bear, D., Invernizzi, M., Templeton, S., & Johnston, F. (2008). *Words their way: Word study for phonics, spelling, and vocabulary instruction* (4th ed.). Upper Saddle River, NJ: Prentice Hall.

Beck, I. L., & McKeown, M. G. (2007). Increasing young low-income children's oral vocabulary repertoires through rich and focused instruction. *Elementary School Journal, 107,* 251–271.

Beck, I. L., McKeown, M. G., & Kucan, L. (2002). *Bringing words to life: Robust vocabulary instruction.* New York: Guilford Press.

Beck, I. L., McKeown, M. G., & Kucan, L. (2008). *Creating robust vocabulary: Frequently asked questions and extended examples.* New York: Guilford Press.

Blaauw-Hara, M. (2006). Why our students need instruction in grammar, and how we should go about it. *Teaching English in the Two-Year College, 34,* 165–178.

Blachowicz, C. L. Z., & Fisher, P. J. (2010). *Teaching vocabulary in all classrooms* (4th ed.). Boston: Allyn & Bacon.

Bloom, L., & Lahey, M. (1978). *Language development and language disorders.* Somerset, NJ: Wiley.

Calfee, R. C., & Miller, R. G. (2007). Best practices in writing assessment. In S. Graham, C. A. MacArthur, & J. Fitzgerald (Eds.), *Best practices in writing instruction* (pp. 265–286). New York: Guilford Press.

Catts, H. W., Adlof, S. M., & Weismer, S. E. (2006). Language deficits in poor comprehenders: A case for the simple view of reading. *Journal of Speech, Language, and Hearing Research, 49,* 278–293.

Collins, M. F. (2010). ELL preschoolers' English vocabulary acquisition from storybook reading. *Early Childhood Research Quarterly, 25,* 84–97.

Cordiero, P. (1988). Children's punctuation: An analysis of errors in period placement. *Research in the Teaching of English, 22,* 62–74.

Cunningham, A. E. (2005). Vocabulary growth through independent reading and reading aloud to children. In E. H. Hiebert & M. Kamil (Eds.), *Teaching and learning vocabulary: Bringing research to practice* (pp. 45–68). Mahwah, NJ: Erlbaum.

Cutting, L. E., & Scarborough, H. S. (2006). Prediction of reading comprehension: Relative contributions of word recognition, language proficiency, and other cognitive skills can depend on how comprehension is measured. *Scientific Studies of Reading, 10*, 277–299.

Dale, E. (1965). Vocabulary measurement: Techniques and major findings. *Elementary English, 42*, 895–901.

Delpit, L. (1995). *Other people's children: Cultural conflict in the classroom.* New York: New Press.

Elley, W. B. (1989). Vocabulary acquisition from listening to stories. *Reading Research Quarterly, 24*, 174–187.

Fearn, L., & Farnan, N. (2007). When is a verb? Using functional grammar to teach writing. *Journal of Basic Writing, 26*, 63–87.

Ferreiro, E. (1984). The underlying logic of literacy development. In H. Goelmann, A. A. Oberg, & F. Smith (Eds.), *Awakening to literacy* (pp. 154–173). Portsmouth, NH: Heinemann.

Ferreiro, E., & Teberosky, A. (1982). *Literacy before schooling.* New York: Heinemann.

Fisher, D., & Frey, N. (2010). Unpacking the language purpose: Vocabulary, structure, and function. *TESOL Journal, 1*(3), 315–337.

Graves, D. H. (1983). *Writing: Teachers and children at work.* Exeter, NH: Heinemann.

Graves, M. F. (2006). *The vocabulary book: Learning and instruction.* New York: Teachers College Press.

Helman, L. (2009). Effective instructional practices for English learners. In L. Helman (Ed.), *Literacy development with English learners: Research-based instruction in Grades K–6* (pp. 234–251). New York: Guilford Press.

Kim, Y., Al-Otaiba, S., Puranik, C., Folsom, J., Gruelich, L., & Wagner, R. (2011). Componential skills of beginning writing: An exploratory study. *Learning and Individual Differences, 21*, 517–525.

Montgomery, J. W., & Evans, J. L. (2009). Complex sentence comprehension and working memory in children with specific language impairment. *Journal of Speech, Language, and Hearing Research, 52*, 269–288.

Nagy, W. E., & Herman, P. A. (1987). Depth and breadth of vocabulary knowledge: Implications for acquisition and instruction. In M. G. McKeown & M. E. Curtis (Eds.), *The nature of vocabulary acquisition* (pp. 19–35). Hillsdale, NJ: Erlbaum.

Nagy, W. E., & Scott, J. A. (2000). Vocabulary processes. In M. L. Kamil, P. B. Mosenthal, P. D. Pearson, & R. Barr (Eds.), *Handbook of reading research* (Vol. III, pp. 269–284). New York: Longman.

National Council of Teachers of English. (2008). *Writing now: A policy research brief produced by the National Council of Teachers of English.* Urbana, IL: Author.

Rescorla, L. (2009). Age 17 language and reading outcomes in late-talking toddlers: Support for a dimensional perspective on language delay. *Journal of Speech, Language, and Hearing Research, 52*, 16–30.

Saddler, B., & Graham, S. (2005). The effects of peer-assisted sentence-combining instruction on the writing performance of more and less skilled young writers. *Journal of Educational Psychology, 97*, 43–54.

Scott, C. (2009). A case for the sentence in reading comprehension. *Language, Speech, and Hearing Services in Schools, 40*, 184–191.

Scott, C. M., & Windsor, J. (2000). General language performance measures in spoken and written narrative and expository discourse of school-age children with language learning disabilities. *Journal of Speech, Language, and Hearing Research, 43*, 324–339.

Stahl, S. A., & Nagy, W. E. (2006). *Teaching word meanings.* Mahwah, NJ: Erlbaum.

Stauffer, R. G. (1970). *The language experience approach to the teaching of reading.* New York: Harper & Row.

Strickland, D., & Schickedanz, J. (2004). *Learning about print in preschool: Working with letters, words, and beginning links with phonemic awareness.* Newark, DE: International Reading Association.

Vukelich, C., Christie, J., & Enz, B. (2012). *Helping young children learn language and literacy: Birth through kindergarten* (3rd ed.). Boston: Pearson.

Wollman-Bonilla, J. (2000). *Family message journals: Teaching writing through family involvement.* Urbana, IL: National Council of Teachers of English.

CHILDREN'S BOOKS CITED

Base, G. (1996). *Animalia.* New York: Puffin.

Charlip, R. (1993). *Fortunately.* New York: Aladdin.

Crews, D. (1993). *School bus.* New York: Greenwillow.

Day, A. (1988). *Frank and Ernest.* New York: Scholastic.

DeGross, M. (1994). *Donavan's word jar.* New York: Harper.

Geisel, T. (1957). *The cat in the hat.* New York: Random House.

Gwynne, F. (1988). *A chocolate moose for dinner.* New York: Aladdin.

Heller, R. (1998). *A cache of jewels and other collective nouns.* New York: Puffin.

Orloff, K., & Catrow, D. (2004). *I wanna iguana.* New York: Putnam.

Pfister, M. (1992). *The rainbow fish.* New York: North-South Books.

Polacco, P. (1988). *The keeping quilt.* New York: Aladdin.

Prelutsky, J. (1983). *The Random House book of poetry.* New York: Random House.

Rathman, P. (1995). *Officer Buckle and Gloria.* New York: Putnam.

Rylant, C. (1990). *Henry and Mudge and the happy cat.* New York: Scholastic.

Scieszka, J. (1996). *The true story of the three little pigs.* New York: Puffin.

Steinberg, L. (2003). *Thesaurus Rex.* Cambridge, MA: Barefoot Books.

Thompson, S. (2003). *Stars and stripes: The story of the American flag.* New York: HarperCollins.

Van Fleet, M. (1995). *Fuzzy yellow ducklings.* New York: Penguin.

CHAPTER 8

Technology and the Common Core Standards

Michael C. McKenna

Kristin Conradi

Craig A. Young

Bong Gee Jang

The Common Core State Standards (CCSS) do not contain a separate technology strand, a fact that might at first suggest a relative lack of importance. Nothing could be further from the truth. Broadly, the college and career readiness anchor standards for K–5 reading include expectations that students integrate content found in digital formats, that they be critical evaluators of content found online and represented in visual formats, and that they strategically use technology, digital media, and visual displays in their presentations. In this way, the standards mark a decided and deliberate shift from a more traditional perspective of reading based solely on printed text.

The standards carry with them expectations that to be literate in the 21st-century students must be adept negotiators of multiple modes and formats. In fact, even in the primary grades, the English language arts (ELA) standards are infused with expectations that involve technology. In this chapter, we address the K–2 standards as they relate to technology and discuss their implications for preschool through second grade. Specifically, we (1) examine issues related to integrating technology into the literacy standards, (2) identify points at which the CCSS explicitly call for the use of technology, (3) interpret the intent of these standards, and (4) describe approaches fulfilling that intent.

DEFINING THE STANDARDS INVOLVING TECHNOLOGY: EXPLORING TERMS AND ISSUES

Because technology integration does not have a strand of its own and because its mention in specific standards is somewhat subtle, we have identified in Table 8.1 the grades, areas, and standards for which its use is explicit.

TABLE 8.1. Technology Use in the CCSS for ELA, Grades K–2

Area	Standard	Kindergarten	Grade 1	Grade 2
Literature	7			Use information gained from the illustrations and words in a print or digital text to demonstrate understanding of its characters, setting, or plot.
Informational text	5		Know and use various text features (e.g., headings, tables of contents, glossaries, electronic menus, icons) to locate key facts or information in a text.	Know and use various text features (e.g., captions, bold print, subheadings, glossaries, indexes, electronic menus, icons) to locate key facts or information in a text efficiently.
Writing	6	With guidance and support from adults, explore a variety of digital tools to produce and publish writing, including in collaboration with peers.	With guidance and support from adults, use a variety of digital tools to produce and publish writing, including in collaboration with peers.	With guidance and support from adults, use a variety of digital tools to produce and publish writing, including in collaboration with peers.
Speaking and Listening	2	Confirm understanding of a text read aloud or information presented orally or through other media by asking and answering questions about key details and requesting clarification if something is not understood.	Ask and answer questions about key details in a text read aloud or information presented orally or through other media.	Recount or describe key ideas or details from a text read aloud or information presented orally or through other media.
	5	Add drawings or other visual displays to descriptions as desired to provide additional detail.	Add drawings or other visual displays to descriptions when appropriate to clarify ideas, thoughts, and feelings.	Create audio recordings of stories or poems; add drawings or other visual displays to stories or recounts of experiences when appropriate to clarify ideas, thoughts, and feelings.
Language	4			Determine or clarify the meaning of unknown and multiple-meaning words and phrases based on *grade 2 reading and content*, choosing flexibly from an array of strategies. Use glossaries and beginning dictionaries, both print and digital, to determine or clarify the meaning of words and phrases.

The frequency and variety of these references underscore the importance of engaging young children in digital as well as print settings. The advent of electronic media necessitates that children not only experience meaningful engagement with text in both print and digital formats, but also become adept at evaluating nontextual presentations of information. Furthermore, children are expected to employ technology both as a resource and as a format for presenting their own information, even in kindergarten.

The anchor standards and the K–2 standards use a variety of terms: Students are called on to *explore, use, gather, interact, integrate, evaluate, publish,* and *collaborate,* taking advantage of and employing *media, visual displays,* and *audio recordings.* In Figure 8.1, we present a word cloud, created at *www.tagxedo.com,* that visually depicts the terms related to technology both in the more general K–5 anchor standards and in the K–2 standards specifically. Words that appear bigger in the cloud appear more frequently in the standards. We find that CCSS word usage is deliberately broad, opening the door to multimedia as an important avenue of learning, either alone or in conjunction with text.

Before moving into the specific applications of the technology-related standards, we feel it is important first to address four issues. We believe that embracing technology in PreK–2 literacy instruction depends on (1) our willingness to believe in the relevance of technology in these grades, (2) our abilitiy to nurture students' growing understanding and use of technology across the early grade levels, (3) our capacity to provide all students with access to technology and teachers with the professional development required to use it, and (4) our knowledge of best practices as informed by research.

Issues of Relevance

Teachers in the early grades tend to vary in the value they ascribe to technology integration (e.g., Castek & Gwinn, 2012; Turbill & Murray, 2006). Indeed, some argue that technology does not belong in the classroom at all, insisting that kids need "real" books, not gadgets, and that computers serve only to distract students from authentic literacy experiences. However, this resistance is problematic for at least two reasons. First, the world in which we are preparing children to live and work is increasingly dominated by digital settings. Second, rejection of technology in favor of conventional print ignores the reality that students are entering school already familiar with digital literacies. Wohlwend (2010) observes that "when young children come to school, they often have to check their technoliteracies at the classroom door" (p. 145) because the instruction they receive takes place in a low-tech environment. As the new standards make clear, achieving them requires a broader perspective of what counts as reading.

FIGURE 8.1. Word cloud of technology terms used in the K–2 CCSS.

Issues of Vertical Articulation

Because technology is not addressed as a distinct area in the CCSS, it may be difficult to infer an incremental sophistication of its use by students. Such increments are often implicit in the wordings of the standards from grade to grade, but the principal focus of the ELA standards is literacy rather than technology. As an example, Standard 6 for writing addresses a "variety of digital tools to produce and publish writing" (see Table 8.1). At the kindergarten level, children are required to "explore" such tools; at first and second grades, they must "use" them. The shift from exploring to using indicates growth in proficiency to be sure, but the standards at grades 1 and 2 are worded identically. Both include the verb *use*. We suggest that growth is still implied, but that it will be evident in the products children create. In Figure 8.2 we present a possible articulation of the Standard 6 for writing as students move across the grades. We situate the figure in the gradual-release model (Pearson & Gallagher, 1983).

Issues of Access and Training

Of course, meeting the new standards also requires access to the technology itself. The extent of such access, in terms of amount and variety, has expanded rapidly since the arrival of the first microcomputers during the 1980s. By the end of the first decade of the 21st century, 100% of American public schools had at least one instructional computer with Internet access, and the average ratio of students to computers was 3.1:1 (Gray & Lewis, 2009). Additionally, 97% of schools had either LCD or DLP projectors, 73% had an interactive white board, and 93% had a digital camera (Gray & Lewis, 2009). These numbers, although impressive, describe a level of access that is not yet universal. Whether the CCSS will provide an impetus for attaining universal access remains to be seen, but it is clear that the standards cannot be achieved without sufficient access to technology.

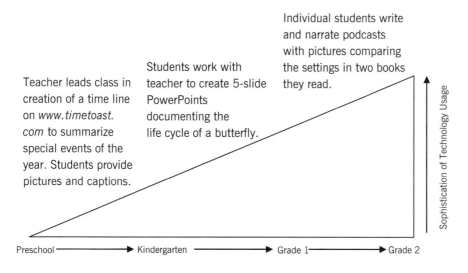

FIGURE 8.2. Vertical articulation of CCSS Writing 6.

Additionally, even if we ensure that all schools have the appropriate technology and Internet access, teachers still must know how to employ the tools effectively in their classrooms. Although most teachers entering the profession today have no recollection of a world without the Internet and technology, this familiarity hardly translates into instructional planning grounded in the knowledge of which applications to include and when (O'Brien & Scharber, 2010). In short, professional development is imperative (Barone & Wright, 2008; Chen & Chang, 2006; Hutchison & Reinking, 2011; Wang, Kinzie, McGuire, & Pan, 2010). Our hope is that the providers of professional development (and literacy coaches in particular) will expend the effort needed to make technology integration a priority (1) for standards that demand its use and (2) for other standards where technology offers a value-added affordance over conventional instruction.

Issues of Best Practice

The fact that the standards oblige teachers to use technology consequently raises questions about best practice. Although research syntheses suggest that reading instruction involving technology is effective (e.g., Blok, Oostdam, Otter, & Overmatt, 2002; Burnett, 2009; Cheung & Slavin, 2011), the traditional process of research validation is hampered by the speed of change. Findings that might guide educators about a particular program or application may not apply to subsequent versions that address problems in a formative manner and that may employ newer hardware. Perhaps the best we can do is seek out applications that embody the principles of good pedagogy.

Some researchers have investigated adapting techniques validated in print environments to digital settings. Linda Labbo's work with approaches such as the Author's Chair (Labbo, 2004), the Morning Message (Labbo, 2005), and the language experience approach (Labbo, Eakle, & Montero, 2002) has demonstrated an advantage when these approaches are undertaken in digital environments. Others have recommended applying the more general findings of literacy research to software design and evaluation, such as the broad body of investigations grounding effective instruction in decoding and fluency (Kuhn & Stahl, 2006). Taking these sources together, we believe that enough is known about the likely effectiveness of applications to offer guidance in meeting the demands of the CCSS.

PUTTING THE STANDARDS INTO PRACTICE

Our inspection of the technology expectations reflected in Table 8.1 reveals recurring applications of three basic kinds: (1) comprehending texts in digital settings (literature, Standard 7, grade 2; speaking and listening, Standard 2, grades K–2); (2) generating texts in digital settings (writing, Standard 6, grades K–2; speaking and listening, Standard 5, grades K–2); and (3) using features available in digital settings (information text, Standard 5, grades 1–2; language, Standard 4, grade 2). We find these categories helpful in planning for systematic technology integration.

Comprehending Texts in Digital Settings

The CCSS acknowledge throughout that students will read in both traditional print and digital settings. We define reading in digital settings to include adult-supported reading of e-storybooks, students reading on the computer, students listening to text read aloud via the computer, and students reading on handheld devices, such as iPads and Kindles. The evident engagement of the first grader shown reading on a tablet in Figure 8.3 suggests the viability of such platforms in the primary grades.

Although early research raised concerns about reading in digital settings (Labbo & Kuhn, 2000), an extensive body of subsequent research has demonstrated that digital environments are at least as effective as their print counterparts and frequently more so (Larson, 2010; Moody, Justice, & Cabell, 2010; Morrow, 2010; Segal-Drori, Korat, Shamir, & Klein, 2010; Shamir, Korat, & Fellah, 2010; Tracy & Young, 2007). For example, Moody and colleagues (2010) examined differences in engagement and story-book interactions in Head Start classrooms when e-storybooks were used versus traditional storybooks. They found that students demonstrated significantly higher levels of persistence with e-readers and found no significant differences in comprehension. Likewise, Larson (2010) examined second graders as they read on Kindles and noted that students not only were motivated but were more likely to take notes while reading. Larson suggested additional benefits for struggling readers with expandable dictionaries, text-to-speech options, and note-taking capabilities.

Because digital environments can include multimedia, we can easily link comprehension of written and oral language. In the following vignette, for example, a kindergartner listens to a read-aloud while following the text. At the same time, highlighting reinforces concepts of print. Note that technology also makes it possible for students to record their impressions long before they are able to articulate them through writing.

FIGURE 8.3. First grader reading from a tablet.

SPEAKING AND LISTENING—ANCHOR STANDARD 2

- **PreK–K:** **Confirm understanding of a text read aloud or information presented orally or through other media by asking and answering questions about key details and requesting clarification if something is not understood.**

- **Grade 1:** **Ask and answer questions about key details in a text read aloud or information presented orally or through other media.**

- **Grade 2:** **Recount or describe key ideas or details from a text read aloud or information presented orally or through other media.**

Miss Carlsen uses several websites in her kindergarten classroom's reading center. A perennial favorite is the "Stories" tab on KOL, Jr.[1] Here, her students can find a series of rhyming books[2] and several books about Arthur,[3] among other reading sources. Having established the routine for the listening center earlier in the year, her students show confidence in participating in an individualized read-aloud experience with the computer.

After sitting at the computer station and putting on headphones, Leilani selects the rhyming stories shortcut on the desktop. This week, her reading group is reading along with *One Hungry Monster* by Susan Heyboer O'Keefe (Lynn Munsinger, illus.). As the text is read aloud, the words appear in red, allowing Leilani to track the text easily. Once she has finished reading, she conferences with Miss Carlsen.

"What story did you read, Leilani?" Miss Carlsen asks.

"*One Hungry Monster.* I really like that one," replies Leilani.

"I like that story, too. Can you tell me about it?"

"Yeah. There is a boy and a lot of monsters live in his house and he has to feed them because they are really hungry."

"Good. Those monsters sure are hungry."

"Uh-huh. I wonder why they're so hungry."

"Leilani, that is a wonderful question. I bet other people who have read the story might have the same question. Today, I want you to post that as our reading center focus question."

The students are familiar with the focus question. Every day, a new student uses a voice recorder to record a question they have about the story being read. Miss Carlsen uses a checklist to ensure that each group member poses at least one question for each book read. A mini-conference, like the one just described, lets Miss Carlsen check her students' comprehension of the story. It also allows her to assist her students' framing a question to pose to their peers. Once the question is posted, all of the other students listen to the focus question and record their answers. Over the course of several days, students experience the same book and have an opportunity to answer all of the focus questions. Miss Carlsen listens to the responses, noting misconceptions that need to be addressed and interesting takes on the story that can be further explored during small-group story time. After this final debriefing in their small group, a new book is selected for the reading center.

---

[1] *http://kids.aol.com/KOL/1/KOLJr.*

[2] *http://kids.aol.com/KOL/2/koljrstories/archive/rhyming-stories.*

[3] *http://kids.aol.com/KOL/2/koljrstories/archive/arthur-stories.*

Generating Texts in Digital Settings

By the first and second grades, the CCSS expect children to be able to use multimedia tools to present their learning. (Likewise, it is reasonable to expect that children in PreK and kindergarten can be cocreators of digital presentations with their teachers.) A suite of presentation software and Web 2.0 tools make multimodal presentations easy, and research has accordingly highlighted their potential in the early childhood classroom. Studies have shown the effectiveness of PowerPoint in the creation of nonlinear texts (Kervin & Mantei, 2010), e-storybooks in engaging and empowering students as authors (Gabriel & Gabriel, 2010), digital photography and creativity software for the digital language experience approach (Labbo et al., 2002), and digital story creation to facilitate the development of students' writing abilities (Sylvester & Greenidge, 2009). Clearly, students of all ages and abilities can use technology to generate language.

We intentionally use the word *generate* because it includes oral and written counterparts, both of which are integral to many of the digital applications now available to young children. A child may listen to a story and then record a spoken response, as in the case of Miss Carlsen's class. But generating language can also include keyboarded text, speech-to-text products, and combinations of text and other media. In the following vignette, second graders begin with a story they have written, using it to anchor a creative multimedia extension of their expression. To accomplish this goal, they produce a digital story using *www.voicethread.com*, a Web application for selecting documents, pictures, or other media. Through this tool, they create a voiceover that links and explains these components.

SPEAKING AND LISTENING—ANCHOR STANDARD 5

- **PreK–K:** Add drawings or other visual displays to descriptions as desired to provide additional detail.

- **Grade 1:** Add drawings or other visual displays to descriptions when appropriate to clarify ideas, thoughts, and feelings.

- **Grade 2:** Create audio recordings of stories or poems; add drawings or other visual displays to stories or recounts of experiences when appropriate to clarify ideas, thoughts, and feelings

As part of reading and writing workshop, Mr. Nardi introduces a digital storytelling center with his second-grade class. They join him in the class meeting area, where he has set up one of the class laptops with speakers and a headset with a microphone. "Good morning, writers. In our exploration of narratives, you have written many stories. Today, I am going to share with you a story that I created entitled 'Getting Lost,' and we are going to look at how we can use pictures to make our stories better." Mr. Nardi opens a voicethread that he created for today's mini-lesson. The voicethread contains several pictures that Mr. Nardi uploaded from his computer and some that he found using a Google Image search. In conjunction with the pictures, Mr. Nardi has recorded a story he wrote recounting an incident that happened when he was a young boy and got separated from his family while on summer vacation at the beach. The students listen attentively to find out what happened. At the end of the story,

Mr. Nardi leads a discussion of this new digital experience. "What do you think of my story, Steph?"

"I was scared when you couldn't find your family. The picture of the little boy crying helped me picture how you felt when you were lost."

Ben adds, "I've never been to the beach. Seeing pictures of the sand and the . . . um, the place with all the people and the video games . . . "

"The boardwalk?" Mr. Nardi assists.

"Yeah, the boardwalk. That really helped me know what you were seeing and that made the story feel real," Ben exclaims.

"That's good. Sometimes pictures help readers understand what writers mean. They help make the author's thoughts and feelings clearer," Mr. Nardi explains. "This is what we are going to focus on during our writing workshop. Each of you is going to select a story that you have published in class and create a voicethread. You may draw your own illustrations or work on the computer to look for pictures and images that help show the ideas, thoughts, and feelings that your words say."

Over the course of the next few days during reading and writing workshop, Mr. Nardi conferences with each student as they make and select pictures for their stories. In mini-lessons, he models uploading the pictures and recording comments using the microphone. As students complete their own voicethreads, they share their work on tablets while sitting at the Author's Chair and receive feedback from their peers.

Because generating oral language is a goal in preschool, technology applications are a natural fit. Although Mr. Nardi's use of a voicethread is too sophisticated for 4-year-olds, a simplified version is developmentally appropriate. The next vignette illustrates how the language experience approach, long a mainstay of beginning reading instruction, can be easily adapted for digital environments. Students discuss still pictures taken during a field trip, select those that contribute to a narrative of events, and then generate captions, which the teacher writes.

WRITING—ANCHOR STANDARD 6

- **PreK–K:**   **With guidance and support from adults, explore a variety of digital tools to produce and publish writing, including in collaboration with peers.**

- **Grade 1:**   **With guidance and support from adults, use a variety of digital tools to produce and publish writing, including in collaboration with peers.**

- **Grade 2:**   **With guidance and support from adults, use a variety of digital tools to produce and publish writing, including in collaboration with peers.**

Mr. Mahidi regularly schedules field trips to a local farm for his preschool class, and finds these trips a perfect opportunity to implement the digital language experience approach (Labbo et al., 2002) with his students. Every spring, the class visits the farm as part of their exploration of how things grow. Throughout the morning, Mr. Mahidi takes pictures of the students as they take a tour, talk with the farmer, and help plant seeds. He purposefully captures images both of individual students and students in groups.

Upon returning to school, the students review and discuss the pictures to decide which ones best illustrate the activities of the day. Once the pictures are selected and placed in sequence, Mr. Mahidi asks the students pictured to provide a caption for each. Individual students dictate their own captions, while small groups of students work together to create an appropriate description of their picture. Mr. Mahidi acts as scribe—embedding the captions on each picture, using an application such as roflbot[1] or captioner.[2]

As the pictures are captioned, Mr. Mahidi leads the class in reading the story through the captions. After the photo story is completed, the class uses the text and pictures as a shared-reading activity. Additionally, Mr. Mahidi makes a printout for each student so that they can practice reading at home and during silent reading time, and he puts a copy on each of the classroom computers in the class digital library so that students gain practice reading the story in both digital and print formats.

[1] *http://wigflip.com/roflbot/.*
[2] *http://bighugelabs.com/captioner.php.*

Digital Supports and Text Complexity

The standards recognize that the texts children face will grow steadily more complex throughout their school experience. To help them meet the challenge of ever-increasing text complexity, teachers must gradually, but relentlessly, raise the bar by selecting texts that push students to read in settings with higher demands. The goal, however, is to challenge without frustrating or discouraging. We believe digital settings have much to offer in reducing the risk of frustration by offering supports that are distracting or unavailable in print settings. When these supports are used in concert, young children can comprehend texts that are surprisingly complex. In fact, McKenna (1998) has suggested that texts with "electronic scaffolding" (p. 47) blur the traditional distinction among the independent, instructional, and frustration levels. Young children are able to read independently texts with digital support that would be frustrating in traditional print environments. For most children, reliance on basic skill scaffolds would decline over time; for those who experience persistent difficulties, such scaffolds offer an affordance that may play a "prosthetic" role through assistive technology (McKenna & Walpole, 2007).

The supportive features found in traditional print books (e.g., table of contents, glossary, index) have digital counterparts. In either setting, some explicit instruction is needed to acquaint students with how to use these features strategically. In addition, it is important that teachers emphasize two differences between print and digital environments. First, the same features may be used in different ways. A table of contents may appear as a sidebar, for example, visible at all times. In the vignette that follows, a first-grade teacher points out that the glossary of a print book is located at the end but does not have a "location" in a digital book. Instead, word meanings are accessed on a point-and-click (or point-and-touch) basis without the reader having to leave the text. Second, some of the features available in digital settings do not have counterparts in print. A particular text, for example, may include on-demand pronunciations, listening options, simplified text, hyperlinked video and audio clips, and links to Internet sources. We cannot assume that children will figure out these resources on their own, which is why the CCSS address their use specifically.

INFORMATIONAL TEXT—ANCHOR STANDARD 5

- **Grade 1:** **Know and use various text features (e.g., headings, tables of contents, glossaries, electronic menus, icons) to locate key facts or information in a text.**

- **Grade 2:** **Know and use various text features (e.g., captions, bold print, subheadings, glossaries, indexes, electronic menus, icons) to locate key facts or information in a text efficiently.**

As part of her reading workshop, Ms. Holohan introduces her first graders to many types of texts in both print and digital formats. This week, she is reinforcing her students' abilities to interact with digital nonfiction texts at the class computer station. After several experiences reading nonfiction big books together, the students are familiar with identifying and using a table of contents and glossary. However, she wants to make sure that her students can transfer this knowledge and access and utilize text features in an online resource. Today, she is working with a small group of students as they navigate an online text using digital features. The children are collaboratively conducting research for a report on dolphins.

"Welcome back to our computer center. I know that you have been looking up information on dolphins, and I found a book that I want you to see. I've put an icon on the desktop that is going to lead you to this book that I found in our TumbleBooks Library.[1] Ginny, please click on the link and let the book load." While the book loads, Ms. Holohan reviews the parts of the nonfiction text with the group, reminding them that nonfiction books do not always need to be read in order.

"OK. Ginny, what information are you looking for about dolphins?"

Looking at the graphic organizer she was given in writing workshop, Ginny explains, "Umm . . . I want to know . . . how do they talk?"

"Great. Do you think you will need to read the whole book to find that out?"

"No?"

"No. Where could you look?"

Alice and Max, Ginny's group partners, eagerly raise their hands to offer help. Ginny looks at the screen and at Ms. Holohan, who points to the Contents icon in the upper left-hand corner of the screen. "Umm . . . the table of contents?"

"Excellent, Ginny. If you don't want to read the whole book, you can look at the table of contents. This lets you skip to the part of the book that you need to read in order to find out what you want to know. You can skip, using the "forward" and "backward" icons on the bottom left and right sides of the screen." The students have used the class CD players to listen to books before and can easily identify and utilize these buttons.

Ms. Holohan checks with Alice and Max about the information they seek. The children then decide to read the book aloud with each other. Before leaving to work with another group, Ms. Holohan gives a reminder. "If you get stuck, you can toggle the sound on by clicking the volume button on the screen. Then the narrator will help you out." Ms. Holohan also reminds the group that the meaning of an unknown word can often be found in a book's glossary. "In a print book," she tells them, "the glossary is at the end, but on the computer the glossary is built in so that you don't need to leave the page. You can click on any word that's underlined and find out what it means right away."

Once Ginny, Alice, and Max have found the information they need, they move back to their writing desks to organize their information. The trio writes and draws pictures that explain what they have learned before sharing it with the class.

---

[1]The subscription to this website costs about $500 per school.

USING THE K–2 TECHNOLOGY-RELATED STANDARDS THROUGHOUT THE SCHOOL DAY

As we noted earlier, the CCSS reference technology throughout rather than providing a specific set of standards for technology. One reason for this is that reading in the 21st century will occur in both print and digital settings. Likewise, locating and presenting knowledge will utilize multiple modes of literacy (moving beyond just text) and will take advantage of the affordances provided by software and the Internet. This seamless integration can and should begin in the primary grades and preschool. In this section, we highlight, through a fifth and extended vignette, how the technology-related CCSS can be integrated throughout the school day.

In PreK and kindergarten, teachers will likely take the lead in the use of technology. Ms. Lofgren's kindergarten class, immersed in a unit on winter, is reading *Bear Snores On* by Karma Wilson. In her preview of the text, Ms. Lofgren notices the word *lair* on the first page and recognizes that it is likely an unknown word. She goes online to Google Images and quickly pulls up two pictures of dens: a bear den and a comfortable den in someone's house. Following her book introduction, but prior to reading the book, she quickly tells her students:

> "In this book we're going to find the word *lair*. A lair is a place where a wild animal lives. A lair is also called a den. When I want to make a picture in my mind of what a word is, I sometimes go online for that information. This time, I went online to find a couple of pictures of dens to help us remember that a lair is a den. When I saw the pictures, I remembered that a den can also be a room in a house. Maybe you have a den in your house, like this picture. [Shows picture.] In this book, the author is referring to a bear's den. Now, that's a little different, isn't it? Here is an example of a bear's den, which we might also call a lair. What is this again? A lair. [Points to bear's den.]"

Later in the day, Ms. Lofgren wants to connect her read-aloud to her science lesson on hibernation. She begins by showing students a very short Sesame Street segment she found on YouTube that defines *hibernation* (see *www.youtube.com/watch?v=AWmckQoDaNE*). Next, the class reads an information book, *Hibernation* by Robin Nelson. Ms. Lofgren leads the class in extending their understanding of the concept. She asks each student to draw a picture of what they would dream about if they hibernated for the winter. The students talk with their table groups about where their lair would be and what things they would miss through the winter or look forward to in the spring. After brainstorming, the students draw a picture of themselves in their lair with a thought bubble picture of their dream.

The next day, Ms. Lofgren's students bring their pictures to the class dramatic play center, which Ms. Lofgren has filled with pillows, blankets, and stuffed bears. She asks each student to nestle in to have their picture taken as if they are hibernating. After Ms. Lofgren takes a picture of each student, she asks the students to dictate a sentence explaining what he or she will dream about. She inserts the photographs, the students' pictures, and their recorded sentences into a digital story maker. The students can then access the digital storybook through the class website.

At the tablet station later that week, students listen to their book and read along, familiarizing themselves with the repetitive nature of the text, finger-pointing as they recite each other's lines, and delighting in the creativity of the class as well as in seeing themselves and their ideas in print and online.

Resources

As demonstrated in the brief snapshot of Ms. Lofgren's kindergarten class and in the vignettes presented earlier in this chapter, effective teachers employ digital resources seamlessly in their instruction and never simply "for the sake of using technology." Our symbaloo site (*www.symbaloo.com/shared/ccs--tech*) contains an extensive list of websites and applications that can be used to teach the K–2 technology-related standards and their natural extension into preschool.

Assessment

A much-discussed problem with digital literacies is the failure to assess progress (Barone & Wright, 2008). We understand that the lack of specificity regarding which tools children will use and how they will orchestrate their use may be a little disconcerting, particularly when it comes to assessing students' proficiency. Standards that explicitly address a progression of technology applications related to literacy have been developed elsewhere and range from basic to advanced (e.g., Leu et al., 2008), and we encourage readers to examine this source for a more fully elaborated list of proficiencies.

In grades K–2, we recommend three types of assessments. The first is formative: Teachers should keep anecdotal records of students' initial familiarity with technology, their willingness to use it, and the frequency with which they use the computers and tools in the classroom. Teachers should also monitor students' proficiency at specific technology applications. Although preschoolers and kindergarten students are not expected to work independently on digital projects, the CCSS acknowledge that students in the first and second grades should be able to use a variety of tools. Following instruction in how to perform various tasks involving technology, teachers can quickly complete specific (but differentiated) checklists of expectations for each task or application. We provide an example in Figure 8.4. Creating a checklist like this one can be useful in building an awareness of what students can do and where they need support.

Finally—and particularly because the standards acknowledge a vertical articulation of the ease with which students will use technology—we recommend incorporating electronic portfolios to track students' growth and progress. Such a portfolio could serve as an electronic collection of students' products across the year. It might include, for example, podcasts, digital presentations, and visual displays.

CONCLUSION

As we close this chapter, it is important to point out the limits of technology within the K–2 ELA standards. It is true that the CCSS infuse technology into many of the standards rather than relegating it to a separate strand. However, this does not mean that technology applies to all standards. Given the expectation for technology applications across many areas and standards, an understandable response would simply be to integrate technology as much as possible into literacy instruction, endeavoring to find ways to apply it to nearly every activity. However, this sweeping interpretation is not the

VOICETHREAD PROFICIENCY CHECKLIST				
Assignment: Students will independently create voicethreads describing their wants versus needs, incorporating at least five images and five sentences. **Addressing CCSS**: Writing 6				
	With significant teacher support	With some teacher support	With peer support	Independently
Accessed the website				
Signed in				
Uploaded images				
Added audio				
Published end product				
End product demonstrated thoughtful integration of image and audio				
End product demonstrated awareness of an audience				

FIGURE 8.4. Example of a teacher-created technology proficiency rubric for grade 2.

intent. In the primary grades, there are 122 ELA standards—across all areas at all three grades—and yet only 13 of these (about one in 10) involve the use of technology. Of these 13, 10 include both digital and nondigital settings. (The three exceptions involve the use of digital writing tools.) Consequently, there was clearly no assumption on the part of the framers that technology use involves an automatic value-added dimension. Rather, the expectation of the CCSS is that teachers will prepare children for literacy in both settings.

In this chapter, we made a case for technology integration on the basis of its particular relevance for young children. We argued that digital settings are already a familiar part of children's lives and will eventually dominate the environments in which they will work. An early start at school, however, requires that technology use progress in a coherent manner from PreK through second grade. Nevertheless, the existence of vertically articulated standards begs the questions of whether access to technology is universal and whether teacher expertise in how to use it is adequate.

We then turned to the issue of best practice and summarized the limited research available regarding young children. Although rapid technological advances make researching technology use difficult, encouraging conclusions are nonetheless warranted. Using vignettes, we suggested a number of instructional applications, ranging from PreK through second grade. These included comprehending and generating texts as well as using technology to scaffold ever-increasing text complexity. We then offered an additional vignette illustrating how the technology-related standards might be addressed throughout the day in a seamless manner. To encourage application of the techniques described, we offered a list of Web resources.

Finally, we described how technology proficiency might be delineated and assessed in relatively straightforward ways. We suggested three approaches to assessment. These included informal data gathering, the use of rubrics for key competencies, and portfolios.

ACTIVITIES AND QUESTIONS

Activities

1. *Literature Standard 7 (Grade 2)*: Create a bookmark on your classroom computers and tablets that includes links to online stories. Send students, in pairs, to computers to choose a story to read. Following the story, direct students to the Story Map student interactive at *www.readwritethink.org*. Here, students are guided step by step as they create maps about the story's characters, conflict, resolution, or setting. Question prompts provide appropriate scaffolding and probing for second graders.

2. *Writing Standard 6 (PreK–2)*: Consider creating a classroom blog through Google, Blogger, or WordPress. At first, you may have to lead in the writing of posts and uploading of pictures, but savvy first and second graders would love to be a part of this process. Send your students' parents the link to your blog and encourage them to comment on various posts. Using blogs with young students is motivating and can instill at an early age the power of communication and audience.

3. *Informational Text Anchor Standard 5 (Grades 1–2)*: Try conducting an extended think-aloud in which you model for children how to make strategic use of the features available on a website (e.g., how to use a table of contents). Begin by choosing a grade-appropriate site that contains the feature(s) you wish to emphasize. Remember that you will be modeling aloud how a proficient reader manages the use of such a feature and your language must make explicit what you have long taken for granted as a reader. Duffy (2009) has offered specific suggestions for language helpful in building students' declarative knowledge (what a table of contents is), procedural knowledge (how we should use a table of contents), and conditional knowledge (in what situations we would consult a table of contents). You will need to address all three types of knowledge in your think-aloud. Project the site and discuss what you expect to gain from your visit to it. Doing so will involve linking the feature to an objective ("Remember, we need to find out . . . "). Describe how you would go about taking stock of what you find on the home page ("First, I want to find out what's on this site, so I look for a list of topics. It's just like the table of contents in our book. Here

it is. This topic looks promising. It may have the information I want"). Pointing out the print counterparts of features whenever possible can lead to useful contrasts.

4. *Speaking and Listening Standard 5 (PreK–2)*: Following a read-aloud, ask your students to respond to the story by drawing a picture. Pictures can be drawn by hand or on various platforms such as Microsoft Drawing Tools, Google Docs, or KidPix. If students draw by hand, scan their pictures in and save them as picture files. Then pair students' work with audio descriptions using the very simple platform found on *www.yodio.com*. What we love about yodio is that you phone in your audio description. Create a free account from your classroom phone and have students call the number and provide their 1-minute audio description. Afterward, you can pair their pictures and audio stories for a wonderful podcast with pictures based on the book.

5. *Language Standard 4 (Grade 2)*: Model different ways of finding word meanings online. Show students (and bookmark) sites such as Merriam Webster's kid-friendly dictionary (*http://wordcentral.com*). Model exactly how you would look up a word and how you would make sense of the results. Consider, too, having your students make vocabulary videos (like those seen on *www.vocabahead.com* and other SAT vocabulary prep sites). In these videos, students provide a definition, act out a word's meaning, and provide a scenario where the word would be appropriately used. After uploading the videos to the computer, have students watch each other's videos. The process will be both motivating and reinforcing.

Questions

1. How would you counter the argument that kids need to learn to read first and that the development of technology proficiency should wait until after students are reading fluently?

2. As students move from PreK through second grade, the expectation is that they transition from exploring to the actual use of technology. What teacher scaffolding is needed for second-grade students to employ Web 2.0 tools effectively to create audio recordings or digital stories?

3. The CCSS clearly call for the integration of technology across grades and content areas. Are there any areas or activities for which technology should be avoided or, on the other hand, privileged above traditional print texts?

4. What are some of the technology-specific skills and strategies children need to learn in order to meet the expectations found in information text anchor Standard 5 (Grades 1–2)?

5. Online tools are encouraged for student writing. How can students' publication through digital tools be related to the writing *process*? How is publication online different from publication offline?

6. How can the integration of multimodality (in particular, image and sound) assist students as they clarify their ideas, thoughts, and feelings?

REFERENCES

Barone, D., & Wright, T. E. (2008). Literacy instruction with digital and media technologies. *The Reading Teacher, 62,* 292–303.

Blok, H., Oostdam, R., Otter, M. E., & Overmatt, M. (2002). Computer-assisted instruction in support of beginning reading instruction: A review. *Review of Educational Research, 72,* 101–130.

Burnett, C. (2009). Research into literacy and technology in primary classrooms: An exploration of understandings generated by recent studies. *Journal of Research in Reading, 32*(1), 22–37.

Castek, J., & Gwinn, C. B. (2012). Technology in the literacy program. In R. M. Bean & A. S. Dagen (Eds.), *Best practices of literacy leaders: Keys to school improvement* (pp. 295–316). New York: Guilford Press.

Chen, J. Q., & Chang, C. (2006). Using computers in early childhood classrooms: Teachers' attitudes, skills, and practices. *Journal of Early Childhood Research, 4,* 169–188.

Cheung, A. C. K., & Slavin, R. E. (2011). The effectiveness of education technology for enhancing reading achievement: A meta-analysis. *Best Evidence Encyclopedia.* Retrieved from *www.bestevidence.org.*

Duffy, G. G. (2009). *Explaining reading: A resource for teaching concepts, skills, and strategies* (2nd ed.). New York: Guilford Press.

Gabriel, R., & Gabriel, M. (2010). Power in pictures: How a schoolwide photo library can build a community of readers and writers. *The Reading Teacher, 63,* 679–682.

Gray, L., & Lewis, L. (2009). *Educational technology in public school districts: Fall 2008* (NCES 2010-003). Washington, DC: National Center for Education Statistics, Institute of Education Sciences, U.S. Department of Education.

Hutchison, A., & Reinking, D. (2011). Teachers' perceptions of integrating information and communication technologies into literacy instruction: A national survey in the United States. *Reading Research Quarterly, 46,* 312–333.

Kervin, L., & Mantei, J. (2010). Incorporating technology within classroom literacy experiences. *Journal of Literacy and Technology, 11,* 77–101.

Kuhn, M. R., & Stahl, S. A. (2006). More than skill and drill: Exploring the potential of computers in decoding and fluency instruction. In M. C. McKenna, L. D. Labbo, R. D. Kieffer, & D. Reinking (Eds.), *International handbook of literacy and technology* (Vol. 2, pp. 295–303). Mahwah, NJ: Erlbaum.

Labbo, L. D. (2004). Author's computer chair. *The Reading Teacher, 57,* 688–691.

Labbo, L. D. (2005). Moving from the tried and true to the new: Digital morning message. *The Reading Teacher, 58,* 782–785.

Labbo, L. D., Eakle, A. J., & Montero, K. M. (2002). Digital language experience approach: Using digital photographs and software as a language experience innovation. *Reading Online, 5*(8). Retrieved from *www.readingonline.org/electronic/elec_index.asp?HREF=labbo2/index.html.*

Labbo, L. D., & Kuhn, M. R. (2000). Weaving chains of affect and cognition: A young child's understanding of CD-ROM talking books. *Journal of Literacy Research, 32,* 187–210.

Larson, L. C. (2010). Digital readers: The next chapter in e-book reading and response. *The Reading Teacher, 64,* 15–22.

Leu, D. J., Jr., Coiro, J., Castek, J., Hartman, D. K., Henry, L. A., & Reinking, D. (2008). Research on instruction and assessment in the new literacies of online reading comprehension. In C. C. Block & S. R. Parris (Eds.), *Comprehension instruction: Research-based best practices* (2nd ed., pp. 321–346). New York: Guilford Press.

McKenna, M. C. (1998). Electronic texts and the transformation of beginning reading. In D. Reinking, M. C. McKenna, L. D. Labbo, & R. D. Kieffer (Eds.), *Handbook of literacy and technology: Transformations in a posttypographic world* (pp. 45–59). Hillsdale, NJ: Erlbaum.

McKenna, M. C., & Walpole, S. (2007). Assistive technology in the reading clinic: Its emerging potential. *Reading Research Quarterly, 42,* 140–145.

Moody, A. K., Justice, L. M., & Cabell, S. Q. (2010). Electronic versus traditional storybooks: Relative influence on preschool children's engagement and communication. *Journal of Early Childhood Literacy, 10,* 294–313.

Morrow, L. M. (2010). Preparing centers and a literacy-rich environment for small-group instruction in Early Reading First preschools. In M. C. McKenna, S. Walpole, & K. Conradi (Eds.), *Promoting early reading: Research, resources, and best practices* (pp. 124–141). New York: Guilford Press.

O'Brien, D., & Scharber, C. (2010). Teaching old dogs new tricks: The luxury of digital abundance. *Journal of Adolescent and Adult Literacy, 53,* 600–603.

Pearson, P. D., & Gallagher, M. C. (1983). The instruction of reading comprehension. *Contemporary Educational Psychology, 8,* 317–344.

Segal-Drori, O., Korat, O., Shamir, A., & Klein, P. S. (2010). Reading electronic and printed books with and without adult instruction: Effects on emergent reading. *Reading and Writing, 23,* 913–930.

Shamir, A., Korat, O., & Fellah, R. (2010). Promoting vocabulary, phonological awareness and concept about print among children at risk for learning disability: Can e-books help? *Reading and Writing, 25,* 45–69.

Sylvester, R., & Greenidge, W. I. (2009). Digital storytelling: Extending the potential for struggling writers. *The Reading Teacher, 63,* 284–295.

Tracy, D. H., & Young, J. W. (2007). Technology and early literacy: The impact of an integrated learning system on high-risk kindergartners' achievement. *Reading Psychology, 28,* 443–467.

Turbill, J., & Murray, J. (2006). Early literacy and new technologies in Australian schools: Policy, research, and practice. In M. C. McKenna, L. D. Labbo, R. Kieffer, & D. Reinking (Eds.), *International handbook of literacy and technology* (Vol. 2, pp. 93–108). Mahwah, NJ: Erlbaum.

Wang, F., Kinzie, M. B., McGuire, P., & Pan, E. (2010). Applying technology to inquiry-based learning in early childhood education. *Early Childhood Education Journal, 37,* 381–389.

Wohlwend, K. E. (2010). A is for avatar: Young children in literacy 2.0 worlds and literacy 1.0 schools. *Language Arts, 88,* 144–152.

CHAPTER 9

Assessment and the Common Core Standards

Peter Afflerbach

A second grader sits at her desk with an oral reading passage close at hand, her high school graduation far in the distance. Across the next 10 years, and following the developmental trajectory that underlies the Common Core State Standards (CCSS; National Governors Association Center for Best Practices [NGA] and Council of Chief State School Officers [CCSSO], 2010), it is expected that this second grader will develop as an engaged and accomplished reader. She will read broadly and deeply in content-area subjects and use reading as a powerful tool in analysis, critique, and application of what is learned. At this moment, the student is reading aloud, demonstrating her ongoing reading development. The teacher listens, noting decoding, fluency, sight word vocabulary, and the student's ability to answer literal and inferential comprehension questions. The teacher uses Running Records, recording successes and challenges, and updates her understanding of the student's reading development. In the here and now of the second grader further developing as a reader, the teacher gathers valuable assessment information.

How can we connect this second-grade student's reading of a relatively simple text and answering comprehension questions with the complexities of text and task that will be demanded by the CCSS in later grades? How can we move from the assessment of early reading skills and strategies to increasingly complex assessment of higher order thinking strategies (e.g., critical reading) that are also foundational to reading? What must happen from this day in second grade through to graduation day in high school for the student to realize her potential? What is the role of assessment in this student's evolution toward superior reading performance?

In this chapter, I examine the requisites of a successful early-grades reading assessment program that is aligned with the CCSS. The chapter is based on seven premises—that reading assessment must:

1. Reflect the most recent and comprehensive understanding of reading.
2. Describe in detail the ongoing development of young readers in relation to both near (daily learning) and far (year-end and school–career CCSS) goals.
3. Combine formative and summative assessments in a symbiotic relationship.
4. Report, support, and teach in relation to student learning.
5. Focus on both the cognitive and the affective aspects of students' reading development.
6. Be developed with clear understanding of the specific roles and responsibilities the CCSS create for teachers and students.
7. Help all students meet the CCSS "raised bar" of achievement, even as some students struggle to meet basic reading levels.

• *Reading assessment must reflect the most recent and comprehensive understanding of reading.* Theory, research, and practice continually contribute information that updates our understanding of reading. They provide the opportunity to reflect on how we regard reading and to determine whether our instructional goals, learning benchmarks, and related assessments are suitable representatives of this evolving knowledge. The CCSS offer an opportunity to examine curriculum and assessment concurrently and to conceptualize them as important partners in the development of effective instructional programs. There are numerous definitions of reading. For this chapter, I focus on one that has much in common with how the CCSS represent reading. The National Assessment Governing Board (2009) defines reading as:

an active and complex process that involves:

- Understanding written text
- Developing and interpreting meaning
- Using meaning as appropriate to type of text, purpose and situation.

According to this definition, constructing meaning from text is no longer the end point of reading: Reading involves the reader's use of that which is understood. This theory of use is a profound shift, one that should effect change in both reading instruction and reading assessment. Many CCSS reflect the fact that applying, analyzing, critiquing, or synthesizing what is understood is an essential part of reading. In addition, the CCSS focus on increasing text and task complexity as students matriculate, developing higher order thinking that will prepare them for success after high school. Under the CCSS, students will be expected to make increasingly detailed critique of increasingly complex texts. They will be expected to conduct accurate syntheses of multiple texts with related but differing viewpoints.

To illustrate how reading becomes more complex across the grades, consider this second-grade reading standard for literature, under the category of Key Ideas and Details:

Describe how characters in a story respond to major events and challenges.

Over the ensuing years, and aided by effective instruction and assessment, the student should develop the ability to perform more complex tasks with more complex texts. Consider, for example, the reading standard for literature for grades 11–12, also in the category of Key Ideas and Details:

> Analyze the impact of the author's choices regarding how to develop and relate elements
> of a story or drama (e.g., where the story is set, how the action is ordered, how the char-
> acters are introduced and developed).

The second grader sitting at her desk is probably not imagining what lies ahead in terms of reading, learning, and assessment. Our careful attention to assessment within the CCSS will help her realize a productive future from the challenging present.

All CCSS-related assessment must have construct validity, and a successful reading assessment program is informed by our most recent and comprehensive understanding of reading. Specifically, valid reading assessment maps onto the construct of reading, focusing on those things that are known to operate in successful reading. While differing perspectives on reading may be characterized more by contention than consensus, the following points are relatively unassailable:

o Reading is a constructive act that combines information from text with information from the reader's prior knowledge.
o Reading varies in the complexity of texts and tasks.
o Reading requires both strategies and skills.
o Reading is influenced by both cognitive and affective factors.

These points help describe the construct of reading, which should inform both the CCSS and the development of related curriculum and assessment.

Figure 9.1 portrays the alignment of four related aspects of the education enterprise: construct, Common Core State Standards and benchmarks, curriculum and instruction, and reading assessment. We can check on an assessment's validity by comparing the construct (Level 1) with an assessment (Level 4). All that is assessed should be part of

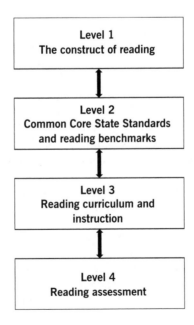

FIGURE 9.1. Necessary alignments for reading assessment.

the construct of reading. The CCSS derive from consensus understanding of what reading and literacy "are:" the construct of reading (Level 1). It follows that the CCSS and related benchmark performances (Level 2) derive from this construct. CCSS are aligned with cognitive understanding of reading: They acknowledge the role of reading strategies and skills and the importance of students' prior knowledge, and they include a focus on higher order thinking. The next alignment involves Levels 2 and 3: the CCSS and classroom curriculum and instruction (Level 3). What is taught and learned in classrooms directly relates to both the CCSS and the construct of reading. The final alignment involves curriculum and instruction and assessment (Levels 3 and 4). We want to assess the important learning and development that are the outcomes of CCSS-related instruction. In a well-functioning assessment system, all four components are aligned; one can examine an assessment and perceive its connection to all other components.

Reading assessment in grades PreK–2 in relation to the CCSS involves a series of challenges and opportunities. Although the CCSS are most often considered in relation to preparation for college and employment, they involve student learning and achievement in the early elementary grades. Becoming an accomplished reader and assessing reading well both have roots in these early grades. Effective assessment helps us consider students' current strengths and needs, and anticipate the future demands that increasingly complex reading texts and tasks will place on them.

The assessments used in conjunction with CCSS must reflect what we know about reading. Assessment must also follow the developmental trajectory that takes the second grader discussing stories and developing fluency to accomplished reading in which the student discusses how the author's craft contributes to a short story or evaluates the value of information provided in a social studies text.

• *Reading assessment must describe in detail the ongoing development of young readers in relation to both daily learning and year-end and school–career CCSS goals.* Many assessments of early reading in grades K–2 have partial construct validity—they focus on important but limited aspects of reading. For example, Dynamic Indicators of Basic Early Literacy (Good & Kaminski, 2011) focuses on phonemic awareness, pronouncing nonsense words, and how many words can be read accurately in 60 seconds. While important, these are only part of the cognitive strategy and skill repertoire that students need to succeed. An immediate challenge is to determine the requisite counterparts to such constrained skills (Paris, 2005), how they are taught, and how they are assessed as developing readers move toward the complex demands of the CCSS. We must have assessments that inform our understanding of young readers' development across the broad base of reading. We cannot focus only on mechanics because this misses the obvious links to students' comprehension strategy use and students' strategic use of what they learn from reading.

For example, reading standards for informational text, grade 2, Craft and Structure is:

> Identify the main purpose of a text, including what the author wants to answer, explain, or describe. (NGA and CCSSO, 2010, p. 13)

The unstated competencies that undergird success at this CCSS include the ability to decode, read fluently, identify and use vocabulary, and comprehend text. Second-grade students are expected to possess those skills and strategies to be able to establish meaning from text as a prerequisite to meeting this standard.

In close affiliation with the CCSS, reading assessment must provide detailed accounts of what students can do when they arrive at school and of their weekly, monthly, and yearly progress in early elementary school experience. Such assessment must be comprehensive—describing the cognitive components of reading development as well as the affective factors that impact development. This assessment is also regular, conducted frequently to provide continual updates of our understanding of individual students. Just as readers update their mental model of the text as they gather information through reading, teachers must update their mental models of students with information from assessment. Using this formative assessment, teachers address the immediate needs of students in relation to the array of cognitive skills and strategies and affective factors that impact reading development. Such assessment is occurring within a curriculum that fosters student growth toward CCSS attainment, and student growth moves them closer to success with text and tasks of increasing complexity.

The standards do not address in detail the prerequisite strategies and skills that are expected of our youngest students. Related to kindergarten, the standards state that:

> Children are expected to demonstrate increasing awareness and competence in the areas that follow: Print Concepts, Phonological Awareness, Phonics and Word Recognition, Fluency.

Thus, curriculum and assessment that focus on print concepts, phonemic awareness, and phonics are essential for ongoing and future attainment related to the CCSS. Maintaining this instruction and assessment focus is part of good practice for the early grades, as indicated by individual student needs. We are not wanting for valid assessments of the basic mechanics of reading (Paris, 2005). We may be wanting for balance in what is assessed in the early elementary grades, and the CCSS help us focus on a more broad array of what is "basic" in reading development. This should be reflected in both our instruction and assessment. When assessment acts as a complement to curriculum, teaching, and learning (and not as a constraint), it can be assigned a passing grade.

• *Reading assessment must combine formative and summative assessments in a symbiotic manner.* Students' reading development in relation to the CCSS will be enhanced by the strategic combination of formative and summative assessments. Formative assessment provides information for understanding individual students and their immediate needs, determining teachable moments during the school day, and creating scaffolded approaches to instruction (Afflerbach, 2012). In contrast, summative assessment provides information about students' literacy products in relation to CCSS benchmarks and performances. A well-functioning assessment program is marked by formative and summative assessment working together toward common goals. However, in many schools the two types of assessment compete for time and resources.

I noted earlier that as assessments associated with the CCSS prove construct valid, they will better represent the complexity of reading. This complexity demands the increased use of formative assessment to inform us of how students are progressing in their ability to do well on summative performance assessments. Consider what is required of our second-grade student by the following grade 2 standard for informational text—integration of Knowledge and Ideas:

7. Explain how specific images (e.g., a diagram showing how a machine works) contribute to and clarify a text.

A cursory task analysis indicates that a second-grade student who meets this standard engages in complex thinking. To demonstrate achievement in the related performance assessment, the student must

- Construct meaning from the text.
- Comprehend a related image.
- Compare the two related understandings.
- Analyze the two for their separate and joint contributions to understanding.
- Explain (through writing or speaking) how the two comprehended parts of the text relate to one another.
- Describe how the image helps comprehension.

We should also assume the student's metacognitive ability to coordinate these skills and strategies and to guide the entire reading process. For the second grader, each of these seven facets of the standard represents significant learning and achievement. Each facet is a necessary focus of instruction and assessment, as is the student's strategic combination of them to meet the standard.

It is difficult to imagine second-grade readers undertaking and succeeding at a related, complex summative assessment task without the prior benefits of ongoing formative assessment and related teacher feedback and instruction. For struggling readers, the need for formative assessment may be more acute. Detailed assessment information is necessary for each of the facets of performance (as well as the coordination of these facets) for students to succeed at the summative performance. Formative assessment related to the CCSS just mentioned helps the classroom teacher identify students' zones of proximal development (Vygotsky, 1978) and related teachable moments. Thus, formative assessment must inform us about how students are faring in the aspects of the performance just listed and how they are combining these aspects in a complex and successful performance. Formative assessment informs the teacher's choice of timely, suitable instruction.

Without formative assessment, the opportunity to understand how students are progressing toward a complex performance is lost, as is the opportunity to influence the process. Without formative assessment, that certain students cannot construct meaning from text (which is an entry point, not an end point in many CCSS) may be missed. Accordingly, the stakes could not be higher for either formative or summative assessment. Should our formative assessment be wanting, we will have little idea of students' development in relation to an upcoming complex performance assessment. We will have diminished ability to determine, through examination of the performance assessment, what was learned and what wasn't in terms of the parts that make the whole.

Assessment that is aligned with CCSS and related complex texts and tasks must reflect text and task complexity. Such complexity demands that formative and summative assessment work together. Over students' K–12 school experience, there should be continuing progress toward the long-term goals of CCSS: The standards are so structured. Assessment must follow this lead, gauging students' progression toward long-term goals that the summative assessment represents, while providing fine-grained information about their near-term work and accomplishments with formative assessment.

- *Reading assessment must be used to report, support, and teach in relation to student learning.* Reading assessment can realize an expanded role and influence as students and teachers work toward attainment of the CCSS. Consider the following reading standard for literature. Second graders will recount stories, including fables and folktales from diverse cultures, and determine their central message, lesson, or moral. (NGA and CCSSO, p. 11)

Reading assessment in the early grades typically focuses on diagnosis and reporting of students' strategies and skills for decoding, fluency, vocabulary, and construction of meaning. Assessment information reports the state of student learning and is useful for teachers, parents, and the students themselves. In relation to this standard, diagnostic assessment can help to identify key aspects of students' cognitive strategy and skill development, including but not restricted to the development of phonemic awareness, phonics, fluency, and literal comprehension. A CCSS-related assessment should help us further determine how (and if) second graders take their understanding of a story and use it to discern a theme, moral, or lesson. The results of such diagnostic assessment are used to inform instruction, helping teachers determine what students need and how students are developing in relation to basic reading ability, on which future CCSS attainment is based.

A second important use of assessment is teaching. In the long view, we hope that students in a CCSS curriculum are on a path to independent and successful reading. Along that path, students must assume increasing responsibility for assessing their own reading. As students become accomplished readers, they must also become independent and accurate assessors of their own work (Afflerbach, 2012; Black & William, 1998). The CCSS expect complex student performance across texts and tasks of increasing difficulty and duration. For example, a CCSS for second grade and informational text is Integration of Knowledge and Ideas. Students are expected to

compare and contrast the most important points presented by two texts on the same topic.

In relation to this and other CCSS, students must develop the ability to manage and assess their reading in the midst of complexity. Thus, a comprehensive assessment program will feature the teaching of reading assessment. Assessment in the early years must help set a foundation on which students can build an understanding of the ways and means of assessment. Rarely a focus on classroom discussion, assessment is worthy of our attention, and discussions about assessment with students help them better understand its value and how it works. As students develop across the early school years, we should assist them in developing the ability to set goals, to plan, to work on increasingly complex tasks, to monitor progress, to note and fix problems, and to eventually gain independence for assessing their own reading.

Formative assessment, conducted regularly by teachers, can help us teach assessment. For example, as teachers ask questions related to the CCSS just presented (comparing and contrasting important points in two texts), they can describe the relationship of the question to the goals of the lesson: "Questions I like to ask myself when I am comparing the important points in two texts are, What is different about these two texts, and what do the two texts have in common?" As students respond to questions, teachers can describe what they are looking for in student responses and how they are evaluating those responses. For example, "I like that you are paying attention to the questions to help guide your thinking. You are right! Both of these texts are about animals that live in the forest. Now, what about a difference? Again, good work! One text is about mammals, and the other is about reptiles. As we continue to read, let's remember that good answers depend on us paying careful attention to the questions that are asked."

Assessment checklists provided to students can serve as one foundation of self-assessment. In addition to questions that directly address CCSS content, we can provide questions that focus on general, powerful self-assessment routines. Second graders vary in their knowledge of self-assessment, but regularly answering the following questions provides introductory experience on which students can build complex self-assessment strategies:

- "Why am I reading?"
- "Does this make sense?"
- "Is there a problem?"
- "What is the problem?"
- "Can I fix it?"
- "Can I get back on track?"

Over time, these questions can become internalized and used as part of second-grade students' independent monitoring routines for increasingly complex reading. With teacher explanation, modeling, and thinking aloud, it is possible to transfer assessment knowledge and strategies from teacher to student, much in the manner of the reciprocal teaching of reading comprehension strategies.

A third important purpose of reading assessment is the support of student learning. Meeting a particular CCSS is arduous work. Our assessment feedback can provide students with guidance, encouragement, and scaffolded instruction that serve to support this work. Support for students can be provided by assessment in two ways. First, our assessment feedback can direct students to immediate areas of concern, focusing attention and preparing them for teachable moments. Assessment feedback helps students make the link between their work and the outcomes of reading. Second, assessment feedback should focus on student effort, building self-efficacy as students realize that their effort can lead to successful reading (Johnston, 2004). We must be aware of how reading assessment information is received and understood by our students. How might a struggling student interpret teacher feedback or a test result? Our continuing work to have students focus on their effort can be influenced by what we say in relation to assessment. Handing back a graded assignment without speaking is different than handing it back and saying, "I know you worked hard on the written assignment to compare and contrast these texts, and your hard work shows." We can also connect effort with specific outcomes: "You included lots of information from each of the two texts that is interesting to the reader. I know that your attention to comparing and contrasting the texts, combined with the effort you put into the drafts of your report, made a difference." Furthermore, self-efficacy matters greatly as students move through grades. Without self-efficacy, it is difficult for students to imagine themselves succeeding at complex tasks. Thus, we should use every opportunity to take our reading assessment information and use it in ways that are supportive of students' growth.

- *Reading assessment must focus on both the cognitive and affective aspects of students' reading development.* Reading assessment dwells on students' cognitive strategy and skill development and the ability to learn content from text. In the early grades, much assessment focuses on the mechanics of reading. There is clear need to chart each student's development through phonemic awareness, sound–symbol correspondences, and fluency, but these aspects of becoming a successful reader are only a part of what we need to assess. Students must also develop large vocabularies and the ability to construct literal, inferential, and critical understanding of text. From grades K through 6, there is a decreasing emphasis on mechanics and increasing focus on reading comprehension and vocabulary. The good news is that many schools' reading assessment programs reflect this dynamic; the bad news is that there is a cognitive monopoly in reading assessment (Afflerbach, Pearson, & Paris, 2008).

We need to ask whether reading strategy and skill, and their use in constructing meaning, are the only things that matter in students' reading development. Consider this stated goal of the CCSS:

> Students will learn in school in a manner that prepares them for success in college, and in life.

Young children must traverse considerable ground to reach this goal. The CCSS demand ever-increasing sophistication and coordination of reading skill and strategy. Throughout their school careers, students will be asked to demonstrate higher order thinking. Despite the importance of gaining in cognitive skill and strategy, we must establish a focus on the noncognitive aspects of school and learning that support student development, and represent legitimate outcomes of schooling in their own right (Afflerbach, Cho, Kim, & Crassas, 2011). We must assess student development in areas that are related to school success but are "other" than skill and strategy. Three areas critical to students' reading development and success include metacognition, motivation and engagement, and self-efficacy. As assessments better reflect the full construct of reading, attending to aspects of reading development that have been heretofore neglected, they can support student growth in all areas relevant to reading development.

Underlying students' success with increasingly complex texts and tasks is metacognition. Students' reading success requires metacognition (Baker & Brown, 1984), and metacognition supports academic learning (Paris & Winograd, 1990). In relation to CCSS, metacognition allows students to set goals, monitor both near and far progress toward those goals, identify problems, fix the problems, and stay "on track." (Zimmerman, 2008). Higher order thinking in reading is a strong thread that runs through all of the CCSS, and we can infer the success of metacognition as students successfully complete complex performance tasks. However, less than competent performance may indicate the lack of appropriate metacognitive strategies. Text complexity gets much attention in CCSS, and it is accompanied by task complexity, reminding us of the need to monitor both the construction of meaning from reading and then how that meaning is used in higher order thinking. If our CCSS-related assessment program does not provide information on how all students are developing a reflective mindset or on the establishment of key metacognitive questions (e.g., "Why am I reading? How am I doing? Do I understand? Is there a problem?"), then we construct only a partial picture of our developing readers. Examples of questions that can help students focus on metacognition were provided earlier in the section on teaching self-assessment.

The CCSS also acknowledge that motivation and engagement are central to reading development and reading achievement. Consider the following:

> Students who meet the *Standards* . . . actively seek the wide, deep, and thoughtful engagement with high-quality literary and informational texts that builds knowledge, enlarges experience, and broadens worldviews. (NGA and CCSSO, 2010, p. 3)

When engagement and motivation are strong, reading instruction improves students' reading comprehension (Guthrie, Wigfield, & You, 2011). Engaged students possess enthusiasm for learning, and motivation is integral to their participation in school (Skinner, Kindermann, & Furrer, 2009). In contrast, students who lack engagement and motivation often struggle with reading. As motivation supports students' learning of strategies and skills and content-domain knowledge, assessment must include it as a focus. Consider the earlier example of the second grader who must "explain how specific images (e.g., a diagram showing how a machine works) contribute to and clarify a text" (NGA and CCSSO, 2010, p. 13). Can we imagine all of our students persevering as they undertake this complex task without adequate motivation? How will second graders succeed if they are not engaged?

Self-efficacy is a third area worthy of assessment attention. The CCSS demand that students undertake increasingly complex tasks. As they read difficult texts and engage in CCSS tasks, students must believe that they can be successful, and this belief is directly tied to student self-efficacy. Self-efficacy influences reading success (Schunk & Zimmerman, 2007), and unless students believe they can produce desired effects by their actions, they have little incentive to act (Bandura, 2006). Consider the different reactions that a successful, self-assured reader and a struggling reader would have to the following assessment task:

> Describe how characters in a story respond to major events and challenges. (NGA and CCSSO, 2010, p. 11)

The student who sees himself as up to the challenge likely will approach the task with confidence and positive motivation, while a student with diminished self-efficacy cannot see himself succeeding.

Including metacognition, motivation and engagement, and self-efficacy as foci within a CCSS assessment program requires that we use appropriate assessments. We are fortunate to have assessment materials and procedures that help us better understand these aspects of students' development related to motivation for reading (Gambrell, Palmer, Codling, & Mazzoni, 1996), students' attitudes toward reading (McKenna & Kear, 1990), and student readers' self-concepts (Chapman & Tunmer, 1995). Each of these assessments might be adapted and used in relation to our early elementary students. In addition, the affective side of students' reading development will benefit from both formative and summative assessment. For example, formative assessment allows us to keep track of students' self-efficacy—whether it improves or declines in relation to ongoing reading challenges and successes. With this information, we can adjust instruction and reading tasks accordingly. Formative assessment also helps us understand the development of students' metacognition, and engagement and motivation. When affective factors are taken seriously, we will see summative assessments that describe engaged and motivated readers, readers who are self-efficacious, and readers who effectively manage complex acts of reading.

- *Reading assessment must be developed with clear understanding of the specific roles and responsibilities the CCSS create for teachers and students.* The CCSS require substantial changes in reading instruction and reading assessment, and these changes create new responsibilities for teachers and students. An assessment program that focuses on detailed, formative assessment demands teacher expertise. Consider the following scenario: Jaime is a second-grade teacher who regularly uses Running Records to help assess his students' growing repertoire of reading strategies and reading knowledge. He has spent hundreds of hours honing his ability to conduct Running Records, analyze the information they yield, and use the information to tailor reading instruction to student needs. The advent of CCSS create new demands related to assessment, and Jaime is preparing for the challenge of meeting these demands. He regularly visits the websites of the Partnership for Assessment of Readiness for College and Careers (PARCC), and the Smarter Balanced Assessment Consortium (SBAC), searching for information and examples of the performance assessments that are to be developed.

In particular, Jaime is interested in using rubrics and related performance assessments. His school district has decided to implement simple performance assessments in the early grades, in part to introduce students to the idea of performance assessments and in part to use in the measure of students' comprehension of narrative and informational texts. Students must also adapt to the new assessments. In the former assessment program, students were assessed through read-alouds, skill sheets, Running Records, and teacher observation. In each of these forms of assessment, students knew what was expected. However, the new performance assessment demands new responsibilities—new levels of activity from the students. Jaime wants to help students better understand the steps that lead toward superior performance.

There are only very limited examples of the assessments that PARCC (2012) and SBAC (2012) are creating on their respective websites, but Jaime is encouraged by his school and district to develop and use checklists that will be tied to the rubrics, so that students can begin to develop independent assessment routines. Jaime needs detailed assessment information to inform instructional decision making, in the midst of lessons and while planning future instruction. With his focus on formative assessment, Jaime must be expert in understanding and using the assessment, interpreting assessment results, taking that assessment information to modify his understanding of individual students, shaping instruction in relation to his knowledge of curriculum and teaching, and using a rubric to scaffold student learning and then to evaluate individual students' performance. As the performance assessments from PARCC and SBAC are developed and released, Jaime and his colleagues will be prepared to conduct a careful linking of their performance checklists with performance assessment rubrics.

Many second-grade students have limited roles and responsibilities with reading assessment. Assessment is done to or for them, and their assessment activity is marked by preparing for and taking quizzes and tests. The complexity and detail of CCSS-related assessments demand that students become more active participants in assessment as opposed to passive contributors. Students need to learn forms of assessment that are new to the classroom and new to their way of thinking about assessment. Students can learn the ways and means of performance assessment, and use related illustrative scoring rubrics and checklists, as demonstrated by the previous example. These student-centered assessment strategies are introduced early in school—and practiced in anticipation of students' reading independence. As their reading develops, students must also become increasingly responsible for assessing their reading. Metacognition, self-regulated learning, and independence all have roots in students' increased role in assessment.

Students' acclimation to the role of assessment user can be enhanced through the use of vertical and horizontal alignment of assessments. The CCSS represent instruction and learning that is connected across the school years and between school subjects. When our assessment programs are aligned across grades and across school subjects, we can enhance students' learning and use of assessment materials and procedures. For example, a district plan to vertically align assessment from grades K through 12 introduces kindergartners to simple performance assessments, checklists, and rubrics early in their school careers. Ensuing years and related assessments encourage students to build on their foundation of assessment knowledge, to move toward independence and self-assessment.

Helping students develop the ability to use assessment is also accomplished by horizontal alignment of assessment. Across content areas, there can be commonalities in assessment forms and uses. For example, students in science, social studies, math, and English become increasingly familiar with performance assessments as they are used throughout the school year in all content areas. The CCSS position reading as an important tool in learning across the curriculum, and the opportunity to develop understanding of the uses and benefits of performance assessment is provided across the school day, leading to competence and then expertise in students' assessment routines.

• *Reading assessment must help all students meet the CCSS "raised bar" of achievement, even as some students struggle to meet basic reading levels.* The CCSS raise the bar in terms of student work and learning outcomes. Students are required to read increasingly complex tasks and to engage in increasingly complex tasks. The CCSS link this raising of the bar to the goal of students being best prepared to realize their potential during and upon completion of school. This approach comes with risk—there are currently millions of students in the United States who do not reach "basic" levels in reading and writing (National Assessment Governing Board, 2009). Creating and teaching to the CCSS does not guarantee that all students will meet them. Students who struggle daily to construct literal understanding of texts will likely be overwhelmed by a task that asks them to comment on the author's craft or to compare and contrast content with another text.

How can students who do not meet basic levels of reading achievement hope to attain the more difficult reading characterized by the CCSS? What are their chances of succeeding at the CCSS, which are arguably more challenging than many extant state reading standards? There are several implications for assessment. We must continue to use assessments that are detailed in the diagnostic information they provide to help teachers identify and teach to readers' basic needs. This diagnostic assessment must be available early and often as our younger students begin their school reading careers. We must have assessments that help us understand both the cognitive strategy and skill profiles of all readers as well as their affective development. We must be able to identify those students who are struggling to develop phonemic awareness, who have imprecise understandings of sound–symbol correspondences, and who are challenged to read fluently and with comprehension. Using the appropriate assessment, we can help students create a foundation from which they can progress toward the attainment of increasingly challenging CCSS.

CONCLUSION

Impetus for change in reading assessment is related to CCSS, but the reading assessment encountered in many districts, schools, and classrooms has been in need of change for some time. The development and maintenance of exemplary reading assessment programs can be in reference to CCSS and informed by the evolving understanding of the nature of reading and of effective assessment. Successful reading assessment programs are developed in concert with curriculum and instruction. They are not added on, after the fact of curriculum development.

A programmatic approach to reading assessment development and use related to the CCSS will have several features. There will be attention to alignments between construct, standards, curriculum and instruction, and reading assessment. In the early elementary grades, assessments must measure basic skills in reading, while anticipating the array of higher order thinking that is at the core of CCSS in later years. The CCSS also require strategic combinations of formative and summative assessment that help teachers and students chart progress across increasingly complex texts and tasks. These assessments help us simultaneously focus on near and far reading goals.

Furthermore, the development of assessment in relation to CCSS should focus on reporting student progress as well as teaching and supporting students. Teaching assessment is critical as students embark on the path toward independent reading marked by increasingly complex texts and tasks. Assessment must also support students in their cognitive and affective growth. Relatedly, our assessments must change to include focus on powerful factors that include motivation and engagement and self-efficacy. Instructional programs that increase reading achievement along with creating positive affect should be documented. New assessments create new roles and responsibilities for teachers and students. With the CCSS, assessment programs must be accompanied by a full accounting of this change. What must teachers do as they regularly collect detailed formative assessment information? How do students become active participants in assessing their reading? Finally, assessment must help all students meet the CCSS raised bar of achievement: those students who struggle to meet basic reading level, and those for whom the CCSS represent an array of doable challenges.

REFERENCES

Afflerbach, P. (2012). *Understanding and using reading assessment, K–12* (2nd ed.). Newark, DE: International Reading Association.

Afflerbach, P., Kim, J.-Y., Crassas, M. E., & Cho, B.-Y. (2011). Best practices in literacy assessment. In L. M. Morrow & L. B. Gambrell (Eds.), *Best practices in literacy instruction* (4th ed., 264–282. New York: Guilford Press.

Afflerbach, P., Pearson, P. D., & Paris, S. (2008). Clarifying differences between reading skills and reading strategies. *The Reading Teacher, 61*, 364–373.

Baker, L., & Brown, A. L. (1984). Metacognitive skills and reading. In P. D. Pearson (Series Ed.), R. Barr, M. L. Kamil, & P. Mosenthal (Vol. Eds.), *Handbook of reading research* (Vol. 1, pp. 353–394). New York: Longman.

Bandura, A. (2006). Toward a psychology of human agency. *Perspectives on Physiological Science, 1*, 164–180.

Black, P., & William, D. (1998). Assessment and classroom learning. *Educational Assessment: Principles, Policy and Practice, 5*, 7–74.

Chapman, J. W., & Tunmer, W. E. (1995). Development of young children's reading self-concepts: An examination of emerging subcomponents and their relationship with reading achievement. *Journal of Educational Psychology, 87*, 154–167.

Gambrell, L., Palmer, B., Codling, R., & Mazzoni, S. (1996). Assessing motivation to read. *The Reading Teacher, 49*, 518–533.

Good, R., & Kaminski, R. (2011). *DIBELS® Next Assessment manual*. Eugene, OR: Institute for the Development of Educational Achievement.

Guthrie, J. T., Wigfield, A., & You, W. (2012). Instructional contexts for engagement and achievement in reading. In S. Christensen, A. Reschly, & C. Wylie (Eds.), *Handbook of research on student engagement* (pp. 601–634). New York: Springer Science.

Johnston, P. (2004). *Choice words: How our language affects children's learning.* Portland, ME: Stenhouse.

McKenna, M., & Kear, D. (1990). Measuring attitude towards reading: a new tool for teachers. *The Reading Teacher, 43,* 626–639.

National Assessment Governing Board. (2008). *Reading framework for the 2009 National Assessment of Educational Progress.* Washington, DC: American Institutes for Research.

National Governors Association Center for Best Practices and Council of Chief State School Officers. (2010). Common core state standards for English language arts & literacy in history/social studies, science, and technical subjects. Washington, DC: Author. Retrieved March 12, 2011, from *www.corestandards.org/assets/CCSSI_ELA%20Standards.pdf.*

Paris, S. (2005). Reinterpreting the development of reading skills. *Reading Research Quarterly, 40,* 184–202.

Paris, S., & Winograd, P. (1990). How metacognition can promote academic learning and instruction. In B. J. Jones & L. Idol (Eds.), *Dimensions of thinking and cognitive instruction* (pp. 15–51). Hillsdale, NJ: Erlbaum.

Partnership for Assessment of Readiness for College and Careers. (2012). PARCC place. Retrieved April 24, 2012, from *http://parcconline.org/sites/parcc/files/March2012PARCCPlaceNewsletter.pdf.*

Schunk, D., & Zimmerman, B. (2007). Influencing children's self-efficacy and self-regulation of reading and writing through modeling. *Reading and Writing Quarterly, 23,* 7–25.

Skinner, E., Kindermann, T., & Furrer, C. (2009). A motivational perspective on engagement and disaffection: Conceptualization and assessment of children's behavioral and emotional participation in academic activities in the classroom. *Educational and Psychological Measurement, 69,* 493–525.

Smarter Balanced Assessment Consortium. (2012). Retrieved April 24, 2012, from *www.smarterbalanced.org/k-12-education/teachers.*

Vygotsky, L. (1978). *Mind in society: The development of higher psychological processes.* Cambridge, MA: Harvard University Press.

Zimmerman, B. (2008). Investigating self-regulation and motivation: Historical background, methodological developments, and future prospects. *American Educational Research Journal, 45,* 166–183.

CHAPTER 10

In Conclusion

On Implementing the Common Core Standards
Successfully in Grades K–2

Timothy Shanahan

As one reads the preceding chapters in this volume, something should be obvious: The new Common Core State Standards (CCSS) are ambitious. The makers of the CCSS espoused the idea of "fewer, clearer, higher" (Bill & Melinda Gates Foundation, 2010), meaning that past standards were too numerous, too foggy, and, if attained, were too low to allow students to graduate from high school with sufficient skills. Nevertheless, the new CCSS English language arts standards still appear to be pretty extensive, though if you know how to read them they should be more manageable than previous standards. Part of the reason there are so many standards has to do with the complexity of language learning itself; it necessarily includes, as the earlier chapters have shown, oral language, writing, reading, and all of the conventions of language too (e.g., mechanics, usage, grammar, spelling). Even that summary list simplifies things more than do the standards themselves: There are standards both for the foundational reading skills (e.g., phonological awareness, decoding, fluency) and for reading comprehension, and reading comprehension is articulated through two lists of standards for each grade level to address the interpretation of literary and informational texts.

Indeed, I believe that the CCSS are clearer and higher and even a bit more manageable than past standards, and their increased rigor has been documented through independent analysis (Carmichael, Wilson, Porter-Magee, & Martino, 2010). Primary-grade teachers are definitely going to be challenged—I hope not overwhelmed—by the extensiveness and complexity of these standards and by how different these standards are from their forerunners.

The purpose of this chapter is both to pull together the strands of thought offered by the various authors of this volume and to provide practical advice to teachers and principals for the successful implementation of the new standards. As good as these standards are—and I do think they are quite good and a real improvement for most states—their attainment is entirely in the hands of the women and men who have to teach them in America's classrooms. Adopting new standards is the easy part, translating them into daily instructional routines that boost children's learning is the real challenge. It is toward the goal of successful implementation that I provide this advice.

READ THE STANDARDS WELL

The chapters in this book offer a great introduction to the primary grades' CCSS. But as good and useful as these chapters are, reading them in no way replaces the need to read the standards themselves. It is imperative that teachers and principals read the standards and read them thoughtfully. The standards are online (National Governors Association Center for Best Practices and the Council of Chief State School Officers, 2010) so that anyone can access them virtually at any time.

Reading the standards will reveal a few surprises. There are, for example, no *reading comprehension* standards per se, but the term *reading* is used to refer to all of the outcomes that deal with comprehension (*Reading Foundations* are treated separately and later in the document, also an unexpected placement). Too, as McKenna, Conradi, Young, and Jang (Chapter 8) explain, there are no technology standards, but technology is explicitly sprinkled throughout the document—in the same way that technology needs to be used in reading, writing, speaking, and listening; not as an end in itself, but as part of the support system that we use to communicate and explore ideas. Another example: Vocabulary is treated as part of reading comprehension (and weighing and evaluating word choices is a big part of reading comprehension and writing in the CCSS), but vocabulary is also included in language, as is described by Watts-Taffe and Breit-Smith (Chapter 7). Language, as they show, still includes mechanics, usage, spelling, and grammar, but academic vocabulary is there too. Thus, teachers are expected to teach students to interpret and evaluate the words in text (reading comprehension), but to build up their academic vocabularies as well (language). Many core programs confound these, teaching vocabulary words just because they appear in a text or focusing on text words during reading, not because of their importance in the specific text but because of their more general value. Sometimes it is necessary to focus on a word in text, not because it is widely used but because the meaning of this text depends on it. Similarly, there are words that students should learn because of the likelihood that they will have long-term value. The varied placement of vocabulary in the CCSS suggests the need for flexibility and thoroughness in such teaching.

Unfortunately, past standards have provided a misleading example of how to read standards effectively. Typically, standards have been little more than random collections of learning goals or objectives. The progressions from grade level to grade level have often been weak or nonexistent, and the connections among sections, such as the connections between reading and writing, have been feeble (often the reading and writing standards were even written by separate committees). Usually teachers have read the standards only for their own grade level and then have swiftly forgotten them, since there was no structure or organization to make them memorable. No wonder so many schools' core instructional program seem to be consistent with their standards; without much memory for specific standards, it is the only way teachers could have any confidence that they were addressing them at all. Similarly, I have seen principals require that teachers staple the standards into their planning books; of course, given the lack of memorability of such standards, no one could be expected to use them during planning without their physical presence.

However, as the preceding chapters have magnificently revealed, these new standards are different than the ones we are used to, but also in how they are organized. In the past, it has made sense to focus on the standards of a single grade level since the information in the other grade level lists was either repetitive or ostensibly unconnected, but with these standards that is not the case. Often the standards of a single grade level cannot be understood fully without tracking that standard across the other grade levels. I provide an example of this shortly, but first let's look at how these standards are structured.

Reading comprehension (or actually "reading" as it is labeled in the standards) includes 10 standards at each grade level. These 10 standards are arranged into four categories. Items 1–3 focus on key ideas and details and are aimed at ensuring that students learn to figure out *what a text says*. The next three items (4–6) emphasize craft and structure, and these guide student attention to making sense of *how a text works*. Items 7–9 stress the integration of knowledge and ideas: *What does a text mean and how do we evaluate its significance?* Item 10 is always about text difficulty and is discussed elsewhere in this chapter. There are two versions of most of these 10 items at all grade levels: one version for literary texts and one for informational texts, and from grades 6–12 there are lists of standards that emphasize science and history reading too.

What you must remember is that all the items that are assigned the number 1 address related or analogous issues no matter what the grade level or text type. The same is true for each of the other nine items assigned to each grade level. Thus, with the CCSS, you can read all the reading comprehension items with the same numbers across the grades to gain a clear sense of progression, and this should be revealing as to the purpose of each of the standards.

One good example of the benefits of this kind of examination is evident for the first section, Key Ideas and Details. Look at this standard from grade 1, for instance:

1. Ask and answer questions about key details in a text.

This standard seems like a pretty traditional and straightforward goal emphasizing the need for readers to understand and remember what an author has said explicitly or implied. And the kindergarten and grade 2 versions of this item are not so different. But look at the analogous item for grade 3:

1. Ask and answer questions to demonstrate understanding of a text, *referring explicitly to the text as a basis for the answers.* (emphasis added)

The emphasis appears to change here, and if you continue to read the versions of this first standard for grades 4–12, the shift becomes even starker. The idea conveyed by these items is that it is not enough for students to just be able to answer questions about what they read—they also need to view text information as evidence that they can collect and use in putting forth their own ideas and arguments. Thus, a traditional literal recall or locate information standard is, here, a standard about collecting and using information, an insight that should color instructional choices but an insight available only from reading the standards across grade levels. Anyone who just reads the first- or second-grade version of such a standard would not have a clue where it is going.

As previously noted, traditional standards have tended to treat speaking, listening, and writing separately from reading. With the Common Core, however, there are important connections across these sets of standards as well. Unlike current standards, the CCSS standards strongly emphasize the importance of writing about text: summarizing, analyzing, synthesizing, and evaluating the text information, which is why Hansen (Chapter 5) so appropriately determined that writing needs to be evident throughout the school day and not just during an isolated writing period. The speaking and listening standards also focus on the use of information found in text; Gillam and Reutzel (Chapter 6) do a masterful job of showing how connected "comprehension and collaboration" are to reading comprehension and "presentation of ideas" are to writing. Given this, I recommend reading the writing standards and the reading standards together (again, connecting them by numbered items, as the writing items, too, are somewhat analogous to the reading items); considering connections in this way will provide valuable insights into the types of activities that might be most profitable in your classroom. The speaking and listening standards are not numbered analogously, but these too would benefit from such a joint reading. Several of the chapters (1, 2, 3, 5, and 6) provide valuable insights into how such connections can play out in the classroom.

One more thing evident from a close examination of the structure of the standards: Many school districts assign standards to be taught during each report card period or to include the standards in pacing guides, so that teachers will aim to accomplish particular goals by particular points in the school year. These new standards are arranged in a way that makes such approaches impractical. For example, an examination of the reading comprehension standards would show them to be not particularly divisible. It makes sense to focus on several standards simultaneously and in conjunction with one another; they don't abstract well into separable items. The same could be said of the writing standards. Given the nature of these standards, rather than trying to parcel them out into marking periods, it would make more sense to closely examine texts to use for instruction and then to determine which combinations of standards fit best with the texts. This means that teachers would teach and reteach a relatively small set of standards throughout a school year, in various combinations depending on the texts. There are exceptions to this: decoding skills and the language standards, for which conventions and vocabulary could profitably be distributed across a school year in a way that the reading, writing, speaking, and listening standards cannot.

THE STANDARDS DO NOT TELL YOU HOW TO TEACH

Standards must be something like an elephant. Everyone likely knows the tale of the blind men trying to describe an elephant and each doing so idiosyncratically in terms that he readily understood—some "seeing" the pachyderm as a wall, others as a snake, and so on. I was struck by that thought as I reviewed the preceding chapters, as many of these authors posited that the best instructional approaches to the standards were akin to those they have always championed. That actually makes sense, however, since the CCSS do not specify how or even what to teach, just what needs to be learned.

Read this from the Common Core Standards Initiative (2010) website established by the National Governors Association and the Council of Chief State School Officers:

Myth: The Standards tell teachers what to teach.

Fact: The best understanding of what works in the classroom comes from the teachers who are in them. That's why these standards will establish *what* students need to learn, but they will not dictate *how* teachers should teach. Instead, schools and teachers will decide how best to help students reach the standards.

It couldn't be clearer—or could it? As Pearson and Hiebert (Chapter 1) note, although the standards themselves neither specify how or what teachers must teach to accomplish these standards, and no states adopted a set of instructional requirements along with the standards, there are many people eager to tell teachers and principals how to accomplish them. We invited the authoritative and highly qualified authors of this volume to weigh in with their thoughts about how best to go about it, and this book is jam-packed with their good ideas.

Many other experts are giving such guidance as well, though not always with as light a hand. Perhaps most influential so far has been "Publishers' Criteria for the Common Core State Standards in English Language Arts and Literacy" for grades K–2 and 3–12 (Coleman & Pimentel, 2012a, 2012b), discussed at length by Pearson and Hiebert. Coleman and Pimentel led the writing team for the common core English language arts standards, so they are certainly authoritative sources, and there is a growing body of useful common core resources on their website (*www.achievethecore.org*). Nevertheless, their widely distributed advice is just advice, and as good as much of it may be, at times it ignores relevant research, generalizes too much from middle/high school experiences to the primary grades, or pushes the pendulum in an attempt to instigate movement in some good direction, without conveying where the pendulum should end up. I have no problem with David and Sue sharing their "advice"; in fact, it has been pretty useful overall. Yet I fear that publishers and states may take this authoritative advice too literally, locking teachers and students into new instructional routines ill-formed.

Similarly, the Bill and Melinda Gates Foundation, which funded the development of the CCSS, has been supporting a plethora of efforts to create exemplary lessons and other tools to support Common Core standards implementation. Thus, there is the Common Core Curriculum Mapping Project (*http://commoncore.org/maps/*), the Literacy Design Collaborative (*https://knowledgebase.newvisions.org/CustomTeamsIndividual.aspx?id=409*), and still other Gates-supported efforts aimed at creating standards-appropriate digital lessons and materials that schools can use to address the Common Core (Gewertz, 2011). To some educators, even the standards themselves seem to be telling them how to teach, since the appendices to the standards included lists of texts illustrative of what *might* be appropriately used for teaching the standards. These appendices seemed to be a very useful resource to schools, and yet some curriculum directors have confided in me, as if they had access to insider information, that those exemplary texts are what they are "supposed" to use. (That, of course, is not true; those text lists are just good examples of the kinds of texts that teachers should choose.)

My point isn't to try to undermine the value of any of these sources, or others that I have not mentioned, but merely to emphasize that it is the teachers and principals who will, ultimately, be held responsible for accomplishing the standards (new testing regimens for grades 3–12 will begin in 2014–2015). Advice and recommendations are just that; teachers need to make sound choices as to how to reach these goals, and it will not be an acceptable excuse that they followed advice, no matter how authoritative it may have seemed at the time. For me, the best approach is to seek methods that have proved effective in raising reading achievement in the past; thus, I rely heavily on research evidence and encourage readers to do the same.

MAKE CHALLENGING TEXT CENTRAL TO YOUR INSTRUCTION

These standards differ from previous standards in many ways, but one of the most important distinctions is that they place relatively greater emphasis on text than on the actions or activities that take place around text (Shanahan, 2011). With standards, typically the verbs have it: *write, read, develop, use, ask, answer, distinguish, compare, analyze, explain, integrate,* and so on. Thus, the stress usually has been on the actions, with little regard for the texts on which those actions must focus. Traditional standards, in other words, have stressed the behaviors the students are supposed to demonstrate, with the assumption that students could show such facility with any text (as such, reading—or writing, speaking, or listening—has been assumed to be highly generalizable, applicable to any text or situation).

There is a fundamental problem with these verb-centric approaches to learning, however; they are not consistent with how individuals read and learn. Much has been made about the distinction between "low-level" questions that require only that students remember or locate information and those "higher level" questions requiring inferencing, interpretation, or reasoning. Studies of student performance data reveal that students do not actually differ in how well they implement these tasks or answer these kinds of questions (ACT, 2006). There are big performance differences when text difficulty varies, however. Thus, in reading, varying the kinds of questions that we ask doesn't make any real difference in how well students can answer the questions, but varying the text difficulty will improve or lower performance markedly.

Think about how I described the reading comprehension standards earlier: three standards about key ideas and details, three about craft and structure, three about integration of knowledge and ideas, and one about text difficulty. That is, in every list of Common Core reading standards, the final item reveals the level of text that the other nine standards must be applied to. There is a difference in interpreting *Dick and Jane* and *War and Peace*, and these standards emphasize that distinction. That means that the 10th reading comprehension standard sets the condition or context within which all the other nine must be carried out. The same scheme is evident with writing as well; it is not enough that students be able to use a writing process or compose a particular type of text, but they must do so while producing texts with appropriate levels of complexity and sophistication.

For the most part, the CCSS require that students work with more difficult text than they have in the past. This means children may be asked to read texts that we once would have claimed to be at a frustration level (so Lexile levels for second and third grade now will include materials written at a slightly higher level than previous Lexile frameworks suggested). Given the centrality of text in student learning, second- and third-grade teachers are asked to "stretch" children to the text rather than to select a text that the children will find relatively easy, an approach that runs counter to years of practice.

There is an important exception to the text difficulty requirement in the Common Core standards worth noting: The CCSS did not set text levels for grades K and 1. This omission was intentional. Lexiles, the readability system the standards use to determine text difficulty, do not go that low; it is hard to reliably specify text difficulty differences at beginner reading levels. Also, much of what beginning readers learn from working with text has to do with figuring out how to decode. If text is too hard (e.g., long complex sentences, varied vocabulary of unfamiliar words), children will struggle to figure out how to read the words themselves, and drawing generalizations about the words will be more difficult.

Once children understand how decoding works, usually by the time they read at a "first-grade reading level," then the harder text specifications of the Common Core start to make sense. In some schools, I fear that teachers will try to ramp up the beginning reading difficulties to ensure that students will be ready to meet the now harder second- and third-grade text requirements. That would be a mistake. Take the time with easier texts to ensure that students can decode text with facility in kindergarten and grade 1; accomplishing that successfully will mean that you do *not* suddenly ramp up text difficulty for the beginners (Hiebert, 1999). With such solid early support, students should be able to handle the more challenging texts that are projected for grades 2 and 3 and beyond.

Pearson and Hiebert (Chapter 1) likewise express concerns that raising text difficulty prematurely could have pernicious effects. They claim that raising text difficulty even by grade 2 would not be justified by research evidence. On this we must disagree. I look at the research conducted at these early grade levels with challenging texts (Morgan, Wilcox, & Eldredge, 2000; Powell, 1968; Stahl & Heulbach, 2005), and conclude that with proper scaffolding, second graders not only can tolerate more challenging texts than they usually are asked to, but that they can thrive when working with them.

Text is central in these standards in some other ways, too. Past standards have usually not emphasized the important distinction between informational and literary text. Such standards may have indicated that students need to read both, but without much explanation of the differences in those texts. With the CCSS standards, each comprehension skill is delineated for both literary and informational text, and if a particular skill has no counterpart across these text types the standard omits it (more on informational text later). Also, much of what is expected of students with regard to writing or speaking and listening is text focused as well, and the quality of texts is thought to be so important that the standards include many examples and lists of the types that would be appropriate.

What does all of this mean? Most basically, these standards recognize the primacy of text in reading comprehension and writing, and that the quality and complexity of texts will determine how well students will be able to demonstrate proficiency with the standards. Just as the CCSS emphasize text, classroom instruction needs to do the same. When selecting programs or creating lessons, make the first decisions about what to read: Is it challenging enough? Rich enough? Is it sufficiently worthwhile to justify its use? And if a text is worthwhile, then questions and activities (e.g., reading, discussion, writing, presentations) need to be designed specifically for the challenges of that text.

PROVIDE SUFFICIENT SUPPORT FOR MORE CHALLENGING TEXTS

Even accepting my caveats for beginning readers, expressed here and in the Pearson and Hiebert chapter, children in grade 2 (and beyond) are going to be asked to read harder texts. The CCSS specify text complexity bands for each grade level starting with grade

2. For example, the grade 2 standards say, "Grade 2 students . . . By the end of the year, read, and comprehend literature . . . in the grades 2–3 complexity band proficiently, with scaffolding as needed at the high end of the range" (National Governors Association Center for Best Practices and Council of Chief State School Officers, 2010, p. 11). The band that this refers to is included in Appendix A, page 8 (reproduced here as Table 10.1). As the table shows, the Common Core standards have stretched the Lexile bands to include harder texts at each grade level than would have been the case in the past. The setting of higher bands of performance in this way means that students, starting in grade 2–3, will be more likely to read so-called frustration-level texts. (The original Lexile levels were aimed at describing student comprehension; that is, how well students at a grade level would understand a text. However, those levels say nothing about learning—how well students can learn from a text.)

If you are like most teachers, you have been taught that students cannot learn from reading materials written at their frustration level. Informal reading inventories (Betts, 1946) and guided reading approaches (Fountas & Pinnell, 1996) are based upon the instructional level idea. Thus, texts are said to be too easy or too hard to learn from, and the appropriateness of the match of text readability level with student reading level is presumed to determine learning. Thus, if texts are easy (i.e., at the independent level), there wouldn't be much to learn from, and if texts are hard, frustration level, they will be too challenging to allow successful learning. Thus, it is best, or so the claim has been, to place students in materials that are at their instructional level.

How to recognize frustration-level text? This is done on the basis of student performance. According to the most widely used scheme (there are variants on this), if a student can read a text aloud with 95–98% accuracy and answer 75% of the questions about a text, then he or she could learn from such material (some systems are less demanding and some more, but they all range between requiring 90–98% oral reading accuracy). This approach has been widely used since the 1940s (Betts, 1946), but even with that it is important to recognize that it is a commonsense approach rather than a research-based one (Shanahan, 1983). Unfortunately, there have been few attempts to determine an optimum level of text difficulty for facilitating learning, but these studies have suggested— much as the CCSS prescribe—that harder texts may be a better way to support student learning at least from second grade up (Morgan et al., 2000; Powell, 1968; Stahl & Heulbach, 2005).

TABLE 10.1. Text Complexity Grade Bands and Associated Lexile Ranges (in Lexiles)

Grade band	Current Lexile band	"Stretch" Lexile band
K–1	N/A	N/A
2–3	450L–725L	450L–790L
4–5	645L–845L	770L–980L
6–8	860L–1010L	955L–1155L
9–10	960L–1115L	1080L–1305L
11–CCR	1070L–1220L	1215L–1355L

Note. From National Governors Association Center for Best Practices and Council of Chief State School Officers (2010, English Language Arts Appendix A, p. 8).

But it might not be text level—or rather it might not be text level *alone*—that is the key factor in student learning. Perhaps this whole approach is just too simplistic to adequately account for literacy learning. Learning to read is an interaction between a learner, a text, and a teacher. Instructional-level theory posits that text difficulty is the important factor or active ingredient in learning. But that ignores the guidance, support, and scaffolding provided by the teacher. What is needed is a two-factor theory, one that encourages teachers to provide greater support with more challenging text and relatively less with easier texts. Rather than trying to place students in relatively simple text all the time—that is, at levels of complexity that should require little teacher support—there might be a greater learning opportunity if students were matched to more challenging texts but with commensurate levels of increased scaffolding, support, and encouragement to allow maximum growth. In other words, using harder text would not necessarily block student learning, but would require increased levels of instructional support and scaffolding.

The last time appreciably harder texts were used in the primary grades was in the late 1980s, when publishers were not allowed to adapt or abridge texts for use in their beginning reading textbooks (Hiebert, 1999). Those texts were so hard that many teachers read them to the children rather than helping the children to read them themselves. Successful work with harder texts is likely to require more vocabulary work, more fluency work, and more thoughtful questioning and scaffolding, and with such extended support students can learn despite the text level. In a study of the impact of text difficulty on learning (Morgan et al., 2000), students did fluency work—repeated reading and paired reading—with frustration-level texts, and made greater gains than "appropriately placed" students (i.e., those who worked in instructional-level materials). But the children placed in the more challenging texts also were more likely to reread the texts and to require greater teacher feedback to be successful (the need for the greater support necessitated by the demands of the harder text). It is essential that instruction with more difficult texts provides such opportunities and supports.

A good deal of what children learn about reading comes not from lessons in specific skills but from opportunities to engage in shared reading, directed reading, or guided reading—that is, from reading and listening to texts and talking about the meaning with others. The degree of text difficulty can be thought of as an "opportunity to learn" variable. The more difficult the text, the more learning opportunities it offers; there is more sophisticated vocabulary to deduce, more complex grammar to detangle, more subtle relationships among characters and ideas to discern. This does not mean that students should be immersed *only* in difficult texts, however. To take advantage of the opportunity to learn that a particular text offers requires teacher support. If there isn't sufficient support, then the opportunity to learn is missed. The trick to successful instruction is to make sure there is adequate opportunity to learn while providing sufficient scaffolding so that the opportunity can be exploited effectively. Teachers cannot be expected to provide maximum support for every reading, and students cannot be expected to always be at their maximum level of motivation and effort. Accordingly, teachers should vary text challenge demands, not just from selection to selection but even in having students engaged in the reading of multiple texts in a single day. Some successful programs of instruction (e.g., Clay, 1993; Cunningham, Hall, & Sigmon, 1999) have long touted the value of having young students confront mixed text difficulty demands on a daily basis, having them read both easy and hard text and varying the degree of teacher support accordingly.

The text complexity demands of the Common Core require that teachers use more challenging texts with their students and that there be greater attention to steadily increasing text difficulty across each school year. Too often teachers work hard to get students placed in the right materials, but the students then languish at those levels, often not changing book levels again until they change teachers. The Common Core standards require that teachers continually stretch students to meet new text demands. For example, the second- and third-grade text range is from 450–790 Lexiles, but students aren't supposed to be able to read independently in that range until toward the end of third grade. Thus, early in second grade, texts that are written in the 450–500 range might be a good high-end text choice, but teachers and programs should try to ratchet this level up to about 600 by the end of the year. That means intentionally choosing more demanding texts throughout the year, perhaps stretching the students at each report card marking. Thus, during the first quarter of the year, teachers might aim to use challenging text that is in the approximate range of 450–500, with the texts during the subsequent quarters spanning Lexile levels 475–550, 525–600, and 575–625, respectively. Third-grade teachers could drop back a bit in this progression early in the year, and then move students up similar amounts along the way, ultimately reaching the 750–790 Lexile span by the end of the year. These spans are wide enough to provide many text choices, and they overlap a bit to provide some flexibility at both the upper and lower ends of the targets. The point isn't that every text needs to be in these ranges—we've already explored the idea of using both easier and more challenging texts—but using texts in these spans should provide students with sufficient experience reading in these ranges as the school year progresses that they can develop the intellectual muscle to handle them proficiently.

Finally, Lexile bands provide an excellent estimate of how hard a text might be, and these specifications allow for good comparisons between texts. What they do not provide is an explanation of why a text might be relatively hard or easy. Texts can be difficult for many reasons, and if a teacher understands what is challenging, it may be possible to provide students with supports that allow them to understand the text better. With young children the most common problem is likely to be the decoding challenge; if you can't read the words, you will have difficulty understanding an author's message. However, even if children can decode the words in a text or read it fluently, there still might be something about the ideas that challenge the reader. For more information on what makes text difficult and what can be done about it, see Shanahan, Fisher, and Frey (2012).

CLOSE READING

Another big shift strongly encouraged by the Common Core standards, and discussed throughout this volume, represents a profound change in how teachers would guide student reading. For generations, reading experts have recommended some form of guided or directed reading in which teachers interact with students in particular ways before reading, during reading, and after reading. The Common Core challenges these reading approaches, suggesting that some form of "close reading" replace these instructional plans. Morrow and Tracey (Chapter 2) and Duke, Halladay, and Roberts (Chapter 3) do an excellent job of illustrating what close reading might look like in the primary grades.

The basic ideas of close reading in the CCSS appear to be drawn from the study of literature, but various disciplines have their own version of this concept (Shanahan & Shanahan, 2012; Shanahan, Shanahan, & Misichia, 2011). Basically, reading lessons have placed a lot of attention on previewing, predicting, purpose setting, background reviews, context setting, connecting to prior knowledge, and similar activities. Supports for this are provided by textbook publishers, tradebook publishers, and various teacher-prepared lesson plans that are widely available.

Nevertheless, the authors of the Common Core have pushed hard to minimize that kind of apparatus and activity. In fact, their "Advice to the Publishers" even goes so far as to say that there should be no prereading at all, and some states may be ready to ban such practices. I think their concerns about prereading are well founded, and yet I do not agree with the solution of proscribing prereading (and in fairness to Coleman and Pimentel, they do not still agree with it either; on April 12, 2012, they issued a revision of their advice that no longer proscribed prereading, but that embraced the approach described here and in the Pearson and Hiebert chapter).

The basic idea of close reading is that reading needs to focus on the ideas in the text, and that all the folderol of activity around the text needs to be minimized so that students can figure out what the text actually says. I must admit I have watched far too many picture walks that were so thorough and so mind-numbing there was absolutely no reason to read the text (the students knew every point before reading a single word). Sometimes the teacher provides some context or gives students purposes that are so specific that reading becomes superfluous (in those classrooms the "good" readers are the ones with the sense to repeat back to the teacher the information he or she revealed before the reading even started).

The idea of stripping away these kinds of supports is disquieting for many teachers, and yet research is supportive of the idea, at least in some contexts. For example, in one study, students were randomly assigned to groups who either completed the typical lessons in core programs (including all the background review and ongoing commentary/activity throughout the reading that may focus on critical skills but that distracts focus from the text content) or worked through the same selections but without all of the apparatus. The lessons that focused on making sense of the text led to better comprehension (McKeown, Beck, & Blake, 2009).

Like Pearson and Hiebert, my problem with surrendering these tools altogether is that if we are asking students to read challenging text, we are going to need to have ways to support their reading. If a text presupposes some information necessary to understand or appreciate it, then by all means we should provide that knowledge or remind students of it. Similarly, I think it is useful for the teacher to direct students to pay attention to particular kinds of information in a text (e.g., "This text makes some important comparisons; be sure to notice what is being compared"). The trick here is balance. Prereading certainly should not take longer than reading the text. Similarly, the preview should reveal little information that can be gleaned from the text itself (giving students a summary of what they are about to read should usually be a no-no). Some texts may not need much of an introduction, and in such cases students can jump right in; in other texts, there might be reason to provide more pretext preparation.

Of course, the idea of close reading is not just about how students are prepared to engage in text reading. It also shapes the questions that students should be asked to encourage their writing or discussion. The Common Core standards stress the idea of "text-dependent questioning," meaning questions that can only be answered successfully by someone who has read the text. For example, in reading a story about a girl who tries to wangle a pet out of her parents, students are often asked about their pets and what kinds of pets they would like to have. The problem with such questions is they are usually an alternative to the actual story (the child's experience takes the place of the story in the book), and as such these questions don't require the students to think much about the ideas in the story. Questions that get at the girl's strategy and the parents' responses would be more evident in a close read.

Close reading also encourages greater use of rereading to deepen students' understanding of a text. Too rarely are students asked to read texts multiple times as a strategy for increasing their grasp of the material. Rereading is a widely used approach for fluency practice, of course, but the idea here is that strategic rereading can enhance and deepen understanding. The point isn't to garner a repetition effect (repetition of something tends to help it to stick in memory) but to actually explore the text ideas more thoroughly upon further reflection. One concept of such rereading is to have students read a text three times, with each reading focused on a different aspect of the text: A first reading might be used to clarify and summarize what the text says, a second reading might evaluate the author's craft and how the text worked, and a third reading might connect the text with other texts and student experiences. Each reading would have a somewhat different purpose and students would be expected to garner a deeper understanding and appreciation of the ideas in the text each time that they read. Needless to say, not all texts justify such thorough consideration, but with selections that are demanding and worthwhile, such an approach is very reasonable.

Of course, all of these suggestions focus on the cognitive supports that teachers need to provide to students so that they can learn to engage in the hard intellectual work of reading challenging and worthwhile materials. As Afflerbach (Chapter 9) emphasizes, there is good reason to consider also the motivational or engagement supports that students will need. It is essential that teachers become proficient in helping students to understand and appreciate what is being asked of them and that they come to recognize that this learning is socially meaningful and worthwhile. That means teachers will need to become more adept at providing students with meaningful choices and challenges, and opportunities to engage in collaborative or cooperative activities (Shanahan et al., 2010).

EMPHASIZE WRITING (AND SPEAKING) ABOUT AND WITH TEXT

This strong emphasis on texts and the ideas that they contain is evident not only in the reading standards but in the writing and oral language standards too. Often writing assignments that have been emphasized in school programs encourage students to write mainly about what they already know. Students are asked to write about "A Favorite Time" or to tell about their family or to keep a daily diary. The Common Core standards, again, push in a different direction: They encourage much more writing about reading.

This is a good direction. Reviews of extensive bodies of research have long shown that reading and writing are connected (Fitzgerald & Shanahan, 2000; Shanahan, 2006; Tierney & Shanahan, 1991), and a recent meta-analysis of 104 studies found that the most effective way to combine reading and writing instruction is to have students writing about what they have read (Graham & Hebert, 2010). These studies show that having students summarize text in writing, writing critical analyses of texts, and synthesizing information from multiple texts all can improve students' reading comprehension. Furthermore, these studies show that writing about text improves reading achievement more powerfully than rereading or discussing text, perhaps because writing requires a more thorough and explicit engagement with the text information.

In many schools, the language arts period is divided into a 90-minute reading block, often with an additional 30 minutes devoted to writing at some other time of the day. Other schools conduct separate reading and writing workshops. Neither of these instructional plans makes much sense with standards that are encouraging so much writing about text. It would certainly be acceptable to assign different texts for the reading and writing periods, but I suspect most teachers will find it more efficient to have students writing about the same texts that they are using for close reading. Hansen's notion (Chapter 5) of having students write throughout the day is a good one, very much in line with CCSS.

Toward that end, I believe that the reading comprehension standards provide useful templates for framing writing prompts or planning writing assignments. For example, in the Key Ideas and Details section of the third-grade reading standards, students are asked to recount stories, stating the central message or lesson and explaining its key supporting ideas. This kind of summary writing could be very powerful in the primary grades (Graham & Hebert, 2010). Likewise, first-grade students are asked to identify the similarities and differences between two texts on the same topic—a great opportunity for close reading, some graphic charting of the information from the two texts, and then a writing assignment that requires the children to convey this information. Similarly, the speaking and listening standards encourage a lot of talk about text, and the comprehension standards offer some wonderful insights as to appropriate prompts for those discussions and presentations too.

DON'T LOSE SIGHT OF THE ADVANCES OF THE PAST 20 YEARS

Gehsmann and Templeton (Chapter 4) emphasize well the importance of foundational skills in the Common Core, and with good reason. Many teachers have labored, during the past decade, to implement solid phonological awareness, phonics, vocabulary, and oral reading fluency instruction in their primary-grade classes. The research findings of the National Reading Panel (National Institute of Child Health and Human Development, 2000) and the National Early Literacy Panel (2008) have had a profound impact on school district programs and policies. Reading First, Early Reading First, Head Start, Title I, the Individuals with Disabilities Education Act, and other federal initiatives have stressed the importance of professional development of teachers in these basic areas as well as valuing well-designed instructional materials, assessments, and interventions aimed at helping to ensure that children can hear and remember the sounds in words, use letter sounds and spelling patterns to decode words, understand the meanings of growing numbers of words, and read text accurately and with sufficient speed and appropriate expression.

But, the Common Core standards do not appear to emphasize these aspects of reading as heavily. For example, in most state standards the first reading standards involve phonological awareness and phonics, with the reading comprehension goals somewhere further back in the pack. With the CCSS, it is the decoding and fluency items that are further back. That has led some to assume that there is no alignment between the requirements of No Child Left Behind and the Common Core. But as Gehsmann and Templeton (Chapter 4) show, this interpretation would be wrong. The authors of the Common Core were careful to ensure that the CCSS did address these aspects of learning appropriately and thoroughly. They wanted to be careful not to reignite the reading wars, and they have not.

The Reading Standards: Foundational Skills (K–5), on pages 16 and 17 of the CCSS document, are quite consistent with the requirements of No Child Left Behind and various federal education initiatives. Additionally, vocabulary is included in the language standards document. Anyone who may have anticipated a retreat from the curricular focus of Reading First will be disappointed. The key pillars of early reading instruction are still intact, now in the form of specific curricular goals that are to be accomplished at particular grade levels. The emphasis on more challenging text from second grade up may even intensify pressure on kindergarten and first-grade teachers to develop these foundational skills successfully. According to the CCSS, primary-grade teachers will need to continue to teach foundational reading skills thoroughly and well.

CONTINUE THE SWING TO INFORMATIONAL TEXT

The relative emphasis on literary and informational text has been shifting over the past decade. The wonderful counterpoint between Morrow and colleagues (Chapter 2) and Duke and colleagues (Chapter 3) is a graphic illustration of where the CCSS positions primary grade reading instruction. As Morrow and her colleagues make clear, there is great value to be gained from the reading of literature and it is essential that children be guided to read stories and poems closely and well. But Duke and her colleagues are equally eloquent in their promotion of the reading of informational text in the same ways. Unfortunately, for more than 50 years, there has been a remarkable imbalance between these kinds of texts in school reading programs (Venezky, 1983). As recently as 2002, studies were showing that about 80% of the selections in core reading programs were literary (Moss & Newton, 2002), and students taught through leveled books (Fountas & Pinnell, 1996) have usually experienced even less exposure to informational texts.

However, that imbalance has improved greatly during the past decade. An informal perusal of recent core reading programs suggests that these days they are averaging something more like a 60–40 split, though still favoring literature, and some programs appear to be even more balanced than that. Also, with the increased availability of informational trade books for the early grades, there may be more informational text in use in guided-reading classes as well. These recent shifts of emphasis are important as the new CCSS require teachers to spend roughly half the time devoted to informational text. This will still be a big shift for some classes (particularly those using older textbook programs or that rely on less up-to-date libraries and book rooms), but it will be less of a shift for many teachers than would have been the case just a few years ago.

This transition to a more balanced emphasis on literature and informational text is important because facility with informational text in later education and beyond is a prerequisite to success. In international comparisons (Mullis, Martin, Kennedy, & Foy, 2007), U.S. fourth graders lag students in 17 other countries in their ability to read informational texts (and the American kids read literary text significantly better than informational text).

Recently, Joanne Yatvin (2012, p. 28), a retired educator, opined in *Education Week*: "The fact that fiction now dominates the elementary curriculum is not the result of educators' decisions about what is best for children, but a reflection of children's developmental states, their interests, and their limited experience in the fields of science, geography, history, and technology." In fact, research clearly shows that young children have strong interest in science, history, technology, and the arts and tend to prefer informational text to literature (Mohr, 2006). And if such text encounters were developmentally inappropriate, why would this hold true only in the United States? The success of children with informational text around the world proves that this approach does not violate some unalterable aspect of child development, as Yatvin claims. Of course, the idea that children have had limited experience in many fields of study goes right to the heart of the matter: Using reading to expand children's horizons beyond the tyranny of their personal experience is strongly endorsed by the Common Core standards.

Yatvin makes another mistake, and it is a useful one in this case because it allows for an important distinction to be made. She confuses literary text with fiction, but there are many factual texts that are literary in character as well, such as biographies and autobiographies. The benefit to teaching with informational text is that it exposes children to many text structures, language, and print conventions that are uncommon in literature. Thus, the use of informational text can expose students to a rich array of text structures or organizational schemes (e.g., enumeration, compare–contrast, nontime sequence, cause–effect, problem–solution), text features (e.g., tables of contents, preface, appendices), print conventions (e.g., bold print, italics, bullets, headings/subheadings), and graphics (e.g., charts, tables, projections). To make these learning opportunities available to children, it would be necessary to use informational text rather than nonfiction.

Of course, teaching children from informational texts requires some shift in instructional approach. Fortunately, given the increases in the availability of informational text for primary grade students, there are many high-quality resources for supporting instruction with such materials (Duke & Bennett-Armistead, 2003; Shanahan et al., 2010).

CONCLUSION

The CCSS represent a major shift in literacy and language teaching for young children. Primary-grade teachers will need to make many adjustments over the next few years to ensure that children reach the high learning goals set by these standards. These shifts will require that teachers diligently study the standards and then transform their classroom instruction in many ways: increasing the difficulty of the texts used to teach reading in grades 2 and on (and escalating these levels of text challenge steadily); providing greater scaffolding to help children meet the challenge of difficult text but without just reading the texts to the children or telling them what the texts say; engaging students in more close reading of text, focusing less on background and more on the ideas expressed in the text; balancing the attention accorded to informational and literary texts; and encouraging and supporting more writing about text. If teachers make this transformation successfully, it will be a bright future for our children indeed.

REFERENCES

ACT. (2006). *Reading between the lines.* Iowa City, IO: American College Testing.

Betts, E. A. (1946). *Foundations of reading instruction.* New York: American Book Company.

Bill & Melinda Gates Foundation. (2010). Fewer, clearer, higher: Moving forward with consistent, rigorous standards for all students [College Ready Monographs]. Seattle, WA: Author. Retrieved from *www.gatesfoundation.org/highschools/Documents/fewer-clearer-higher-standards.pdf.*

Carmichael, S. B., Wilson, W. S., Porter-Magee, K., & Martino, G. (2010). The state of state standards—and the common core—in 2010. Washington, DC: Thomas Fordham Institute. Retrieved from *www.edexcellence.net/publications/the-state-of-state-of-standards-and-the-common-core-in-2010.html.*

Clay, M. (1993). *Reading Recovery: A guidebook for teachers in training.* Portsmouth, NH: Heinemann.

Coleman, D., & Pimentel, S. (2012a). Revised publishers' criteria for the Common Core State Standards in English language arts and literacy, grades K–2. Retrieved from *www.achievethecore.org/downloads/Publishers%20Criteria%20for%20Literacy%20for%20Grades%20K-2.pdf.*

Coleman, D., & Pimentel, S. (2012b). Revised publishers' criteria for the Common Core State Standards in English language arts and literacy, grades 3–12. Retrieved from *www.achievethecore.org/downloads/Publishers%20Criteria%20for%20Literacy%20for%20Grades%203-12.pdf.*

Common Core State Standards Initiative. (2010). Myths vs. facts. Retrieved from *www.corestandards.org/about-the-standards/myths-vs-facts.*

Cunningham, P. M., Hall, D. P., & Sigmon, C. M. (1999). *The teacher's guide to the four blocks, grades 1–3: A multimethod, multilevel framework for grades 1–3.* Greensboro, NC: Carson-Dellosa.

Duke, N. K. (2000). 3.6 minutes per day: The scarcity of informational texts in first grade. *Reading Research Quarterly, 35,* 202–224.

Duke, N. K., & Bennett-Armistead, S. (2003). *Reading & writing informational text in the primary grades: Research-based practices.* New York: Scholastic.

Fitzgerald, J., & Shanahan, T. (2000). Reading and writing relations and their development. *Educational Psychologist, 35,* 39–51.

Fountas, I. C., & Pinnell, G. C. (1996). *Guided reading: Good first teaching for all children.* Portsmouth, NH: Heinemann.

Gewertz, C. (2011, April 27). Foundations creating online common-standards coursework. *Education Week: Curriculum Matters.* Retrieved from *http://blogs.edweek.org/edweek/curriculum/2011/04/gates_pearson_foundation_to_cr.html?qs=sally+hampton.*

Graham, S., & Hebert, M. (2010). Writing to read: Evidence for how writing can improve reading. New York: Carnegie Corporation of New York. Retrieved from *http://www.all4ed.org/files/WritingToRead.pdf.*

Hiebert, E. H. (1999). Text matters in learning to read (Distinguished Educators Series). *The Reading Teacher, 52,* 552–568.

McKeown, M. G., Beck, I. L., & Blake, R. G. K. (2009). Rethinking comprehension instruction: Comparing strategies and content instructional approaches. *Reading Research Quarterly, 44,* 218–253.

Mohr, K. A. J. (2006). Children's choices for recreational reading: A three-part investigation of selection preferences, rationales, and processes. *Journal of Literacy Research, 38,* 81–104.

Morgan, A., Wilcox, B. R., & Eldredge, J. L. (2000). Effect of difficulty levels on second-grade delayed readers using dyad reading. *Journal of Educational Research, 94,* 113–119.

Moss, B., & Newton, E. (2002). An examination of the informational text genre in basal readers. *Reading Psychology, 23,* 1–13.

Mullis, I. V. S., Martin, M. O., Kennedy, A. M., & Foy, P. (2007). *PIRLS 2006 International Report: IEA's progress in international literacy study in primary schools in 40 countries.* Boston: TIMMS & PIRLS International Study Center, Lynch School of Education, Boston College.

National Early Literacy Panel. (2008). Developing early literacy: Report of the National Early

Literacy Panel. Washington, DC: National Institute for Literacy. Retrieved from *http://lincs.
ed.gov/publications/pdf/NELPReport09.pdf.*

National Governors Association Center for Best Practices and Council of Chief State School Officers. (2010). *Common Core State Standards for English language arts & literacy in history/
social studies, science, and technical subjects.* Washington, DC: Author.

National Institute of Child Health and Human Development. (2000). Report of the National
Reading Panel. Teaching children to read: An evidence-based assessment of the scientific
research literature on reading and its implications for reading instruction (NIH Publication
No. 00-4769). Washington, DC: U.S. Government Printing Office. Retrieved from *http://
www.nichd.nih.gov/publications/nrp/upload.smallbook_pdf.pdf.*

Powell, W. R. (1968). Reappraising the criteria for interpreting informal inventories. In *International Reading Association Conference Proceedings* (Vol. 12, pt. 4, pp. 100–109). Reproduc-
tion Service No. ERIC 5194164.

Shanahan, C., Shanahan, T., & Misichia, C. (2011). Analysis of expert readers in three disciplines:
History, mathematics, and chemistry. *Journal of Literacy Research, 3,* 393–429.

Shanahan, T. (1983). The informal reading inventory and the instructional level: The study that
never took place. In L. Gentile, M. L. Kamil, & J. Blanchard (Eds.), *Reading research revisited* (pp. 577–580). Columbus, OH: Merrill.

Shanahan, T. (2006). Relations among oral language, reading, and writing development. In C.
A. MacArthur, S. Graham, & J. Fitzgerald (Eds.), *Handbook of writing research* (pp. 171—
186). New York: Guilford Press.

Shanahan, T. (2011). Common Core standards: Are we going to lower the fences or teach kids to
climb? *Reading Today, 29*(1), 20–21.

Shanahan, T., Callison, K., Carriere, C., Duke, N. K., Pearson, P. D., Schatschneider, C., et al.
(2010). Improving reading comprehension in kindergarten through 3rd grade: A practice
guide (NCEE 2010-4038). Washington, DC: National Center for Education Evaluation
and Regional Assistance, Institute of Education Sciences, U.S. Department of Education.
Retrieved from *http://ies.ed.gov/ncee/wwc/practiceguide.aspx?sid=14.*

Shanahan, T., Fisher, D., & Frey, N. (2012). The challenge of challenging text. *Educational Leadership, 69*(6), 58–63.

Shanahan, T., & Shanahan, C. (2012). What is disciplinary literacy and why does it matter? *Topics in Language Disorders, 32,* 1–12.

Stahl, S., & Heulbach, K. M. (2005). Fluency-oriented reading instruction. *Journal of Literacy
Research, 37,* 25–60.

Tierney, R., & Shanahan, T. (1991). Reading-writing relationships: Processes, transactions, outcomes. In P. D. Pearson, R. Barr, M. Kamil, & P. Mosenthal (Eds.), *Handbook of reading
research* (pp. 246–280). New York: Longman.

Venezky, R. L. (1983). The origins of the present-day chasm between adult literacy needs and
school literacy instruction. *Visible Language, 16,* 113–136.

Yatvin, J. (2012, February 29). A flawed approach to reading in the common-core standards.
Education Week, p. 28.

APPENDIX A

Common Core State Standards for English Language Arts, Grades K–2

ENGLISH LANGUAGE ARTS STANDARDS FOR KINDERGARTEN

Reading: Literature 》 *Kindergarten*

Key Ideas and Details

- RL.K.1. With prompting and support, ask and answer questions about key details in a text.
- RL.K.2. With prompting and support, retell familiar stories, including key details.
- RL.K.3. With prompting and support, identify characters, settings, and major events in a story.

Craft and Structure

- RL.K.4. Ask and answer questions about unknown words in a text.
- RL.K.5. Recognize common types of texts (e.g., storybooks, poems).
- RL.K.6. With prompting and support, name the author and illustrator of a story and define the role of each in telling the story.

Integration of Knowledge and Ideas

- RL.K.7. With prompting and support, describe the relationship between illustrations and the story in which they appear (e.g., what moment in a story an illustration depicts).
- RL.K.8. (Not applicable to literature)
- RL.K.9. With prompting and support, compare and contrast the adventures and experiences of characters in familiar stories.

Range of Reading and Level of Text Complexity

- RL.K.10. Actively engage in group reading activities with purpose and understanding.

From the Common Core State Standards Initiative. Copyright 2010 by the National Governors Association Center for Best Practices and Council of Chief State School Officers. All rights reserved.

Reading: Informational Text 》 Kindergarten

Key Ideas and Details

- RI.K.1. With prompting and support, ask and answer questions about key details in a text.
- RI.K.2. With prompting and support, identify the main topic and retell key details of a text.
- RI.K.3. With prompting and support, describe the connection between two individuals, events, ideas, or pieces of information in a text.

Craft and Structure

- RI.K.4. With prompting and support, ask and answer questions about unknown words in a text.
- RI.K.5. Identify the front cover, back cover, and title page of a book.
- RI.K.6. Name the author and illustrator of a text and define the role of each in presenting the ideas or information in a text.

Integration of Knowledge and Ideas

- RI.K.7. With prompting and support, describe the relationship between illustrations and the text in which they appear (e.g., what person, place, thing, or idea in the text an illustration depicts).
- RI.K.8. With prompting and support, identify the reasons an author gives to support points in a text.
- RI.K.9. With prompting and support, identify basic similarities in and differences between two texts on the same topic (e.g., in illustrations, descriptions, or procedures).

Range of Reading and Level of Text Complexity

- RI.K.10. Actively engage in group reading activities with purpose and understanding.

Reading: Foundational Skills 》 Kindergarten

Print Concepts

- RF.K.1. Demonstrate understanding of the organization and basic features of print.
  - ○ Follow words from left to right, top to bottom, and page by page.
  - ○ Recognize that spoken words are represented in written language by specific sequences of letters.
  - ○ Understand that words are separated by spaces in print.
  - ○ Recognize and name all upper- and lowercase letters of the alphabet.

Phonological Awareness

- RF.K.2. Demonstrate understanding of spoken words, syllables, and sounds (phonemes).
  - ○ Recognize and produce rhyming words.
  - ○ Count, pronounce, blend, and segment syllables in spoken words.
  - ○ Blend and segment onsets and rimes of single-syllable spoken words.
  - ○ Isolate and pronounce the initial, medial vowel, and final sounds (phonemes) in three-phoneme (consonant–vowel–consonant, or CVC) words.[1] (This does not include CVCs ending with /l/, /r/, or /x/.)
  - ○ Add or substitute individual sounds (phonemes) in simple, one-syllable words to make new words.

Phonics and Word Recognition

- RF.K.3. Know and apply grade-level phonics and word analysis skills in decoding words.
  - o Demonstrate basic knowledge of letter–sound correspondences by producing the primary or most frequent sound for each consonant.
  - o Associate the long and short sounds with the common spellings (graphemes) for the five major vowels.
  - o Read common high-frequency words by sight (e.g., *the, of, to, you, she, my, is, are, do, does*).
  - o Distinguish between similarly spelled words by identifying the sounds of the letters that differ.

Fluency

- RF.K.4. Read emergent-reader texts with purpose and understanding.

Writing » Kindergarten

Text Types and Purposes

- W.K.1. Use a combination of drawing, dictating, and writing to compose opinion pieces in which they tell a reader the topic or the name of the book they are writing about and state an opinion or preference about the topic or book (e.g., *My favorite book is . . .*).
- W.K.2. Use a combination of drawing, dictating, and writing to compose informative/explanatory texts in which they name what they are writing about and supply some information about the topic.
- W.K.3. Use a combination of drawing, dictating, and writing to narrate a single event or several loosely linked events, tell about the events in the order in which they occurred, and provide a reaction to what happened.

Production and Distribution of Writing

- W.K.4. (Begins in grade 3)
- W.K.5. With guidance and support from adults, respond to questions and suggestions from peers and add details to strengthen writing as needed.
- W.K.6. With guidance and support from adults, explore a variety of digital tools to produce and publish writing, including in collaboration with peers.

Research to Build and Present Knowledge

- W.K.7. Participate in shared research and writing projects (e.g., explore a number of books by a favorite author and express opinions about them).
- W.K.8. With guidance and support from adults, recall information from experiences or gather information from provided sources to answer a question.
- W.K.9. (Begins in grade 4)

Range of Writing

- W.K.10. (Begins in grade 3)

Speaking and Listening 》 *Kindergarten*

Comprehension and Collaboration

- SL.K.1. Participate in collaborative conversations with diverse partners about *kindergarten topics and texts* with peers and adults in small and larger groups.
  - Follow agreed-upon rules for discussions (e.g., listening to others and taking turns speaking about the topics and texts under discussion).
  - Continue a conversation through multiple exchanges.
- SL.K.2. Confirm understanding of a text read aloud or information presented orally or through other media by asking and answering questions about key details and requesting clarification if something is not understood.
- SL.K.3. Ask and answer questions in order to seek help, get information, or clarify something that is not understood.

Presentation of Knowledge and Ideas

- SL.K.4. Describe familiar people, places, things, and events and, with prompting and support, provide additional detail.
- SL.K.5. Add drawings or other visual displays to descriptions as desired to provide additional detail.
- SL.K.6. Speak audibly and express thoughts, feelings, and ideas clearly.

Language 》 *Kindergarten*

Conventions of Standard English

- L.K.1. Demonstrate command of the conventions of standard English grammar and usage when writing or speaking.
  - Print many upper- and lowercase letters.
  - Use frequently occurring nouns and verbs.
  - Form regular plural nouns orally by adding /s/ or /es/ (e.g., *dog*, *dogs*; *wish*, *wishes*).
  - Understand and use question words (interrogatives) (e.g., *who, what, where, when, why, how*).
  - Use the most frequently occurring prepositions (e.g., *to, from, in, out, on, off, for, of, by, with*).
  - Produce and expand complete sentences in shared language activities.
- L.K.2. Demonstrate command of the conventions of standard English capitalization, punctuation, and spelling when writing.
  - Capitalize the first word in a sentence and the pronoun *I*.
  - Recognize and name end punctuation.
  - Write a letter or letters for most consonant and short-vowel sounds (phonemes).
  - Spell simple words phonetically, drawing on knowledge of sound–letter relationships.

Knowledge of Language

- L.K.3. (Begins in grade 2)

Vocabulary Acquisition and Use

- L.K.4. Determine or clarify the meaning of unknown and multiple-meaning words and phrases based on kindergarten reading and content.
  - o Identify new meanings for familiar words and apply them accurately (e.g., knowing *duck* is a bird and learning the verb to *duck*).
  - o Use the most frequently occurring inflections and affixes (e.g., *-ed, -s, re-, un-, pre-, -ful, -less*) as a clue to the meaning of an unknown word.
- L.K.5. With guidance and support from adults, explore word relationships and nuances in word meanings.
  - o Sort common objects into categories (e.g., shapes, foods) to gain a sense of the concepts the categories represent.
  - o Demonstrate understanding of frequently occurring verbs and adjectives by relating them to their opposites (antonyms).
  - o Identify real-life connections between words and their use (e.g., note places at school that are colorful).
  - o Distinguish shades of meaning among verbs describing the same general action (e.g., *walk, march, strut, prance*) by acting out the meanings.
- L.K.6. Use words and phrases acquired through conversations, reading and being read to, and responding to texts.

ENGLISH LANGUAGE ARTS STANDARDS FOR GRADE 1

Reading: Literature 》 *Grade 1*

Key Ideas and Details

- RL.1.1. Ask and answer questions about key details in a text.
- RL.1.2. Retell stories, including key details, and demonstrate understanding of their central message or lesson.
- RL.1.3. Describe characters, settings, and major events in a story, using key details.

Craft and Structure

- RL.1.4. Identify words and phrases in stories or poems that suggest feelings or appeal to the senses.
- RL.1.5. Explain major differences between books that tell stories and books that give information, drawing on a wide reading of a range of text types.
- RL.1.6. Identify who is telling the story at various points in a text.

Integration of Knowledge and Ideas

- RL.1.7. Use illustrations and details in a story to describe its characters, setting, or events.
- RL.1.8. (Not applicable to literature)
- RL.1.9. Compare and contrast the adventures and experiences of characters in stories.

Range of Reading and Level of Text Complexity

- RL.1.10. With prompting and support, read prose and poetry of appropriate complexity for grade 1.

Reading: Informational Text 》 *Grade 1*

Key Ideas and Details

- RI.1.1. Ask and answer questions about key details in a text.
- RI.1.2. Identify the main topic and retell key details of a text.
- RI.1.3. Describe the connection between two individuals, events, ideas, or pieces of information in a text.

Craft and Structure

- RI.1.4. Ask and answer questions to help determine or clarify the meaning of words and phrases in a text.
- RI.1.5. Know and use various text features (e.g., headings, tables of contents, glossaries, electronic menus, icons) to locate key facts or information in a text.
- RI.1.6. Distinguish between information provided by pictures or other illustrations and information provided by the words in a text.

Integration of Knowledge and Ideas

- RI.1.7. Use the illustrations and details in a text to describe its key ideas.
- RI.1.8. Identify the reasons an author gives to support points in a text.
- RI.1.9. Identify basic similarities in and differences between two texts on the same topic (e.g., in illustrations, descriptions, or procedures).

Range of Reading and Level of Text Complexity

- RI.1.10. With prompting and support, read informational texts appropriately complex for grade 1.

Reading: Foundational Skills 》 *Grade 1*

Print Concepts

- RF.1.1. Demonstrate understanding of the organization and basic features of print.
  - Recognize the distinguishing features of a sentence (e.g., first word, capitalization, ending punctuation).

Phonological Awareness

- RF.1.2. Demonstrate understanding of spoken words, syllables, and sounds (phonemes).
  - Distinguish long from short vowel sounds in spoken single-syllable words.
  - Orally produce single-syllable words by blending sounds (phonemes), including consonant blends.
  - Isolate and pronounce initial, medial vowel, and final sounds (phonemes) in spoken single-syllable words.
  - Segment spoken single-syllable words into their complete sequence of individual sounds (phonemes).

Phonics and Word Recognition

- RF.1.3. Know and apply grade-level phonics and word analysis skills in decoding words.
  - Know the spelling–sound correspondences for common consonant digraphs (two letters that represent one sound).
  - Decode regularly spelled one-syllable words.
  - Know final -e and common vowel team conventions for representing long vowel sounds.
  - Use knowledge that every syllable must have a vowel sound to determine the number of syllables in a printed word.
  - Decode two-syllable words following basic patterns by breaking the words into syllables.
  - Read words with inflectional endings.
  - Recognize and read grade-appropriate irregularly spelled words.

Fluency

- RF.1.4. Read with sufficient accuracy and fluency to support comprehension.
  - Read grade-level text with purpose and understanding.
  - Read grade-level text orally with accuracy, appropriate rate, and expression.
  - Use context to confirm or self-correct word recognition and understanding, rereading as necessary.

Writing 》 Grade 1

Text Types and Purposes

- W.1.1. Write opinion pieces in which they introduce the topic or name the book they are writing about, state an opinion, supply a reason for the opinion, and provide some sense of closure.
- W.1.2. Write informative/explanatory texts in which they name a topic, supply some facts about the topic, and provide some sense of closure.
- W.1.3. Write narratives in which they recount two or more appropriately sequenced events, include some details regarding what happened, use temporal words to signal event order, and provide some sense of closure.

Production and Distribution of Writing

- W.1.4. (Begins in grade 3)
- W.1.5. With guidance and support from adults, focus on a topic, respond to questions and suggestions from peers, and add details to strengthen writing as needed.
- W.1.6. With guidance and support from adults, use a variety of digital tools to produce and publish writing, including in collaboration with peers.

Research to Build and Present Knowledge

- W.1.7. Participate in shared research and writing projects (e.g., explore a number of "how-to" books on a given topic and use them to write a sequence of instructions).
- W.1.8. With guidance and support from adults, recall information from experiences or gather information from provided sources to answer a question.
- W.1.9. (Begins in grade 4)

Range of Writing

- W.1.10. (Begins in grade 3)

Speaking and Listening » *Grade 1*

Comprehension and Collaboration

- SL.1.1. Participate in collaborative conversations with diverse partners about *grade 1 topics and texts* with peers and adults in small and larger groups.
    - o Follow agreed-upon rules for discussions (e.g., listening to others with care, speaking one at a time about the topics and texts under discussion).
    - o Build on others' talk in conversations by responding to the comments of others through multiple exchanges.
    - o Ask questions to clear up any confusion about the topics and texts under discussion.
- SL.1.2. Ask and answer questions about key details in a text read aloud or information presented orally or through other media.
- SL.1.3. Ask and answer questions about what a speaker says in order to gather additional information or clarify something that is not understood.

Presentation of Knowledge and Ideas

- SL.1.4. Describe people, places, things, and events with relevant details, expressing ideas and feelings clearly.
- SL.1.5. Add drawings or other visual displays to descriptions when appropriate to clarify ideas, thoughts, and feelings.
- SL.1.6. Produce complete sentences when appropriate to task and situation.

Language » *Grade 1*

Conventions of Standard English

- L.1.1. Demonstrate command of the conventions of standard English grammar and usage when writing or speaking.
    - o Print all upper- and lowercase letters.
    - o Use common, proper, and possessive nouns.
    - o Use singular and plural nouns with matching verbs in basic sentences (e.g., *He hops*; *We hop*).
    - o Use personal, possessive, and indefinite pronouns (e.g., *I, me, my; they, them, their, anyone, everything*).
    - o Use verbs to convey a sense of past, present, and future (e.g., *Yesterday I walked home*; *Today I walk home*; *Tomorrow I will walk home*).
    - o Use frequently occurring adjectives.
    - o Use frequently occurring conjunctions (e.g., *and, but, or, so, because*).
    - o Use determiners (e.g., articles, demonstratives).
    - o Use frequently occurring prepositions (e.g., *during, beyond, toward*).
    - o Produce and expand complete simple and compound declarative, interrogative, imperative, and exclamatory sentences in response to prompts.
- L.1.2. Demonstrate command of the conventions of standard English capitalization, punctuation, and spelling when writing.
    - o Capitalize dates and names of people.
    - o Use end punctuation for sentences.
    - o Use commas in dates and to separate single words in a series.
    - o Use conventional spelling for words with common spelling patterns and for frequently occurring irregular words.
    - o Spell untaught words phonetically, drawing on phonemic awareness and spelling conventions.

Knowledge of Language

- L.1.3. (Begins in grade 2)

Vocabulary Acquisition and Use

- L.1.4. Determine or clarify the meaning of unknown and multiple-meaning words and phrases based on *grade 1 reading and content*, choosing flexibly from an array of strategies.
  - Use sentence-level context as a clue to the meaning of a word or phrase.
  - Use frequently occurring affixes as a clue to the meaning of a word.
  - Identify frequently occurring root words (e.g., *look*) and their inflectional forms (e.g., *looks, looked, looking*).
- L.1.5. With guidance and support from adults, demonstrate understanding of figurative language, word relationships and nuances in word meanings.
  - Sort words into categories (e.g., colors, clothing) to gain a sense of the concepts the categories represent.
  - Define words by category and by one or more key attributes (e.g., a *duck* is a bird that swims; a *tiger* is a large cat with stripes).
  - Identify real-life connections between words and their use (e.g., note places at home that are *cozy*).
  - Distinguish shades of meaning among verbs differing in manner (e.g., *look, peek, glance, stare, glare, scowl*) and adjectives differing in intensity (e.g., large, gigantic) by defining or choosing them or by acting out the meanings.
- L.1.6. Use words and phrases acquired through conversations, reading and being read to, and responding to texts, including using frequently occurring conjunctions to signal simple relationships (e.g., *because*).

ENGLISH LANGUAGE ARTS STANDARDS FOR GRADE 2

Reading: Literature 》 Grade 2

Key Ideas and Details

- RL.2.1. Ask and answer such questions as *who, what, where, when, why*, and *how* to demonstrate understanding of key details in a text.
- RL.2.2. Recount stories, including fables and folktales from diverse cultures, and determine their central message, lesson, or moral.
- RL.2.3. Describe how characters in a story respond to major events and challenges.

Craft and Structure

- RL.2.4. Describe how words and phrases (e.g., regular beats, alliteration, rhymes, repeated lines) supply rhythm and meaning in a story, poem, or song.
- RL.2.5. Describe the overall structure of a story, including describing how the beginning introduces the story and the ending concludes the action.
- RL.2.6. Acknowledge differences in the points of view of characters, including by speaking in a different voice for each character when reading dialogue aloud.

Integration of Knowledge and Ideas

- RL.2.7. Use information gained from the illustrations and words in a print or digital text to demonstrate understanding of its characters, setting, or plot.
- RL.2.8. (Not applicable to literature)
- RL.2.9. Compare and contrast two or more versions of the same story (e.g., Cinderella stories) by different authors or from different cultures.

Range of Reading and Level of Text Complexity

- RL.2.10. By the end of the year, read and comprehend literature, including stories and poetry, in the grades 2–3 text complexity band proficiently, with scaffolding as needed at the high end of the range.

Reading: Informational Text » Grade 2

Key Ideas and Details

- RI.2.1. Ask and answer such questions as *who*, *what*, *where*, *when*, *why*, and *how* to demonstrate understanding of key details in a text.
- RI.2.2. Identify the main topic of a multiparagraph text as well as the focus of specific paragraphs within the text.
- RI.2.3. Describe the connection between a series of historical events, scientific ideas or concepts, or steps in technical procedures in a text.

Craft and Structure

- RI.2.4. Determine the meaning of words and phrases in a text relevant to a *grade 2 topic or subject area.*
- RI.2.5. Know and use various text features (e.g., captions, bold print, subheadings, glossaries, indexes, electronic menus, icons) to locate key facts or information in a text efficiently.
- RI.2.6. Identify the main purpose of a text, including what the author wants to answer, explain, or describe.

Integration of Knowledge and Ideas

- RI.2.7. Explain how specific images (e.g., a diagram showing how a machine works) contribute to and clarify a text.
- RI.2.8. Describe how reasons support specific points the author makes in a text.
- RI.2.9. Compare and contrast the most important points presented by two texts on the same topic.

Range of Reading and Level of Text Complexity

- RI.2.10. By the end of year, read and comprehend informational texts, including history/social studies, science, and technical texts, in the grades 2–3 text complexity band proficiently, with scaffolding as needed at the high end of the range.

Reading: Foundational Skills » Grade 2

Phonics and Word Recognition

- RF.2.3. Know and apply grade-level phonics and word analysis skills in decoding words.
  - ○ Distinguish long and short vowels when reading regularly spelled one-syllable words.
  - ○ Know spelling–sound correspondences for additional common vowel teams.
  - ○ Decode regularly spelled two-syllable words with long vowels.
  - ○ Decode words with common prefixes and suffixes.
  - ○ Identify words with inconsistent but common spelling–sound correspondences.
  - ○ Recognize and read grade-appropriate irregularly spelled words.

Fluency

- RF.2.4. Read with sufficient accuracy and fluency to support comprehension.
  - ○ Read grade-level text with purpose and understanding.
  - ○ Read grade-level text orally with accuracy, appropriate rate, and expression.
  - ○ Use context to confirm or self-correct word recognition and understanding, rereading as necessary.

Writing » Grade 2

Text Types and Purposes

- W.2.1. Write opinion pieces in which they introduce the topic or book they are writing about, state an opinion, supply reasons that support the opinion, use linking words (e.g., *because, and, also*) to connect opinion and reasons, and provide a concluding statement or section.
- W.2.2. Write informative/explanatory texts in which they introduce a topic, use facts and definitions to develop points, and provide a concluding statement or section.
- W.2.3. Write narratives in which they recount a well-elaborated event or short sequence of events, include details to describe actions, thoughts, and feelings, use temporal words to signal event order, and provide a sense of closure.

Production and Distribution of Writing

- W.2.4. (Begins in grade 3)
- W.2.5. With guidance and support from adults and peers, focus on a topic and strengthen writing as needed by revising and editing.
- W.2.6. With guidance and support from adults, use a variety of digital tools to produce and publish writing, including in collaboration with peers.

Research to Build and Present Knowledge

- W.2.7. Participate in shared research and writing projects (e.g., read a number of books on a single topic to produce a report; record science observations).
- W.2.8. Recall information from experiences or gather information from provided sources to answer a question.
- W.2.9. (Begins in grade 4)

Range of Writing

- W.2.10. (Begins in grade 3)

Speaking & Listening 》 Grade 2

Comprehension and Collaboration

- SL.2.1. Participate in collaborative conversations with diverse partners about *grade 2 topics and texts* with peers and adults in small and larger groups.
  - Follow agreed-upon rules for discussions (e.g., gaining the floor in respectful ways, listening to others with care, speaking one at a time about the topics and texts under discussion).
  - Build on others' talk in conversations by linking their comments to the remarks of others.
  - Ask for clarification and further explanation as needed about the topics and texts under discussion.
- SL.2.2. Recount or describe key ideas or details from a text read aloud or information presented orally or through other media.
- SL.2.3. Ask and answer questions about what a speaker says in order to clarify comprehension, gather additional information, or deepen understanding of a topic or issue.

Presentation of Knowledge and Ideas

- SL.2.4. Tell a story or recount an experience with appropriate facts and relevant, descriptive details, speaking audibly in coherent sentences.
- SL.2.5. Create audio recordings of stories or poems; add drawings or other visual displays to stories or recounts of experiences when appropriate to clarify ideas, thoughts, and feelings.
- SL.2.6. Produce complete sentences when appropriate to task and situation in order to provide requested detail or clarification.

Language 》 Grade 2

Conventions of Standard English

- L.2.1. Demonstrate command of the conventions of standard English grammar and usage when writing or speaking.
  - Use collective nouns (e.g., *group*).
  - Form and use frequently occurring irregular plural nouns (e.g., *feet, children, teeth, mice, fish*).
  - Use reflexive pronouns (e.g., *myself, ourselves*).
  - Form and use the past tense of frequently occurring irregular verbs (e.g., *sat, hid, told*).
  - Use adjectives and adverbs, and choose between them depending on what is to be modified.
  - Produce, expand, and rearrange complete simple and compound sentences (e.g., *The boy watched the movie; The little boy watched the movie; The action movie was watched by the little boy*).
- L.2.2. Demonstrate command of the conventions of standard English capitalization, punctuation, and spelling when writing.
  - Capitalize holidays, product names, and geographic names.
  - Use commas in greetings and closings of letters.
  - Use an apostrophe to form contractions and frequently occurring possessives.
  - Generalize learned spelling patterns when writing words (e.g., *cage* → badge; *boy* → boil).
  - Consult reference materials, including beginning dictionaries, as needed to check and correct spellings.

Knowledge of Language

- L.2.3. Use knowledge of language and its conventions when writing, speaking, reading, or listening.

  o Compare formal and informal uses of English.

Vocabulary Acquisition and Use

- L.2.4. Determine or clarify the meaning of unknown and multiple-meaning words and phrases based on grade 2 reading and content, choosing flexibly from an array of strategies.

  o Use sentence-level context as a clue to the meaning of a word or phrase.
  o Determine the meaning of the new word formed when a known prefix is added to a known word (e.g., *happy/unhappy, tell/retell*).
  o Use a known root word as a clue to the meaning of an unknown word with the same root (e.g., *addition, additional*).
  o Use knowledge of the meaning of individual words to predict the meaning of compound words (e.g., *birdhouse, lighthouse, housefly; bookshelf, notebook, bookmark*).
  o Use glossaries and beginning dictionaries, both print and digital, to determine or clarify the meaning of words and phrases.

- L.2.5. Demonstrate understanding of figurative language, word relationships and nuances in word meanings.

  o Identify real-life connections between words and their use (e.g., *describe foods that are spicy or juicy*).
  o Distinguish shades of meaning among closely related verbs (e.g., *toss, throw, hurl*) and closely related adjectives (e.g., *thin, slender, skinny, scrawny*).

- L.2.6. Use words and phrases acquired through conversations, reading and being read to, and responding to texts, including using adjectives and adverbs to describe (e.g., *When other kids are happy that makes me happy*).

APPENDIX B

Thematic Units for Grades K–2, with Common Core State Standards Embedded

Erin Kramer
Kelly Lovejoy
Mary Rodgers
Jessica Sullivan
Rutgers University

EARTH—GRADE K

Desired results: Literacy	Desired results: Science
Established Goals Common Core State Standards for English language arts grade K* *Standards articulated in the Learning Plan below.	**Established Goals** • Describe Earth materials using appropriate terms, such as *hard*, *soft*, *dry*, *wet*, *heavy*, and *light*. • Identify and use water conservation practices. • Identify the natural resources used in the process of making various manufactured products. • Communicate ways that humans protect habitats and/or improve conditions for the growth of the plants and animals that live there or ways that humans might harm habitats. (N.J. Department of Education, 2010)

Enduring Understandings	Enduring Understandings
• What is spoken can be written. • What is written can be read and spoken. • Reading is for enjoyment and learning. • Writing and spoken language are for sharing ideas, opinions, experiences, or asking questions. • Effective communication involves clarity of ideas.	• The Earth is a system, continuously moving resources from one part of the system to another. • Soil is a product of the interactions of the Earth system components. • The Earth system includes a variety of materials in solid, liquid, or gaseous form. • All animals and most plants depend on both other organisms and their environments for their basic needs. (N.J. Department of Education, 2010)
Essential Questions • How are reading, writing, and spoken language related and what are they for? • How can I effectively communicate an idea, opinion, or experience or ask a question?	**Essential Questions** • How can rocks be described and sorted? • What is soil? • Where is water found, and how is it used? • What can be made from Earth's natural materials? • What can I do to take care of the Earth?
Knowledge Students will know: • Print is read from left to right, top to bottom, and page by page. • Spoken words are represented in written language. • Words are separated by spaces. • Questions are useful when we want to find out something.	**Knowledge** Students will know: • Soils are made of many living and nonliving substances. The attributes and properties of soil (e.g., moisture, kind and size of particles, living/organic elements) vary depending on location. • There are many sources and uses of water. • The origin of everyday manufactured products such as paper and aluminum cans can be traced back to natural resources. • Humans can change natural habitats in ways that can be helpful or harmful for the plants and animals that live there. (N.J. Department of Education, 2010)
Skills Students will be able to: • Read *made, is, from,* and *are* by sight. • Write for authentic purposes using knowledge of letter–sound correspondences. • Listen to others and take turns while speaking. • Ask and answer questions. • Use question words (*who, what, where, when, why, how*). • Use and expand complete sentences in shared language activities speaking audibly and clearly. • Expand understanding of descriptive words through categorization and comparison of real-life objects.	**Skills** Students will be able to: • Explore and name properties of rocks. • Explore and identify things found in soil. • Name water sources (lake, river, ocean). • Name uses for and ways to conserve water. • Identify the natural source of common objects. • Name and follow healthy Earth practices.

Assessment Evidence

Performance Task
- **Creating Room Labels for Healthy Earth Practices**
  - Goal and Role: As a member of the classroom community, create labels for the classroom to remind the community of specific healthy Earth practices.
  - Audience: The class
  - Situation: The challenge involves knowing healthy Earth practices for the classroom and being able to draw and write about it.
  - Product: A label with pictures and words
  - Standards: Students will think of a healthy Earth practice and may receive help from an adult (*What can we say about the sink?*). The picture must fill the index card (4″ × 6″) and have realistic colors. The writing will be done at students' developmental levels, and the teacher can note progress (adult writing should be written below student writing before hanging the label on the wall).

Other Evidence
- Earth Test
- Checklist for Print Concepts
- Oral Language Checklist
- Word List for Sight Words

LEARNING PLAN

Routines and Morning Meeting

CCSS in English Language Arts: RF.K.1, RF.K.2, RF.K.3, RF.K.4, SL.K.1, SL.K.4, SL.K.6, L.K.1, L.K.5.c, L.K.6

Objectives: Students will be able to:
- Perform classroom responsibilities that demonstrate healthy Earth practices.
- Use concrete objects as a way to build vocabulary.
- Participate in conversations, speaking in complete sentences when necessary, and exhibit listening, turn taking, and building on others' talk.
- Identify beat, rhymes, known letters, syllables, word chunks, and sight words in familiar songs.

Activities:
- Classroom Job: Lights person turns out the lights when the classroom is empty.
- Classroom Job: Spy checks the floor for supplies (e.g., pencils, crayons, markers) and saves them from being wasted.
- Classroom Job: Recycler brings the classroom bottles and cans down to the big bin for recycling.
- Classroom Job: Plants person waters the classroom plants.
- Students bring in unique rocks to start a class rock collection.
- Dramatic Play Area: Set up a geology center in the classroom with the following items:
  - Tools—magnifying glasses, paint brushes for brushing off rocks, flashlights
  - Clothing—headlamps, goggles, white button-down shirts for lab coats or child-sized aprons

o The rocks from the class rock collection and soil in plastic zipper bags

o Literacy materials—pencils, clipboards with paper or notebooks, rock types chart, soil classification chart, geological rock color chart

• Share: One way I take care of the Earth is . . .

• Activity: Sing an Earth song. Print text on chart paper. Clap out beat or syllables, and identify known letters, sight words, known word chunks, and rhyming words where appropriate. Several are available at *www.songs4teachers.com/earthday.htm* and *www.preschoolexpress.com/music_station07/earth_day_songs_apr07.shtml*.

• Activity: Adjective Game. Take a rock from the collection. Hold it and say one descriptive word. Pass the rock to the next person, who has to come up with a new word. Continue passing and saying adjectives (no repeats). When someone is stumped, present a new rock and continue the game with that one. The round ends when everyone has had a turn. Multiple rounds can be played where students try to "beat their score," coming up with more words than the time before.

• Science Word Wall: Keep a running list of science vocabulary words throughout the unit.

Lesson Assessment: Participation will be checked. Notes and recordings can be made to assess students' language use.

LESSON 1: CLASS ROCK COLLECTION LANGUAGE ACTIVITY

CCSS in English Language Arts: RF.K.1, RF.K.3, W.K.7, W.K.8, SL.K.1, SL.K.6, L.K.1, L.K.2, L.K.5

Objectives: Students will be able to:

• Explore and name properties of rocks.

• Use phonics knowledge to suggest letters to spell words.

• Develop print concepts.

• Use and expand complete sentences speaking audibly and clearly.

• Expand understanding of descriptive words through categorization and comparison of real-life objects.

Activities:

• Prior to the start of the unit, send a note home asking students to hunt for unique rocks to bring in to start a class rock collection. Allow the rock collection to grow throughout the unit. Place the rocks in a special spot.

• For this lesson, have students gather the rocks they brought in and sit with them in a circle on the carpet.

• Ask students to observe the rocks using their sense of sight and touch. If desired provide them with a hand lens. Allow a couple minutes for observation.

• Go around the circle and have students describe their rocks. Prompt them to use complete sentences. Add in comments that compare and contrast the rocks and invite students to expand on their descriptions by asking leading questions.

- Decide on a way to sort the rocks (e.g., by color, size, texture). Work together to spell the words you have chosen as labels for the different categories.

- Create a language experience chart together, recounting the experience and reviewing the descriptive words. Example text: *Our rock collection has lots of different rocks. _____'s rocks are _____. (List students' names and what they said.) We sorted them by _____.*

Lesson Assessment: Participation will be checked. Teacher can note students having difficulty describing the rocks.

LESSON 2: LEARNING MORE ABOUT ROCKS WITH INFORMATIONAL TEXT

CCSS in English Language Arts: RI.K.1, RI.K.2, RI.K.5, RI.K.6, RI.K.7, RI.K.10, RF.K.1, RF.K.4, SL.K.2, L.K.6

Objectives: Students will be able to:
- Explore and name properties of rocks.
- Develop print concepts.
- Ask and answer questions, retell key ideas using the text's pictures, and actively participate in an informational text reading.
- Use rock vocabulary learned from the text and active exploration.

Activities:
- Reread language experience chart to review Lesson 1.
- Big book read-aloud—*Rocks* by Brenda Parks
  - Before: Have the students identify the parts of the book: front cover, back cover, title, author, and title page. Review the job of the author. Review that this book does not have an illustrator because many photographers took the pictures.
  - Set purpose: *Listen to find out the groups this author puts rocks in.*
  - During: Ask the students where to begin reading. Track the print with a pointing device and model fluent reading. Pause to think aloud about the rock groups: *Big rocks is a group. The other groups are small rocks and sand, which is tiny rocks. All of those groups talk about size.* Ask questions that guide students to identifying other groups: *So what was that group? What are we sorting by if the rocks are in groups like egg-shaped, triangle, tall and thin, or short and wide? (shape)*
  - After: Use the photographs to review the places rocks can be found and the different properties (groups) the author uses to identify rocks. Have students retell the details of the text by describing what the illustration shows.

Lesson Assessment: Participation will be checked. Teacher should maintain a checklist or anecdotal notes to track students' print concepts.

LESSON 3: OUTDOOR EXPERIENCE FOR REFINING UNDERSTANDING OF VOCABULARY

CCSS in English Language Arts: SL.K.1, SL.K.2, SL.K.4, SL.K.6, L.K.1, L.K.5, L.K.6

Objectives: Students will be able to:

- Explore and name properties of rocks.
- Expand understanding of descriptive words through categorization and comparison of real-life objects.
- Ask and answer *what* questions using question words.
- Use and expand complete sentences, speaking audibly and clearly.

Activities:

- Review the descriptive words students used when observing their rocks. Write one word for each child on an index card. Put the card and a rock that matches that description in a plastic zipper bag. If possible, give students words that they can remember or read.
- Go outside and gather students in a circle. Model showing the rock, using a complete sentence to describe the rock, and asking a question: *My rock is smooth. What else out here is smooth?*
- Allow students to explore within a designated area and a designated time. Then call them back and select students to share what they found. Objects that are small enough can be added to the plastic zipper bag.
- Students take turns "being the teacher" using the model you provided. You may wish to have up to five students go at a time so that they can search for multiple descriptive words at a time.
- Once everyone has had a turn, return indoors to review the contents of the plastic zipper bags.

Lesson Assessment: Participation will be checked.

LESSON 4: READING FOR ENJOYMENT WITH NARRATIVE TEXT

CCSS in English Language Arts: RL.K.1, RL.K.5, SL.K.2, L.K.4.a, L.K.6

Objectives: Students will be able to:

- Name properties of rocks.
- Develop print concepts.
- Ask and answer questions about a text.
- Identify different types of texts and purposes for reading.
- Expand descriptive vocabulary and clarify meaning of a multiple-meaning word.

Activities:

- Read-aloud—*A Gift from the Sea* by Kate Banks.
  - Before: Have the students identify the parts of the book: front cover, back cover, title, author, illustrator, and title page. Review the jobs of the author and illustrator. Display the story next to *Rocks* by Brenda Parks. Have students identify the differences between the two texts and why we might read them. (Rocks *is an informational text for learning.* A Gift from the Sea *is a storybook to enjoy.*)
  - Set purpose: *Listen for the words used to describe the rock the boy finds in this story and what happened to make the rock what it is today.*

- During: Pause to ask and answer questions. Make connections to the properties they studied and the language they used.
- After: Review the descriptive language. Point out the description of the sand as *cool*. Use the context to review the meaning of this multiple-meaning word. Discuss the following question: *Do you think the things that happened to the rock were things that could happen in real life?*

Lesson Assessment: Participation will be checked.

LESSON 5: SOIL LANGUAGE ACTIVITY

CCSS in English Language Arts: W.K.2, W.K.8, SL.K.1, SL.K.3, SL.K.4, L.K.1, W.K.2, W.K.6

Objectives: Students will be able to:

- Ask and answer questions to explore and identify things found in soil.
- Understand that soils are made of many living and nonliving substances. The attributes and properties of soil (e.g., moisture, kind and size of particles, living/organic elements) vary depending on location.
- Write for authentic purposes.

Activities:

- Take students outside to collect some soil samples if there is a good place to dig or bring in some soil from a garden.
- Show question cards with picture cues for each of the question words: *who, what, where, when, why,* and *how.* Challenge students to think of questions about the soil beginning with one of these words. Example questions: *Who/what uses soil? What is soil for? What is in soil? Where does soil come from? When is soil needed? Why do plants need soil? How can I find out more about soil?* You may wish to record and post the questions for reference. Some questions will be addressed in this unit, and others may be addressed in a future unit on plants.
- Have students sift through the soil to discover what is in the soil (e.g., rocks, roots, worms, insects, plant matter).
- Discuss what students found and then ask them to record their findings in a science journal. Students may draw, write, or use a combination of both depending on their developmental level.

Lesson Assessment: Participation will be checked. Teacher will note each student's ability to use question words. Written work can be analyzed.

LESSON 6: USING INFORMATIONAL TEXT TO EXPAND KNOWLEDGE OF SOIL

CCSS in English Language Arts: RI.K.1, RI.K.10, RF.K.1, RF.K.3, RF.K.4, SL.K.1, SL.K.4, L.K.6

Objectives: Students will be able to:

- Understand that soils are made of many living and nonliving substances. The attributes and properties of soil (e.g., moisture, kind and size of particles, living/organic elements) vary depending on location.

- Report on a recent experience.
- Ask and answer questions and participate in collaborative conversations surrounding a text.
- Identify words in a text using phonics knowledge.

Activities:

- Have students review their science journals to recall what they found in soil and share with the class.
- Read-aloud—*Soil Basics* by Carol K. Lindeen
    - o Set purpose: *Listen to find out if the author writes about some of the things we found in the soil.*
    - o During: Stop to ask questions and emphasize content on the composition and types of soil.
    - o After: Find the words and pictures in the book that match what the students found in the soil (e.g., plants, animals, rocks, leaves). Have them point out the pictures and frame the words with their fingers by placing an index finger on either side of the word so that the word may be seen in between. Use length of word, initial/final consonants, and word chunks to find words.

Lesson Assessment: Participation will be checked.

LESSON 7: READING AND WRITING SIGHT WORDS

CCSS in English Language Arts: RF.K.3.c, L.K.1.e, L.K.2, L.K.6

Objectives: Students will be able to:
- Read the sight words *is* and *are*.
- Use ending marks.
- Use phonics knowledge to spell words.

Activities:

- Introduce the sight words: *is* and *are*.
    - o Read the word and use it in a sentence. Have students repeat.
    - o Chant the spelling of the word.
    - o Write the word demonstrating proper formation of the letters.
    - o Put the word on the word wall.
    - o Repeat lesson multiple times as needed.

(Cunningham, 2009)

- Hunt for sight words:
    - o Look around the classroom to hunt for the sight words in the charts and posters on the walls.
    - o Reread the texts you've read together to hunt for the sight words.
    - o Identify sight words in future texts read within the unit.
- Make and read sentences with the sight words:
    - o Give the students cards with the sight words, cards with both pictures and the words *rocks* and *soil*, cards with punctuation, and blank cards with writing lines. Each of the word cards can have the word written with a capital letter on the back of the card.
    - o Model how to use the materials to make sentences. Example sentences: *Rocks are hard. Is soil cool?* Demonstrate lining up the cards, leaving spaces between the words. Show students how to use letter sounds to spell the missing word the best you can. Emphasize the need to use punctuation.
    - o Have students work independently to build and read sentences.

Lesson Assessment: Teacher will circulate and check students' sentences.

LESSON 8: SOIL COMPARISON LANGUAGE ACTIVITY

CCSS in English Language Arts: RF.K.3, W.K.2, W.K.7, W.K.8, SL.K.1, SL.K.3, L.K.5, L.K.6

Objectives: Students will be able to:

- Ask and answer questions to explore and identify things found in soil.
- Understand that the attributes and properties of soil (e.g., moisture, kind and size of particles, living/organic elements) vary depending on location.
- Write using phonics knowledge.

Activities:

- Provide samples of soil that represent at least three different types. Use the garden soil from Lesson 5 and other options that have obvious differences (e.g., sand, clay). If possible, gather the soil for this lesson yourself and document this process with photographs or a video recording.
- Set out the soil samples. Tell students that they will explore each of the soil types to decide how they are similar and different.
- Use the question cards to write a set of science questions together to guide this exploration: *What does the soil feel like? What is in the soil? What color is the soil? Where is the soil from? Why does it feel different? How big are the pieces in the soil?*
- Come up with procedures together to guide the exploration. For example:
  - Touch it.
  - Spread it out.
  - Look at it with a hand lens.
  - Squeeze it.
- After students have had sufficient time for exploration, refer to the science questions to discuss similarities and differences together. If necessary, prompt students to discuss the moisture level, kind and size of particles, and living/organic elements. Create a chart together with a column and appropriate heading for each soil sample. Use shared-writing procedures to record key words in each column.
- If you were able to gather the soil yourself, show the students where the soils came from by sharing your photographs or video recording.

Lesson Assessment: Participation will be checked.

LESSON 9: USING INFORMATIONAL TEXT TO BRIDGE EXPERIENCE WITH SOIL AND HEALTHY EARLY PRACTICES

CCSS in English Language Arts: RI.K.1, RI.K.3, RI.K.4, RI.K.8, L.K.4

Objectives: Students will be able to:

- Ask and answer questions, describe connections between ideas, and identify reasons the author gives to support points in order to demonstrate an understanding that soils are made of many living and nonliving substances, and that humans can change natural habitats in ways that can be helpful or harmful for the plants and animals that live there.

- Identify things found in soil.
- Ask and answer questions about unknown words in a text.

Activities:

- Read-aloud—*Garbage Helps Our Garden Grow: A Compost Story* by Linda Glaser
  - Before: Write the words *moist*, *decay*, and *landfill* on the board. Have students raise their hand if they have heard the words before. Have them keep their hand raised if they think they can tell what they mean. Address the students with their hands down: *What question could we ask if we don't know what* moist *means?* (*What does* moist *mean?*) Give students individual question cards for the word *what*. Place Post-it notes in the text with the word *what* above the words *moist*, *decay*, and *landfill* to cue students to ask the question.
  - Set purpose: Ask students to raise their question card when they see one of the Post-it notes or want to ask a question about another word.
  - During: When students give the signal, select a student to ask the question. Use context clues and pictures to determine the meaning of the words. Ask students questions about the meaning of other words.
  - After: Review the meaning of each word.
- Review key ideas through questioning. Display the appropriate question cards as you pose questions to the students. Prompt and support their attempts.
  - *This story tells us that worms help compost. What are some reasons the author gave that tell us why? (They eat the rotting plant matter. They change the garbage into soil.)*
  - *What can we add to the soil that makes it good for gardens? (Plant matter)*
  - *How is composting good for the Earth? (It lessens the amount of garbage going to land fills. It helps gardens grow.)*

Lesson Assessment: Participation will be checked.

LESSON 10: MULTIPLE READINGS OF A HIGH-QUALITY PIECE OF CHILDREN'S LITERATURE FOR MULTIPLE PURPOSES

CCSS in English Language Arts: RL.K.1, RL.K.2, RL.K.4, RL.K.6, RL.K.7, RL.K.10, RI.K.9, RF.K.1, RF.K.2, RF.K.3, RF.K.4, SL.K.1, SL.K.2, L.K.2, L.K.6

Objectives: Students will be able to:

- Ask and answer questions to demonstrate an understanding that soils are made of many living and nonliving substances, and that humans can change natural habitats in ways that can be helpful or harmful for the plants and animals that live there.
- Compare and contrast two similar stories to identify things found in soil.
- Develop print concepts.
- Identify alphabet letters and their sounds.
- Use picture clues and context to assist in identifying words.
- Identify and produce rhymes.
- Read and spell words using known chunks and letters.
- Retell a story.

Activities:

- Part A: Comprehension of Science Content
  - Revisit *Garbage Helps Our Garden Grow: A Compost Story* by Linda Glaser to review that soil can be improved for plant growth by adding compost—decayed plants. Review what kinds of plants went into the compost in that story.
  - Review the chart from Lesson 8 to decide which soil samples had plant matter in them.
  - Read-aloud—*Compost Stew: An A to Z Recipe for the Earth* by Mary McKenna Siddals
    - Before: Identify the parts of the books, author, and illustrator. Read the Author's Note.
    - Set purpose: *Listen to find out what kinds of things this story says can go into compost.*
    - During: Pause every few pages and allow students to share some of the things they heard. Prompt if necessary using the letters of the alphabet.
    - After: *Turn and tell a friend some things that can go into compost. Share what a friend said.* Compare and contrast the information presented in both compost stories.

- Part B: Reviewing the Alphabet and Making Text–Picture Connections
  - Display *Compost Stew: An A to Z Recipe for the Earth* by Mary McKenna Siddals. Ask students to summarize what the story was about.
  - Cover some of the words for the alphabet letters you wish to emphasize using sticky notes.
  - Read the text and pause at the alphabet letters, identifying the letter by stating its name and sound. Then have students use the picture clues to help them search for items that would make sense as something that could go in compost and match with the initial consonant.
  - Write their guesses on the sticky notes. Uncover and read the text together.

- Part C: Identifying Rhyme and Making Words
  - Reread *Compost Stew: An A to Z Recipe for the Earth* by Mary McKenna Siddals.
  - Pause to allow students to identify some of the rhyming pairs (be sure to include the –ot words *pot, rot, got*). When necessary, scaffold this for students by providing the first word and asking them to identify its pair.
  - Identify the two letters that make up the –ot word family. Have students hold letter cards to "be the letters."
  - Give out the letters *p*, *r*, and *g*. Students take turns standing together to make the words from the story. Blend the sounds together and then say the word (*p-o-t, pot*).
  - Ask students if they can think of any other words that rhyme with *pot, rot*, and *got*. When they come up with a word, have them decide which letter they need for the initial consonant and hand out letter cards. Blend the sounds together and then say the word.
  - Include a few words with digraphs and blends, like *plot* and *shot*, to make this lesson more multilevel.

(Cunningham, 2009)

- Part D: Prop Storytelling
  - Create paper representations of the different items from the alphabet letters in the book *Compost Stew: An A to Z Recipe for the Earth* by Mary McKenna Siddals. Write the letter of the alphabet on it. Gather a plastic cauldron left over from Halloween.
  - Give out the pieces to the students. As you model a fluent reading of the book, have the students come up and put the items into the cauldron.
  - Place the book and the storytelling pieces into the literacy center for the students to use as a retelling activity.

(Morrow, 2002)

Lesson Assessment: Students' responses to questions and contributions during discussions will be noted. Students may perform storytelling for the class in small groups.

LESSON 11: INFORMATIONAL TEXT AS AN INTRODUCTION TO WATER

CCSS in English Language Arts: RI.K.2, RI.K.5, RI.K.6, RI.K.7, RI.K.10, RF.K.1, RF.K.3, RF.K.4, W.K.1, W.K.5, SL.K.5, L.K.1, L.K.2, L.K.6

Objectives: Students will be able to:
- Name water sources (lake, river, ocean).
- Name uses for water.
- Develop print concepts.
- Retell key details using the text's pictures.
- Draw and write about an opinion and add details to strengthen writing.

Activities:
- Big book read-aloud—*I Am Water* by Jean Marzollo
  o Before: Identify the parts of the book, author, and illustrator.
  o Set purpose: *Listen to find out where we find water and how it's used.*
  o During: Ask the students where to begin reading. Track the print with a pointing device and model fluent reading. Pause to "read" the pictures, emphasizing information gained from the illustrations.
  o After: Revisit the text and make a T-chart with the headings *Things Made of Water* and *Uses for Water*. Help students use the pictures to fill out the chart.
- Students draw and write about something they like to do in water. Compile writing into a class book.

Lesson Assessment: Participation will be checked. Teacher will circulate during writing activity and prompt students who could add details to strengthen writing.

LESSON 12: WATER POLLUTION AND CONSERVATION EXPERIMENT

CCSS in English Language Arts: K.W.3, K.W.5, K.W.6, K.W.8, SL.K.1, SL.K.3, SL.K.4, SL.K.5, L.K.6

Objectives: Students will be able to:
- Name water sources (lake, river, ocean).
- Name uses for and ways to conserve water.
- Ask and answer questions and participate in collaborative conversations.
- Use phonics knowledge to write in order to record an experience and a reaction.
- Use digital tools to publish writing.

Activities:
- Review chart from Lesson 11. Pose the question: *What will happen to the plants and animals if the lake, river, or ocean is not healthy? What will happen if there is not enough water?*
- Water Pollution Experiment Day 1:
  o Cut stalks of celery for each child.
  o Give out cups of clean water.
  o Have the child place the celery in the clean water.
  o Staple a page into the science journals that has two pictures of celery for the children to color.

- o Help them label the pictures *Clean* and *Dirty.*
- o Students color in the picture of the clean celery.
- o "Pollute" the water by putting red food dye in each of the children's cups. Have them swirl the water around gently using their celery stalk.
- o Set the celery in a safe spot to be checked the next day.
- o Put the remaining celery in a cup without water.
- Water Pollution Experiment Day 2:
  - o Check the cups of celery and color the picture in the science journals.
  - o Check the celery without water.
  - o Turn and tell a friend what happened to the celery.
  - o Share what your friend said.
- Hold up the question cards as you pose questions: *The pollution was in the water. Where is it now? Where will it be if an animal comes by and eats this plant? Where will it be if a bigger animal comes by and eats that animal? Where will it be if we eat it? What happened to the plant that had no water? What will happen to animals that have no water? How can we help in the classroom and at home?*
- Students use their phonics knowledge to write a reaction to this experiment under the pictures. Teacher circulates and supports.
- Blog about the experience together. Help them recall the events in order. Have them read their reaction to you as you type it in. Scan in pictures from the students' science journals.

(Wilkes, 1991)

Lesson Assessment: Students science journals and discussion will be assessed.

LESSON 14: GUIDED READING LESSON REINFORCING WATER CONCEPTS

CCSS in English Language Arts: RI.K.10, RF.K.1, RF.K.2, RF.K.3, RF.K.4, L.K.4, LK.6

Objectives: Students will be able to:

- Name water sources and uses for water.
- Read and comprehend informational texts at their reading level.
- Apply grade-level phonics and word analysis skills in decoding.
- Read with sufficient accuracy and fluency.

Activities:

- Specific literacy skills practiced in guided reading should be based on the students' needs and the text selected. Keep a balanced focus on learning the science content (vocabulary/comprehension) and literacy skills (decoding/fluency).
- Some suggestions include one-to-one matching, sight words, using letter sounds and chunks to figure out words, using pictures to figure out words, asking and answering questions, and print concepts.
- Suggested texts
  - o DRA 1, Guided Reading A: *The Water* by Jill Eggleton
  - o DRA 2, Guided Reading B: *Water* by Susan Canizares and Pamela Chanko
  - o DRA 3, Guided Reading C: *Wonderful Water* by Joshua Douglas
  - o DRA 3, Guided Reading C: *Water, Water* by Monica Hughes
  - o DRA 8, Guided Reading E: *Water* by Emily Neye
  - o DRA 8, Guided Reading E: *Where Is Water?* by Reginald Lewis

o DRA 8, Guided Reading E: *Water Everywhere!* by Christine Taylor-Butler
o DRA 12, Guided Reading G: *Everyone Needs Water* by Brenda Parkes

Lesson Assessment: Running records and anecdotal notes can be taken.

LESSON 13: PRODUCTS MADE FROM NATURE WITH AN ART CONNECTION

CCSS in English Language Arts: SL.K.1, SL.K.3, L.K.1

Objectives: Students will be able to:
- Identify the natural source of common objects.
- Follow a set of oral directions and ask questions for clarification to make a paper planter.
- Participate in collaborative conversations.

Activities:
- Gather classroom supplies made from nature. The following are suggestions: paper, pencils, books, cotton art smock, extra snacks (e.g., pretzels, carrot sticks), small chalkboard, chalk, paintbrushes with natural hair bristles, paper plate, wool mittens, leather shoes, and wooden rulers.
- Give out the items. Have students sort them into three piles: made from plants, made from animals, and made from rocks. Discuss each one.
- Why is it important not to waste classroom supplies? What can we do to make sure everyone is taking care of our supplies?
- Art connection: Have students make their own recycled paper planter. Demonstrate directions and have students use question cards to ask questions if they need to clarify directions. Directions for this activity available at *www.calrecycle.ca.gov/Education/curriculum/ctl/K3Module/ Unit2/Lesson4.pdf*.

Lesson Assessment: Participation will be checked.

LESSON 14: READING AND WRITING SIGHT WORDS

CCSS in English Language Arts: RF.K.3.c, L.K.1.e, L.K.2, L.K.6

Objectives: Students will be able to:
- Read the sight words *made* and *from*.
- Use ending marks.
- Use phonics knowledge to spell words.

Activities:
- Introduce the sight words: *made* and *from*.
  o Read the word and use it in a sentence. Have students repeat.
  o Chant the spelling of the word.
  o Write the word demonstrating proper formation of the letters.

o Put the word on the word wall.
o Repeat lesson multiple times as needed.

(Cunningham, 2009)

- Hunt for sight words:
  o Look around the classroom to hunt for the sight words in the charts and posters on the walls.
  o Reread the texts you've read together to hunt for the sight words.
  o Identify sight words in future texts read within the unit.
- Make and read sentences with the sight words:
  o Give the students cards with the sight words, cards with both pictures and the words from Lesson 13, cards with punctuation, and blank cards with writing lines. Each of the word cards can have the word written with a capital letter on the back of the card.
  o Model how to use the materials to make sentences. Example sentences: *Chalk is made from rocks. Pencils are from plants.* Demonstrate lining up the cards, leaving spaces between the words. Show students how to use letter sounds to spell the missing word the best they can. Emphasize the need to use punctuation.
  o Have students work independently to build and read sentences.

Lesson Assessment: Teacher will circulate and check students' sentences.

Lesson 15: Narrative Text About Taking Care of the Earth

CCSS in English Language Arts: RL.K.3, RL.K.9, RL.K.4, RF.K.3, W.K.2, W.K.8, SL.K.1, L.K.1, L.K.2, L.K.6

Objectives: Students will be able to:

- Understand that humans can change natural habitats in ways that can be helpful or harmful for the plants and animals that live there.
- Name and follow healthy Earth practices.
- Identify story elements.
- Write informational texts, drawing on knowledge of print conventions, sight words, and phonics.

Activities:

- Listen and sing along to John Farrell's "Kids Who Want to Help the Earth."
- Have students discuss things they could do to help take care of the Earth.
- Read-aloud—*Recycle Every Day!* By Nancy Elizabeth Wallace
  o Set purpose: *Listen to find out who the characters are, where this story takes place, and what happens in the story.*
  o During: Pause to fill out a story map with the follow headings: *Characters, Setting,* and *Events.*
  o After: Review the story map. Compare and contrast the way Minna's family takes care of the Earth to the way the family in *Garbage Helps Our Garden Grow: A Compost Story* takes care of the Earth.
- Have students draw and write about one way they could take care of the Earth in their science journals.

Lesson Assessment: Participation will be checked.

LESSON 16: LITERACY CENTER ACTIVITY: GARBAGE SORT

CCSS in English Language Arts: FS.K.3, W.K.2, L.K.1, L.K.6

Objectives: Students will be able to:

- Understand that humans can change natural habitats in ways that can be helpful or harmful for the plants and animals that live there.
- Name and follow healthy Earth practices.
- Draw and label items using phonics knowledge.

Activities:

- Clean a variety of discarded items. Be sure to include garbage that won't be recycled, cans, plastic, and paper.
- Place the items together in one trash bag.
- Have the students take turns removing an item from the bag and sorting it into the appropriate bin.
- Provide a worksheet with the appropriate number of bins. Have students draw and label the items they sorted into each bin.
- Students clean up by placing all of the items back into the trash bag for the next group.

Lesson Assessment: Sheets will be checked.

LESSON 17: CREATING ROOM LABELS FOR HEALTHY EARTH PRACTICES PERFORMANCE TASK

CCSS in English Language Arts: RF.K.1, W.K.2, W.K.8, SL.K.5, L.K.1, L.K.2, L.K.6

Objectives: Students will be able to:

- Create labels describing healthy Earth practices for the classroom using pictures and words.

Activities:

- Introduce the performance task to the whole group. Tell students that their help is needed to create labels that the class can look at everyday to remind them of things to do in the classroom that help the Earth.
- Demonstrate how to create a label by making a picture that fills the index card and uses realistic colors and words that give a direction.
- For this performance task it would be best to work one on one with each student. Prompting is allowed and may be necessary.

Lesson Assessment: Student performance will be judged based on the standards set forth in the Assessment Evidence box.

---

*Unit plan format from Wiggins and McTighe (2005).

REFERENCES

Cunningham, P. M. (2009). *Phonics they use: Words for reading and writing.* Boston: Pearson.

Morrow, L. M. (2002). *The literacy center: Contexts for reading and writing.* Portland, ME: Stenhouse.

N.J. Department of Education. (2010). New Jersey Core Curriculum content standards: Classroom applications document—science: Earth system science (by the end of grade 2). Retrieved from *www.state.nj.us/education/cccs/cad/5.*

Wilkes, A. (1991). *My first green book: A life-size guide to caring for our environment.* New York: Knopf.

Wiggins, G. P., & McTighe, J. (2005). *Understanding by design.* Alexandria, VA: ASCD.

FAMILY—GRADE 1

Desired results: Literacy	Desired results: Social studies
Established Goals • Common Core State Standards for English language arts grade 1* *Standards articulated in the Learning Plan below.	**Established Goals** • Compare and contrast different kinds of families locally and globally. • Distinguish the roles and responsibilities of different family members. • Determine the factors that contribute to healthy relationships. • Describe how culture is expressed through and influenced by the behavior of people. • Explain how an individual's beliefs, values, and traditions may reflect more than one culture. • Describe why it is important to understand the perspectives of other cultures in an interconnected world. (N.J. Department of Education, 2010)
Enduring Understandings • The purpose of reading is to understand the message of the author. • The purpose of writing and speaking is to communicate your ideas, opinions, experiences, and questions. • Effective communicators take into account their audience when they organize their thoughts and select their language. • Effective communicators actively listen and clearly convey their ideas when having conversations.	**Enduring Understandings** • The family unit is defined differently by different cultures and the composition of a family unit differs between families. • People of various cultures live in the United States. • Roles and responsibilities of family members are influenced by culture. • Traditions are derived from cultural practices and may combine practices from multiple cultures. • Respect for all cultures is essential in a diverse world.
Essential Questions • Why do we read and write? • What do good readers sound like? • How can I effectively communicate?	**Essential Questions** • What is a family and who is in it? • What are the roles and responsibilities of my family members?

	• What are some of my traditions and cultural practices? What are some traditions and practices of other families and cultures? How are they alike and different? • How do I demonstrate respect for other cultures?
Knowledge Students will know: • Pictures in texts can tell you more than the text alone. • A fluent reader sounds like they are talking. • Writers and speakers think about their audience when they are communicating. • An active listener responds to the text and to a speaker. • Technology is a tool that can be used to communicate. • Words have patterns and rules that are useful to know in order to encode and decode words.	**Knowledge** Students will know: • The family unit encompasses the diversity of family forms in contemporary society. • Cultures include traditions, popular beliefs, and commonly held values, ideas, and assumptions that are generally accepted by a particular group of people. • The cultures with which an individual or group identifies change and evolve in response to interactions with other groups and/or in response to needs or concerns. (N.J. Department of Education, 2010)
Skills Students will be able to: • "Read" visual information for details and use it to make inferences. • Compare/contrast characters in stories. • Describe the connection between two individuals in an informational text. • Make connections between the text and themselves. • Demonstrate fluency. • Write informational texts. • Practice conversation skills such as speaking clearly, turn taking, and asking and answering questions. • Collaborate with others. • Use technology as a tool to convey information and share ideas. • Perform skits to convey ideas.	**Skills** Students will be able to: • Define a family as a group of people usually related by blood, marriage, or adoption, but may also include people who are unrelated and living together. • Identify the people in their immediate and extended families. • Identify roles and responsibilities of family members. • List ways to be a good family member. • Identify what country(s) their family is from. • Identify some of their family traditions and cultural practices. • Compare and contrast their family unit, traditions, and practices to others' family unit, traditions, and practices. • Identify ways the United States and the world are diverse. • Identify ways one can show respect for another culture.

Assessment Evidence

Performance Tasks
• **Family Photo Album**
  ○ Goal and Role: As a family member, you will create a "photo" album of your family.
  ○ Audience: Your classmates
  ○ Situation: The challenge involves creating an album that you enjoy looking at that also teaches others about your family.

- o Product: A digital or print album of photographs or drawings with captions and labels that will be shared in the class library or on the class website.
- o Standards: You must include visual images of your family members with labels identifying their names and relationship to you and some of their roles/responsibilities. Visual images and captions of two or more family traditions must also be included. Handwriting must be legible and the final product must be neat.

- **A New Tradition**
  - o Goal and Role: As a family member, you will tell your family about a new tradition you would like to start.
  - o Audience: Your family
  - o Situation: The challenge involves creating a whole new tradition that you have not had before.
  - o Product: An informational letter to your family
  - o Standards: You must state what your new tradition would be, describe it in detail, and tell how you would feel if you could do it together from now on.

Other Evidence
- Family Test

LEARNING PLAN

Routines and Morning Meeting

CCSS in English Language Arts: RL.1.4, RF.1.4, SL.1.1, SL.1.2, SL.1.3, SL.1.4, L.1.1, L.1.5.c, L.1.6

Objectives: Students will be able to:
- Perform classroom responsibilities that resemble family roles/responsibilities.
- Explore literacy in authentic and spontaneous contexts.
- Practice conversation skills such as speaking clearly, turn taking, and asking and answering questions.
- Use concrete objects to build vocabulary.
- Identify sensory language.
- Demonstrate fluency.

Activities:
- Class Job: "Parents" tie the shoes of the children who need help.
- Class Job: "Brothers and sisters" look around for someone who is playing alone and invite them to play.
- Class Job: "Babies" crawl around on the floor to pick up items.
- Dramatic Play Area: Set up a play kitchen in the classroom with the following items:
  - o Furniture: play stove, table and chairs, sink, cupboard, refrigerator. (If play furniture is not available, make these from large cardboard boxes. For the sink, set a large plastic tub into a rectangle cut just large enough so the lip of the tub can rest on the box.)
  - o Garbage and recycling cans
  - o Dinnerware and play food

- o Family activity supplies (e.g., board games, fake computer, fake game system)
- o Supplies for celebration (e.g., decorative tablecloth, festive plates)
- o Literacy materials: List paper, drawing paper, writing utensils, store circulars, calendar, cookbooks, menus from take-out places, packaging from real food products, telephone, mail, photo albums
- Greeting: Share several greetings from different languages each day/week. On a map point to the country where the greeting is from.
- Share: Parents come in to share a tradition with the class.
- Share: I live with _____ people.
- Activity: Print the words to a family-themed song on chart paper. Read and reread together. Identify the sensory words and family vocabulary. Several are available from *http://www.childfun. com/index.php/activity-themes/people-house-home/240-family-activity-theme.html?start=4.*
- Activity: Tell jokes from the book *Family Follies: A Book of Family Jokes* by Jill L. Donahue
- Activity: Read picture books that include words from other languages.
- Monthly Poem: Select family poetry to read and reread throughout the month. Introduce students to the "magic trick" of poetry; identify sensory words that help the poem come to life. Small groups of students record themselves and podcast the monthly poem.
- Social Studies Word Wall: Keep a running list of social studies vocabulary words throughout the unit.

Lesson Assessment: Participation will be checked. Notes and recordings can be taken to assess students' conversation skills and reading fluency.

LESSON 1: INTRODUCTION TO FAMILY/DEFINE INDIVIDUAL FAMILY

CCSS in English Language Arts: RL.1.1, RL.1.2, W.1.2, SL.1.1, SL.1.6, L.1.1, L.1.2, L.1.6

Objectives:
  Students will be able to:
- Define families.
- Listen and recall details of a story read orally.
- Create an illustration of their family and write a matching sentence.
- Speak audibly when sharing family illustration.

Activities:
- Allow students to activate prior knowledge by brainstorming everything they know about families. Create a list together on chart paper.
- Read-aloud—*Families Are Different* by Nina Pellegrini
  - o Set purpose: *Listen to see if this book makes you think of something about your own family.*
  - o During: Pause to have the students share connections they are making with the book.
  - o After: Discuss the new information that students have learned about families from the book. Add to the list the students started.
- Introduce students to their *My Family* books: *In these books you will use what you have learned to draw and write about your family. You will fill in the pages of this book throughout the unit. Today you will draw a picture of your family and write a sentence telling who is in your family.*
- Students share their illustrations in cooperative pairs.

Lesson Assessment: Participation and writing will be checked. Teacher will circulate during sharing time to evaluate speaking skills and write anecdotal notes.

LESSON 2: PETS IN THE FAMILY

CCSS in English Language Arts: RL.1.1, RL.1.10, RF.1.3, RF.1.4, W.1.2, W.1.7, W.1.8, SL.1.1, L.1.1, L.1.2

Objectives: Students will be able to:

- Identify members of their family.
- Read fluently.
- Write a sentence using correct grammar and punctuation to convey an idea.
- Write a how-to guide with a partner.
- Encode plural words whose singular word ends in -*y*.

Activities:

- Part A: Read-aloud—"Love Your Pets" from *http://www.canteach.ca/elementary/songspoems49.html*

Love Your Pets
(to the tune of "Row, Row, Row Your Boat")
Love, love
Love your pets,
Love them
Every day.
Give them food
And water, too,
Then let them
Run and play.

  - Set purpose: *This is a song that teaches you about taking care of pets. Listen to find out what you should do to take care of a pet.*
  - During: Track the print while singing fluently.
  - After: Discuss how pets can be a part of a family. Review that families who have pets need to give them food, water, exercise, and love. *Turn and tell a friend if you have pets in your family and if so share a little about each pet.*
  - Students write and illustrate a sentence describing their pet(s), if any, or a pet they would like to have in their *My Family* books.
- Part B: Writing How-to Guides
  - Reread the poem together using echo and choral reading procedures.
  - Review the things that pets need (*food, water, exercise, and love*).
  - Students work in small groups to write a how-to guide using small booklets. Model each step of the process and allow students to work together immediately following each modeling session.
    - Select one pet from one of their families and determine what materials are needed to care for that pet while filling out the Materials page.
    - Write the steps that need to be followed to care for that pet on the Sequence of Steps page.
    - Draw and label a picture of the pet being cared for on the Picture page.
    - Fill out the Glossary page by selecting important words from the text and defining them.

- Fill out the Table of Contents page by writing the headings of the different sections and the pages where they are found.
- Complete the cover, adding a title, picture, author, and publication date.

(Morrow, 2012)

- Part C: Plural Nouns Ending in -y
  o Write *family* and *families* on the board. Have the students identify the letters that are the same in each word and underline them. Repeat for the letters that are different in each word and underline them in a second color. Review that you change the *y* to an *i* and add *-es* to make *family* plural.
  o Interactive writing—Students take turns with the marker to create a list of pets that end in -y (e.g. *bunny, puppy*) and write the plural form of the words.

Lesson Assessment: Evaluate the students' writing, list of plural words, and their *My Family* books.

Lesson 3: Define Characteristics of Families/Roles Responsibilities

CCSS in English Language Arts: W.1.2, SL.1.1, SL.1.6, L.1.1, L.1.2

Objectives: Students will be able to:
- Define the characteristics of families.
- Write and draw a picture that shows their family role.
- Design and perform skits on a designated topic.

Activities:
- Review chart from Lesson 1 defining families.
- Students get together with their cooperative pairs from Lesson 1 and compare/contrast the first picture they created in their *My Family* books. Students identify one way the picture of their family was the same and/or different from their partner's picture. Select a few cooperative pairs to share with the class.
- Discuss how the class is like a family. Ask students how the class family helps out and works together (e.g., class jobs, protect each other, work together, play together). Review that families work together to keep all of the members of the family safe, healthy, and supported.
- Organize groups of four students who will work together to create a short skit about a family working together to create a party. Have students select a family member card (e.g., mom, dad, grandpa, aunt) and define their role in working with their "family" to create a party. Props should be available to students.
- Students present their skits to the class.
- Students write and illustrate a sentence defining their role in their families in their *My Family* books.

Lesson Assessment: Writing in *My Family* books will be checked. Ability to define the role and responsibility of their character in the skit will be evaluated.

LESSON 4: LITERACY CENTER ACTIVITY: COMPUTER CENTER

CCSS in English Language Arts: SL.1.2, SL.1.4

Objectives: Students will be able to:

- Define a family as a group of people usually related by blood, marriage, or adoption, but may also include people who are unrelated and living together.

Activities:

- Have a pair of students access "Oh, Can't You See, We Are Family" at *www.watchknowlearn. org/Video.aspx?VideoID=20829&CategoryID=6204.*
- Have students write their name on a log to show they viewed the video.
- Student pairs discuss information presented in the video.

Lesson Assessment: Check the log to ensure participation.

LESSON 5: READING NARRATIVE TEXT TO EXTEND UNDERSTANDING OF FAMILY ROLES

CCSS in English Language Arts: RL.1.1, RL.1.2, RL.1.9, RL.1.10, RF.1.4, W.1.8, SL.1.1, SL.1.2, SL.1.5, L.1.6

Objectives: Students will be able to:

- Identify roles and responsibilities of family members.
- Participate in collaborative conversations to compare and contrast characters' actions, developing an understanding that mothers and fathers can have the same role in the family unit.
- Ask and answer questions and retell a story including key details.
- Read with fluency.
- Respond to a story by writing/drawing a text-to-self connection.

Activities:

- Read-aloud—*What Mommies Do Best/What Daddies Do Best* by Laura Numeroff
  - Picture walk: Flip through the pages of the book. Allow students to comment on what they see. Additionally, ask them to predict who the characters are based on what they see in the pictures.
  - Set purpose: *As you listen, think about what your mom and/or dad do for you and your brothers and sisters.*
  - During: Pause to model how to make text-to-self connections. Allow the students to comment and share their own text-to-self connections.
  - After: Make a list together of what the mommies and daddies in the story did for their children. Compare the two stories, noting that the mommies and the daddies had the same roles. In reader-response journals, students draw and write about a connection they had when listening to this story.
- Retelling and fluency: Copy the pictures from this book, number them, and turn them into felt board pieces. Retell the story using the felt board pieces. Reread the book multiple times throughout the unit and put the felt board pieces and a copy of the story in the literacy center.

Students can work with a partner or small group, taking turns manipulating the pieces and reading the text.

(Morrow, 2012)

Lesson Assessment: Participation and reader-response journals will be checked. Groups can perform their retelling/reading for the class.

LESSON 6: NEEDS AND WANTS OF A FAMILY/ROLES AND RESPONSIBILITIES OF FAMILY MEMBERS

CCSS in English Language Arts: RL.1.1, RL.1.3, W.1.2, SL.1.1, SL.1.4, SL.1.6, L.1.1, L1.2, L.1.6,

Objectives: Students will be able to:
- Participate in collaborative conversations to identify needs and wants.
- Identify roles and responsibilities of family members and how they relate to needs/wants.
- Ask and answer questions regarding the text read-aloud.
- Write and draw pictures to explain the needs/wants of their families and the roles and responsibilities of the members of their families.

Activities:
- Define the words *need* and *want*. Present the idea that students have needs and wants at school.
- Shared Writing—Create a T-chart of the needs and wants of students at school.
- Explain that families have needs and wants too.
- Students work in groups of three to briefly discuss the needs and wants their families have and then share their thoughts with the larger group. Record the information on a new T-chart and think aloud: *All families need the same basic things:* [read the list]. *Not all families want the same things though. Some families might want* [appropriate item from the list], *while others do not.*
- Read-aloud—*Daddy Makes the Best Spaghetti* by Anna Grossnickle Hines.
  - Set purpose: *Listen to find out how the family in this story gets their needs and wants.*
  - During: Pause to allow students to think–pair–share about how the family is getting their needs and wants met (e.g., *parent(s) work, father/son take time to buy groceries, father prepares food, family eats together*).
  - After: Read cards stating a family member's role or responsibility from the book and have the students decide which need(s) or want(s) it relates to. Emphasize that roles and responsibilities of family members in each family may be different to meet the needs and wants of the family.
- Students write and illustrate two sentences in their *My Family* books, each showing a different family members' role/responsibility: one meeting a need and one meeting a want.

Lesson Assessment: *My Family* books will be evaluated for students' ability to correctly identify a need and want of their family and correctly state a role and/or responsibility of at least two family members.

LESSON 7: POETRY CONNECTION, FLUENCY, AND WORD STUDY

CCSS in English Language Arts: RL.1.2, RL.1.3, RL.1.10, RF.1.2, RF.1.3, RF.1.4, SL.1.2, L.1.2, L.1.4, L.1.6

Objectives: Students will be able to:

- Identify roles and responsibilities of family members and list ways to be a good family member.
- Describe the characters, retell the main ideas, and explain the message/lesson of a poem.
- Identify rhyming pairs and use rimes to read and spell new words.
- Sort words based on spelling principles.
- Read a text with a high level of accuracy and fluency.

Activities:

- Write the text of "Chad the Cheater" on a piece of chart paper.

> **Chad the Cheater**, by Erin Kramer
> Chad the Cheater was a lad
> Who was oh so bad, bad, bad.
> He cheated at games and his chores
> Skipping out and changing scores.
> "What to do?" wondered his dad.
> Oh he'd be so sad, sad, sad.
> He scratched his head for a plan,
> "Chad can be a better man!"
> Valiant Vlad, a high school grad,
> Who Chad thought was rad, rad, rad,
> He showed Chad a better way
> One day when he came to play.
> Good examples the grad had.
> This made Chad's dad glad, glad, glad.
> "I'm just like Vlad!" Chad exclaimed.
> Chad the Chum he was renamed.

- Part A: Read-aloud—"Chad the Cheater" by Erin Kramer
  - Summary statement: This is a poem about a boy who cheats—he doesn't play fairly or help out with his chores, which makes his dad upset.
  - Activate prior knowledge: *What happens in your families if you are being unfair or do not take care of your responsibilities?* Review the challenging words and phrases (e.g., *lad, chores, "skipping out," grad, chum, renamed*).
  - Set purpose: *Listen to find out who helps with Chad's problem.*
  - During: Model fluent reading.
  - After: Discuss Vlad and how older children and adults can be good role models for younger family members.

- Part B: Reread "Chad the Cheater"
  - Before: Select students to describe the characters, retell the main ideas, and explain the message/lesson of the poem.
  - Set purpose: *As I read, see if you can hear some rhyming pairs.*
  - During: Pause to highlight the rhyming pairs using different colors for each.
  - After: *Look at the letters that are the same in each of the rhyming pairs.* Segment and blend those words. Make a list of new words to read and spell using those rimes.

- Part C: Differentiated Word Sorts
  - Provide students different word sorts featuring some of the words from the poem based on their developmental level.
    - Letter Name–Alphabetic Sort: short *a*: *lad, bad, dad, sad, rad, had, man, can, Dan, ran, fan, tan*
    - Letter Name–Alphabetic Sort: short *a, i, u*: *lad, bad, dad, grad, glad, did, bid, lid, grid, skid, mud, bud, dud, thud, stud, crud*
    - Letter Name–Alphabetic Sort: short *a* and short *o*: *dad, man, cat, bag, mad, cab, jam, not, job, top, fox, pop, got, top, was, for*
    - Letter Name–Alphabetic Sort: two-step sort with *l, r, and s* blends and short *a, i, o*: *Vlad, glad, glop, plan, plop, grad, crab, crib, grip, drop, spot, spin, snap, stop, stick*
    - Within-Word Pattern Sort: short/long *a*: *dad, grad, plan, man, jack, ask, slap, fast, pass, path, way, play, day, stay, clay, may, plain, paid, sail, wait, paid, what, said*
    - Within-Word Pattern Sort: long *a* patterns: *way, play, say, clay, hay, came, name, made, grape, chase, waste, shave, flake, claim, chain, waist, brain, train, have, said*
- Part D: Follow-Up Activities/Centers
  - Fluency: Choral, echo, and partner read the poem. Record students reading and post on class podcast.
  - Provide word family wheels, sliders, and flipbooks. Have students make and then record words on paper.
  - Dice: Set dice up for students based on their word study focus. The dice can have word families, short vowels, and long-vowel spellings. Each student rolls the die. If they can come up with a word that matches their roll, they record it. This can be turned into a game by having students work with partners. Include faces with "lose a turn" and "roll again" if playing as a game.

(Bear, Invernizzi, Templeton, & Johnston, 2008)

Lesson Assessment: Participation will be checked. Word sorts can be glued on paper to be handed in and checked, recording sheets for follow-up activities will be checked, and recorded poetry reading can be student work sample.

LESSON 8: REINFORCING AND DEEPENING KNOWLEDGE OF FAMILY ROLES AND RESPONSIBILITIES THROUGH GUIDED READING

CCSS in English Language Arts: RL.1.10, RF.1.1, RF.1.2, RF.1.3, RF.1.4, L.1.4, L.1.6

Objectives: Students will be able to:

- Identify family members and their roles and responsibilities.
- Read and comprehend literature at their reading level.
- Apply grade-level phonics and word analysis skills in decoding.
- Read with sufficient accuracy and fluency.

Activities:

- Specific literacy skills practiced in guided reading should be based on the students' needs and the text selected. Keep a balanced focus on learning the social studies content (vocabulary/comprehension) and literacy skills (decoding/fluency).
- Some suggestions include: Compare/contrast families and characters, making inferences based

on the picture clues, using picture clues to figure out words, making connections, and print concepts.

- Suggested texts
  - DRA 2, Guided Reading B: *Silly Sally* by Betsy Franco
  - DRA 6, Guided Reading D: *I Do Not Want To* by Kathy Schulz
  - DRA 8, Guided Reading E: *Eat Your Peas, Louise!* by Pegeen Snow
  - DRA 10, Guided Reading F: *Bear's Busy Family* by Stella Blackstone
  - DRA 12, Guided Reading G: *I Shop With My Daddy* by Grace Maccarone
  - DRA 14, Guided Reading H: *Rex and Lilly: Family Time* by Laurie Krasny Brown
  - DRA 16, Guided Reading I: *The Berenstain Bears Are a Family* by Stan Berenstain and Jan Berenstain
  - DRA 18, Guided Reading J: *Henry and Mudge in the Family Trees* by Cynthia Rylant
  - DRA 20, Guided Reading L: *Super-Completely and Totally the Messiest* by Judith Viorst

Lesson Assessment: Running records and anecdotal notes can be taken.

LESSON 9: LITERACY CENTER ACTIVITY: COMPUTER CENTER

CCSS in English Language Arts: W.1.2, W.1.6, SL.1.2

Objectives: Students will be able to:

- Identify roles and responsibilities of family members.
- Draw and write about ways to be a good family member.

Activities:

- Have students access "Helping Out Around the House" at *www.watchknowlearn.org/Video.aspx?VideoID=20834&CategoryID=6207*
- Students use Artpad at *http://artpad.art.com/artpad/painter/* or Kerpoof at *www.kerpoof.com/#/activity/draw* to draw and write about the things they do to help around the house. These can be saved and/or sent to the teacher.

Lesson Assessment: Drawing and writing will be checked.

LESSON 10: FAMILIES DO SPECIAL ACTIVITIES TOGETHER

CCSS in English Language Arts: RL.1.1, W.1.3, W.1.5, W.1.8, SL1.1, SL.1.2, SL.1.3, SL.1.4, SL.1.5, SL.1.6, L.1.1, L1.2, L.1.6

Objectives: Students will be able to:

- Ask and answer questions about a narrative text.
- Illustrate and orally describe special activities they have done with their families using complete sentences.
- Write a narrative with a sequence of events, details, temporal words, and a sense of closure.
- Use correct spacing, letter formation, and complete sentences.

Activities

- Read-aloud—*Arthur's Family Vacation* by Marc Brown
  - Set purpose: *Listen to find out what special things Arthur does with his family in this book.*
  - During: Pause to ask and answer questions. Have students share their responses with a partner.
  - After: Discuss the special activities Arthur did with his family.
- Narrative writing in *My Family* books
  - Brainstorming: Students work in small groups to share one activity they have done with their family.
  - Prewriting: On a graphic organizer with three picture frames labeled *first*, *then*, and *last*, model drawing three detailed "photographs" from a single event depicting a family activity. Students work individually to complete their graphic organizers.
  - Oral rehearsal: Model for the students how to share the photographs by describing the details of the activity, using temporal words, and ending by sharing your feelings. Circulate as students share their photographs in their small groups and prompt as needed.
  - Drafting: Model the drafting process before students begin. Cut out the pictures from the graphic organizer and glue them into the *My Family* book. Think aloud as you write, making connections to the pictures as you recount the events, include details and temporal words, and end by sharing your feelings about the event. Student work session should immediately follow.
  - Share: Allow students to share their writing in small groups. Peers may praise the work or ask questions in the form of "I like how you . . . " and "I wonder . . . "
- Discuss how the activities that people share with their families are all different but all valuable.

Lesson Assessment: Anecdotal notes can be taken to assess students' ability to orally describe a family activity using complete thoughts that correlate with their pictures. Writing will be evaluated against a rubric based on the first-grade narrative writing standards, and letter spacing, letter formation, and complete sentences may also be noted.

LESSON 11: FAMILIES SUPPORT EACH OTHER

CCSS in English Language Arts: RL1.1, RL1.2, RL.1.10, W.1.2, W.1.3, SL.1.1, SL.1.2, L1.1, L1.2, L1.5

Objectives: Students will be able to:

- Ask and answer questions about a narrative text describing the ways families support each other.
- Retell a story and demonstrate how characters help each other.
- Write a thank you card.
- Write about the ways their family supports them and they support their family.
- Read a first-grade-level text with the support of a partner.
- Write a new version of a familiar story with a different outcome.

Activities:

- Read-aloud—*A Sick Day for Amos McGee* by Philip C. Stead
  - Before: Discuss the word *support*. Brainstorm ways that people can show support.
  - Set purpose: *Listen to find out the ways the animals offer Amos McGee support.*

- During: Pause to allow students to share about the ways the animals offer Amos McGee support and record their ideas on chart paper.
- After: Review the chart together and allow students to share connections they have made with the story.
- Follow-up centers
  - Felt board: Provide felt pieces and a copy of the book *A Sick Day for Amos McGee*. Students retell the story showing how the animals support Amos.

(Morrow, 2002)

  - Card making: Students create thank you cards for people in their families that support them. Students address the card and write a message explaining the support they are thankful for.
  - *My Family* books: Students draw and write on two pages in their books. The first should include a picture and a sentence explaining how a family member supports them. The second should show how they support their family.
  - *The Little Red Hen*: Students partner read a version of the folktale *The Little Red Hen*. Together, they retell the story showing how the animals could have supported the hen. Students can use props or a storyboard to write and draw their new story.

Lesson Assessment: Observation and anecdotal notes will be used to assess students' strengths and weaknesses in the different centers.

LESSON 12: LINKING EXPOSITORY AND NARRATIVE TEXTS TO LEARN ABOUT EXTENDED FAMILIES

CCSS in English Language Arts: RL.1.1, RL.1.3, RL.1.4, RL.1.7, RI.1.1, RI.1.3, RI.1.6, RI.1.7, RI.1.10, W.1.2, W.1.5, W.1.8, SL.1.1, SL.1.2, SL.1.4, SL.1.5, L.1.1, L.1.2, L.1.6

Objectives: Students will be able to:

- Define a family as a group of people usually related by blood, marriage, or adoption, but may also include people who are unrelated and living together.
- Ask and answer questions about key details in texts.
- Use pictures to describe people and characters in texts making connections between individuals and identifying information that is provided in the illustrations alone.
- Identify words that appeal to the senses.
- Write and talk about the people in their immediate and extended families.

Activities:

- Part A: Read-aloud—*Families* by Ann Morris
  - Picture walk: Flip through the pages of the book. Allow students to comment on what they see. Additionally, ask them to predict who the people are based on what they see in the pictures.
  - Set purpose: *As you listen read the pictures carefully. Sometimes the pictures tell you more than the words.*
  - During: Pause to ask and answer questions reinforcing content already covered in the unit (e.g., families are different, families work together, families care for one another).
  - After: Prompt students to share what they read in the pictures. Introduce the idea that families include more than just the people you live with. Use the words *extended family*. Look back through the text, reading the pictures together to describe the connection between people, and identify individuals who might be included in an extended family.

- Part B: Initial Reading—*The Relatives Came* by Cynthia Rylant
  - Before: Read the title and the cover illustration for information. *What are relatives? Who are the people on the cover? What's on the roof of their car? Why is it there?*
  - Set purpose: *As you listen, read the pictures carefully. See if you can figure out who are the members of this extended family and how they visit, work, and play together.*
  - During: Pause to ask and answer questions, pointing out specific images. Allow students to comment as well.
  - After: Turn and tell a friend about your relatives—the members of your extended family.
- Part C: Author's Craft
  - Before: Cynthia Rylant thinks of her audience as she writes. She tries to connect with the reader's feelings. Discuss some of the words and phrases below that suggest feelings and appeal to the senses.
    - Build anticipation: *all day long, waiting, traveled up all those miles*
    - Suggest feelings: *hugging time, crying sometimes, so much laughing, shining faces, quiet talk, busy hugging and eating and breathing together, beds felt too big and too quiet, they missed us*
  - Set purpose: *As we read see if Cynthia Rylant helps you connect with the family in her book. Can you think of a time when you felt the way the characters do in this story?*
  - During: Model identifying words and phrases that suggest feelings and appeal to the senses. Allow students to take over. Ask questions to prompt students to make emotional and personal connections.
  - After: Discuss text-to-self connections and emotions the story evokes. Draw extended families in *My Family* book. If students were able to make a connection with the book, encourage them to include that experience in their picture of their extended family. Label and write a sentence. Allow students to share.

Lesson Assessment: Participation and *My Family* books will be checked.

LESSON 13: THINKING ABOUT YOUR AUDIENCE WHEN WRITING INFORMATIONAL TEXTS

CCSS in English Language Arts: RL.1.5, RI.1.2, RI.1.3, RI.1.7, RI.1.8, W.1.2, W.1.5, W.1.8, L.1.1, L.1.2

Objectives: Students will be able to:
- Define a family as a group of people usually related by blood, marriage, or adoption, but may also include people who are unrelated and living together.
- Identify roles and responsibilities of family members.
- Understand that the purpose of informational writing is to teach about something.
- Identify the main idea and key details of a text referring to the illustrations.
- Write an informational text with purpose and awareness of audience.

Activities:
- Review the story *Families* by flipping through and looking at the pictures. Think aloud to identify the main idea: *In this book we saw pictures of many different kinds of families working, playing, and caring for one another. So I think the main idea of this book is "Families can be so different, but all of them care for and help one another."*

- *Since this is an informational book, the job of the author is to teach her audience something. Ann Morris definitely thinks of her audience when she makes a book. What do you see that helps you understand this main idea?* Students compare and contrast the photographs. Emphasize that she selects a lot of different pictures to teach us how families are different and alike.

- *In informational writing we want to teach someone something. We need to think of our audience when we decide what to write and what pictures to include so they can learn from our writing.*

- Model selecting a topic, including key details, and making an illustration that furthers the reader's understanding. Throughout the process, ask yourself, "What can I do to help my reader understand?" and "Will my reader learn from this?"

- Students are to use the writing process you have modeled to write an informational text. Circulate and conference with students, guiding them to think about their audience as they write and assist as needed.

- Students share their writing.

Lesson Assessment: Writing will be kept in a portfolio as a student work sample.

LESSON 14: FAMILY AND CULTURE

CCSS in English Language Arts: RL.1.1, RL.1.2, RL1.3, RL.1.10, RF.1.3, RF.1.4, W.1.1, W.1.2, L.1.1, L.1.2

Objectives: Students will be able to:
- Compare and contrast families from different cultures.
- Write an opinion piece that provides an opinion, reasons, and a sense of closure.
- Encode and identify words ending with -*ice*.
- Retell a story using puppets.
- Map a story identifying the central message, characters, setting, and events.
- Read books at their independent reading level.
- Draw and write about one traditional food that their family eats.

Activities:
- Read-aloud—*Everybody Cooks Rice* by Norah Dooley
  - Set purpose: *Listen to see if you can name all of the different kinds of rice the families eat.*
  - During: Pause to allow students to name the kinds of rice and create a list together.
  - After: Compare and contrast the families in the story.
- Follow-up centers
  - Writing Center: Provide rice-shaped paper for students to write an opinion piece where they state an opinion about their favorite kind of rice (or dislike for rice), include a reason for their opinion, and provide some sense of closure.
  - Making Words Center: Students make words that rhyme with rice using magnetic letters and then record the words they make on paper.

o Retelling Center: Students work together to draw the main character and houses in *Everybody Cooks Rice*. Popsicle sticks are added to the drawings to make puppets. Students use their puppets, copies of the pictures of rice from the book, and the text to retell the story.
o Guided reading: Guide the students in a story-mapping activity where they identify the central message, characters, setting, and events of *Everybody Cooks Rice*. Provide leveled books for students and select activities based on the students' needs and the text selected. If appropriate, have students repeat the story-mapping activity for their guided reading books and complete word work activities with the initial consonant *r* or the word family *-ice*.

• Students write a sentence explaining one traditional meal that their family eats and draw a picture in their *My Family* books.

Lesson Assessment: Participation and written work will be checked. Groups can perform their retelling for the class. Opinion writing will be evaluated against a rubric based on the first-grade opinion writing standards, and grammar/punctuation may also be noted. Running records and anecdotal notes may be taken during guided reading.

LESSON 15: FAMILIES SHARE TRADITIONS

CCSS in English Language Arts: RI.1.7, RF.1.4, W.1.2, W.1.8, L.1.1, L.1.2, L.1.6

Objectives: Students will be able to:
• Provide examples of family traditions.
• Encode two- to four-letter words.
• Write and identify words ending in *-ing*.
• Read fluently.
• Compare/contrast traditions from around the world to their own family traditions.
• Write and illustrate a sentence explaining a tradition in their family.

Activities:
• Discuss and define *traditions*. Provide examples of traditions: singing happy birthday, meeting up with family during holidays, etc.
• Center activities
  o Making Little Words Out of a Big Word Center
    ▪ Give students the following letters on slips of paper: *a, i, i, o, d, n, r, t, t.*
    ▪ Students manipulate the letters to make little words out of the word *tradition.*
    ▪ Students record their words on paper with columns for *Two Letter Words, Three Letter Words,* and *Four Letter Words.*

(Morrow, 2002)

  o Top Ten Center
    ▪ Students write a list of "Top Ten Things to Do for the Holidays with *-ing*" and highlight the *-ing* words (e.g., making cookies on Christmas).
  o Poetry Center
    ▪ Write the poem from *www.canteach.ca/elementary/songspoems3.html* on a piece of chart paper.
    ▪ Read the poem several times during morning meeting following choral and echo reading procedures.

> Our family comes
> From many homes,
> Our hair is straight,
> Our hair is brown,
> Our hair is curled,
> Our eyes are blue,
> Our skins are different
> Colors, too.
> We're girls and boys,
> We're big and small,
> We're young and old,
> We're short and tall.
> We're everything
> That we can be
> And still we are
> A family.
> We laugh and cry,
> We work and play,
> We help each other
> Every day.
> The world's a lovely
> Place to be
> Because we are
> A family.

  - Students take turns pointing and whisper reading the poem.
  o Teacher-Led Traditions Around The World Center
    - Show pictures of people participating in traditions, discuss the traditions, and identify on a map the countries the pictures are from. After the first few, allow students to predict which countries the traditions are from.
    - Students compare and contrast their own traditions with those in the pictures.
- For homework students will work with a family member to draw a picture of a family tradition in their *My Family* book. The students will write a sentence using an *-ing* word, and describe the tradition and its country of origin.

Lesson Assessment: Participation and written work will be checked.

LESSON 16: FAMILIES CELEBRATE TOGETHER

CCSS in English Language Arts: W.1.6, W.1.7, SL1.1, SL.1.4, SL1.5, L.1.1

Objectives: Students will be able to:
- Identify and discuss ways families celebrate together.
- Work collaboratively to create a skit depicting a family celebrating together.
- Speak clearly, use full sentences, and use proper grammar.
- Provide feedback to others.

Activities:

- Shared writing—*Our Classroom Family*. The students share celebrations their classroom family participates in together.
- Divide the class into small groups of six. Students select one of the following roles:
  - Scene Setter: This person will use props to set a scene for the skit.
  - Video Recorder: This person will video record the skit.
  - Presenter: This person will introduce and present the skit.
  - Actors (3): These students will perform the skit.
- Students discuss ways that their families celebrate together. Then they decide on one idea together to perform as a skit. Their skit should demonstrate one way a family celebrates together. Students practice and then record their skit.
- Watch the videos together. Students give feedback in the form of "I like how you . . . " and "I wonder . . . "

Lesson Assessment: Participation will be checked. Videos will serve as student work sample.

LESSON 17: FAMILIES ARE UNIQUE AND WE MUST RESPECT DIFFERENCES

CCSS in English Language Arts: RI.1.1, RI.1.2, RI.1.4, W.1.2, W.1.6, W.1.8, SL.1.1, L.1.1, L.1.2

Objectives: Students will be able to:

- Compare and contrast their family unit, traditions, and practices with other family units, traditions, and practices.
- Identify ways the United States and the world are diverse.
- Write a friendly letter.
- Listen to and write words that describe music from around the world.
- Write a family-themed alphabet book.
- Create a PowerPoint slide stating a way to show respect to a family that is different than their own.

Activities:

- Read-aloud—*How My Family Lives in America* by Susan Kuklin
  - Before: Review the vocabulary. Write sentences from the text containing the following vocabulary words on sentence strips: *heritage, village, Hispanic, calligraphy, chopsticks*. Ask questions to help students develop an understanding of the vocabulary words.
  - Set purpose: *As you listen, think about the ways your family is like the families in the book and the ways your family is different.*
  - During: Pause to allow students to share differences and similarities between their own family and the families depicted in the book.
  - After: Discuss the traditions of the families in the book. Allow students to make a text-to-self connection by drawing and writing in their reader-response journals.
- Follow-up centers
  - Writing Center: Students write a letter to a classmate asking them a question about their family.
  - Listening Center: Students listen to music from around the world and write three words to describe one of the country's songs.

o Computer Center: Students create a PowerPoint slide to add to the presentation entitled "Respect Families and Their Differences." Students are to write an idea of how to show respect for another family's traditions and will add clip art to match the text.

o Alphabet books: Students work with a partner to make a family-themed alphabet book. The students think of words that have to do with family for each letter of the alphabet. Students can use the alphabet organizer located at *www.readwritethink.org/files/resources/interac-tives/alphabet/.*

• Students draw and write a sentence stating how they can show respect to another person's family and traditions in their *My Family* books.

Lesson Assessment: Participation and written work will be checked.

LESSON 18: FAMILIES TRADITION AND CULTURE SHARE DAY

CCSS in English Language Arts: SL.1.4, SL.1.6, L.1.1

Objectives: Students will be able to:

• Identify and orally present a family tradition and cultural food, speaking clearly and using complete sentences.

• Share their *My Family* books.

Activities:

• Invite families to the classroom for Culture Share Day. At home children work with their families to decide on a cultural food they would like to bring in and one tradition they'd like to share with the class.

• Students take turns presenting their family tradition and cultural food.

• Students and families share their foods, their *My Family* books, and converse.

Lesson Assessment: Anecdotal notes may be taken to note students' ability to speak clearly and in complete sentences.

---

*Unit plan format from Wiggins and McTighe (2005).

REFERENCES

Bear, D. R., Invernizzi, M., Templeton, S., & Johnston, F. (2008). *Words their way: Word study for phonics, vocabulary, and spelling instruction.* Upper Saddle River, NJ: Pearson.

Morrow, L. (2002). *The Literacy Center.* Portland, ME: Stenhouse.

Morrow, L. M. (2012). *Literacy development in the early years: Helping children read and write.* Boston: Pearson.

N.J. Department of Education. (2010). New Jersey Core Curriculum content standards: Social studies. Retrieved from *www.state.nj.us/education/cccs/standards/6/index.html.*

Wiggins, G. P., & McTighe, J. (2005). *Understanding by design.* Alexandria, VA: ASCD.

WEATHER—GRADE 2

Desired Results: Literacy	Desired Results: Science
Established Goals • Common Core State Standards for English language arts grade 2* *Standards articulated in the Learning Plan below	**Established Goals** • Observe and document daily weather conditions and discuss how the weather influences your activities for the day. • Observe and discuss evaporation and condensation. (N.J. Department of Education, 2010)
Enduring Understandings • Knowledge can be shared through written text and oral communication and by using digital tools. • Effective communication involves clarity and fluency of ideas in writing and speaking. • Reading and listening can be effective methods for learning new information.	**Enduring Understandings** • Earth's components form systems. These systems continually interact at different rates of time, affecting the Earth regionally and globally. • The Earth is a system, continuously moving resources from one part of the system to another. (N.J. Department of Education, 2010)
Essential Questions • How can I effectively communicate my thoughts, knowledge, and understandings? • What are the purposes for and benefits of reading? • What do good readers do?	**Essential Questions** • How does the weather affect our daily activities? • How can the weather be observed, described, measured and reported? • Where does precipitation come from?
Knowledge Students will know: • Good readers can employ a variety of strategies in order to assist in decoding and comprehension. • Texts have structure related to the author's purpose. • Authors carefully select the language they use to convey feelings, ideas, and information.	**Knowledge** Students will know: • Current weather conditions include air movement, clouds, and precipitation. • Weather conditions affect our daily lives. • Water can disappear (evaporate) and collect (condense) on surfaces. (N.J. Department of Education, 2010)
Skills Students will be able to: • Use context and beginning dictionaries/glossaries to determine meaning of unknown words. • Use and connect vocabulary with real-life situations. • Ask and answer questions about texts. • Use visualization to aid comprehension. • Use text structure to aid comprehension and organize writing. • Exhibit fluency when reading and speaking. • Identify and use sensory language in reading, writing, and speaking. • Record science observations. • Use digital tools to publish writing.	**Skills** Students will be able to: • Describe reasons for knowing the weather and ways to find out about the weather. • Observe and measure to collect weather data. • Report the weather. • Create a weather map. • Identify and classify the different types of clouds. • Tell about the water cycle.

Assessment Evidence

Performance Tasks
- **Weather Report**
  - Goal and Role: As a team of meteorologists, your group will produce a weather broadcast.
  - Audience: Community members
  - Situation: The challenge involves not only predicting the weather based on gathered data but also effectively describing the weather using words and images as well as making suggestions for the day's preparations/activities.
  - Product: A television weather broadcast
  - Standards: Weather prediction and daily preparations/activities must be reasonable based on collected data. Speak clearly and with an appropriate pace. Weather map must match the report and be neat.
- **Children's Picture Book**
  - Goal and Role: As an author/illustrator, create a narrative children's picture book.
  - Audience: Other children your age
  - Situation: The challenge involves understanding what makes a good book.
  - Product: Create a picture book that has characters, a strong sense of setting, descriptive/sensory language, and a weather-based problem/solution.
  - Standards: Your book must have illustrations that tell a story and words that paint a picture, characters, and a strong sense of setting; use time-order words; and have evidence of organization/structure (chain of events, problem/solution).

Other Evidence
- Weather test

LEARNING PLAN

Routines and Morning Meeting

CCSS in English Language Arts: RL.2.4, RF.2.4, SL.2.4, SL.2.5, L.2.4 L.2.5

Objectives: Students will be able to:
- Identify rhythm in songs and poetry.
- Read fluently.
- Speak audibly when reporting weather.
- Create recordings of poetry readings.
- Use context and beginning dictionaries/glossaries to determine meaning of unknown words.
- Use and connect weather vocabulary with real-life situations.

Activities:
- Have a student helper identify the weather each morning. The helper can set the weather information for all to see and dress a character with the appropriate attire. At Morning Meeting he or she can report their observations.
- Weather station: Set up a center in the classroom with the following items:
  - Weather data chart with the headings *Date, Temperature, Sky, Precipitation, Wind, Humidity,* and *Air Pressure*
  - Weather tools—a thermometer, hygrometer, barometer, and pinwheel

- ○ Meteorologist work schedule assigning students to dates for data collection
- ○ Sign with the logo for the local news/weather channel
- ○ Clipboard with copies of a weather data collection sheet and an attached pencil
- Greeting: "Good morning [name], it sure is [adjective] out today . . . " Students have to come up with a different adjective as they pass the greeting down the line.
- Share: My favorite type of weather . . .
- Activity: Make a rainstorm—all students simultaneously follow each step: rub palms together, snap fingers, clap two fingers to palm, clap, pat your lap and stamp your feet, and then reverse steps back to quiet.
- Activity: Sing a weather song. Print text on chart paper. Discuss how words and phrases supply rhythm and meaning. Several are available from Jean Warren at *www.preschoolexpress.com/ music_station01/music_station_sept01.shtml.*
- Monthly poem: Select weather poetry to read and reread throughout the month. (See Lesson 7 for suggestions.) Identify and determine meaning of unknown words. Small groups of students record themselves and podcast the monthly poem.
- Science Word Wall: Keep a running list of science vocabulary words throughout the unit.

Lesson Assessment: Take anecdotal notes on students' vocabulary use and speech. Audio recording can be student work sample.

LESSON 1: INTRODUCTION TO UNIT USING INFORMATIONAL TEXT

CCSS in English Language Arts: RI.2.1, RI.2.4, RI.2.10, SL.2.1.a, SL.2.2, SL.2.3, L.2.4.a, L.2.4.e, L.2.6

Objectives: Students will be able to:
- Use context and beginning dictionaries/glossaries to determine meaning of unknown words.
- Ask and answer questions about informational text.
- Describe reasons for knowing the weather.

Activities:
- Discuss performance task—peak interest by telling students they will be meteorologists, or weather forecasters, by observing and collecting information and measurements of the weather and then producing a weather broadcast.
- Allow students to activate prior knowledge to explain vocabulary, and then use glossaries/dictionaries to find the precise definition. Add words to science word wall: *meteorologist, forecast, observe, measure,* and *broadcast.* Continue to add other words to the science word wall throughout the unit.
- Read-aloud—*What Will the Weather Be?* by Lynda DeWitt.
  - ○ Set purpose: *Listen to find out why knowing the weather is important and how meteorologists predict the weather.*
  - ○ During: Pause to ask and answer questions about the text, emphasize information, and model using context clues to determine meaning of unfamiliar words using think-alouds.
  - ○ After: *Turn and tell a friend why knowing the weather is important. Share what your friend said.*

Lesson Assessment: Responses will be noted.

LESSON 2: USING FUNCTIONAL TEXTS TO FIND OUT ABOUT THE WEATHER AND PLAN FOR THE DAY

CCSS in English Language Arts: RI.2.5, RI.2.7, SL.2.1.a

Objectives: Students will be able to:

- Use functional texts to check the weather forecast and plan for the day.
- Use text features and images to aid comprehension.

Activities:

- Discussion—*What are some ways we can find out information about the weather?* (*Check the television, newspaper, or Internet; observe and measure.*) As students make suggestions, show examples. Identify text features together and use them to guide the reading. Have students explain how the images enhance the text. Discuss the types of activities you could do and appropriate clothing to wear based on the reports.
  - Distribute or project newspaper weather report.
  - Watch a weather broadcast on television, streamed from the Internet, or on the Weather Channel app for the iPad.
  - Check weather on the Internet or using an app for the iPad (use a printed Internet weather report if necessary).
  - If students do not include *observe* and *measure*, suggest it and show weather tools: thermometer, barometer, rain gauge, hygrometer, and anemometer/weather vane/pinwheel. Inform students they will learn how each works in another lesson.

Lesson Assessment: Participation will be checked.

LESSON 3: WEATHER TOOL WORDS AND WORD PARTS

CCSS in English Language Arts: RF.2.3.d, L.2.4.b, L.2.4.c

Objectives: Students will be able to:

- Decode words using morphemes, or meaning-bearing word parts.

Activities:

- Write *thermometer, hygrometer, barometer,* and *thermostat* on the board and remind students which tool is which and what they do.
- Have students tell how the words are alike. Have them make an inference for the meaning of *-meter* and *thermo-/therm-* (*measuring tool, heat*).
- *-stat* means keeping something stable/still, *hygro-* means moisture, *baro-* means pressure.
- Review exceptions: <u>*statement*</u>—a sentence that ends with a period, <u>*baron*</u>—member of the nobility not as powerful as the king.
- Write other words with *thermo-/therm-* and *-meter* (*thermos, thermal, centimeter, speedometer*).
- Add morphemes to the word wall.

Lesson Assessment: Participation will be checked.

LESSON 4: OBSERVING AND MEASURING TO COLLECT DATA ON THE WEATHER

CCSS in English Language Arts: W.2.6, W.2.7, L.2.3

Objectives: Students will be able to:
- Observe and measure to collect weather data.
- Record observations and measurements.
- Use digital tools to publish writing.

Activities:
- Review reasons why it is important to know about the weather.
- Introduce the weather station and weather tools to the students. Name weather tools and explain what they measure. Review data collection procedures: how to read tools, fill out the data collection form, and transfer data to weather data chart.
- Model process by being the meteorologist of the day.
- Students will work in small groups on a rotating schedule to collect data for an extended period of time.
- Weather data may be shared and compared with data from students in another region through collaborative online websites such as wikis or ePals.

Lesson Assessment: Recorded data will be checked for accuracy.

LESSON 5: USING LITERATURE TO REINFORCE IDEAS ABOUT BEING PREPARED FOR THE WEATHER

CCSS in English Language Arts: RL.2.1, RL.2.2, RL.2.6, RL.2.9, RL.2.10, RF.2.4

Objectives: Students will be able to:
- Ask and answer questions about a piece of literature.
- Describe reasons for knowing the weather.
- Compare/contrast and evaluate two versions of the same story.
- Retell a piece of literature and speak in different voices for each character.

Activities:
- Part A: Read-aloud—*The Mitten* by Jan Brett
  - Activate prior knowledge: *What might you do to prepare yourself to go outside in the snow?*
  - Set purpose: *Listen to find out what happens to Nicki's snow-white mitten.*
  - During: Pause to ask and answer questions and have students make predictions.
  - After: *Turn and tell a friend why it is important to be prepared for the weather.*
- Part B: Read-aloud—*The Mitten* by Alvin Tresselt
  - Use the felt board pieces to lead a retelling of Jan Brett's *The Mitten.*
  - Set purpose: *Listen to find out what is the same and what is different in this version of the story.*
  - During: Pause to fill out Venn diagram.
  - After: *Turn and tell a friend which story you liked best and why.*

- Part C: Storytelling
  - o Model how to use the felt board pieces to retell *The Mitten* by Jan Brett.
  - o Emphasize changing your voice for the different characters.
  - o Place storytelling pieces and text in literacy center.

Lesson Assessment: Responses will be noted. Take anecdotal notes on students' retellings.

LESSON 6: LITERACY CENTER ACTIVITY: SEASONS REVIEW AND MINI-BOOKS FOR KINDERGARTEN BUDDIES

CCSS in English Language Arts: W.2.2, W.2.6, W.2.8, L.2.1.f, L.2.2.a, L.2.3

Objectives: Students will be able to:
- Recall information about the weather from personal experiences to answer a question.
- Write and illustrate informational texts using complete sentences.
- Use digital tools to publish writing.

Activities:
- Guiding research question—What are typical weather conditions and activities in the four seasons? During a whole-group discussion, students recall information and create a chart together.
- In centers students write informational texts on the four seasons for a kindergartner. Story writing software such as Storybird, Storybook Weaver, and StoryJumper may be used.
  - o Use pictures and captions that show typical weather and seasonal activities
  - o Use simple language, including kindergarten sight words (*I, see, like, my, a, and, to, go, for, from*), in complete sentences.
  - o Create a cover and a dedication page.

Lesson Assessment: Completed writing will be evaluated.

LESSON 7: IN-DEPTH INFORMATIONAL TEXT STUDY ON SEVERE WEATHER WITH A POETRY CONNECTION

CCSS in English Language Arts: RL.2.4, RI.2.1, RI.2.2, RI.2.4, RI.2.5, SL.2.1, L.2.4.a

Objectives: Students will be able to:
- Describe reasons for knowing the weather.
- Use context and beginning dictionaries/glossaries to determine meaning of unknown words.
- Identify the main topic of an informational text and the focus of each section within the text.
- Participate in collaborative conversations surrounding an informational text.
- Use visualization to aid comprehension.

Activities:

- Part A: Initial reading of *Super Storms* by Seymour Simon in small- or whole-group setting
  - Allow students to activate prior knowledge to explain vocabulary, and then use glossaries/ dictionaries to find the precise definition. Add words to science word wall.
  - Introduce nonfiction text structure: Main idea/details—*The whole story is going to have one main idea. I can use the title to help me figure it out. I bet it's going to be:* Some storms are super storms. *Then I can read to find out the different types of super storms. Those would be the details.*
  - Set purpose: *Listen to find out the different types of super storms.*
  - During: Pause to fill out main idea/details graphic organizer together.
  - After: *Turn and tell a friend why knowing the weather is important. Share what your friend said.*
- Part B: Adding headings and identifying main idea/details of text sections
  - Revisit yesterday's main idea/details graphic organizer.
  - Together, add headings to each section using sticky notes: *Thunderstorms, Hail Tornadoes,* and *Hurricanes.*
  - Review nonfiction text structure: Main idea/details—*The whole story has one main idea. The title helped me decide the main idea of the whole story:* Some storms are super storms. *The different types of super storms were the details. Now that we have added headings we have divided the story into sections, kind of like chapters. Each of those sections is going to have their own main idea and details.*
  - Model how to fill out the main idea/details graphic organizer for the thunderstorms section. (*Main idea: Thunderstorms are super storms. Details: They can drop millions of gallons of water in 1 minute. Lightning can destroy a tree or small house. Lightning can start fires. Hail damages crops, buildings, and cars.*)
  - Students select which section they will become the expert on and form small groups. Have students fill out the main idea/details graphic organizer together for their section.
  - Group speaker share their organizer with the class.
- Part C: Sensory language and visualization
  - Review comprehension strategy: Visualize—*A good reader naturally creates a picture in their mind of what they are reading. This picture could be like a photograph or more like a movie that plays in your mind.*
  - Review writing strategy: Sensory language—*A good writer uses words that help the reader imagine what it is like. They help us see, smell, hear, taste, and feel.*
  - Revisit the text to visualize the super storms. Work together to identify the words Seymour Simon uses to help the reader imagine what each storm is like. Determine which of the five senses they help the reader use.
- Part D: Poetry connection to extend understanding of visualization and sensory language
  - Review that poetry is an artistic type of writing where the author may use sensory language to help the reader imagine the way something looks, sounds, feels, tastes, or smells.
  - Read selected weather poetry and have students use their five senses to visualize. Allow them to draw or discuss what they saw in their mind.
  - Suggested texts:
    - Frank, J. (1990). *Snow toward evening: A year in a river valley.* New York: Dial.
    - Goldish, M. (1996). *101 Science poems & songs for young learners.* New York: Scholastic.
    - Moore, H. H. (1997). *A poem a day.* New York: Scholastic.
    - Katz, B. (1999). *Poems just for us.* New York: Scholastic.

                                                                    (Bauman et al., 2011)

Lesson Assessment: Responses will be noted. Graphic organizers will be checked.

LESSON 8: LITERACY CENTER ACTIVITY: SEVERE WEATHER REPORT

CCSS in English Language Arts: RI.2.3, RF.2.4, W.2.2, SL.2.5

Objectives: Students will be able to:

- Describe connections between scientific ideas in informational texts.
- Write an informational report and read it fluently.
- Create audio recording to present knowledge.

Activities:

- Students work with a buddy to select a type of severe weather to report on gathering information from informational texts.
- Identify conditions people should expect, the cause of the weather, typical effects of the weather, and an interesting fact about the weather within the weather report.
- Draw a picture of the extreme weather.
- Practice reading your report until fluency is reached. Record the reading.

Lesson Assessment: Informational writing will be checked for accuracy. Assess fluency using a rubric.

LESSON 9: LITERACY CENTER ACTIVITY: FIVE SENSES POEM

CCSS in English Language Arts: W.2.8, L.2.5.a

Objectives: Students will be able to:

- Use sensory language gathered from firsthand experience to write descriptive poetry.

Activities:

- Students use a web graphic organizer with the headings *Feel, Hear, Smell, See* to plan for a poem about a seasonal article of clothing (e.g. gloves, mittens, hats, scarves, ear warmers, hats, rain boots, rain coats, bathing suit, flip-flops).
- Students write a poem.

Lesson Assessment: Poems will be kept as student work sample.

LESSON 10: IN-DEPTH NARRATIVE LITERATURE STUDY WITH CHILDREN'S PICTURE BOOK PERFORMANCE TASK (SEVERAL DAYS WILL BE NEEDED FOR EACH LESSON PART)

CCSS in English Language Arts: RL.2.3, RL.2.5, RL.2.7, RL.2.10, W.2.3, W.2.5, SL.2.4, L.2.1, L.2.2, L.2.5.b, L.2.6

Objectives: Students will be able to:

- Describe reasons for knowing the weather.
- Identify story elements, including characters, setting, problem, and solution.

- ○ Write and illustrate a children's picture book with a problem/solution story structure; a strong sense of setting; and temporal, descriptive, and sensory language.
- ○ Create a lead picture that introduces the setting and characters and establishes the mood; a problem picture that depicts a problem caused by a super storm; and a solution picture that shows how the problem was resolved.

Activities:

- Part A: Initial reading of *Wild Horse Winter* by Tetsuya Honda in whole-group setting
  - ○ Predict: *If you're not prepared for severe weather, you could have a problem. What problem could horses have in a blizzard?*
  - ○ Set purpose: *Read to find out where the story takes place, who the characters are, what their problem is, and how they solve it.*
  - ○ During: Pause to fill out story map: setting, character, problem, and solution.
  - ○ After: *What kind of storm do you want to write about? What problem could that type of weather cause?* Students can flip through *Super Storms* by Seymour Simon to focus on their topic and discuss their thoughts with a friend.

- Part B: Exploring and creating illustrations that enhance characters, setting, and plot
  - ○ Creating the lead picture:
    - ■ Review the lead picture in *Wild Horse Winter*. Cover up the text and identify the information learned from the illustration alone. *Where does the story take place? What season is it? What time of day is it? Who are the characters? What is the mood? What details in the picture give us clues that help answer these questions?*
    - ■ Model creating a lead picture thinking aloud as you go. Demonstrate filling the entire page; selecting appropriate colors for the time of day, season, and mood you wish to depict; adding in extra details to give setting clues; and making decisions about the characters such as facial expressions.
    - ■ Students begin work on their own picture. Following the student work session, have a group share time where selected students share their picture and the process they used to create them.
  - ○ Creating the problem picture:
    - ■ Review information given in the problem picture in *Wild Horse Winter*. Cover up the text and identify the problem. *What details in the picture give us clues to the problem?*
    - ■ Model creating a problem picture thinking aloud as you go. Demonstrate selecting a real problem that could occur as a result of a super storm; selecting appropriate colors for the weather and mood you wish to depict; adding in extra details to give clues about the problem and emotions of the characters.
    - ■ Student work session and group share.
  - ○ Creating the solution picture:
    - ■ Review information given in the solution picture in *Wild Horse Winter*. Cover up the text and identify the solution. *What details in the picture give us clues that the problem was solved?*
    - ■ Model creating a solution picture thinking aloud as you go. Demonstrate selecting a possible solution related to the super storm; selecting appropriate colors for the weather and mood you wish to depict; adding in extra details to give clues about the solution and emotions of the characters.
    - ■ Student work session and group share.

- Part C: Oral rehearsal of narrative writing
  - ○ Model reading pictures for details pointing to the picture as you tell about it. *What is happening in this picture? Where does it take place? What time of day is it? What kind of day is it?*
  - ○ Choose students to read their pictures and orally rehearse their story. Prompt if needed: *I notice in your picture. Can you tell me about it? What is your _____ doing?*
  - ○ Record particularly excellent language shared by students that they might wish to include in their writing.

- Part D: Identifying descriptive language
  - Discuss the "magic trick" of really good writing: When the words are so good, the reader can visualize the illustration moving. For example, they might see the wind blowing the trees and the grass bending and swaying.
  - Reread *Wild Horse Winter* and have students check for the "magic trick," share what they saw in the pictures, and recall some of the words that helped them imagine it was moving.
  - Model using a four-column graphic organizer and thinking questions to brainstorm excellent language while viewing the lead picture you have created.
    - *What four important nouns in my picture will I put as the headings in my graphic organizer?*
    - *What is my [noun] doing?*
    - *How is the [noun] [verb]ing?*
    - *How would I describe my [noun]?*
  - Student work session and group share.
- Part E: Writing to the picture
  - Revisit *Wild Horse Winter* and make a list of the things Honda includes in the lead paragraphs (weather, season, setting details, place, and character). Make particular note of how the first sentence begins.
  - Display your lead picture.
- Model how to select the very best words from the graphic organizer filled out in Part D.
  - Have students suggest what to write for the lead sentences.
  - Model making changes by adding in and taking away words emphasizing the process of thinking of better ideas as we go along.
  - Student work session and group share.
  - Repeat Part D and Part E for the problem and solution pages and include a model of using temporal words.
- Part F: Revision
  - Show pictures and text that reflect the types of errors your students made and have students make suggestions on how to improve them.
  - Guide students through the revision process.

(Olshansky, 2008)

Lesson Assessment: Performance task will be evaluated based on the standards listed and children's books will become student work samples.

LESSON 11: USING A COMMON EXPERIENCE WITH CLOUDS TO PRACTICE OPINION WRITING

CCSS in English Language Arts: W.2.1, SL.2.1.a, SL.2.1.b, L.2.6

Objectives: Students will be able to:
- Observe to collect weather data.
- Participate in collaborative conversations, taking turns talking and building on what others say.
- Write opinion pieces.

Activities:
- Take students outside to observe clouds. Students use their imaginations to describe what shapes they see. Try to build on what the last person said.
- Create a language experience chart together to record students' opinions. Review opinion

writing structure: introduce topic, state opinion, supply reasons, and provide a concluding statement. Allow students to supply language for writing. Example text: *We went outside to look at the clouds. We all thought of different words to describe these clouds.* (List students' names and what they saw, with reasons.) *It was fun to see how differently everyone thinks.*

Lesson Assessment: Participation will be checked. Language experience chart will be displayed as opinion writing sample.

LESSON 12: USING INFORMATIONAL TEXT TO LEARN ABOUT CLASSIFYING CLOUDS

CCSS in English Language Arts: RI.2.1, RI.2.4, RI.2.6, RI.2.7, RI.2.8

Objectives: Students will be able to:
- Use context to determine meaning of unknown words.
- Ask and answer questions about informational text.
- Identify and classify the different types of clouds.

Activities:
- Think aloud to identify the purpose of the opinion paragraph created on the language experience chart in Lesson 11: *The purpose of this text is to tell our different opinions of how the clouds looked.* Reread the language experience chart together to recall the events of the last lesson. Discuss how the reasons support the purpose by giving specific examples of different views.
- Discussion—Do all clouds look the same? Are there names we can use to describe the different clouds?
- Read-aloud—*Clouds* by Anne Rockwell
  o Set purpose: *Listen to find out the names of the clouds and what type of weather they bring.*
  o During: Pause to ask and answer questions about the text, emphasize information and images, and model using context clues to determine meaning of unfamiliar words using think-alouds.
  o After: Select students to help look back in the text and make a list of cloud names and the type of weather they bring.

Lesson Assessment: Participation will be checked.

LESSON 13: USING LANGUAGE, ART, AND MATH TO REVIEW CLOUD CLASSIFICATIONS

CCSS in English Language Arts: RI.2.9, L.2.4.b, L.2.4.c

Objectives: Students will be able to:
- Use affixes to determine meaning of vocabulary words.
- Identify and classify the different types of clouds.
- Compare and contrast information presented by two texts on the same topic.

Activities:
- Review list of cloud names. Point out the word parts that are similar and determine meaning of word parts.

- Share "Common Types of Clouds in the Troposphere" from *http://eo.ucar.edu/webweather/cloud3.html* or a similar poster that visually represents cloud types and the weather they are associated with. Compare/contrast information in this text and the informational text read yesterday.
- Make cloud mobile.
  - See NASA's *http://spaceplace.nasa.gov/cloud-mobile/* for directions.
- Add cloud types graph to weather station.

(N.J. Department of Education, 2010)

Lesson Assessment: Cloud mobiles will be hung as student work samples. Cloud Types graph will be checked for accuracy.

LESSON 14: CONSTRUCTING KNOWLEDGE OF THE WATER CYCLE THROUGH EXPERIMENTATION

CCSS in English Language Arts: W.2.7, SL.2.4, L.2.5.a

Objectives: Students will be able to:

- Record science observations.
- Recount an experience with appropriate facts and relevant, descriptive details.
- Tell about the water cycle.
- Use and connect water cycle vocabulary with real-life situations.

Activities:

- Create KWL chart together.
  - *What We Know* (K)—Students suggest what they already know about precipitation. Include information on clouds if they do not suggest it: *Stratus and cumulonimbus clouds carry rain or snow.*
  - *What We Want to Find Out* (W)—Students suggest what they want to find out. Include questions on the water cycle if they did not suggest them: *How did the water get in the clouds?*
  - *What We Learned* (L)—Fill out as the class discovers information and recounts their experiences through discussion.
- Water Cycle Lab Day 1
  - Each student (or group of students) gets three cups. Label them 1, 2, and 3.
  - Cup 1 gets water and the level is marked and dated. The cup gets placed on the windowsill. It will stay there for a few days. The students record their predictions for the water in this cup.
  - Cup 2 gets ice. The cup gets placed on the windowsill. It will stay there overnight. The students record their predictions for the ice in this cup.
  - Cup 3 gets hot water (boiled from an electric kettle is best), covered in plastic wrap, and sealed with a rubber band. This cup stays on students' desks for immediate observation. The students record what they see. *If you were inside this cup, what type of weather would you be having? (rainy/foggy weather)*
- Water Cycle Lab Day 2
  - Observe Cup 2. Students record what happened to the ice. (*It melted.*) *Where do we see ice in nature? (icicles, glaciers, icebergs, snow, hail, frozen bodies of water) What type of weather is needed to see ice? (cold weather, winter weather) Based on what you see happening what type of weather is your cup having? (warmer weather, spring weather)*
  - Observe Cup 1. Students mark and date the water level. *Did anything happen yet?* Replace

Cup 1 on the windowsill and check it again a few days later. Every time this cup is checked the water level gets marked and dated. Cups 2 and 3 can also be kept for the same purpose.

Lesson Assessment: Student record sheets will be checked and evaluated.

LESSON 15: REINFORCING AND DEEPENING KNOWLEDGE OF WATER CYCLE THROUGH GUIDED READING

CCSS in English Language Arts: RI.2.10, RF.2.3, RF.2.4

Objectives: Students will be able to:
- Read and comprehend informational texts at their reading level.
- Apply grade-level phonics and word analysis skills in decoding.
- Read with sufficient accuracy and fluency.
- Tell about the water cycle.

Activities:
- Specific literacy skills practiced in guided reading should be based on the students' needs and the text selected. Keep a balanced focus on learning the science content (vocabulary/comprehension) and literacy skills (decoding/fluency).
- Some suggestions include: Repeating KWL activity, questioning, predicting, identifying the main topic of the text/paragraphs, making connections, using text features, and describing how reasons support specific points.
- Suggested texts
  o DRA 8, Guided Reading E: *I Am Water* by Jean Marzollo
  o DRA 16, Guided Reading I: *Where Do Puddles Go?* by Fay Robinson
  o DRA 18/20, Guided Reading J: *Water* by Alice K. Flanagan
  o DRA 28, Guided Reading M: *The Water Cycle* by Helen Frost
  o DRA 28, Guided Reading M: *Splish, Splash, Splosh!: A Book about Water* by Mick Manning and Brita Granström
  o DRA 30-34, Guided Reading N: *Down Comes the Rain* by Franklyn Mansfield Branley and James Graham Hale

Lesson Assessment: Running records and anecdotal notes can be taken.

LESSON 16: READER'S THEATRE TO REVIEW WEATHER CONCEPTS

CCSS in English Language Arts: SL.2.4, RF.2.4

Objectives: Students will be able to:
- Review weather concepts.
- Read with fluency.

Activities:

- Discuss how a fluent reader sounds.
- Pass out "Weather Readers Theatre Script" by Dr. Rosalind M. Flynn (*www.rosalindflynn. com/EdThtrScripts.html#science*) and have students highlight and read their parts. Assist students who need help with a word.
- Read and reread script until fluency is reached.
- Students create their props with construction paper.

Lesson Assessment: Assess fluency using a rubric.

---

*Unit plan format from Wiggins and McTighe (2005).

REFERENCES

Bauman, J. F., Chard, D. J., Cooks, J., Cooper, J. D., Gersten, R., Lipson, M., et al. (2011). *Journeys grade 2 teacher's edition*. Orlando, FL: Houghton Mifflin Harcourt.

N.J. Department of Education. (2010). New Jersey Core Curriculum content standards: Classroom applications document – science. Earth system science (by the end of grade 2). Retrieved from *www.state.nj.us/education/cccs/cad/5/*.

Olshansky, B. (2008). *The power of pictures: Creating pathways to literacy through art*. San Francisco: Jossey-Bass.

Wiggins, G. P., & McTighe, J. (2005). *Understanding by design*. Alexandria, VA: ASCD.

Index

Page numbers followed by *f* indicate figure, *t* indicate table